Crafting Coalitions
for Reform

Peter R. Kingstone

Crafting Coalitions for Reform

Business Preferences, Political Institutions, and Neoliberal Reform in Brazil

The Pennsylvania State University Press
University Park, Pennsylvania

Library of Congress Cataloging-in-Publication Data

Kingstone, Peter R., 1964–
    Crafting coalitions for reform : business preferences, political
institutions, and neoliberal reform in Brazil / Peter R. Kingstone.
        p.   cm.
    Includes bibliographical references and index.
    ISBN 0-271-01938-7 (cloth : alk. paper)
    ISBN 0-271-01939-5 (pbk. : alk. paper)
    1. Business and politics—Brazil.   2. Industrialists—Brazil
—Attitudes.   3. Industrial policy—Brazil.   4. Brazil—
Economic policy.   I. Title.
JL2469.P7K56   1999
338.981′009′048—dc21   98-54928
                                                                         CIP

It is the policy of The Pennsylvania State University Press to use acid-free paper for
the first printing of all clothbound books. Publications on uncoated stock satisfy the
minimum requirements of American National Standard for Information Sciences—
Permanence of Paper for Printed Library Materials, ANSI Z39.48-1992.

Contents

Abbreviations

ABDIB	Associação Brasileira para o Desenvolvimento das Indústrias de Base
ABIMAQ/SINDIMAQ	Associação Brasileira da Indústria de Máquinas e Equipamentos/Sindicato Nacional da Indústria de Máquinas
ABINEE/SINAEES	Associação Brasileira da Indústria Eletro-Eletrônica/Sindicato Nacional da Indústria de Aparelhos Elêtricos, Eletrônicos, e Similares do Estado de São Paulo
ABIPEÇAS/SINDIPEÇAS	Associação Brasileira da Indústria do Componentes para Veículos Automotores/ Sindicato Nacional da Indústria do Componentes para Veículos Automotores
ADR	American depository receipts
ANFAVEA	Associação Nacional dos Fabricantes de Veículos Automotores
ANFPC	Associação Nacional dos Fabricantes do Papel e Celulose
BEFIEX	Benefícios Fiscais a Programas Especiais de Exportação
BNDES	Banco Nacional de Desenvolvimento Econômico e Social
CACEX	Carteira de Comércio Exterior
CAD/CAM	Computer-aided design / computer-aided manufacturing
CCE	Consejo Coordinador de Empresarial
CDI	Conselho de Desenvolvimento Industrial
CEPB	Confederación de Empresarios Privados de Bolivia

CGT	Central Geral dos Trabalhadores
CIP	Conselho Interministerial de Preços
CLT	Consolidação das Leis do Trabalho
CNC	Computer numerically controlled
CNI	Confederação Nacional da Indústria
CPA	Conselho de Política Aduaneira
CPI	Comissão Parlamentaria de Inquerito
CUT	Central Única dos Trabalhadores
DECEX	Departamento de Comércio Exterior
DECON	Departamento de Economia
FEBRABAN	Federaçao Brasileira de Associaçãoes de Bancos
FGTS	Fundo de Garantia por Tempo de Serviço
FDI	Foreign direct investment
FIERGS	Federação das Indústrias do Estado de Rio Grande do Sul
FIESP/CIESP	Federação das Indústrias do Estado de São Paulo/Centro das Indústrias do Estado de São Paulo
FINAME	Agência Especial de Financiamento Industrial
FIRJAN	Federação de Indústrias do Estado de Rio de Janeiro
GDP	Gross Domestic Product
GNP	Gross National Product
IBGE	Fundação Instituto Brasileiro de Geografia e Estatística
ICMS	Imposto Sobre a Circulação de Mercadorias e Serviços
IEDI	Instituto de Estudos para o Desenvolvimento Industrial
IMF	International Monetary Fund
INSS	Instituto Nacional do Seguro Social
ISI	Import-substitution industrialization
LIBOR	London interbank offer rate
MNC	Multinational corporation
OECD	Organization for Economic Cooperation and Development
OEM	Original equipment manufacturer
PBQP	Programa Brasileiro de Qualidade e Produtividade

PDS	Partido Democrático Social
PDT	Partido Democrático Trabalhista
PFL	Partido da Frente Liberal
PL	Partido Liberal
PMDB	Partido do Movimento Democrático Brasileiro
PNBE	Pensamento Nacional das Bases Empresariais
PPB	Partido Progressista Brasileiro
PRN	Partido de Reconstrução Nacional
PROER	Programa de Estimulo para a Reestruturação do sistema financeiro
PSDB	Partido da Social Democracia Brasileira
PT	Partido dos Trabalhadores
PTB	Partido Trabalhista Brasileira
SENAI	Serviço Nacional de Apredizagem Industrial
SESI	Serviço Social da Indústria
SIMEFRE	Sindicato da Indústria de Materiais e Equipamentos Ferroviários e Rodoviários no Estado de São Paulo
UBE	União Brasileira de Empresários

Tables and Figures

Tables

Figures

Acknowledgments

First and foremost, I am grateful to David Collier for his support, advice, and wisdom over the eleven years since we met. It is a testament to David's teaching that the older and more experienced I become as a political scientist, the more I appreciate both his direct advice and his example. Ruth Collier's incisive questions and comments have repeatedly challenged me to sharpen my thinking.

John Zysman's approach to political economy profoundly shaped my understanding, and his contacts in the Brazilian business community led to extensive access to industrialists. I am also grateful to Peter Evans, Ernst Haas, and Oliver Williamson for their guidance at various stages of this project.

Berkeley is blessed with an invigorating and inspiring group of graduate students. Among many over the years, Carol Medlin, Ken Shadlen, and Andy Schwartz contributed comments and encouragement. I want to especially acknowledge the central role that Max Cameron, Arun Swamy, David Waldner, and Deborah Yashar have played and continue to play in my life—as colleagues, companions, and teachers. I also want to thank another Berkeley alumnus, Ben Ross Schneider, for his helpful comments.

While in Brazil, a number of people have helped me understand Brazilian politics better. Some read and commented on portions of this book or on variations of the central argument: Lourdes Sola, Rubens Figueiredo, Brasilio Sallum, João Paulo Candia Veiga, Scott Martin, José Afonso Alves Castanheira, Gerald Reiss, Norman Gall, José Roberto Ferro, Bill Hinchberger, Diomedes Christodoulou, Jamal Khokhar, Wendy Barker, Luciano Coutinho, Luis Ornstein, Mario Bernardini, Jorge Hori, Emerson Kapaz, Oded Grajew, Mauro Arruda, Guilherme Dias, Helio Nogueira da Cruz, Wilson Suzigan, Geraldo Gardenalli, and Gesner Oliveira. I conducted roughly one hundred interviews in the Brazilian industrial community, and Brazilian businesspeople were remarkably accessible and candid in their dealings with me. For their openness and the ease of access they afforded me to their community, I am grateful.

A number of people have read and commented on portions of the manuscript and/or have provided important commentary on the arguments herein: Leslie Armijo, Jeff Cason, Greg Gause, John Echeverri-Gent, Robert Gordon Kaufman, Sylvia Maxfield, Al Montero, Sayid Abu Rizvi, Stephanie Seguino, Cherie Steele, Ross Thomson, and Curt Ventriss.

I have benefited from the opportunity to present arguments based on this work at the Centre for Brazilian Studies at Oxford University and at the Economics Department of the University of Vermont. I also benefited from the chance to present this work to the new generation of graduate students working with David and Ruth Collier at Berkeley. As always, their seminars remain among the most challenging and stimulating venues for presenting work.

Finally, I have benefited from Fran Hagopian's close reading and insightful comments. Her challenges and suggestions pushed me to substantially rethink my claims. The insights of this book depend greatly on the help I received from these individuals—all remaining faults are mine.

Initial financial support for this research came from the Institute of International Studies at the University of California at Berkeley through the John L. Simpson Fellowship. While in Brazil, the Fundação Getúlio Vargas provided me with an office and other logistical support. Through the auspices of Rubens Figueiredo, I was afforded access and the help of the staff at the archives of the Federação das Indústrias do Estado de São Paulo. Finally, the subsequent research and writing were supported by the University of Vermont through the Direct Faculty Support Grant of the College of Arts and Sciences and the University Committee on Research and Scholarship Grant of the Graduate College. I am grateful to the University of Connecticut for providing a stimulating environment for continuing to pursue the questions raised by this work.

I would like to thank my parents for their encouragement and support throughout this process. My father's visit to São Paulo in 1991 was a welcome treat. I have appreciated the opportunity to discuss with him, as a businessperson, my observations about the way businesspeople think. My parents have also provided financial help, emotional encouragement, and most important, child care. Their loving care of my children has greatly eased my wife and my efforts to complete our respective scholarly pursuits.

I especially want to thank my wife, Lisa. In the time since this project began, my wife has become a creative and thoughtful scholar in her own discipline, American literature. Her excitement for learning has been a helpful reminder of why I went into this business in the first place. She has read portions of the manuscript, tracked down split infinitives and run-on sentences, and reminded me that good writing is simple and clear. To the extent that I have achieved that end, the credit is due to her. She has supported me with her pride, her enthusiasm, her taking over the household when I really needed it, and her reminding me that I have a life outside this book when I really needed that. My debt to her exceeds what my words can repay.

Finally, I want to thank my children, Ben and Lara. I remember as a graduate student finding Peter Evans's acknowledgment to his sons particularly moving. At the time, I did not have children, or any plans to have them soon. Now, I understand his gratitude. Watching my children run through the house, capes flying behind them as they yell "SuperBen!" and "SuperLara!" has brought me greater delight than anything professional can ever deliver. In loving appreciation of the richness they have brought me, I dedicate this book to Lisa, Ben, and Lara.

Introduction

Understanding business is critical to understanding neoliberal reform. One key assumption underlying neoliberalism is that the private sector becomes the engine of growth. The program also presents significant challenges to business survival, however, particularly to domestic producers long accustomed to protectionism and state promotion. Politically, business groups (whether domestic or foreign) are presumed to be central to preserving the reform process as well as the democratic process, even though many analyses assume they are hostile to both.[1]

Unfortunately, business remains one of the least studied and least understood social groups in Latin American society. Many prominent approaches to Latin American politics assume business preferences rather than subject the preferences to empirical investigation. One consequence is that very few theoretical accounts address one of the central empirical puzzles of neoliberal reform: What explains domestic business elites' relative acquiescence to, and at times even enthusiastic support

---

1. There is some schizophrenia in the field with respect to business. On the one hand, analysts like Catherine Conaghan, *Restructuring Domination: Industrialists and the State in Ecuador* (Pittsburgh: University of Pittsburgh Press, 1988); James Petras, Fernando Ignacio Leiva, and Henry Veltmeyer, *Democracy and Poverty in Chile: The Limits of Electoral Politics* (Boulder, Colo.: Westview Press, 1994); and Edward Gibson, "Conservative Electoral Movements and Democratic Politics: Core Constituencies, Coalition Building, and the Latin American Right," in Douglas A. Chalmers, Maria Carmo Campello de Souza, and Atilio A. Boron, eds., *The Right and Democracy in Latin America* (New York: Praeger, 1992), suggest that neoliberalism is a business project and that neoliberalism's natural constituency is politically a right-wing, elite one. On the other hand, discussions about domestic industrialists typically assume that industrialists are hostile to neoliberalism because they cannot compete. See, for example, Eduardo Silva, *The State and Capital in Chile* (Boulder, Colo.: Westview Press, 1996), or Ernest Bartell, "Perceptions by Business Leaders and the Transition in Chile," in Ernest Bartell C.S.C. and Leigh Payne, eds., *Business and Democracy in Latin America* (Pittsburgh: University of Pittsburgh Press, 1995). These conflicting views are not easily reconciled, and certainly few proponents of these views have tried to reconcile them.

of, neoliberal reform? In turn, how does the character of the support affect the sustainability of the reform process and the consequences for development?

This book addresses these questions by focusing on industrialists and neoliberal reform in Brazil. It approaches the problem by examining how market factors interact with political factors to shape business preferences and behavior. Specifically, I examine how industrialists' preferences are affected by four factors: their sectoral location; the specific political institutions in which their sector is embedded; the adjustment options that the government's policy commitment make possible; and the way that the credibility of those commitments shapes industrialists' perceptions of the costs and benefits of those adjustment options. I argue that industrialists judge credibility by watching and evaluating the government's tactical choices for maneuvering reforms through the political system. These factors affect the character of industrialists' political support and private adjustment strategies. In turn, these influence the sustainability of the reform process and the development consequences of reform. Thus, the book links political institutions to business strategies for the political arena and the market.

In this book, I show that the economic crisis of the 1980s ruptured the existing relations between business and the state—which I have called the import-substitution–industrialization (ISI)–corporatist model. I further examine how that rupture left industrialists open to new growth strategies, including neoliberalism. Their openness reflected a substantial margin for industrial adjustments and a revitalization of interest associations that facilitated more effective political participation. Their ability to adjust and their willingness to accept the costs of reform, however, depended on government's credibly delivering on policy promises. In the absence of that credibility, industrialists mobilized opposition to reform.

Once they had sufficient stability of expectations, adjustments occurred rapidly so that their strategic market choices quickly foreclosed other options. Thus, the reform process became more politically sustainable as industrialists became increasingly dependent on the continuation of government policy. Nevertheless, uncertainty about political performance led private actors to craft risk-averse strategies. In turn, those strategies translated into a series of suboptimal outcomes for economic development. Thus, politicians were able to craft and maintain coalitions in favor of neoliberal reform, but they could not ensure that reforms produced the desired results.

SOME POINTS OF CLARIFICATION

In writing this work, I use four critical concepts that are subject to considerable confusion: business, support, coalition, and preferences. Here, I offer some points of clarification on how I have used them in this book.

Business

Business is a large and diffuse category. On the one hand, it can encompass entrepreneurs in industry, finance, agriculture, commerce, and services. Each of these distinct categories of business has different interests and characteristics that affect them as political actors. On the other hand, analysts can also focus on business by class, by sectors, by firms, by organizations, or by personal networks.[2] These conceptual subtleties mean that one must treat the concept of business with some care.

In this book, I have used industrialists interchangeably with businesspeople, but the book is only about industrialists. Although ideally I would include other business segments, the research strategy would make that approach a prohibitively time-consuming and complex task. Brazil is not Chile or Peru where a review of a few conglomerate heads can tell a surprisingly complete story. On the contrary, it is much more like advanced industrial societies than it is like other Latin American societies in the complexity and diversity of its producing sectors. Brazilian industry encompasses all those sectors engaged in manufacturing, whether they are seeds, shoes, or nuclear power plants. That segment of the economy generates sufficient variation on its own. This variability coupled with the distinctly privileged position held by industrialists in Brazil since the 1930s warrants a study of industrialists on their own.

Similarly, I have had to choose among the categories listed above (class, sectors, firms, organizations, and networks): This book does not treat business as a class. At times, I have used the term *business community* to refer to the industrial community, but that is a shorthand reference. Treating business as a class would require considering the interests of capital in contrast to the other societal concerns. To some extent, that is implicit

---

2. This categorization was articulated by Stephan Haggard, Sylvia Maxfield, and Ben Ross Schneider, "Theories of Business and Business-State Relations," in Sylvia Maxfield and Ben Ross Schneider, eds., *Business and the State in Developing Countries* (Ithaca: Cornell University Press, 1997), 37.

in the consideration of investors' needs. It is not the implicit focus of this research.

My research *did* explicitly focus on industrialists with reference to the other four categories. I examined industrialists as owners (or managers) of firms with specific characteristics, operating in sectors with specific characteristics. Those industrialists brought their market concerns to the political organizations and personal networks in which they operated. Thus, I have sought to link these four categories systematically and causally. Industrialists' experience at the micro- and sectoral levels shaped their political behavior at higher levels of aggregation.

Support

Charting industrialists' support is not a simple task. Business activity often takes place behind closed doors where it is impossible to document. Extensive and candid interviews supported by or consistent with other overt acts can demonstrate the existence of support or opposition. Another approach I followed in the course of this research was to connect micro-level issues with public positions expressed by industrial leaders. Many studies of business operate only at the level of class or organization. At that level of aggregation, there is no mechanism for examining the basis of public statements. It is easier to make judgments about the reliability of public statements when one can test them against the problems that industrialists face in their own plants.

In this book, I have taken a broad view of the notion of support, ranging from acquiescence to enthusiasm. Acquiescence is not exactly the same thing as support, but there are several reasons to treat the two together. For one, industrialists who acquiesce politically are still required to act in the market in response. Capital flight and other decisions that lead industrialists to withdraw from production have important political consequences. Although the concept of support implies political behavior, it is also connected to market decisions. Second, acquiescence suggests a willingness to accept the policy direction that is distinct from opposition. In particular, executives or industrial associations may still draw on acquiescent industrialists for expressions of support in contrast to opponents. The mobilization of industrialists in mid-1996 called on such industrialists for support. Political expression can be thought of as a continuum ranging from overt opposition to overt support, with private market decisions falling in between (Fig. 1).

Fig. 1. Continuum of political responses to economic reform

Aggressive Opposition	Passive Opposition	Acquiescence	Enthusiastic Support
Active mobilizations Participation in antigovernment activities Alternative coalition building	Capital flight Sale of assets Speculative activities against government policy Unavailable for government support Might be available for opposition	Investment in restructuring Engaging in competitive adjustments Unavailable for alternative coalitions Might be available for government support	Active mobilizations in favor or in support of government policy Lobbying in support of government agenda

Coalition

As with business, the term *coalition* can mean different things in different contexts. It can refer to a legislative coalition linking legislators behind a program or policy. Electoral coalitions can refer to the network of disparate voters who unite politically behind a party or candidate. Finally, a governing coalition can refer to the set of social groups that support government policy. In all these cases, coalitions may be more or less defined, more or less explicit, more or less formalized, and more or less mobilized. The terms of participation in a coalition may vary substantially and may be highly unequal. In view of the qualities noted earlier, coalitions may be stable or unstable—weak or strong.

In this study, I have thought of industrialists as members of both electoral coalitions and governing coalitions. They have repeatedly brought their political resources to bear in elections. They have also constituted important bases of social support for the reform process. At times, presidents have tried to call on their political support in their conflicts with the legislature. At times, presidents have benefited from unsolicited expressions of support.

Neither Fernando Collor nor Fernando Henrique Cardoso could claim particularly strong business participation in governing coalitions. Both Collor and Cardoso privileged some segments of industry. In general, Collor remained hostile and distant until it was too late. His efforts to grant privileges to new business organizations gained him little leverage with the industrial community. Cardoso privileged multinational corporations (MNC) generally and the auto industry specifically, but because that strategy soured in 1996, Cardoso actively worked to include larger segments of the industrial community. In that event, Cardoso's efforts paid off in greater stability in business participation in his governing coalition. In particular, it effectively stopped efforts in the industrial community to build alternative coalitions.

Preferences

I do not offer a theory of preferences. When economists speak of a theory of preferences, they refer to assumptions about behavior. Specifically, they assume that entrepreneurs are utility maximizers or satisfiers, and so on. The operative theory of preferences in this book is that industrialists are utility maximizers operating under conditions of imperfect information. In other words, industrialists would like to earn as much as they can, and to that end, they would like to pursue the optimal adjustment strategy. Because they lack reliable information about the sustainability of government policy and its ultimate impact, however, they must make choices based on limited information.

When I speak of preferences, I refer to preferences for policy. I examine how market factors constrain business choices and how that constraint interacts with the political process. In turn, I ask how that interaction affects what industrialists believe is the best policy, political strategy, and market strategy for them.

RESEARCH STRATEGY

I designed my field research to explore how members of the business community experienced neoliberal reform at the micro-level. I focused on three sectors that represented a continuum of preparedness for a commercial opening: pulp and paper (highly competitive), auto parts (competitive, but facing significant challenges), and machine tools and equipment (seriously challenged). Conducting research along this continuum allowed me to test the hypotheses about which sectors support liberalization and which do not. It also provided a comparative understanding of the range of issues that both the collapse of state-led development and neoliberal reforms posed. With help from economists, businesspeople, and sectoral representatives, I chose firms to get a sample that reflected the cleavages in each sector. I tested the findings of my interviews with economists, businesspeople, and sectoral representatives. In this way, I could identify observations that contradicted what others involved in the sector observed.

I used several forms of data. First, I conducted extensive interviews in the business community—more than one hundred interviews between 1991 and 1992 and then again in 1996. The interviews were divided between plant-level interviews that focused on issues of industrial adjustment and on policymaking and political participation and business association–level interviews (both sectoral and nonsectoral) that focused on political roles.

In my interviews, I used open-ended questions about four issue areas. Each interview began with a broad evaluation of the economic reform program, including but not limited to commercial liberalization. I followed these questions with questions about the individuals' assessments of their sectors' performance, strengths, and weaknesses. I pursued these questions, then, with reference to the individuals' own companies. Finally, I returned to the overall program to specify more precisely an individual's assessment of different aspects of the reform program and its progress. Respondents generally answered the first set of questions with blandly positive and essentially uninformative answers, but questions about the sector and the company generated detailed and energetic responses. The advantage of this strategy is that it provided a detailed map of the concrete micro-level issues facing these businesspeople. I could then use these maps to get more informative evaluations of the actual program. This latter stage generated some of the most interesting and provocative observations, including the surprising degree to which businesspeople watched executive tactics to reach conclusions about the sustainability of reform.

I corroborated interview evidence and gathered further data in several ways. Various business associations (in particular, Federation of Industry of the State of São Paulo [FIESP], National Thought of the Business Bases [PNBE], Institute for Industrial Development Studies [IEDI]) print material that sets out their perspectives on issues of concern. Businesspeople also actively voice their views in the press through opinion pieces. In general, I found that these views were consistent with what businesspeople said in private, although they tended to be more critical in private. There is also extensive newspaper coverage of the political expressions and activities of business associations, including association elections, such as in FIESP. Several institutions have gathered substantial survey data, which I used to complement interview and newspaper evidence.

Finally, I relied on the large body of scholarly work in Brazil on a wide range of topics: work on the institutional structure of ISI in Brazil and its impact on business; extensive work and data on the performance of various sectors and their competitiveness relative to foreign producers; extensive analyses of the Collor Plan, the *Plano real* (Real Plan) and previous anti-inflation plans and their effects on business; political analyses of Collor's election, Cardoso's election, and their subsequent terms in office. Throughout the text, I have interspersed both business sources of information and independent and scholarly sources.

The research at the micro-level inexorably pushed me to higher levels of political life. Rather than finding that the micro-bases of politics were where the story lay, I found that policymaking at the national level drove the micro-level. In each sector, businesses faced a range of possible choices so that their preferences were more malleable than much of the literature on political economy suggests. What they chose to do and how well they succeeded depended on the policy decisions governments made and the ways in which governments tried to pass these decisions through the legislature. Thus, my research increasingly included interviews with participants in policymaking as well as journalistic and scholarly discussions of the policymaking process.

Ultimately, studying politics in a relatively closed, elitist society poses distinct methodological challenges. Much of what happens occurs behind closed doors (*nos bastidores*), away from the eyes of the public and the press. It is difficult to document some of the most interesting revelations—those expressed in interviews with participants in elite politics. I chose to keep my interviewees anonymous, and that decision paid off in the extraordinary candor that many interviewees displayed. Several members of the business community confessed to using Collor's scandals as an opportunity to attack both him and neoliberalism. Others precisely detailed existing corruption schemes and methods of tax evasion. Others spoke candidly about the behind-the-scenes machinations of leaders in the industrial community. At times, these insights appear in the analysis; otherwise, they certainly inform the general discussion. Although I have chosen to keep the interviewees confident, I have included a list of the firms and organizations in which I conducted interviews (see Fig. 2).

ORGANIZATION OF THIS BOOK

In Chapter 1, I consider the problem of explaining industrialists' preferences for free trade. I explore the limitations of arguments based on class,

Fig. 2. Interview list

The most important firms and organizations in which interviews were conducted. Some firms or organizations were visited more than once. Some of the interviewees were interviewed in 1991–92 and then again in 1996. All interviews were confidential.

A. *Firms*

Alberto Cestini and Companhia	Elka Plasticos	MGM Mecânica
	Enron	Nakata
Aldo Ciola	Equipamentos Clark	Papirus
Arteb	Freios Varga	Parker Hannifin (Filtros
Bardella	General Electric do Brasil	Irlemp)
Celso Miori Assessoria	Gradiente	Phillips do Brasil
Empresárial	Grano Ltda.	Planasa
Champion Paper	Grow Toys	Rockwell Braseixos
Citibank	Jack Strauss	Rockwell Fumagalli
Cobrasma	Kentinha	Romi
Companhia Iochpe-	Klabín Fabricadora	Royal Bank
Maxion	Kostal Eletromecânica	Sulmecânica
Confab	Metal Dois	Technoplan
Consemp	Metal Leve	Vila Romana
Cotía Trading	Metalpó	Villares
Dante Ramenzoni	Moinho Santista	Westmerchant
Degremão		

B. *Organizations (business and government)*

American Chamber of Commerce (São Paulo, Brazil)
Associação Brasileira da Indústria de Brinquedos (ABRINQ)
Associação Brasileira da Indústria de Fundição (ABIFA)
Associação Brasileira da Indústria do Componentes para Veículos Automotores / Sindicato Nacional da Indústria do Componentes para Veículos Automotores (ABIPEÇAS/SINDIPEÇAS)
Associação Brasileira da Indústria de Máquinas e Equipamentos / Sindicato Nacional da Indústria de Máquinas (ABIMAQ/SINDIMAQ)
Associação Brasileira da Indústria Eletro-Eletrônica (ABINEE)
Associação Brasileira para o Desenvolvimento das Indústrias de Base (ABDIB)
Associação Nacional dos Fabricantes de Papel e Celulose (ANFPC)
Banco Nacional de Desenvolvimento Econômico e Social (BNDES)
Brazil–Canada Chamber of Commerce
Business Council on National Issues—Canada (BCNI)
Confederação Nacional da Indústria (CNI)
Eletros
Federação das Indústrias do Estado de São Paulo / Centro das Indústrias do Estado de São Paulo (FIESP/CIESP)
Instituto de Estudos para o Desenvolvimento Industrial (IEDI)
Pensamento Nacional das Bases Empresariais (PNBE)
Secretaría da Ciencia e Tecnología (SCT) de São Paulo
Sindicato da Indústria de Materiais e Equipamentos Ferroviários e Rodoviários no Estado de São Paulo (SIMEFRE)
União pela Modernização do Setor de Auto Peças

organizational factors, and market position and observe that perceptions of crisis and a variety of adjustment options make industrialists available for reform coalitions. I argue that their availability, however, depends on the credibility of the executive's tactical decisions for maneuvering reforms through the legislature.

In Chapter 2, I examine the crisis of the 1980s and how it helped produce the conditions for a neoliberal coalition. The chapter traces the breakdown of the state's finances and its impact on the private sector at the micro-level. It explores some of the José Sarney administration's efforts at managing the crisis and how mismanagement helped shift business to support neoliberal reform. Finally, it also reviews how the 1988 Constitution exacerbated business concerns about the economy and further strengthened business commitment to reforms.

In Chapter 3, I examine the micro-level bases of political support and opposition. The chapter explores three sectors differentiated by their preparedness for international competition across four areas: sectoral history, linkages to the state, costs and benefits of neoliberal reform, and adjustment decisions between 1990 and 1992. The chapter shows that these sectors believed they had adjustment options and demonstrates the relations between micro-level options and government policy performance.

In Chapter 4, I examine the corporatist structure of business organization. Business frustration with the corporatist system erupted at the sectoral level and in peak associations through the late 1980s and 1990s. Industrialists complained that their organizations had lost their utility as the ISI-corporatist model broke down. Instead, members pressured their organizations to reform to better serve micro-level needs and to better reflect changes in business–state relations. As a consequence, business organizations were more effective conduits of both political support and opposition during the neoliberal reform period.

In Chapters 5 and 6, I explore the relations between political signals and business behavior. Chapter 5 reviews Fernando Collor's election and subsequent initiation of neoliberal reform. The chapter is organized in terms of a series of tactical choices about how to maneuver reforms through a fragmented political system. Each episode of reform efforts is treated as a separate set of tactical choices by Collor and responses by the industrial community. Thus, the chapter covers the formation and ultimate collapse of Collor's neoliberal reform coalition.

Chapter 6 explores Fernando Henrique Cardoso's recrafting of the coalition for reform. After Collor's impeachment, Cardoso established himself as a credible presidential candidate while acting as finance minister to the interim president, Itamar Franco. Building on his successful stabilization plan, the Real Plan, Cardoso built support for continued liberalization. Despite some successes, Cardoso's institutional obstacles have forced him to repeatedly change his tactics as well. Overall, Cardoso has successfully used his tactical shifts to maintain business support for neoliberal reform. This chapter is also organized in terms of a series of tactical choices and industrialists' responses, but the chapter points to the consolidation of the reform process rather than its collapse.

Finally, Chapter 7 provides a postscript since 1997 and addresses five broad lessons about industrialists and economic reform in the Brazilian case. First, it points to a preference for qualitative, small-N research as the key to explaining the dynamics of support and opposition to free trade. Second, the study suggests that industrialists are adaptive. Neither analysts nor policymakers need look at economic reform as a choice between rent-seeking, uncompetitive domestic industrialists versus modern, competitive MNCs. Domestic industrialists retain the ability to adjust as long as policy and political conditions permit them. Third, given the second lesson, policymakers could and probably should take a more heterodox approach to economic reform. Fourth, industrialists need a strategic framework to orient their investment strategies. In its absence, they are more inclined to pursue their own course, regardless of its public welfare consequences. Finally, political institutions matter because they shape government's capacity to define a strategic framework and because they influence private actors' adjustment strategies. The extent that economic reform could and should serve public welfare concerns is very much shaped by the efficacy of political institutions.

1

Explaining Support for Free Trade

Industrial Adjustment and Political Signals

Neoliberal reform was slow to arrive in Brazil, but when it finally did, it provoked an intriguing and surprising response from the country's politically powerful industrial community. Between 1985 and 1997, successive Brazilian governments gradually implemented a neoliberal economic reform program, including a substantial commercial liberalization. The reform proceeded in fits and starts—an erratic pattern that reflected the fragmented and inchoate character of Brazil's political system. One component, free trade, proceeded virtually unimpeded, however, beginning in earnest in 1990 and reaching its conclusion in 1994. After fifty years of protection and nurturing by the state, observers of Brazilian political economy would have expected Brazilian industrialists to actively oppose the reform process. Instead, the industrialists displayed an erratic pattern of behavior that mirrored the confusion of the policy process. This pattern featured repeated shifts between aggressive support of and aggressive opposition to neoliberal reform generally and free trade specifically. The late 1980s witnessed growing, intense mobilization of industrialists in favor of neoliberal reform (including commercial liberalization). Brazilian industrialists sharply and critically attacked the state, decrying it for its excessive size and interventionist role. Yet by 1991–92, most industry leaders had retreated and attacked the government for its commitment to neoliberalism and for President Fernando Collor de Mello's tactics to promote this policy. Business criticism erupted from a wide range of existing and new business organizations, and businesspeople helped bring down the incumbent president. In 1994–95, they again mobilized in favor of a presidential candidate, Fernando Henrique Cardoso, and called for neoliberal reforms. Through early 1996, substantial business opposition again surfaced to both the government's commitment to neoliberalism and to the president's tactics. By the end of 1996, business opposition had largely quieted, and the business community had again mobilized behind the potential re-election of the incumbent president.

This book offers an explanation for business behavior in Brazil from 1985 to 1997. Understanding this pattern of surprising and erratic behavior is central to understanding critical underlying questions about business and economic reform: What shapes business preferences? What factors explain why businesspeople choose to support a reform program or to oppose it? How do business preferences and behavior change in "hard times," and what effect do politicians and the political process have on how businesspeople perceive their choices? The answers to these questions have important implications for another set of crucial questions. How does business contribute to the sustainability of economic reform, particularly neoliberal reforms? How do business choices influence development? Finally, how powerful is business in Latin America's capitalist societies? The question of business power has spawned a significant debate among scholars of developed countries, particularly of the United States, but the question remains relatively unexplored empirically in Latin America. These issues are considered in the conclusion of this book.

Observers of Brazilian politics typically explain away industrialists' erratic behavior by declaring that businesspeople are hypocrites who say one thing but mean another or that businesspeople simply fear import competition. Unfortunately, these explanations, commonly spoken although rarely published, are ad hoc, atheoretical, and unconnected to empirical research.[1] This shortcoming reflects a widespread problem. As Barbara Geddes noted, analysts of neoliberal reforms have failed to adequately account for the behavior of several social groups, among them business.[2] Business behavior has defied the expectations expressed in the

1. For published versions of this argument, see William Nylen, "Liberalismo para Todo Mundo Menos Eu: Brazil and the Neoliberal Solution," in Chalmers, de Souza, and Boron, eds., *The Right and Democracy in Latin America*; Fernando Henrique Cardoso and José Rubens de Lima Figueiredo Jr., "Reconciling the Capitalists with Democracy" (paper presented at the Conference on Economic Reform and Democratic Consolidation, Forli, Italy, April 2–4, 1992).

2. Barbara Geddes, "The Politics of Economic Liberalization," *Latin American Research Review* 30, no. 2 (1996): 196. Stephan Haggard and Steven Webb make the same observation in Haggard and Webb, eds., *Voting for Reform: Democracy, Liberalization, and Economic Adjustment* (Oxford: Oxford University Press, 1994), 18.

literature on Latin American politics and general political economy literature. The reasons for the analytical shortcomings are clear. First, Latin Americanists have conducted very few studies of business.[3] Second, the general political economy literature on business-state relations in developing countries[4] and on business support for free trade is underdeveloped.[5]

3. This situation has begun to change in the 1990s with the work of many scholars. For example, Blanca Heredia, "Mexican Business and the State: The Political Economy of a 'Muddled' Transition," Conaghan, "The Private Sector and the Public Transcript: The Political Mobilization of Business in Bolivia," and Carlos Acuña, "Business Interests, Dictatorship, and Democracy in Argentina," all in Bartell and Payne, eds., *Business and Democracy in Latin America*; and Sylvia Maxfield, *Gatekeepers of Growth: The International Political Economy of Central Banking in Developing of Growth* (Princeton: Princeton University Press, 1997), have added to a body of work they began in the late 1980s. They have been joined by a new generation of writers on business in Latin America, including Ben Ross Schneider, "The Elusive Embrace: Synergy Between Business and the State in Developing Countries" (paper presented at the annual meeting of the American Political Science Association, Washington, D.C., August 1993) and "Organized Business Interests in Democratic Brazil," *Journal of Interamerican Studies and World Affairs* 39, no. 4 (1997); Payne, *Brazilian Industrialists and Democratic Change* (Baltimore: Johns Hopkins University Press, 1994); Kurt Weyland, "How Much Political Power Do Economic Forces Have? Conflicts over Social Insurance Reform in Brazil," *Journal of Public Policy* 16, no. 1 (1996): 59–84; Silva, *State and Capital in Chile*; Francisco Durand, *Business and Politics in Peru* (Boulder, Colo.: Westview Press, 1994); Strom Thacker, "Big Business, the State, and Free Trade in Mexico: Interests, Structure, and Political Access" (paper presented at the annual meeting of the American Political Science Association, Washington, D.C., August 1997); Kenneth Shadlen, "Small Industry and the Mexican Left: Neoliberalism, Corporatism, and Dissident Populism" (paper presented at the annual meeting of the American Political Science Association, Washington, D.C., August 1997); Alfred Montero, "Shifting States in Uneven Markets: Political Decentralization and Subnational Industrial Policy in Contemporary Brazil and Spain" (Ph.D. diss., Columbia University, 1997); Nylen, "Small Business Owners Fight Back: Non-Elite Capital Activism in Democratizing Brazil (1978–1990)" (Ph.D. diss., Columbia University, 1992), as well as my own work. In addition, Peter Evans has continued his influential work on business-state relations and development in *Embedded Autonomy: States and Industrial Transformation* (Princeton: Princeton University Press, 1995).

4. Maxfield and Schneider, *Business and the State*, 4, criticize the general political economy literature in their study of business-state relations in developing countries. In particular, they note that business-state cooperation has been necessary to create capacity and promote growth in virtually all developing nations. In turn, that cooperation has depended on effective interaction and partnership in contrast to the hypotheses about rent seeking that the literature on developed countries has produced.

5. Helen Milner first made this observation in her study *Resisting Protectionism: Global Industries and the Politics of International Trade* (Princeton: Princeton University Press, 1988). Milner noted that the literature explaining why firms and sectors support protection is well developed, whereas few explanations exist for why firms and sectors may support free trade. In a more recent review, James Alt and colleagues observe that the existing literature on trade coalitions has generally failed to adequately explain the available data. James Alt, Jeffry Frieden, Michael Gilligan, Dani Rodrik, and Ronald Rogowski, "The Political Economy of Inter-

As a consequence, large theoretical gaps limit our understanding of business behavior. In turn, this shortcoming hinders our efforts to understand what makes the reform process sustainable or unsustainable.

The answers to these questions lie in understanding how the political process shapes the way businesspeople view their own preferences for policy. Market position and class identity clearly limit the range of policies that businesspeople may support. Nevertheless, both factors allow them considerable latitude, especially during a crisis when they may well understand that the status quo is no longer viable.[6] In that context, politicians play a crucial role in framing the choices available to businesses and in shaping how they perceive the mix of costs and benefits of alternative programs. Businesspeople may be willing to accept the costs of reform in exchange for promises of offsetting benefits. Politicians are able to craft coalitions in support of economic reforms by offering policies that influence business adjustment strategies and business perceptions of the benefits of reform. Thus, business preferences reflect the interaction of politics and the market.[7]

In the Brazilian case, the collapse of the import substitution industrialization strategy opened a wide range of business groups to neoliberal reform. Their support, however, hinged on the government's fulfilling its

---

national Trade: Enduring Puzzles and an Agenda for Inquiry," *Comparative Political Studies* 29 (December 1996): 699.

6. The most important statement on the impact of crisis is Peter Gourevitch, *Politics in Hard Times* (Ithaca: Cornell University Press, 1986).

7. The idea that the market interacts with politics is a well-developed one. For example, it forms the basis of the entire literature on industrial adjustment, including important works such as Gourevitch, *Politics in Hard Times*; John Zysman, *Government, Markets, and Growth: Financial Systems and the Politics of Industrial Change* (Ithaca: Cornell University Press, 1985); Peter Katzenstein, *Small States in World Markets: Industrial Policy in Europe* (Ithaca: Cornell University Press, 1985); Katzenstein, ed., *Between Power and Plenty: Foreign Economic Policies of Advanced Industrial States* (Madison: University of Wisconsin Press, 1978); Richard Locke, *Remaking the Italian Economy* (Ithaca: Cornell University Press, 1995); J. Rogers Hollingsworth and Robert Boyer, eds., *Contemporary Capitalism: The Embeddedness of Institutions* (Cambridge: Cambridge University Press, 1997); Charles Sabel, *Work and Politics* (New York: Cambridge University Press, 1982); Peter Hall, *Governing the Economy: The Politics of State Intervention in Britain and France* (New York: Oxford University Press, 1986). In the Latin America field, works such as Evans, *Dependent Development: The Alliance of Multinational, State, and Local Capital in Brazil* (Princeton: Princeton University Press, 1979), and Helen Shapiro, *Engines of Growth: The State and Transnational Auto Companies in Brazil* (New York: Cambridge University Press, 1994), have demonstrated that the interaction of the private sector and policymakers led to specific policy choices that profoundly affected the character of the market. The argument in this book draws on these works and situates itself in the same analytical tradition.

policy commitments to address the fiscal crisis of the state[8] and related systemic economic problems. Business support eroded as government policy and tactics became increasingly erratic and unpredictable and made the promised benefits of reform uncertain even as the costs became increasingly real. In that context, businesspeople increasingly preferred the status quo to further reforms. Despite Fernando Collor's well-documented weaknesses as a president, the government's performance primarily reflected a flawed political system that promoted extremes of patronage-based politics, political party weakness, and unusually lengthy, complicated, and frequently unsuccessful bargaining between the legislature and executive.[9] The resulting uncertainty about the sustainability and future direction of policy led businesspeople to put off extensive adjustment efforts.

With Collor's impeachment in 1992, the business community in 1994 endorsed Fernando Henrique Cardoso—a candidate who appeared able to implement the policies that Collor could not. By 1996, Cardoso faced the same pattern of eroding support, and his legislative failures and criticism of his tactical choices mounted. Business support renewed in late 1996 as Cardoso rapidly changed his tactics for implementing his reforms, offered a host of new benefits to alleviate business concerns, and promoted his own re-election as a way to forestall emerging opposition. By 1997, Cardoso appeared to be the only presidential candidate capable of continuing a reform process on which industrialists increasingly depended. Businesspeople had intensified their commitment to the reform process as they increasingly invested in a variety of adjustment strategies and thus foreclosed on other alternatives. Nevertheless, many firms still expressed concerns about the sustainability of the reform process and therefore left themselves exit strategies should Cardoso fail to deliver on his promises.

In making this argument, I advance four central distinctive claims about business preferences. First, business preferences are not static or mechanical reflections of the market or of businesspeople's class posi-

---

8. The nature of the fiscal crisis in Brazil and its far-reaching consequences is explicitly addressed in Luis Carlos Bresser Pereira, *Economic Crisis and State Reform in Brazil: Toward a New Interpretation of Latin America* (Boulder, Colo.: Lynne Rienner, 1996).

9. Brazil's political system has been widely recognized as one of the least coherent in Latin America. Discussions of its problems with presidentialism and multipartism can be found in Scott Mainwaring, "Politicians, Parties, and Electoral Systems: Brazil in Comparative Perspective," *Comparative Politics* (October 1991): 21–44; Mainwaring and Timothy R. Scully, *Building Democratic Institutions: Party Systems in Latin America* (Stanford: Stanford University Press, 1995).

tion.[10] Businesspeople, like scholars, can and do look both backward in time and toward the future. They can and do make determinations about the viability of the status quo, and they can and do consider alternatives for the future. Observers of Latin American politics have typically portrayed Latin American businesspeople as passive, weak, and dependent on state protection. Yet, by the late 1980s, it was equally apparent to scholars *and* businesspeople that import substitution was no longer viable. Businesspeople understood that fact and accepted the need for change—even if in an ideal world they would have preferred continued state promotion. Thus, businesspeople in Latin America generally and Brazil specifically embraced what Eduardo Silva has labeled "pragmatic neoliberalism."[11]

Second, markets allow more room for adjustment than the literature on economic reform typically assumes. Firms have more alternatives than simply to compete in the same market and in the same manner as previously or go under. Markets allow a wide range of specialty niches in which firms may choose to operate: They provide substantial subcontracting opportunities; they provide substantial opportunities to alter the mix of goods produced by firms as well as the sources of inputs; they allow for substantial changes in the degree of verticalization; they allow for substantial variety in the use of labor; they allow for a wide range of mergers, acquisitions, and other associations; finally, they create numerous opportunities to diversify out of uncompetitive activities. Thus, firms face many possible adjustment strategies in a period of economic reform, particularly in a large and complex market such as Brazil. Ultimately, the best choice is contingent, reflecting both the character of the market and the particular government policies.

Third, given the room to adjust, the decision to pursue commercial liberalization may not have sharp distributional consequences as trade theory often assumes. Thus, one important explanation for limited business resistance to neoliberalism is that the "losers" from open trade may not lose. As Brazil's policy course became clearer after 1994, industrialists adopted appropriate strategies for adjustment. For many Brazilian firms, adjustment meant joint ventures or mergers with foreign capital. For others, it meant some sort of licensing, subcontracting, or importing arrangement with foreign capital. Overall, trade liberalization may cause sectoral

10. Ben Ross Schneider has also made the case to treat business preferences as malleable and dynamic in a review article. "Elusive Synergy: Business-State Relations and Development," *Comparative Politics* 31, no. 1 (1998): 101–22.

11. Silva, *State and Capital in Chile*, 173–213.

changes and shifting resources, but many of the losers in this process remain leading figures in the industrial community through successful adjustment strategies.

Finally, given the possibility of adjustment, firms depend on clear signals from the government about both the policy direction and the sustainability of the program. Governments can publicly announce policies or privately commit themselves to a particular policy, and businesspeople can verify the government's performance, but sustainability is a subjective variable that reflects the perceptions of all actors involved. The government's track record on meeting commitments and the tactics it uses to pursue its program influence the credibility of its policy promises. Businesspeople read these political signals to determine the relative merits of supporting or opposing a reform program. These political signals reflect a contingent variable, tactics, and a structural variable, the electoral and related party system that affects legislative-executive bargaining. Thus, the factors that affect governability and government performance also significantly shape business participation in support coalitions.

The remainder of this chapter discusses the analytical framework used to analyze industrialists' behavior and their support for neoliberal reform broadly and commercial liberalization specifically. The first section considers the evidence of business support for neoliberalism in Latin America and the effects of organizational factors on business passivity. The second section considers how micro-level factors shape business preferences. The third section explores the ways in which the political process interacts with micro-level factors.

NEOLIBERALISM AND BUSINESS IN LATIN AMERICA

Many analysts view the arrival of neoliberalism in Latin America as a combination of an imposition from abroad—the "Washington consensus"—and an imposition by insulated technocrats with strong neoliberal orientations.[12] In this view, the shock of the debt crisis allowed techno-

---

12. This viewpoint has been mildly expressed in Bresser Pereira, *Economic Crisis and State Reform,* 15–30, which provides a review and a critique of the Washington consensus. A more scathing critique is in Petras, Leiva, and Veltmeyer, *Democracy and Poverty in Chile.* For a strong critique of the view that neoliberal reform was the product of technocrats versed in neoliberal theory and divorced from interest-group input, see Silva, *State and Capital in Chile,* 2–7.

crats with neoliberal agendas to assume positions of influence in the state structure. These technocrats put in place the largely unpopular reform measures supported by international pressure through the institutions of the Washington consensus, such as the International Monetary Fund (IMF), the World Bank, and the U.S. State Department. For the most part, these analyses typically see little domestic constituency, except for a narrow coalition of bankers and right-wing elites.

The empirical record, however, calls this view into question. Neoliberals have repeatedly won elections. Some who won as "stealth" neoliberal candidates—candidates who campaigned on a non-neoliberal program—implemented neoliberal reforms on winning. Yet, in some instances, these same stealth candidates, such as Carlos Menem of Argentina or Alberto Fujimori of Peru, were able to win re-election. Even more telling was the relative absence of opposition from groups most expected to oppose, such as labor and domestic industrial elites.

Domestic industrialists figure prominently among those groups that analysts usually expect to resist neoliberal reforms, and for good reason. Neoliberal reforms typically include a host of measures that threaten domestic industrialists. Reductions in state spending affect subsidies for business; privatizations can lead to price increases on previously subsidized inputs; commercial liberalization exposes domestic producers to import competition as well as competition from new foreign direct investment. Sixty years of protection and extensive state promotion hardly prepared domestic industrialists to compete in an open market. As numerous observers have pointed out, increasing exposure to trade can effect a rapid and profound redistribution of wealth.

Yet, domestic industrial elites in several Latin American countries not only failed to resist neoliberal reforms, but actually organized to support them. In Mexico, the Business Coordinating Council (CCE), mobilized against the populist tactics of Luis Echeverría in the 1970s, then became a source of business mobilization in favor of neoliberalism in the 1980s.[13] The Bolivian Confederation of Private Entrepreneurs (CEPB) emerged in Bolivia to push for the same set of reforms.[14] In Chile, industrialists joined with landowners to support neoliberal reform and to pressure the democratic opposition to Pinochet to continue supporting the reform process.[15] In Argentina, industrialists participated in repeated negotiations with the

---

13. Discussed in Heredia, "Mexican Business and the State," 203.
14. See Conaghan, "The Private Sector," 114ff.
15. See Bartell, "Perceptions," in Bartell and Payne, eds., *Business and Democracy in Latin America,* and in Silva, *State and Capital in Chile.*

Alfonsin government to support neoliberal-type reforms and then again supported Menem after 1989.[16] In Peru, business leaders also mobilized in favor of reform.[17] The same pattern of mobilizing to support neoliberal reforms appeared in Brazil as well. Support for the reform process emerged from a diverse group of new organizations including the small-business–dominated National Thought of the Business Bases (PNBE), the Liberal Institutes of São Paulo and Rio de Janeiro, the big business re-formers of the Institute for the Study of Industrial Development (IEDI), as well as umbrella groups like the Ação Empresarial (Business Action).[18]

This pattern of support for neoliberal reforms is particularly surprising in view of the way most Latin America studies have typically portrayed domestic industrialists. According to these common views, Latin American business elites are weak, passive, and dependent on state protection. Latin American business elites fail through their inability to act as a hege-monic class. Their risk aversion prevents them from defining a hegemonic project to lead society toward a true liberal, capitalist order, as business elites in developed societies supposedly did.

This analytic perspective identifies businesspeople's passivity as a func-tion of their character as a class. Delayed industrialization led to a late-blooming industrial class, dependent on state promotion. Domestic indus-trialists were never forced to face risks and remained risk averse through the period of import-substitution industrialization; therefore, they pre-ferred state protection. They were and remained dependent and passive; therefore, they preferred authoritarian controls on labor and privileged access to policymakers, which authoritarian regimes supposedly gave to businesspeople. In this perspective, the only explanation for the appear-ance of business support for reform is hypocrisy and/or fear of imports (i.e., support until imports enter).

The characterization of Latin American businesspeople as weak, pas-

16. See Acuña, "Business Interests," as well as Luigi Manzetti, *Institutions, Parties, and Coalitions in Argentina* (Pittsburgh: University of Pittsburgh Press, 1994), chap. 8. The two perspectives differ somewhat. Acuña's view of the industrialists' position was that of relative weakness in the face of the Menem government and little active input into policy deliberation. Manzetti's analysis suggests a much more active negotiating role for domestic industrialists and greater support for neoliberal reform among smaller, domestic-market–oriented industrialists.

17. See Durand, "From Fragile Crystal to Solid Rock: The Formation and Consolidation of a Business Peak Association in Peru," in Bartell and Payne, eds., *Business and Democracy in Latin America.* For an extended discussion, see Durand, *Business and Politics in Peru.*

18. For a discussion of Ação Empresarial and Brazilian business efforts to organize in the 1990s, see Ben Ross Schneider, "Organized Business Politics in Democratic Brazil," *Journal of Interamerican Studies and World Affairs* 39, no. 4 (1997): 95.

sive, and dependent may well have been partially correct, particularly with respect to the market,[19] but it presents several problems. First, it may significantly underestimate the effect of the political and economic context on business behavior. That is, given the strength of ISI and the range of benefits available under it, Latin American industrialists did not need to overcome their "fear of the market."[20] Second, this view sinks under the weight of evidence of business support. The sources of evidence include interviews, surveys, business documents, public statements, business mobilizations, and other explicit political acts. Furthermore, studies have documented this evidence in several countries.[21] Finally, even if business behavior did reflect hypocrisy, we would still need an additional theoretical basis for explaining the hypocrisy. No empirical examination of business has offered one.

A second type of explanation identifies business passivity as a function of the organization of business interests.[22] This explanation takes several

19. This understanding of business has been sharply criticized in recent empirical studies of Latin American business: Bartell, "Perceptions"; Conaghan, *Restructuring Domination*; Durand, *Business and Politics in Peru*; Payne, *Brazilian Industrialists,* and "Brazilian Business," in Bartell and Payne, eds., *Business and Democracy in Latin America*; Silva, *State and Capital in Chile*. Their analyses of business in Argentina, Chile, Bolivia, Ecuador, Peru, Mexico, as well as Brazil point to a much more nuanced reality. For example, Payne's work on Brazilian industrialists' attitudes toward democracy reveals a wide range of differing attitudes. Her study further pointed to a range of organizational factors that influence business decisions to mobilize and that are effective in influencing policy.

20. Cardoso and Rubens Figueiredo, "Reconciling the Capitalists." This notion that Brazilian industrialists feared the market (as opposed to democracy) is the central thesis of the article. I emphatically disagree with this view.

21. Note particularly the set of essays in Bartell and Payne, eds., *Business and Democracy in Latin America*. See also Carol Wise, "The Trade Scenario for Other Latin American Reformers in the NAFTA Era," in Carol Wise, ed., *The Post-NAFTA Political Economy: Mexico and the Western Hemisphere* (University Park: The Pennsylvania State University Press, 1998).

22. The study of business organizations has generated a large and impressive bibliography, particularly in Organization for Economic Cooperation and Development (OECD) countries. These have included studies linking the form of business interest organizations to rent seeking, such as Mancur Olson, *The Rise and Decline of Nations* (New Haven: Yale University Press, 1982); the role of business organizations in helping states create local capacity, such as Evans, *Embedded Autonomy,* or Richard Doner, "Limits of State Strength: Towards an Institutionalist View of Economic Development," *World Politics* 44 (April 1992); studies linking business organizations to particular styles of policymaking, such as the vast literature on neocorporatism: Katzenstein, *Small States in World Markets*; Philippe Schmitter, "Modes of Interest Intermediation and Models of Societal Change in Western Europe," *Comparative Political Studies* 10, no. 1 (1977); John Goldthorpe, *Order and Conflict in Contemporary Capitalism: Studies in the Political Economy of Western European Nations* (Oxford: Clarendon Press, 1984); as well as the impact of organizations on business efforts to influence policy, such as David Vogel, *Fluctuating Fortunes: The Political Power of Business in America* (New York: Basic Books,

alternative lines of argument: Businesspeople failed to resist reforms because of the passivity of business organizations and their focus on rent seeking;[23] businesspeople supported reforms, and resistance failed to develop because pro-reform businesses dominated organizations representing business interests;[24] businesspeople supported reforms, and resistance failed to develop because the state privileged pro-reform groups and marginalized antireform groups.[25]

This claim about business passivity locates the source of business weakness in the corporatist system of interest representation. According to this view, business organizations, especially in Brazil, have been organized in ways that diffuse business influence. Business organizations seek benefits from the state, which in turn grants them official recognition.[26] Thus, they are reluctant to challenge the state. These organizations reflect weak civil societies, poorly equipped to address grassroots concerns. This second claim about Latin American businesspeople certainly accurately describes the pattern of business representation for much of modern industrial history. It is supported by empirical and theoretical work on developed societies, work that identifies business organizations as a crucial variable that affects how well business defends its interests.

Yet it is easy to exaggerate this claim.[27] First, it is important not to

1989); Payne, *Brazilian Industrialists*; Elizabeth McQuerry, "Economic Liberalization in Brazil: Business Responses and Changing Patterns of Behavior" (Ph.D. diss., University of Texas, Austin, 1995).

23. Weyland, "The Fragmentation of Business in Brazil," in Durand and Silva, eds., *Business Peak Associations in Latin America* (Miami: North-South Center, forthcoming); Eli Diniz and Renato Raul Boschi, "Lideranças Empresariais e Problemas do Estratégia Liberal no Brasil" (paper presented at the International Seminar on Estratégias Liberais de Refundação, Dilemas Contemporâneos do Desenvolvimento, IUPERJ/CLACSO/ISA, Rio de Janeiro, 1992).

24. Manuel Pastor and Carol Wise, "The Origins and Sustainability of Mexico's Free Trade Policy," *International Organization* 48 (Summer 1994): 466.

25. Pastor and Wise, "Origins and Sustainability"; Shadlen, "Small Industry"; Aaron Tornell, "Are Economic Crises Necessary for Trade Liberalization and Fiscal Reform: The Mexican Experience," in Rudiger Dornbusch and Sebastian Edwards, eds., *Reform, Recovery, and Growth: Latin America and the Middle East* (Chicago: University of Chicago Press, 1995).

26. This view has been expressed by Weyland, "The Fragmentation of Business in Brazil," and Eli Diniz and Olavo Brasil Lima Jr., *Modernização Autoritaria: O Empresariado e a Intervenção do Estado na Economia* (Brasília: IPEA-CEPAL, 1986). The view goes back to earlier examinations of business organizations, most important, Schmitter, *Interest Conflict and Political Change in Brazil* (Stanford: Stanford University Press, 1971).

27. One case in point is Sebastião Velasco e Cruz's "Os Empresários e o Regime: A Campanha contra a Estatização" (Ph.D. diss., University of São Paulo, 1984), a study of the campaign against "statization." Velasco e Cruz documented the business campaign against excessive state growth implied by the first and second national development plans. He noted, however, that the movement grew out of liberal intellectual circles, such as the owner of Bra-

overstate the weakness of business organizations. For example, as René Dreifuss and Maria Antoinetta Leopoldi have demonstrated in Brazil, business organizations were active and effective in helping to orchestrate the 1964 coup as well as the 1950s import-substitution industrialization program.[28] Second, as Suzanne Berger has argued, interest organizations reflect the character of the state and change in response to changes in the state.[29] Latin American business organizations emerged to obtain benefits from a state that offered them. The state corporatist system functioned well to channel all manner of rents to the business community. In Brazil in the 1970s, an explosion of new associations occurred as firms sought to take advantage of the resources of the first and second National Development Plans,[30] but the combination of declining state resources and pressure from member firms provoked real changes in the 1980s and 1990s. New associations formed to better represent the interests of the business

---

zil's *Wall Street Journal* equivalent, the *Gazeta Mercantil*. Business opponents revealed themselves only after the movement had begun. Casual observers have suggested that this study shows that business is passive and purely reactive, but Velasco e Cruz's work suggests a different understanding. First, the business community had sharply diverging views of the plans. Luis Eulalio de Bueno Vidigal Filho, a leading figure in the transport material sector, saw state expansion as a threat to the production and sales of his family-owned firm, Cobrasma. As a consequence, he braved critical attacks from both the federal government and the state government of São Paulo to voice his opposition. On the other hand, Paulo Aguiar Cunha, principal owner and chief executive officer of Grupo Ultra, stood to benefit from the state's expansion into the petrochemical sector. As a consequence, Cunha was a supporter. Thus, the argument for business passivity ignores the importance of widely divergent views of the National Development Plans in the business community. A second limitation to Velasco e Cruz's passivity argument is that the plans did not threaten any firms until they resulted in investments that actually competed with important business interests. The initial reaction was an ideological reaction, from people without tangible business concerns. Businesspeople were broadly supportive of the state's role in the economy. Businesspeople joined the opposition only when that role directly threatened them.

28. René Dreifuss, *1964: A Conquista do Estado: Ação Política, Poder, e Golpe de Classe* (Petrópolis: Vozes, 1987). Maria Antoinetta Leopoldi, "Industrial Associations and Politics in Contemporary Brazil" (Ph.D. diss., Oxford University, 1984).

29. Suzanne Berger, "Regime and Interest Representation: The French Traditional Middle Classes," in Berger, ed., *Organizing Interests in Western Europe: Pluralism, Corporatism, and the Transformation of Politics* (New York: Cambridge University Press, 1981), 83–84.

30. This process is discussed in Diniz and Boschi, *Agregação e Representação de Interesses do Empresariado Industrial: Sindicatos e Associações de Classes* (Rio de Janeiro: Edições IUPERJ, 1979), 29–46. These authors showed that businesses rapidly created new voluntary associations parallel to the corporatist system and that these simultaneously afforded them lobbying power vis-à-vis the state while protecting them from the factors that made the corporatist, mandatory associations vulnerable to state intervention. Their study points to how rapidly business leaders developed new organizations capable of responding to changes in the state.

community.[31] In turn, these new associations pressured Brazil's leading industrialist organization, the Federation of Industry of the State of São Paulo (FIESP), to improve its leadership as well. In addition, sectoral associations reformed themselves, and shifted their focus from rent seeking to providing better member services. As a consequence, business associations were better able to serve as bases of support or opposition to reforms. Thus, business organizations proved more dynamic and more capable of reforming themselves then earlier analyses suggested.

The Brazilian case presents two further problems for the organizational perspective. First, the interests represented in several business organizations shifted in the period of this book. Voices that had been marginalized grew louder as a significant "modernization" movement swept through business organizations. This movement (actually three distinct strands of modernizers) brought a range of new voices into play, including small firms, pro-democracy firms, and pro-market or antistatism firms. Second, many of these new voices shifted from support to opposition back to support. Clearly, organizational factors alone could not account for that pattern.

In ten to fifteen years, businesspeople largely revealed themselves as more dynamic and more receptive to neoliberal reforms than the literature on Latin American politics suggested. In addition, the speed and extent to which business organizations reformed themselves point to the need for a better explanation of business behavior. To understand this pattern of behavior, we need a theoretical account of how businesspeople determine their preferences and what neoliberal reforms offered them.

INDUSTRIAL ADJUSTMENT AND MICRO-LEVEL INFLUENCES ON BUSINESS PREFERENCES

Most political science explanations of business preferences come from economics. These explanations can be loosely divided into three

31. For a discussion of small and microbusinesses, see Nylen, "Small Business Owners Fight Back." Discussions of big business changes are in Denise Barbosa Gros, "Empresariado e Ação Política na Nova República: Os Institutos Liberais de São Paulo e Rio Grande do Sul," in Diniz, ed., *Empresários e Modernização Econômica: Brasil Anos 90* (Florianópolis: Editora da UFSC/IDACON, 1992); Payne, *Brazilian Industrialists,* and "Brazilian Business"; Diniz and Boschi, "Lideranças Empresariais," and "Brasil: Um Novo Empresariado? Balanço de Tendências Recentes," in Diniz, ed., *Empresários.*

groups: production-profile explanations,[32] factor-endowment explanations (Heckscher–Olin Theory),[33] and specific factors (Ricardo–Viner Theory).[34]

Production-profile explanations derive preferences as a function of firms' market positions. Thus, for Milner, preferences are a function of the degree of export dependence and multinationality. For Gourevitch, they are primarily a function of international competitiveness and the stability of demand. In either case, export-oriented firms that are globally competitive prefer free trade, whereas domestic-market–oriented firms that are less competitive prefer protection.

Factor-endowment explanations derive preferences from the scarcity or abundance of a country's resources: land, labor, and capital. This explanation draws on the Heckscher–Olin theorem (and the Stolper–Samuelson refinement), which argues that increasing exposure to trade tends to benefit those factors in which a society is abundant and to hurt those factors in which a society is scarce. Thus, developing countries rich in land and labor, but scarce in capital, probably generate coalitions of labor and the countryside in favor of free trade against protectionist capital. Assuming that factors are not mobile has severe weaknesses in the modern global economy, however; even the primary champion of this view, Ronald Rogowski, suggested that his model was valid only until roughly 1960.[35]

Finally, specific factors arguments derive preferences based on the mobility of the specific factors that firms or sectors use to produce. This argument draws on the Ricardo–Viner theorem's critique of Heckscher-Olin for assuming little to no factor mobility. Instead, Ricardo-Viner assumes that at least some producers can shift factors from one use to another. Those producers who can shift easily—those who do not use highly specific factors—should support free trade. Alternatively, users of highly specific factors face high costs and possibly large losses from changing

---

32. For example, Milner, *Resisting Protectionism;* Gourevitch, *Politics in Hard Times;* Vinod Aggarwal, Robert Keohane, and David Yoffie, "The Dynamics of Negotiated Protectionism," *American Political Science Review* 81 (June 1987): 345–66; and Milner and David Yoffie, "Between Free Trade and Protectionism: Strategic Trade Policy and a Theory of Corporate Preferences," *International Organization* 43 (Spring 1989): 239–72.

33. Ronald Rogowski, *Commerce and Coalitions: How Trade Affects Domestic Political Alignments* (Princeton: Princeton University Press, 1989).

34. Jeffry Frieden, *Debt, Development, and Democracy: Modern Political Economy and Latin America, 1965–1985* (Princeton: Princeton University Press, 1991).

35. Rogowski, *Commerce and Coalitions,* 18.

patterns of trade. Thus, they are more likely to have intense preferences and to invest their resources in lobbying against free trade.

All three categories have yielded parsimonious, powerful explanations. Yet, all three generate inaccurate predictions about firm behavior in Brazil. Some reasons for this failure are discussed in a 1996 review of the literature on the political economy of international trade by James Alt, Jeffry Frieden, Michael Gilligan, Dani Rodrik, and Ronald Rogowski. The authors noted two problems with the existing literature. First, the politics of international trade are complex and varied enough that no single model can claim a monopoly on the truth. The authors further suggested that these models are not mutually exclusive and that they all operate to some degree depending on the circumstances. Thus, none of them alone performs particularly well in explaining the available data. The authors concluded that explaining trade coalitions requires more models rather than one universal model.[36]

The second problem facing these models is the importance of intra-industry as opposed to interindustry trade. If countries primarily trade differentiated products in the same sectors, increasing trade need not result in sectors losing out. In other words, intraindustry trade may sharply mitigate the redistributive effects of increasing exposure to trade. In that context, the dynamics of support or opposition to free trade may be much more ambiguous.[37] In general, the dynamics of coalition building are ambiguous if increasing trade does not represent absolute losses for some sectors and absolute gains for others.

We can illustrate some of these difficulties by briefly considering the Brazilian case. For example, pulp and paper firms require very large in-

---

36. Alt, Frieden, Gilligan, Rodrik, and Rogowski, "The Political Economy of International Trade," 691.

37. Alt, Friedan, Gilligan, Rodrik, and Rogowski, "The Political Economy of International Trade," 704–5, looked to the literature on the economics of institutions for a solution to the problem of explaining trade coalitions. In particular, they pointed to the work of Oliver Williamson and others on asset specificity and industrial organization. What emerges from their review is that asset specificity is a very difficult concept to measure because of the variety of ways in which an asset may be specific. For example, they noted that Williamson identifies four different kinds of specificity: site specificity, meaning that assets are highly immobile; physical specificity, meaning the asset is designed for highly specific transactions; human specificity, meaning the asset lies in human capital and specific relations or patterns of learning by doing (although presumably political relations should be able to create specificity as well); and dedicated assets, meaning assets dedicated to a specific customer so that the loss of the customer would result in significant excess capacity (705). One consequence not discussed by Alt and colleagues is that firm preferences and thus trade coalitions probably cannot be specified a priori.

vestments in highly specific assets, including very expensive, specialized machinery as well as a range of specific needs related to ownership of large forests of a particular kind of tree—eucalyptus. According to the specific factors argument, pulp and paper producers should have intense preferences about trade policy and should lobby aggressively to protect them. Instead, pulp and paper producers were relatively indifferent to commercial liberalization: They could survive either way. In contrast, the financial sector, holders of presumably highly mobile assets, was much warier of neoliberal reforms. In particular, as Leslie Elliott Armijo has argued, financial-sector regulations allowed banks to earn substantial profits from inflation.[38] As a result, neoliberalism's emphasis on stabilization and financial liberalization significantly threatened them.

The preferences of the pulp and paper sector tended to support production-profile explanations. As globally competitive producers, the most vertically integrated firms in the sector (primarily domestic) exported as much as 50 percent of their production. Their preferences conformed more to Helen Milner's prediction that firms with low degrees of multinationality but high export dependence would prefer open markets abroad but protected markets at home. Nevertheless, Milner's otherwise powerful framework fails to account for the reasons that majorities of machine tool and auto parts producers (both heavily domestic, nonexporting producers) would support commercial liberalization.

In addition to the limitations that Alt and colleagues identified, several other factors demonstrate that market complexity makes a priori specifications difficult. First, commercial liberalization did not imply the wholesale disappearance of entire sectors, especially in cases like Brazil where the large internal market justifies and supports a wide range of industrial activities. Some analysts have noted that the benefits of free trade are diffuse whereas the losses are specific,[39] but in a large, complex market with diverse opportunities for adjustment, the losses may be diffuse as well. Second, neoliberal reforms also entailed a relaxation of foreign direct investment (FDI) rules. The inflow of FDI threatened to displace some economic actors while creating new adjustment possibilities for others. Thus, even for firms that could not compete with imports, new capital inflows opened possibilities of licensing or subcontracting arrangements as well as mergers and joint ventures. Finally, the fact that many leading

38. Leslie Elliott Armijo, "Inflation and Insouciance: The Peculiar Brazilian Game," *Latin American Research Review* 31, no. 3 (1996): 7–46.

39. Raquel Fernandez and Dani Rodrik, "Resistance to Reform: Status Quo Bias in the Presence of Individual-Specific Uncertainty," *American Economic Review* 81, no. 5 (1991).

Brazilian firms are part of large conglomerates *(grupos econômicos)* meant that decision makers had interests that transcended particular sectors. These elements contributed to much more flexible and contingent attitudes vis-à-vis commercial liberalization than much of the existing literature suggests.[40]

Another important reason that these views fail to predict business preferences is that Latin American businesses made their choices in "hard times"—times of crisis in which the status quo was no longer tenable. As Peter Gourevitch has noted, behavior changes in times of crisis. Routinized responses to problems do not work and thus make actors aware of the need to try new solutions. Brazilian businesspeople faced a host of related problems that clearly pointed to the need for change: declining state revenues coupled with a rapidly growing need to finance state operations through massive domestic borrowing; intractable inflation, partially fueled by state borrowing (at constantly rising costs as state credibility dwindled) and partially maintained through inertia; rapidly dwindling resources for investment and declining infrastructure; shrinking internal market managed through increasing financial speculation and by ever-higher profit margins charged on ever-shrinking production volumes; finally, ever-more politicized and erratic state regulation of the economy. For Brazilian businesspeople, it grew increasingly clear through the 1980s that import substitution generally and protectionism specifically no longer offered answers.

Finally, businesspeople did not make simple choices between higher or lower tariffs. The breakdown in Latin America in the 1980s is more analogous to the global crisis of the 1930s, in that it provoked a fundamental reconsideration of each country's growth strategy. Latin American policymakers and businesspeople had to address larger questions involving the role of the state, the character of the integration into the global economy, the character of labor relations. Thus, businesspeople faced tariff policy as part of a bundle of policies associated with neoliberal reforms. Even if they preferred protection, commercial liberalization figured as an essential component of the overall program.[41] In turn, the overall program

---

40. This is one of the crucial claims of Eduardo Silva in *State and Capital in Chile.*

41. This is consistent with Albert Hirschman's observation that opponents of reforms may be induced to support in that beneficial policies may compensate them for losses they may suffer as a consequence of reforms. Pastor and Wise, "Origins and Sustainability," made the case that Mexican business elites supported commercial liberalization because it came with a promise of stabilization. Nevertheless, their argument is made without specific empirical exmaination of the preferences or behavior of these Mexican business leaders. In the Brazilian case, it is unlikely that stabilization would have been sufficient to overcome concerns about

promised many benefits that offset some costs of reform and facilitated competitive adjustments. Those promised benefits directly addressed the problems related to the fiscal crisis of the state: renewed investment in crucial areas of infrastructure; new sources of financing; improvement of the tax system; decrease in state borrowing and thus crowding out private investment; easing of state regulation; shifting consumption from the unreliable state to more creditworthy private owners; elimination of all manner of perverse distortions in the price system; opportunities related to commercial liberalization, such as importing lower-cost, higher-quality inputs; finally stabilization.

All these issues point to the need for a more nuanced framework to explain free-trade coalitions. The role of crisis, the ways in which policies are bundled, and the ambiguity that market size, conglomerates, intra-industry trade, and FDI added to adjustment possibilities all point to the need to understand how particular policies and politicians interact with the nuances of the market. One possible solution is suggested by the literature on industrial adjustment. A central tenet of this literature is that states and markets interact in a wide variety of ways.[42] The specific ways in which they interact have important consequences for how the state and the private sector manage the challenges of economic change. Thus, the character of business coalitions is inherently political. Businesses always have choices, but what they choose to do reflects the ways in which they can influence the political process and in turn the ways in which the political process influences them. Business choices vary widely depending on such questions as how decision making occurs, who participates in deci-

---

losing out to imported products because indexation was so much more effective and extensive in Brazil. Indexation meant and still means that important segments of Brazilian society can contemplate political programs that result in renewed inflation because they know there are mechanisms to protect them.

42. For example, in the 1980s, scholarship on industrial adjustment identified several different typologies of models of adjustment. Thus, Zysman, *Governments, Markets, and Growth,* identified the actors responsible for coordinating the adjustment process: company-led, state-led, and negotiated. Katzenstein, *Small States in World Markets,* framed his discussion in terms of exporting or internalizing the costs of adjustment. Harold Wilensky, *Democratic Corporatism and Policy Linkages: The Interdependence of Industrial, Labor-Market, Incomes, and Social Policies in Eight Countries* (Berkeley: Institute of International Studies, University of California, 1987), included pluralist, corporatist, and corporatist without labor. The number of categories has increased as the industrial adjustment literature has refined its appreciation of the variety of forms of economic coordination. Thus, Hollingsworth and Boyer, *Contemporary Capitalism,* 9–19, identified a range of coordinating mechanisms that can exist simultaneously in one region or nation, including networks, communities, associations, markets, private hierarchies, and the state.

sion making, the ways in which participants are allowed to participate in decision making, the ways in which interests are organized and whose interests are organized, the ways labor and capital interact, as well as the myriad ways in which the political process links social actors to the state and to one another.[43] Although this framework itself does not necessarily generate parsimonious theories, it does allow a systematic analysis of business-state relations in a period of change. After all, in a period of significant reform, such as the turn to neoliberalism, changes may be occurring simultaneously in almost all these areas as well as in their interactions with one another.

Thus, posing the problem of explaining support for neoliberal reform as a problem of industrial adjustment allows for a more nuanced understanding of coalition dynamics. Firms have opportunities to adjust. Yet, politicians have a significant impact on whether they choose to support or oppose reforms and which adjustment strategies they choose to pursue.

CRAFTING COALITIONS FOR REFORM

Why do businesspeople support commercial reforms that impose high costs on them? This book argues that politicians play a vital role in crafting such coalitions through the choices they present in the electoral arena, the policy commitments they make, and the credibility of their commitment to deliver, particularly in times of crisis.[44] Businesspeople understand that the status quo may no longer be viable in a crisis. Politicians'

43. On this point, Stephan Haggard, Sylvia Maxfield, and Ben Ross Schneider have made an important contribution in discussing the variety of ways in which analysts can understand and examine business: business as a class; business as sector; business as firms; business as associations; and business as networks. Haggard, Maxfield, and Schneider, "Theories of Business," 37 in Maxfield and Schneider, eds., *Business and the State.*

44. Gourevitch, *Politics in Hard Times,* framed his whole discussion in terms of crisis but did not discuss the issue of credibility. As for coalition formation, Gourevitch noted that many factors influence market position and that both the state and intermediary associations play a critical role in determining which interests have a voice. His framework, then, is not deterministic, but he still tends to treat preferences mechanically as functions of market position rather than as something that may be shaped by the political process. Both John Keeler, "Opening the Window for Reform: Mandates, Crises, and Extraordinary Policy-Making," *Comparative Political Studies* 25 (January 1993): 433–86, and Tornell, "Are Economic Crises Necessary," in Dornbusch and Edwards, eds., *Reform, Recovery, and Growth,* made explicit cases for the importance of crisis as a factor that gives policymakers the autonomy they need from social groups to implement reform policies.

policy commitments influence how firms see their adjustment options. In turn, the credibility of politicians' commitments affects their perceptions of the costs and benefits of supporting reform.

Thus, to some extent, the problem of crafting reform coalitions is a bargaining problem. Scholars have noted that there are several ways in which policymakers can compensate potential losers from trade liberalization.[45] Those compensatory commitments include stabilization[46] or policies such as exchange-rate devaluations,[47] pursuing gradual reforms or eliminating import licenses.[48] To a certain extent, the problem is one of simply providing a stable economic environment with clear signals about future policy. In that context, even potential losers can successfully work out adjustment alternatives.

Yet the problem of crafting a support coalition does not disappear after the initiation of reforms.[49] Although analysts and scholars have debated the merits of shock programs versus gradualism,[50] time has proved the question somewhat moot. As of the late 1990s, it is clear that all neoliberal programs are by necessity gradual: Getting "the prices right" has turned out to be a necessary but not sufficient condition for resuming growth. As a consequence, governments must continuously adjust their policy programs to maintain political support for reforms. To build support, politicians must be able to bargain credibly with social actors.

Dani Rodrik noted that under conditions of uncertainty about a government's intentions, investors would prefer the status quo to reforms. To avoid this behavior, Rodrik suggested that reform governments needed to act boldly so as to send a powerful, credible signal of their intent to pursue reforms.[51] In the Brazilian case, Fernando Collor pursued a gradual

---

45. Javier Corrales, "Coalitions and Corporate Choices in Argentina, 1976–1994: The Recent Private Sector Support for Privatization," *Studies in Comparative International Development* 32, no. 4 (1998): 24–51; and Hector Schamis, "Distributional Coalitions and the Politics of Economic Reform in Latin America," *World Politics* 51, no. 2 (1999): 236–68, are two recent studies of business support for neoliberal reforms also making coalitional arguments that turn on bargains between executives and leading domestic businesses.

46. Dani Rodrik, "The Rush to Free Trade," in Haggard and Webb, *Voting for Reform,* 83; Pastor and Wise, "Origins and Sustainability," 467.

47. Rodrik, "The Rush to Free Trade," 76–77.

48. Haggard and Webb, *Voting for Reform,* 18–19.

49. Alberto Alesina and Allan Drazen, "Why Are Stabilizations Delayed?" *American Economic Review* 81, no. 5 (1991) made the point about stabilization. They argued that because stabilization is not a "one-shot affair," actors have to resolve the distribution of costs over an extended period.

50. This debate is reviewed in Haggard and Webb, *Voting for Reform,* 22–24.

51. Rodrik, "Promises, Promises: Credible Policy Reform via Signalling," *Economic Journal* 99 (September 1989): 758.

commercial liberalization, but he initiated his reform program with a dramatic anti-inflation shock and a host of deregulatory measures during his first three months in office.

As important as it is for government to signal the credibility of its intent to pursue reforms, it must also maintain credibility beyond the initial reforms. Crafting and maintaining a coalition in favor of reform also depend on the credibility of a government's future policy commitments. Businesspeople must make adjustment decisions that may have implications or may show no results for years after the initial decision. Thus, they must evaluate not only the government's past performance, but also the credibility of the government's policy commitments. The choices a government makes about how to implement its program send important signals to private actors. Those signals influence businesses' perceptions of the government's ability to deliver in the future.

In turn, government tactics reflect the way the political system shapes executive-legislative bargaining. In particular, the organization of political parties and the electoral system affect the incentives facing individual legislators. The more autonomous the individual legislators, the more complex, costly, and unpredictable the bargaining process. By contrast, political systems with disciplined parties may have a much easier time bargaining with the executive.[52] Clearly, the more complex the bargaining process, the more difficult it is for executives to make credible commitments on future policy.

Bargaining in the Brazilian political system is particularly complex, costly, and unpredictable.[53] Brazilian legislators are elected through pro-

52. The most extensive discussion of how the internal characteristics of political parties shape governing performance in Latin America is in Mainwaring and Scully, eds., *Building Democratic Institutions*. The most important discussion of the relations of presidents and assemblies in Latin America is Matthew Soberg Shugart and John M. Carey, *Presidents and Assemblies: Constitutional Designs and Electoral Dynamics* (New York: Cambridge University Press, 1992). One work that combines some of the insights of these two volumes is Mainwaring and Shugart, *Presidentialism and Democracy in Latin America* (New York: Cambridge University Press, 1997).

53. Timothy J. Power, "The Pen Is Mightier Than the Congress: Presidential Decree Power in Brazil," in John Carey and Shugart, eds., *Executive Decree Authority: Calling Out the Tanks or Filling Out the Forms* (New York: Cambridge University Press, 1998). See also Mainwaring, "Presidentialism, Multipartism, and Democracy: The Difficult Combination," *Comparative Political Studies* 26 (July 1993): 198–228. Discussions of the effects of patronage on congressional behavior can be found in Barry Ames, "Electoral Rules, Constituency Pressures, and Pork Barrel: Bases of Voting in the Brazilian Congress," *Journal of Politics* 57 (May 1995): 324–43; Ames, "Electoral Strategy Under Open-List Proportional Representation," *American Journal of Political Science* 39 (May 1995): 406–33.

portional representation in statewide districts with open lists. This clustering of characteristics has produced what Scott Mainwaring and Timothy R. Scully[54] have labeled an "inchoate" party system, in which electoral patterns are unstable, political parties lack roots in society, voters do not perceive the electoral process as either legitimate or important, and party organizations do not matter. In fact, Brazilian legislators are notoriously independent of political parties.[55]

As Mainwaring[56] and Barry Ames[57] have shown, however, the legislators maintain strong links to particular functional or geographic constituencies. To win elections in a statewide district, candidates tend to concentrate their efforts on distinct voter groups in a state. To maintain those ties, they must remain sensitive to the demands of the groups and depend on their ability to deliver patronage resources. Overall, Brazilian legislators face little incentive to worry about good government and tend to primarily concern themselves with satisfying narrow, particularistic groups.

This system, labeled *corporativismo*[58] by Brazilians, forces government and political party leaders into new negotiations for every piece of legislation. Presidents must construct a new ad hoc governing coalition for each piece of their program. Presidents' social support is of limited help because power is diffused through the system and legislators respond to narrow, elite groups. Neither the mass of low-income voters nor the encompassing business groups sway legislative votes on any consistent basis.

For the purpose of this book, there are two important consequences of this system. First, presidents must pay out large sums of patronage to maintain legislative coalitions. In principle there is nothing wrong with this practice as long as it works, but in practice, the cost can be very

54. Mainwaring and Scully, *Building Democratic Institutions*, 4–5.

55. This argument differs somewhat from the emphasis Haggard and Robert Kaufman, *The Political Economy of Democratic Transitions* (Princeton: Princeton University Press, 1995), put on polarization and fragmentation of the party system. Instead, this argument focuses more on the characteristics of political parties and the ways those characteristics affect executive-legislative relations.

56. Mainwaring, "Politicians, Parties, and Electoral Systems," and "Brazil," in Mainwaring and Scully, eds., *Building Democratic Institutions*.

57. Ames, "Electoral Rules," and "Electoral Strategy," as well as *Political Survival: Politicians and Public Policy in Latin America* (Berkeley and Los Angeles: University of California Press, 1987).

58. The term *corporativismo* does not have the same meaning as *corporatism*. Brazilians use this term to refer to the very narrow interest groups represented by specific politicians in the legislature, distinct from the formal interest organizations with state-sanctioned monopolies on representation, as described by Schmitter, *Interest Conflict*.

high. In addition, Brazilian legislators have proved unwilling to support measures that significantly penalize well-organized voting groups or significantly restrict their own access to patronage resources. Unfortunately, both the neoliberal program specifically and sound macroeconomic policy generally have demanded exactly such measures. Thus, successive presidents have attempted a series of constitutional reforms needed to address what Luis Carlos Bresser Pereira labeled "the fiscal crisis of the state."[59] As of 1997, they have made only limited progress.

The second consequence stemming from the Brazilian electoral system is that presidents are forced to repeatedly change tactics to reconstruct legislative support and maintain social support. Each tactical change sends out political signals that businesspeople use to evaluate the credibility of government commitments. The frequency of tactical shifts leads businesspeople to continuously reevaluate the costs and benefits of supporting reforms. In that context, businesses hold off adopting adjustment strategies or hedge their bets even after they do. Politically, this erratic process leaves coalitions more fragile and fluid. Figure 3 traces this argument in Brazil.

There are two important limitations to the fluidity of support coalitions. First, businesspeople are takers of what politicians offer them in the electoral arena. Thus, in coalitional terms, business preferences sometimes point to the lesser of two evils. In 1989, business elites backed Fernando Collor—an apparently rash, impulsive neoliberal, neopopulist elite basher. They had preferred several other more moderate neoliberal candidates, but Collor emerged as the only viable right-of-center candidate. In 1996, business criticism and pressure mounted against Fernando Henrique Cardoso, but as soon as Cardoso forced a choice between re-electing him or electing anybody else, business leaders rallied to his side.

The second limitation arises as a consequence of investing in specific adjustment strategies. Once firms choose a specific path and sink costs in that path, they become more dependent on continuation of the same policy course. This fact is consistent with the argument in this book because firms are likely to invest in a particular strategy only once there is some policy stability and coherence. In this context, coalition fluidity is likely to diminish somewhat. Nevertheless, the unpredictability of the Brazilian process has consequences for how private firms define their adjustment strategies.

59. Bresser Pereira has devoted considerable intellectual energy to describing and explaining the fiscal crisis of the state in Brazil, although the original term is not his—he credits James O'Connor (see Bresser Pereira, *Economic Crisis and State Reform,* 24).

Fig. 3. Political signals and business responses, 1990–1996

Year/Event	Attempted Reform	Tactical Signals	Business Response
March 1990: Inauguration	Drastic stabilization, deregulation, commercial liberalization	Collor uses popular legitimacy and executive decrees to impose his program on a defensive congress	Business groups express support; begin adjustments; express concern about long-term reforms and policy plans
October 1990: Midterm elections	Contain inflation (Collor II) through intervention and controls on business	After Collor's electoral strategy fails, attacks business elites as part of new political strategy	Business anger mounts—increasing charges of government incompetence, calls for noncompliance
March 1991: The "soft style"	Industrial policy and constitutional amendments *(emendão)*	Collor changes economic team; pledges no more shocks; labels new style the "soft style"	Business groups respond well; leading groups help negotiate social pact for constitutional reform
November 1991: Failed social pact	Emergency tax increases; abandonment of real fiscal reform; legislative agenda stalled	Collor sharply increases patronage spending and rolls over state debt in exchange for tax hike—needed to secure IMF standby loan	Business opposition emerges publicly in the period—first among more threatened sectors, then everywhere by early 1992
October 1992: Suspension of President Collor	None: Government loses policy direction; privatizations slow; inflation rises rapidly	Frequent finance minister changes; public disputes over policy direction	Business adjustment strategies on hold; short-term profits earned on old high-inflation strategies
March–October 1994: The Real Plan and the Cardoso election	Real Plan. Continued privatization and accelerated commercial liberalization	Cardoso mixes consensus building and hardball politics to secure plan	Business support very high; new FDI inflows and business adjustment renews

Year/Event	Attempted Reform	Tactical Signals	Business Response
January–June 1996: The failure of constitutional reform	Reform of social security, civil service, and tax system	Mixture of consensus building, patronage dispensing, and occasional hardball politics (including insults)	Business associations engaging Cardoso critics; lobbying pressure mounts; business organizes "march to Brasília"
June–December 1996: Public admission of failed tactics. Tactical changes and the re-election amendment	Incremental changes to production taxes; new lines of credit; new import control; re-election amendment	Cardoso admits failure of tactics; promises new "incremental" approach; offers new benefits to industry; announces support for re-election	Business criticism diminishes; business leaders publicly rally to support Cardoso as only candidate who can pass reforms

In sum then, this book offers an analytic framework for studying business preferences (as opposed to a theory of preferences), a framework sensitive to the complexity of the market and the ways in which the political process interacts with it. The study's central claims are summarized in Figure 4 (page 26).

Fig. 4.   Crafting coalitions: Principal hypotheses

1. Crises disrupt institutionalized patterns of business-state, business-business, and business-labor relations. As a consequence, businesses become available for alternative (and even costly) reform programs.

2. Even the most challenged sectors and many of the most challenged firms could support neoliberal reforms because they could conceive viable adjustment strategies. However, their viability depended on the government's delivering on its policy commitments.

3. Because successful adjustments depended on the governments resolving the practical problems each sector faced, even the least threatened firms and sectors could shift into opposition if they believed that the government could not credibly deliver on its policy commitments.

4. Although the potential for support was widely distributed across the industrial community, the strength of support for neoliberal reform varied with the degree to which firms and sectors were internationally competitive and independent of the state.

5. Crises lead businesspeople to pressure for changes to their organizations as they seek effective political expression that addresses changing micro-level circumstances and business–state relations.

6. Businesspeople make strategic decisions about industrial adjustment and political support for reform efforts with reference to the credibility of government policy commitments. Businesspeople judge credibility by evaluating government's tactical choices for implementing reforms.

7. Politicians make tactical choices with reference to their institutional environments. Fragmented political systems with weak political parties significantly increase the uncertainty and instability of executive strategies.

8. Support for reforms tend to consolidate as businesspeople invest in particular adjustment strategies. Thus, even though the distribution of losses may become more defined, businesspeople foreclose other alternatives and depend on policy continuity.

9. Businesspeople are to a large extent takers of what is offered in the electoral system. Thus, business leaders may support a candidate of whom they are unsure or critical if this is the best available choice.

2

Breaking with the Past

Fiscal Crises, Constitutional Messes, and the Business Revolt Against the State

From 1930 through the 1970s, the Brazilian business community prospered under a state-led development model. The model prompted growth through import-substitution industrialization and linked business to the state through corporatist interest organizations. Business support for this ISI–corporatist model dissipated after the debt crisis and the resulting fiscal crisis of the state. High and rising inflation, rapidly increasing public debt, erratic government policy, and a fiscally destabilizing new constitution combined to undermine business performance and erode the legitimacy of the state's presence in the economy. Thus, by the late 1980s, the micro-level consequences of these tangible problems left Brazilian industrialists available for new policy coalitions. Neoliberalism was not the only plausible alternative, but, it was the most successful one politically. This chapter explores the character of the Brazilian crisis of the 1980s, the problems that affected the business community, and the basis of industrialists' support for neoliberalism.

CRISES, PREFERENCES, AND THE POLITICAL BASES OF REFORM

Many observers of politics have noted that crises play an important role in promoting or facilitating reform. This observation has led to a variety of hypotheses about the linkages between crises and the initiation of difficult reforms. For example, Haggard and Kaufman argued that crisis leads to a pervasive sense that "something must be done," thus granting executives wide leeway for promoting reform.[1] In a similar vein, Tornell argued that crises are necessary for stabilization because they weaken opponents and allow policymakers room to impose the costs of the policy.[2] Keeler argued that crises create windows of opportunity in which executives are freer to act.[3] David Collier argued that the perception of crisis among elites helps contribute to the breakdown of democracy.[4] Gourevitch argued that international economic crises break existing coalitions and lead social actors to seek new coalitions in support of alternative economic policies.[5] In an earlier study, Binder and colleagues argued that modern polities evolved in response to their particular sequence of developmental crises.[6]

Scholars have focused less on how crises affect business preferences for policy. One prevalent view, articulated by Haggard (1987) and Fernandez and Rodrik (1991), suggests that businesspeople have weak policy preferences in times of economic reform because they do not know a priori how reforms affect them. This absence of preferences tends to enhance policymakers' autonomy, even though it may weaken efforts to mobilize political support from potential beneficiaries. This argument tends to downplay the role of social actors in supporting and facilitating reforms.[7]

That actors cannot foresee the future during a crisis does not mean that crises do not affect how actors perceive their situations or that they do not have strong preferences for policies. Businesspeople may not know the correct strategic program for solving a crisis, but they are conscious of the practical problems they face at the micro-level. They remain capable of evaluating and expressing preferences for specific policies related to their micro-level problems. What they seek is a complement between

---

1. Haggard and Kaufman, *Political Economy of Democratic Transitions,* 160.

2. Tornell, "Are Economic Crises Necessary?"

3. Keeler, "Opening the Window for Reform."

4. David Collier, ed., *The New Authoritarianism in Latin America* (Princeton: Princeton University Press, 1979).

5. Gourevitch, *Politics in Hard Times.*

6. Leonard Binder, *Crises and Sequences in Political Development* (Princeton: Princeton University Press, 1971).

7. John Echeverri-Gent made this point in "The Dynamic Constraints of India's Economic Reform: A Critique of Game-Theoretical Approaches to Interest Representation" (paper presented at the American Political Science Association Meeting, Washington, D.C., August 1993). Echeverri-Gent argued that gradual domestic changes may support the emergence of pro-reform coalitions.

the policy programs that politicians offer and the practical problems they face at the micro-level.

To see how actors look for practical solutions to their problems, it is worthwhile considering a definition of a *crisis*. Sidney Verba defined crises as "situations in which the basic institutional patterns of the political system are challenged and routine response is inadequate."[8] During crises, actors become aware that routinized strategies for solving problems do not work. Instead, they look for reforms that permit them to successfully address the challenges they face. In that context, social actors are open to alternative coalitions and institutions, and politicians have to offer institutional innovations to mobilize support.

Under the ISI-corporatist model, Brazilian industrialists had found relatively stable, successful, and institutionalized patterns of interacting with one another, with the state, and with labor. Each firm could rely on relatively routine responses to the challenges of growing and competing in the Brazilian market, but the combination of fiscal crisis and the dilemmas posed by the 1988 Constitution profoundly called into question this growth model. By 1989, Brazilian industrialists were seeking a new growth model that could resolve conflicts between business and the state, between firms, in and among sectoral and peak associations, and between business and labor. They did not have well-defined preferences for an overall growth model, but they did have well-defined preferences for policies that addressed the concrete and easily defined problems associated with the collapse of the ISI-corporatist model.

A BRIEF HISTORY OF THE ISI-CORPORATIST MODEL

Brazil's basic industrial development model dates back at least to Getúlio Vargas and the *Estado Nôvo* in 1937. This model rested on two key principles: large-scale state intervention and participation in the economy[9] and extensive use of patronage resources passed through clientelist prac-

---

8. Sidney Verba, "Sequences and Development," in Binder, *Crises and Sequences,* 302.

9. This principle is one of the defining features of Brazilian development and is very well documented. For example, see Thomas Skidmore, *Politics in Brazil, 1930–1964: An Experiment in Democracy* (Oxford: Oxford University Press, 1967); Werner Baer, *The Brazilian Economy: Growth and Development* (New York: Praeger, 1995).

tices and corporatist institutions.[10] The model generated benefits in terms of economic growth, although at a very real price. In particular, it tended toward generating recurring fiscal crises, politically excluding much of the population, and weakening already weak political institutions such as parties and interest organizations. Getúlio Vargas laid down its basic framework by establishing the first corporatist institutions[11] and promoting import-substitution industrialization (ISI) and state involvement in production.[12]

ISI emerged under Vargas largely as a consequence of the Great Depression and World War II. With supplies from abroad disrupted, the Vargas administration created the first state industries. From that starting point, state production continued to expand to substitute imported goods. The state expanded its leadership role to foster local private production and to contain and regulate the participation of foreign capital. The state also invested heavily in infrastructure development. One of the central goals was rapid industrialization; for example, President Kubitschek (1955–60) stated that he intended to move Brazil fifty years in only five.[13]

State officials interacted with relevant interest groups through the network of corporatist institutions established by Vargas in the 1930s. Borrowing heavily from the fascist constitutions of the day, Vargas constructed a series of institutions that vertically tied segments of labor and business into the state.[14] The result was a civil society that depended on the state for resources and was more state focused than member focused.[15] The state conferred legal status on approved organizations and negotiated only with those it recognized. Forging links with bureaucratic agencies paid off much better than grassroots organizing or forming horizontal linkages with other organizations (which was in many cases ille-

---

10. For a discussion of clientelism, corporatism, and their consequences for political parties and bureaucratic politics, see Kaufman, "The Politics of Economic Stabilization in Post War Latin America," in James Malloy, ed., *Authoritarianism and Corporatism in Latin America* (Pittsburgh: University of Pittsburgh Press, 1977), 111–16.

11. Kenneth Paul Erickson, *The Brazilian Corporative State and Working Class Politics* (Berkeley and Los Angeles: University of California Press, 1977), 11–26.

12. See, for example, Skidmore, *Politics in Brazil,* 41–47.

13. Cited in Paulo Rabello Castro and Marcio Ronci, "Sixty Years of Populism in Brazil," in Dornbusch and Edwards, eds., *The Macroeconomics of Populism in Latin America* (Chicago: University of Chicago Press, 1991), 160.

14. See Skidmore, *Politics in Brazil,* 3–47, for a discussion of the development of Vargas's constitution and the origins of corporatist institutions.

15. The classic study of the weakness of Brazilian civil society remains Schmitter, *Interest Conflict.*

gal). Not surprisingly, this corporatist system created privileged, self-interested leaderships in both labor and business organizations.

The model continued to develop with the restoration of democracy in 1945. From 1945 to 1960, under Presidents Dutra, Vargas, and Kubitschek, the state expanded its productive role, pursued ISI more aggressively, and bought continued social support by distributing extensive benefits through the corporatist structure. As industrialization progressed in the 1940s and 1950s, the coalition expanded to formally include previously excluded members of society, particularly labor. State elites purchased social support through an array of nonproductive and frequently inflationary benefits. Business was bought off with protected markets, subsidies, tax incentives, cheap utilities, and favorable manipulations of the exchange-rate system. Labor was bought off with access to the social security institute[16] and with wages indexed to the rate of inflation (unconnected to productivity). Labor also benefited from ample access to the critical labor ministry with its influence over labor-management conflicts.[17] The middle class was bought off with an expansion of opportunities and services, at least in part through the dramatic expansion of the civil service and increases in civil service salaries.

Professional politicians formed an important segment of the coalition. Politicians were the principal agents of patronage such as road work, hospitals, bridges, and rail systems, as well as government-contracting and civil service jobs. Although they were important conduits of patronage, their spirited defense of the patronage system went beyond merely defending client interests. Patronage offered politicians opportunities for tremendous self-enrichment and career promotion. Politicians' defense of particularistic interests was also a defense of a system in which they flourished.

Landed elites suffered economic costs through the manipulation of the exchange-rate system that indirectly taxed agricultural producers to support industrial financing. A gerrymander in the electoral system disproportionately weighted rural votes in the North and Northeast. This weighting protected the local elite's political power by allowing it to veto any effort at land reform or other efforts to restructure rural politics or economics. It also assured the elite of a sizable share of patronage resources.

---

16. See Malloy, *The Politics of Social Security in Brazil* (Pittsburgh: University of Pittsburgh Press, 1979).

17. Erickson, *Brazilian Corporative State.*

Thus, the model incorporated a defining strategic orientation: import-substitution industrialization; specific policies to implement the strategy's goals, such as Brazil's variable exchange-rate policy in the 1950s;[18] a support base made up of business, workers, technocrats, and politicians; and a set of corporatist institutions that linked the social base to the state. Brazil's ISI growth strategy fused into the development model a political logic based on patronage and clientelism and mediated through corporatist institutions.

This model's principal political weakness lay in politicians' dependence on patronage and clientelism to purchase support. Consequently, political parties did not develop a role as vehicles of popular mobilization and did not form ideological appeals or offer programmatic solutions to Brazilian problems.[19] They were primarily regionally based providers of patronage benefits.[20] They did not vote as parties in Congress. In fact, Brazilian legislators continually crossed party lines to vote in blocs on single issues of concern to them. This fact coupled with the weakness of civil society and the shallowness of participation in social organizations[21] made programmatic coalition building very difficult.

This model's principal economic weakness was that it used more resources than it generated.[22] To maintain political support while pursuing developmental goals, successive governments relied heavily on foreign borrowing and deficit financing. Although it continued to work until the early 1960s, the model created politically unresolvable problems with inflation, balance of payments, and the budget deficit. From 1960 to 1964, Presidents Quadros and Goulart faced increasingly difficult conflicts over state spending. International creditors' concern about Brazil's balance-of-payment problems provoked a balance-of-payments crisis and squeezed the state's dependence on borrowing. Business, workers, and international creditors all demanded continued or increased government resources.

By 1964, the Brazilian government faced an extremely difficult situation. It was heavily in debt, had lost control of inflation, was facing enor-

18. Leopoldi, "Industrial Associations," 194–236.

19. The UDN is a partial exception to this pattern. Udenistas tended to oppose Vargas on more programmatic grounds and to concern themselves less with patronage benefits than did either the PTB or PSD. See Ames, *Political Survival,* 107–8.

20. Ames, *Political Survival,* 107–8.

21. See Schmitter, *Interest Conflict.*

22. Albert Fishlow, "Some Reflections on Post 1964 Brazilian Economic Policy," in Alfred Stepan, ed., *Authoritarian Brazil* (New Haven: Yale University Press, 1973), 106–8.

mous pressure from foreign creditors, and could not build an anti-inflation coalition in Congress. Brazilian political actors expressed their concerns about the crisis with the word *ungovernability*.[23] Eventually, the conflicts intensified beyond the political system's capacity to manage them, and the democracy fell to a military-civilian alliance. Under the military dictatorship, the model remained intact, except that labor was excluded from the support base.[24]

From 1964 to 1967, the military imposed a harsh stabilization program.[25] By 1967, inflation had fallen to more moderate and manageable levels. The military felt it had restored the country's fiscal health and subsequently chose to replicate the earlier policy orientation.[26] It renewed massive state spending and provided extensive benefits to its principal beneficiaries—the private sector through the corporatist system. The number of state firms and agencies grew dramatically and with it the opportunities for business access. Although business remained the privileged class, the rapid expansion of the economy provided some benefits for most organized segments of society.

The model broke down in the face of powerful shocks from the international economy. When the oil shocks of 1973 and 1979 hit, the military could not impose painful adjustments again. Its legitimacy as the ruler of Brazil rested on maintaining rapid growth and extensive benefits.[27] Instead, it chose to rely more heavily on foreign debt and to grow out of the crisis.[28] This choice led to increasing indebtedness and unmanageable fiscal difficulties.

General João Figueiredo succeeded General Ernesto Geisel as president in 1979. Geisel's presidency had been marked by a transition from miraculous growth to inconsistent performance. During that period, the military attempted to avoid oil shock adjustments by expanding the economy

23. Stepan, "Political Leadership and Regime Breakdown: Brazil," in Juan J. Linz and Stepan, eds., *The Breakdown of Democratic Regimes: Latin America* (Baltimore: Johns Hopkins University Press, 1978), 116–19.

24. Lourdes Sola, "The Political and Ideological Constraints to Economic Management in Brazil, 1945–1964" (Ph.D. diss., Oxford University, 1982).

25. James Dinsmoor, *Brazil: Responses to the Debt Crisis* (Washington, D.C.: Inter-American Development Bank, 1990).

26. Fishlow, "Some Reflections"; Baer, *Brazilian Economy.*

27. Bolivar Lamounier, "Abertura Revisited: The Impact of Elections on the Abertura," in Stepan, ed., *Democratizing Brazil: Problems of Transition and Consolidation* (New York: Oxford University Press, 1989).

28. Fishlow, "A Tale of Two Presidents: The Political Economy of Crisis Management," in Stepan, ed., *Democratizing Brazil,* 88–105.

through massive foreign borrowing and state investment. When the second oil shock occurred, Figueiredo tried to avoid the pain by applying the brakes to inflation while holding off recession. His (or actually Planning Minister Delfim Netto's) heterodox policy combined currency devaluation and export incentives with selective subsidies and incentives for private foreign borrowing. As inflation worsened, the international lending community pressured Netto to move to more orthodox stabilization in late 1980.[29] The results were felt quickly.

Over the period 1981–84, Brazil performed poorly on virtually every economic indicator. Foreign debt ballooned as did domestic debt, which in fact grew faster than foreign debt as a percentage of total debt. Public-sector deficits as a percentage of gross national product (GNP) grew, nearly doubling from 1981 to 1982.[30] Although the federal budget performed well, the monetary and state enterprise budgets generated enormous deficits.[31] Industrial production and employment declined rapidly, especially in the once-favored capital goods sector.[32] Credit was tightly rationed, and this, coupled with large devaluations, made private industrial debts overwhelming and sources of financing extremely scarce. Finally, inflation continued seemingly unaffected by the state's stabilization efforts, rising from 91.2 percent per year in 1981 to 203.3 percent per year in 1984.[33]

The stabilization efforts of 1964–67 and 1982–84 differed in a number of important respects. Those differences help account for the great success of the effort in the 1960s and its failure in the 1980s. First, indexing was introduced only gradually throughout the period in the 1960s, and therefore inertial inflation, the institutionalized memory of inflation, was not a factor earlier. Second, the foreign debt was much smaller in the 1960s, and more important, the state did not turn so heavily to private-sector lending to finance its debt obligations. Third, the public sector was much larger in the 1980s as a result of the military's ambitious state investment programs through the 1970s. Thus, the continuing operational deficits of the public sector placed a great burden on the state. Finally, the

---

29. Fishlow, "Tale of Two Presidents."

30. Fishlow, "Tale of Two Presidents."

31. Baer, *Brazilian Economy,* 208–17.

32. Fábio Stéfano Erber and Roberto Vermulm, "Ajuste Estrutural e Estratégias Empresariais—Um Estudo dos Setores Petroquímico e de Máquinas-Ferramenta no Brasil" (unpublished study, Banco Nacional de Desenvolvimento Econômico e Social/Universidade de São Paulo, 1992), 199–201.

33. Ian Roxborough, "Inflation and Social Pacts in Brazil and Mexico," *Journal of Latin American Studies* 24, no. 3 (1992): 640.

return of competitive elections after 1982 made printing money and deficit financing to win elections more prevalent.[34]

The industrial community responded to the recession and the new export incentives, but even sizable increases in industrial exports from 1981 to 1983 did not offset the pain felt at home. Industrial production still lagged well below the high of 1980, and profit margins on the export market were well below domestic margins. Private wealth holders could not protect the value of their productive assets or improve the rate of return on productive investment. They could preserve their wealth by turning to speculation because the state's decision to finance its debt depended on borrowing from private wealth holders. As the tap of foreign lending had been shut off, the state introduced new debt papers for the private financial markets. By 1981, the amount of federal debt held by the public had begun to grow at fantastic rates.[35] The relations between the state and business had changed from patrimonial and protective to predatory.[36]

The business community was quick to voice criticism of the military's stabilization efforts and growing dependence on domestic borrowing. By mid-1983, nearly half of the business community was critical of the government with only 13 percent supporting it. This was a dramatic turn from 69 percent approving Delfim Netto with 5 percent disapproving in 1980.[37] Industrialists charged the government with being more closed to business despite the political opening (abertura).[38] They charged the financial community with running the government and betraying the business community.[39] In 1982, the largest opposition party, the Party of the Brazilian Democratic Movement (PMDB), came to power in the state of São Paulo in the first truly contested election of the military dictatorship.

34. This alternative set of explanations is reviewed in Sola, "Heterodox Shock in Brazil: Técnicos, Politicians, and Democracy," *Journal of Latin American Studies* 23 (1988): 165–66.

35. Dinsmoor, *Brazil,* 27–31.

36. Peter Evans, "Predation, Embedded Autonomy, and Adjustment," in Haggard and Kaufman, eds., *The Politics of Economic Adjustment* (Princeton: Princeton University Press, 1992), 149–51. Clearly, there is a difference between Evans's archetype case of state predation, Zaire, and Brazil, especially because the state's borrowing created ample opportunities for private capital holders to earn significant returns. The state's borrowing also systematically undermined productive investments by making capital too expensive and the potential returns on productive investments too risky. Thus, the state borrowed money from individuals who accepted gains on private holdings at the expense of productive assets, frequently family owned firms. In turn, that money financed the black hole of state deficit financing.

37. Datafolha, cited in Frieden, *Debt, Development, and Democracy,* 130.

38. Discussed in Eli Diniz and Olavo Brasil de Lima Jr., *Modernização Autoritaria: O Empresariado e a Intervenção do Estado na Economia Brasileira* (IPEA-CEPAL, 1986).

39. Datafolha, Frieden, *Debt, Development, and Democracy,* 131.

One of the prominent platform issues (although certainly not decisive) was the government's interest-rate policy.

Business criticism had changed considerably since 1978, when the eight most influential businesspeople of São Paulo published an open letter calling for a new industrial policy and a return to democracy.[40] That call was mildly worded and lacked the urgency of later demands.[41] Mostly, it reflected a belief that the military's rule should have been only a brief interlude and that the time for departure was overdue. It further argued that the country could reorient its development policy only through a full debate among all Brazilians. The calls for the return to democracy beginning in 1982–83 were much more strident and widespread.[42] By late 1983, even the banking sector turned against government policy as the easy profits on high interest rates were threatened by widespread bankruptcies in industry and commerce.

The military violated the terms of its coalition when it shifted the costs of adjustment onto the privileged members of the alliance. It further abused its partners by turning to them to finance its own enormous and steadily worsening accounts. State debt, monetary policy, and public borrowing helped shift the returns on investment away from production and to speculation. This trend heaped even greater pain on industry while privately industrialists could maintain their fortunes. The state had reached the limits of its expansion. No longer able to expand, it reached the limits of its capacity to buy its support. Broke, it turned to its own supporters to finance itself. With the middle class shrinking in the face of austerity, industry bruised, inflation spiraling up, and foreign lending over, the ISI-corporatist coalition broke. By 1981, there was no choice but to resort to painful, orthodox austerity measures.

This decision pushed business groups decisively into the democratic opposition, despite some improvements in economic indicators by 1984. The policy persisted until the election of 1984 when large numbers of military party (Democratic Social Party [PDS]) members defected in the electoral college vote and chose a civilian, Tancredo Neves, over the PDS candidate, Paulo Maluf. The military dictatorship ended almost by surprise, but democracy set the stage for even greater conflict and struggle. The military's legacy to Brazil was the largest debt in the developing world, high inflation, and fiscal chaos.

40. Democratic Manifesto of the Bourgeoisie, published in the *Gazeta Mercantil* (São Paulo), July 1978.
41. Confidential author interview with one of the signatories.
42. Frieden, *Debt, Development, and Democracy.*

REDEMOCRATIZATION, INFLATION, AND FISCAL CHAOS, 1985–1989

By the end of the military's rule, the orthodox stabilization espoused by the IMF and implemented by Delfim Netto had clearly failed. Although the balance of payments improved through a large increase in exports, inflation and public deficits grew seemingly out of control.[43] The demands placed by foreign creditors created even greater internal strains than had existed before as the government sought new ways to finance itself and its debt. Growing public deficits, increased state borrowing, and high interest rates, all indexed to the rate of inflation, fueled inflation even more. The greater the debt grew, the more the state had to borrow to finance it; the more the debt grew, the higher inflation rose, and so on.[44]

The failure of stabilization under the military left the new democracy in difficult straits. The growth of the debt, both foreign and domestic, had a number of perverse consequences that Sarney had to reverse, but ultimately could not. First, financing the debt brought the state into a complicated game with private creditors. To obtain financing, the state had to borrow from private wealth holders at interest rates high enough to induce their investment. This lending went to pay off obligations to other creditors, foreign and domestic. Borrowing created new obligations that required new rounds of borrowing to pay off new creditors. This Ponzi scheme, although unavoidable, contributed to inflation and produced a burgeoning demand for debt paper in the new market for government deficit financing.

Second, high interest rates made credit expensive for investors in productive assets. Export, import, and industrial adjustment financing became scarce in both state and private capital markets. Even when financing was available from the state, high interest rates and high inflation made productive investment extremely risky. Overall, the climate of uncertainty deeply discouraged productive investment. Businesspeople did move to protect their financial wealth even if they could not protect the value of their productive assets. They did this by heavily participating in the speculative activity of lending to the indebted state. The result was a further loss of state revenues from a shrinking industrial tax base.

As a third perverse consequence, this scheme undermined the govern-

43. Fishlow, "Tale of Two Presidents"; Dinsmoor, *Brazil*.
44. Fishlow, "Tale of Two Presidents"; Dinsmoor, *Brazil*.

ment's credibility and the credibility of the currency.[45] To continue financing itself, the government had to offer ever-higher risk premiums on shorter and shorter maturities to encourage new investment in state debt. Maturities finally reached one day by the late 1980s as private investors became increasingly reluctant to hold government debt. Eventually, this dynamic led to the creation of an overnight savings market where banks paid interest daily on private savings accounts.

Along with these macroproblems, by 1990 Brazil had suffered a gradual but steady decline in the competitiveness of its industrial structure.[46] Virtually every industrial sector put off needed investments in new equipment. A lack of infrastructure investments, declining dramatically throughout the decade, left Brazil with systemic problems in the overall competitiveness of its economy.[47] Inflation soared throughout the decade from 228 percent per year in 1985 to 1,764.9 percent per year by 1989.[48] Brazil's nominal fiscal deficit jumped from 16.6 percent of gross domestic product (GDP) in 1982 to 48.5 percent of GDP in 1988. Public-sector borrowing requirements exceeded national revenues by over 70 percent.[49]

This environment was chaotic for business. The state interacted with the private sector as a consumer, a regulator, and an investor, but growing financial problems undermined all three functions. More and more, access to resources became arbitrary and politicized. Firms depending on state purchases found the process increasingly uncertain. Although price indexation still allowed some businesses to successfully pass on their costs to consumers, the results became much more erratic and politicized.[50] As resources dried up, access to financing came to depend much more heavily on political connections than previously.

A new constitution, negotiated in 1987 and 1988 and instituted by the

45. This problem is discussed in Baer, *Brazilian Economy,* 198.

46. Wilson Suzigan, "Situação Atual da Indústria Brasileira e Implicações para a Política Industrial" (unpublished paper, Universidade de São Paulo, December 4, 1991), 1–2. See also Wilson Suzigan and Annibal V. Villela, *Industrial Policy in Brazil* (Campinas: Universidade Estadual de Campinas: Instituto de Economia, 1997), 64; Luciano Coutinho and João Carlos Ferraz, *Estudo da Competitividade do Indústria Brasileira* (Campinas: Papirus/Editoria da Universidade Estadual de Campinas, 1995), 151–58.

47. Baer, *Brazilian Economy,* 198.

48. Roxborough, "Inflation and Social Pacts," 640.

49. Norman Gall, "The Floating World of Brazilian Inflation" (São Paulo: Instituto Fernand Braudel, September 1991), 37.

50. Winston Fritsch and Gustavo H. B. Franco, "Import Compression, Productivity Slowdown, and Manufactured Export Dynamism," in G. K. Helleiner, ed., *Trade Policy and Industrialization in Turbulent Times* (New York: Routledge, 1994), 76. The politicization of price controls is also discussed in Baer, *Brazilian Economy,* 142–43.

Congress in 1988, only made matters worse. Despite business efforts to influence the course of the debates, the new constitution angered the business community in several ways: It created a vast array of new labor rights that business felt belonged in the realm of normal law and that exceeded the capacity of a developing country; it expanded the scope of legitimate state intervention in business affairs; and it passed several measures that directly worsened the state's fiscal problems.

By the 1989 presidential elections, the business community overwhelmingly called for neoliberal solutions to get the state out of business affairs, to contain inflation, and to ease the pressure of the state's fiscal chaos on business. Import substitution had clearly failed to adjust to the crisis of the 1980s. The corporatist system was riddled with modernizing revolts as diminishing state resources rendered it ineffective. Business operations had become chaotic. While state benefits had dried up, high inflation, high and rising taxes, increasingly arbitrary or politicized regulation, price distortions, and tremendous uncertainty came to define the state's relation to business. The rest of this chapter examines the elements of crisis that made support for neoliberalism plausible: President José Sarney's failure to stabilize inflation; the impact of the fiscal crisis on industry and on business-state relations; and the effect of the 1988 Constitution on industrialists' perceptions of the crisis. Finally, the chapter concludes by considering some of the limits to industrialists' support for neoliberalism.

THE CRUZADO PLAN AND THE FAILED ASSAULT ON INFLATION

Sarney made several efforts to address inflation. The best-known and the most important of these experiments was the heterodox stabilization plan known as the Cruzado Plan.[51] The theory behind the plan was that the

---

51. Sola, "Heterodox Shock"; William Smith, "Heterodox Shocks and the Political Economy of Democratic Transition in Argentina and Brazil," in William Canak, ed., *Lost Promises: Debt, Austerity, and Development in Latin America* (London: Westview Press, 1989); Roxborough, "Inflation and Social Pacts"; Paul Singer, "Democracy and Inflation, in the Light of the Brazilian Experience," in Canak, ed., *Lost Promises;* Kaufman, *The Politics of Debt in Argentina, Brazil, and Mexico: Economic Stabilization in the 1980s* (Berkeley and Los Angeles: Institute of International Studies, University of California Press, 1988). See also the extensive discussion in Baer, *Brazilian Economy,* chap. 8.

principal underlying cause of inflation was the inertial memory of inflation preserved in the pervasive indexation system in Brazil's economy.
The argument was that a combination of a short wage and price freeze,
elimination of all indexation, and monetary reform would wipe out the
inertial component.

Sarney anticipated the plan with a small tax reform to improve the
state's fiscal balances. In a climate of modest growth and relatively improved state balances, Sarney passed the plan, which had been developed
in isolation from any organized group and was completely unanticipated.
It contained four basic points: (1) the conversion of the currency from
cruzeiros to *cruzados,* pegged at a rate of one thousand to one; (2) the
elimination of all official inflation indices and the conversion of all contracts into *cruzados* without monetary correction; (3) a small redistribution of wealth to workers and the middle class through the formula for
converting wages into *cruzados;* (4) and finally, a temporary wage and
price freeze.

After several months of low inflation and high levels of support from
virtually all segments of society, inflationary pressure re-emerged in the
economy. Sarney passed a new set of adjustments to the plan, called the
cruzadinho (literally, little *cruzado*), but postponed further adjustments
until after the November congressional elections. At that point, prices
were adjusted in the private sector and in public utilities, and the currency
was further devalued. Inflation steadily worsened until Sarney finally fired
Finance Minister Dilson Funaro and abandoned the plan.

The analyses of its failure vary widely. To some extent, the fact that
Sarney implemented it without consultation with key social groups increased the difficulty of maintaining support from key segments of society.[52] Because heterodox wage and price plans require cooperation from
labor and business to avoid seeking increases in wages and prices, impos-
ing the freeze made failure more likely. Labor, and especially business,
had strong incentives to defect and little incentive to cooperate with a
plan that Sarney imposed on them from above. This was particularly a
problem given the weakness of Brazilian institutions and conflict-resolu-
tion mechanisms.[53]

In addition, Sarney politicized the plan, undermining its integrity. For
political purposes, Sarney failed to carry out fiscal adjustments that would
have helped to secure the new currency as well as enhance its credibility.

52. Roxborough, "Inflation and Social Pacts"; Smith, "Heterodox Shocks."
53. Roxborough, "Inflation and Social Pacts," particularly emphasizes this point.

That failure drove up fiscal deficits, adding to inflationary pressure. Furthermore, Sarney violated the neutrality of the plan by manipulating the conversion of *cruzeiros* to *cruzados* to raise workers' wages. The resulting consumption boom produced a euphoria that allowed Sarney's party, the PMDB, to profit from congressional elections, but produced an additional source of inflationary pressure.[54] Inflation quickly returned to even higher levels.

In many respects, Sarney's stabilization efforts paralleled those of General Figueiredo. An initial dismal failure with heterodoxy led to the firing of the finance minister and a turn toward more orthodox efforts. When heterodoxy failed, the increasingly bankrupt state resorted to a series of additional heterodox plans that incorporated more and more orthodox measures. The Cruzado Plans were followed by Finance Minister Luis Carlos Bresser Pereira's plan for macroeconomic stability, which was followed by the policy of "beans and rice," which was followed by Finance Minister Maílson da Nobrega's Summer Plan.

All the plans displayed the same basic dynamics. After a brief interlude of success in containing inflation, the plans crumbled in the explosion of suppressed inflation. Persistent fiscal imbalances and distributional struggles produced inflationary pressures that could not be expressed because of price controls. The result was a buildup of price distortions and an intensification of distributional conflict, which put real inflation out of line with official measures of inflation. Black markets, withholding of supply, vicious disputes over pricing and wages all helped erode support for the plans. When Sarney's economic team loosened controls, in each case official inflation measures flew upward to reach their real level.

The problem for Sarney was that the weakness of political mechanisms to resolve conflict coupled with Sarney's poor command of the Congress forced him to resort to methods to try to stabilize the economy without having to confront any organized groups. The only institutional mechanism of conflict resolution in the Brazilian state (short of military intervention) was the system of indexation. Indexing all monetary instruments, contracts, wages, and prices was a way to try to insulate all organized members of society from the effects of inflation. Brazilian society had no alternative means to settle its struggles over resources when Sarney removed indexation.

Heterodoxy was tempting exactly because of the state's institutional weakness, but that institutional weakness was the same factor that under-

---

54. Sola, "Heterodox Shock," 181–84.

mined the possibility of heterodoxy's working. Fragmented, weak, and poorly institutionalized political parties forced Sarney to rely heavily on patronage in his relation with Congress. Weak connections to the electorate led to massive state spending to win congressional elections. Making the rules of the freeze and the monetary reform neutral and managing fiscal deficits were too hard politically.

To have succeeded, Sarney would have to have settled the distributional struggles through some mechanism that did not simply pump fuel into the economy to avoid pain. His inability to do just that ratcheted those struggles up a notch in intensity. The glaring failures of government efforts, including the frequency of the shocks and the speed with which they failed, generated unmanageable levels of uncertainty. Business groups grew much warier of government efforts to control inflation. As Cardoso and Rubens Figueiredo pointed out, business support for the initial Cruzado Plan was high, with business leaders openly expressing their enthusiasm for the plan.[55]

The political manipulation that drove deficits higher and prevented correcting price distortions, however, destroyed Sarney's credibility. With Bresser Pereira's heterodox plan in June 1987, business groups quickly geared up in opposition. ANFAVEA, the automobile producers' association and probably the most powerful business organization by a long measure, actively opposed Bresser Pereira on price and wage rules. Within six months, Bresser Pereira resigned under pressure, hampered by business opposition and Sarney's lack of support. Neither of the plans that followed, the policy of rice and beans and the Summer Plan, was nearly as ambitiously heterodox or any more successful.

FISCAL CRISIS OF THE STATE AND ITS IMPLICATIONS FOR INDUSTRY

At the heart of Brazil's problems lay a financial crisis of sizable proportions. Much of Brazil's elite supported some degree of neoliberal reform by the 1989 election, and the consensus about this liberalizing path of "modernization" even embraced some members of the Workers' Party by the end of 1991. Consensus over the need for modernizing reforms did

55. Cardoso and Figueiredo, "Reconciling the Capitalists," 11–13.

not translate into consensus over how to restore the state's fiscal health, however, particularly because the existing allocation of resources and its reliance on debt (both domestic and foreign) were institutionalized in the political system.[56]

Despite the consensus on the need to modernize the economy, reallocating resources confronted powerful political opposition. Every democratically elected president from Kubitschek to Collor had tried to reform or contain government spending and had failed to pass reform through Congress. The 1988 Constitution made Collor's particular obstacles even more formidable by protecting the sources of his greatest financial burdens.

Specifically, three aspects of the budget tightly constrained presidents up through Fernando Collor: payroll payments, transfers to the states and municipalities, and debt servicing. The three items combined to consume roughly 95 percent of the federal operational budget[57] and were guaranteed by the constitution. The growth of all three elements during the 1980s steadily worsened the federal government's position. Through the 1980s, a less and less legitimate military government, followed by a weak and unpopular democratic government, pushed the domestic debt ever higher. In all, the government's nominal deficit had risen to 73 percent of GDP by 1989. By 1990, public debt service exceeded Treasury income by over 70 percent.[58]

Payrolls played an important role in election spending at all levels of government. In fact, according to one report by the *Folha de São Paulo,* some state government's payroll expenditures actually represented over 100 percent of their revenues. Despite rhetoric to the contrary, each of the three previous governors of São Paulo significantly increased public-service hiring on election.[59] The constitution exacerbated the political abuses of public-service employment by increasingly guaranteeing civil service employment stability and by maintaining retirement by years of service, not by age.

Payroll expenses had risen 71 percent in real terms between 1982 and 1988, consuming 70 percent of federal revenues. Federal employment

---

56. Extended discussions of Brazil's fiscal problems can be found in Baer, *Brazilian Economy;* Bresser Pereira, *Economic Crisis and State Reform;* and Alfred Montero, "Devolving Democracy? Politicial Decentralization and the New Brazilian Federalism," in Kingstone and Power, *Democratic Brazil.*

57. Maílson da Nóbrega, talk at CEDEC, São Paulo, 1991.

58. Gall, "The Floating World," 37.

59. Datafolha, *Folha de São Paulo,* November 12, 1991.

rose to 700,000 jobs, with an additional 860,000 in parastatals. The problem in the states and municipalities was particularly acute. State and local employment had climbed to 4.5 million jobs by 1988. The same political patronage logic that drove constant public-sector hiring also drove constant, real-wage increases. This dynamic played an important role in increasing public-sector debt.

As of 1998, transfer payments to the states and municipalities remained one of the thorniest fiscal problems in Brazil. The 1988 Constitution introduced an article passing resources without corresponding spending obligations from the federal government to the states and municipalities. The expressed intention behind the successful amendment was to attack the centralizing and authoritarian power that the military dictatorship's president had exercised over all resources.[60] The result was an increasing gap between the federal government's share of tax receipts and its share of public spending (52 percent and 73 percent respectively in 1987).[61] Under the new constitution, the federal government transferred almost 63 percent of its two most important sources of tax revenue: the income tax (IR) and the tax on industrial production (IPI).[62]

Decreasing revenues over the course of the decade compounded the problems of the fiscal crisis. Gross tax revenues as a percent of GNP declined from 26 percent in 1970 to 22 percent of GNP in 1987, whereas net revenues declined from 17 percent to 12 percent of GNP.[63] Spending in this period actually increased in state-level payrolls, especially after 1985. Consequently, government savings declined from over 6 percent in the early 1970s to 2 percent in 1980 to rapidly growing deficits by the mid-80s.

Claudio Maciel set out several reasons for the decline in tax revenues: the loss of their value through inflation; the increase in importance of nontaxed or less taxed economic assets; the shift to less taxed industrial activities, principally industrial and agricultural exports; and the growth of the informal sector and other forms of evasion.[64] The growth of the

60. Eduardo Kugelmas and Brasílio Sallum Jr., "O Leviathan Accorrentado," in Lourdes Sola, ed., *Estado, Mercado, e Democracia: Política e Economia Comparadoas* (São Paulo: Paz e Terra, 1993), 17–18.

61. Gall, "Floating World," 9.

62. SINDIMAQ report prepared for the Auto Sectoral Accord, 1992. Not publicly circulated.

63. SINDIMAQ report, 72.

64. Claudio Maciel, "Padrão de Investimento Industrial nos Anos 90 e Suas Implicações para a Política Tecnológica," in Coutinho and Suzigan, eds., *Desenvolvimento Tecnológico da Indústria e a Constituição de um Sistema Nacional de Inovação no Brasil* (Campinas, IPT/FECAMP contract, Instituto de Economia/UNICAMP, 1990), 74–75.

informal sector and the evasion resulted directly from the government's increasing use of the tax system to finance itself. Burdened with constantly growing deficits, the government continuously raised tax rates and created new taxes on the same narrow set of payers. As it did so, those businesses that could, moved into the informal sector and brought labor with them. This trend led some to estimate that by 1990, the informal sector accounted for 50 percent of all national employment.[65]

A look at the tax system in Brazil reveals a range of perverse consequences for the country, which help explain the high level of evasion. In a study conducted by the Institute for the Study of Industrial Development (IEDI) on taxation in Brazil, the imbalances of the tax system clearly emerge. Brazil taxed businesses much more than did the OECD nations, but obtained fewer revenues from them as a percentage of total revenues. Although Brazilian revenues came overwhelmingly from workers (payroll and social security taxes), OECD nations obtained much greater percentages of their revenues from property, corporate taxes, and especially personal income taxes.[66]

Despite the regressiveness of Brazil's tax system, Brazil taxed businesses much more heavily than the rest of the sample in IEDI's study: United States, Canada, England, Japan, and Mexico. Although much of the developed and developing world lowered its corporate tax rates over the decade, Brazil consistently raised them.[67] IEDI's study further noted that the structure of Brazil's tax system favored nonexport goods over export goods, hurting Brazil's export position. Overall, the study concluded that the tax system hurt the competitive position of Brazilian industry more than any other factor did (Table 2.1).[68]

In 1991, Stephen Kanitz conducted a study confirming these findings (and those of the Booz, Allen, and Hamilton study on auto parts cited in Chapter 3). He reported an average of 42.3 percent taxes on value added for thirty-four sectors of industry, commerce, and services.[69] Taxes fell particularly hard on private-sector firms, with almost double the rate of that on parastatals.[70] A study in 1991 by the International Advisory Ser-

65. Ofelia de Lanna Sette Torres, Fundação Getúlio Vargas, interview, September 1991.
66. IEDI, "Carga Fiscal, Competitividade Industrial, e Potencial de Crescimento Econômico" (São Paulo, 1991): 5.
67. IEDI, "Carga Fiscal," 2.
68. IEDI, "Carga Fiscal," 6–10.
69. Stephen Kanitz, "O Peso da Carga Tributária nas Empresas" (unpublished study conducted for the periodical *Exame;* São Paulo, 1991): 2.
70. Kanitz, "O peso," 6.

Table 2.1.   Comparative tax revenues, total receipts (percentages)

	OECD		U.S.A.		Brazil	
	1965	1986	1980	1987	1980	1987
Income tax	26.3	31.5	40	39	12	12
Corporation taxes	9.2	7.9	11	9	4	6
Social security	18.2	24.2	22	25	31	28
Payroll taxes	1.1	1.0	—	—	—	8
Property taxes	7.9	4.9	11	11	—	8
Goods and services tax	37.1	30	17	17	54	48
Total	100	100	100	100	100	100

SOURCE: IEDI, *Mudar para Competir*, 1990.

vices Group (an independent consulting firm) compared the tax burden on Brazilian steel exports with ten of its strongest competitors. The group reported that the tax burden on exported steel had risen from 12.15 percent of the value of each ton in 1985 to 31.98 percent in 1989. Among its ten competitors, tax burdens on exported steel ranged from 10 percent in South Korea to a high of 18.38 percent for Germany, slightly more than one-half of Brazil's rate.[71] In the same vein of analysis, a study by the Brazilian Federation of Banks (FEBRABAN) reported that the high rate of taxation appeared in bank interest rates as well. According to the study, the government appropriated 59.84 percent of the difference between the rates paid to depositors and the rates paid by borrowers. The bank retained 21.64 percent to cover risks, operational costs, and profits and returned 18.52 percent to investors.[72] It further reported that at a monthly inflation rate of 14 percent, the government consumed 71 percent of banks' spreads on loans.

The cost of Brazil's tax system had an additional effect through the number, complexity, and bureaucratic awkwardness of the system. A report by the National Machinery Syndicate (SINDIMAQ) observed that Brazil had fifty-three different taxes on industrial activity. Each of these taxes had a different schedule for payment, was corrected for inflation by several different inflation indices, and required a different and complex set of documents.[73] The bookkeeping requirements posed by the complex-

71. International Advisory Services Group, "The Tax Burden and Effective Rates of Protection for Various International Producers" (private consulting report; Washington, D.C., 1991).
72. FEBRABAN, "O Impacto da Carga Tributaria na Taxa de Juros" (private, unpublished report; São Paulo, September 1991).
73. SINDIMAQ report.

ity of the tax system were substantial, involving seventy different documents and almost thirty different due dates.[74]

Meanwhile, the democratic government had lowered the highest marginal tax rate on personal income below the level of the United States, Japan, Mexico, England, and Canada.[75] The high levels of evasion on both personal and corporate taxes led the government to derive most of its income from those who could not escape the tax system: large corporations and especially workers. The tremendous impact on corporate competitiveness was overshadowed only by the tremendous regressiveness of Brazil's tax system.

The overwhelmingly negative impact of Brazil's financial crisis extended beyond the tax system. Several other critical effects arose from the crisis. The government's need to finance itself drove a high interest-rate policy. The government maintained high interest rates almost continuously since 1987 despite opposition from most business groups. Those rates made the cost of capital prohibitive, encouraged speculation over production, and increased public-sector debt. Although the dire consequences of these interest rates were well understood, this understanding did not eliminate the government's need to resort to them to finance itself.

The interest-rate policy contributed to Brazil's dizzying inflationary spiral by increasing public debt, especially through indexation and its money-creating effect. A former finance minister, Maílson da Nobrega, summed up the danger of indexation by comparing it to anesthesia: Indexation anesthetized Brazilian society so it would not feel the pain of inflation. Unfortunately, as da Nobrega argued, Brazil needed surgery, not just anesthesia. Lacking the political means to actually attack the real roots of inflation (public-sector debt), the government continued to resort to indexation.[76] In place of surgery, the government simply borrowed more, by printing money and by borrowing from the private sector.

Another consequence of the enormous public debt was the collapse of infrastructure investments. Public investment by all levels of government fell from 4.5 percent of GNP in 1975 to less than 1.5 percent of GNP in 1990 and was slated for 0.3 percent of GNP in the 1990 budget.[77] Although one 1992 survey of multinational corporations (MNC) suggested that Brazil's infrastructure remained among the best in Latin America,[78]

---

74. SINDIMAQ report.
75. IEDI, "Carga Fiscal," 2.
76. Maílson da Nóbrega, cited in Gall, "Floating World," 42.
77. Gall, "Floating World," 10.
78. *Latin Finance* 33 (Coral Gables; January–February 1992): 20. Infrastructure investment

the country's expenditures could not maintain that quality, particularly in energy and transportation. Furthermore, in a market highly dependent on government bank lending, funds for industry finance became increasingly scarce. Private banks did not compensate for the decline in state lending because in a highly inflationary economy, private banks rarely lent money for longer terms than twenty-five days.[79]

EFFECTS OF THE FISCAL CHAOS ON INDUSTRY

The continuing erosion of the state as the pillar of the development model made itself felt on the micro-level in distinct ways. The obvious failure of the state to address its structural weaknesses in macroeconomic management hurt its credibility. Sarney's tenure was marked by frequent policy changes that borrowed from different ideologies. His five-year rule was marked by three major stabilization plans, three different currencies, four different finance ministers, and a major industrial policy announcement that amounted to little in the end. To add to this policy atmosphere, the Brazilian Congress wrote a new constitution for the nation in 1988, which by many accounts is a disaster, notably for its impact on state finances (discussed further below).[80]

The sharp policy changes contributed to high inflation and produced unmanageable uncertainties. Key industrial sectors, like automobiles with their tremendous multiplier effect, simply stopped investing. Some sectors previously privileged by state policy, such as machine tools and equipment, suffered wild swings in profit rates. The state, which had been the source of most benefits, now became the source of most problems for businesses.

The state's financial difficulties filtered down to the micro-level through the state's links with the private sector. The state occupied space in four

---

rates are listed in Suzigan and Villela, *Industrial Policy in Brazil*, 96. Total infrastructure investments fell by more than 50 percent between 1980 and 1990, with energy falling by 70 percent and transportation falling to only one-eighth of its level in 1980.

79. Confidential author interviews, Citibank and Royal Bank of Canada, September–October 1991.

80. For example, see Kugelmas and Sallum, "O Leviathan," 18. Sola, "Estado, Regime Fiscal, e Ordem Monetaria: Qual Estado?" *Revista Brasileira de Ciências Sociais* 10 (February 1995); Keith Rosenn, "Brazil's New Constitution: An Exercise in Transient Constitutionalism for a Transitional Society," *American Journal of Comparative Law* 38 (1996): 773–802.

distinct ways: as producer, as consumer, as investor or lender, and as regulator. Over the course of the model's development, the state interaction with the business community varied by sector along these four dimensions. As a producer, the state's relation was primarily in the supply chain as a supplier of subsidized inputs of production, such as steel, energy, telecommunications, and naphtha for petrochemicals. As a consumer, the state purchased domestic products from diverse sectors such as machine tools and equipment, transport equipment, and construction services. As an investor and lender, the state provided almost all financial resources aside from the very short money for working capital, which private banks loaned. Finally, as a regulator, the state controlled prices, imports and exports, joint ventures, and contractual negotiations.

The differences in how sectors experienced the decline of the state led to intense conflicts over government policy between and even within sectors. For example, in the electroelectronics sector, producers of electronic components fought with producers of durable consumer goods (such as stereos and cameras) over appropriate levels of protection and policies aimed at absorbing technology.[81] Differences in the relation to the state also meant that sectors were unequally privileged or punished by regulation. During the 1980s, among steel, auto, auto parts, and machine tool producers, steel and auto prices were tightly controlled (steel in fact was priced well below international prices, prompting charges of dumping).[82] Auto parts and especially machine tools managed much larger price increases through more relaxed regulation. This difference generated intense conflict over pricing policies and charges of unfair transfers of wealth among sectors. It is probably not coincidence that steel is dominated by parastatals, autos by MNCs and auto parts and machine tools overwhelmingly by domestic private capitalists.

These differences among sectors produced new cleavages in the business community around the differences in the relation to the state. As size became an important cleavage in organizational politics, the origin of capital lost its salience as a universal cleavage. Instead, sectoral differences created new cleavages with foreign and domestic firms uniting in some cases and competing in others. The most conflictual points of divergence

81. Mariano Francisco Laplane, "Competitive Assessment of Brazilian Industrial Robots and Computer Numerical Control Industries" (unpublished paper; Campinas: Universidade Estadual de Campinas/Instituto de Economia, 1988): 53–56.

82. Confidential author interview, Usiminas Seminar, Instituto Fernand Braudel, São Paulo, November 13, 1991.

came between firms that sought to import components and technology versus the local producers of that technology.

The recession of 1981–83 pushed many firms to begin exporting for the first time or at much higher levels than before. Those firms that did so confronted a changing global economy in which rapid changes in technology and production techniques were occurring. The greater consciousness of the need to modernize placed exporting firms and sectors in confrontation with the state and its policies of protecting key sectors, including electronic components, computers, telecommunications, and machine tools and equipment.

These battles were waged through the Foreign Trade Department (CACEX), the agency that issued import licenses. CACEX was ideologically committed to market protection and worked with the appropriate *sindicatos* (corporatist interest organizations, discussed in Chapter 4) to impede all import requests through the Law of National Similars. This law, or set of laws, was originally intended less to prevent imports than to set higher import duties on domestically produced products. Through CACEX's ideological commitment and the *sindicatos'* ability to use the law to their advantage, however, the law became more of an absolute barrier to importing.

The area of greatest conflict on the micro-level was over prices. A declining market, high chronic inflation, and state regulation made pricing particularly important for businesses. Naturally, in difficult economic conditions, price negotiations were often battles over which firm would bear the costs. The Interministerial Price Council's (CIP's) intervention in this area further politicized an already difficult negotiation process. CIP's awkward formula requiring firms and *sindicatos* to submit detailed cost plans and making rulings sometimes months later made a mess of price negotiations. As long as Brazil's economy was expanding, CIP's intervention guaranteed all members of the business community protection from the effects of inflation. With the market shrinking and resources declining, CIP's intervention resulted in transfers of wealth to favored sectors and produced intense conflict between suppliers and buyers, particularly after the Cruzado Plan.

Rumors of the price freeze led to speculative price increases as businesses tried to set their prices as high as possible in anticipation. The result was an incoherent pattern of profits and losses. Those firms that had guessed well made profits, and those that had not correctly anticipated the freeze lost. Moreover, Sarney's maintenance of the freeze beyond the three-month mark exaggerated price distortions and prevented businesses from adjusting. In response, firms used a range of tactics, from stopping production to withholding supplies to refusing to supply unless black market prices (the *agio*) were paid. This pattern of behavior carried through all of Sarney's stabilization plans.

Overall, the Sarney period's fiscal crisis had four effects on the micro-level. First and foremost, businesses faced unmanageable uncertainties in every facet of operations. Continuous policy changes (including several changes of the official inflation indices), high interest rates and taxes, sharp swings in consumption and production, and intense supply and price conflicts discouraged investment and made production risky. Second, as a result, short-term thinking dominated business attitudes. Despite a changing global economy, business survival strategy had to concern itself with the happenings of the month, not the possible happenings of next year. Third, state borrowing and uncertainty made speculation on financial instruments more appealing than was productive investment. The state's need to encourage private-sector lending guaranteed a high real return on short-term debt paper. On the other hand, investment in production posed serious risks. Finally, uncertainty, uneven effects of regulation, problems of nonpayment and late payment, unequal access to state resources, and conflicts over policy made the supply chain the scene of overt and brutal conflict. By 1989, the entire industrial community was looking for change.

EFFECTS OF THE 1988 CONSTITUTION

Significant numbers of industrialists began expressing a set of positions consistent with neoliberalism around the time of the constitutional debates in 1987. Diverse business groups as well as individual prominent businesspeople called for reducing the state's role. They explicitly framed their rhetoric in the language of free markets and private initiative.

Although the press, many businesspeople, and many academics saw this as an expression of business's conversion to neoliberal ideology, the issues were specific. With few exceptions, businesspeople and their representatives were not ideologically neoliberals. They did not have any specific neoliberal blueprint for rebuilding Brazil or any desire to completely eliminate the role of the state in the economy. These businesspeople directed their calls to a limited number of concrete problems, including the public deficit and its impact on business management, the state's regulation of prices, and the threat of new constitutional and interventionist regulation of labor issues. Neoliberalism offered a diagnosis, a rhetoric, and a set of prescriptions for those problems.

In that sense, important segments of the business community embraced neoliberal positions as a tactical choice in their conflict with the state. Neoliberalism offered the solution to the business community's dilemma. The ever-worsening condition of the state's financial health had enormous impact on the micro-level. The state's increasingly hurtful participation produced intense conflicts that fragmented the business community around new cleavages. Neoliberalism appealed to many businesspeople because its prescriptions and language identified the state as the villain and business entrepreneurs as embattled heroes.

Leading industrialists began expressing neoliberal sentiments at the time of the constituent assembly's work on the new constitution. The initial document contained strong nationalist tendencies and a strong labor orientation, which reflected the successful mobilization of labor groups and their allies in Congress and the lack of mobilization on the business side. In response, the business community mobilized for the first time. Two new organizations emerged as critical vehicles mobilizing efforts against the first draft of the constitution. The National Thought of the Business Bases (PNBE),[83] actually only an informal group of the Federation of Industry of the State of São Paulo (FIESP—the official corporatist federation) dissidents until 1990, emerged as one. The other, the União Brasileira de Empresários (Brazilian Union of Entrepreneurs [UBE]), unified various branches of the official corporative structure. The UBE, in conjunction with a private group called the National Front for Free Initiative, raised and invested U.S.$35 million in their lobbying campaign among members of Congress.

Although the PNBE consisted of a small number of dissident *sindicato* heads representing small- and medium-size firms and the UBE spokespersons were among the biggest businesspeople in Brazil, their messages were largely the same: Get government off business's back. They targeted this message at a specific set of issues: the large number of labor regulations in the new constitution; the nationalist discrimination against foreign capital; and the absence of measures to address public deficits.

---

83. The PNBE had an influence disproportionate to its size and the economic importance of its members. Its influence came from the attention showered on it by the press, by its proven ability to mobilize interest and political expression, and by its ability to forge alliances with other social groups. As a consequence, it was influential insofar as it could generate attention on an issue but less important as a representative of all business.

Labor

Brazil's constitution of 1988 is an extremely detailed document, particularly in reference to labor rights. The initial draft was even more so. More than anything else, the business community objected to a provision that guaranteed job stability. Beyond that provision, business also objected to a series of measures that it felt should be matters of law, not constitutional rights. These included limiting continuous shifts to six hours, limiting the length of the workday, a 120-day maternity leave as well as an 8-day paternity leave, an unrestricted right to strike, the protection of workers from the effects of automation, and the prohibition of arbitrary firing or firing without just cause (which businesspeople particularly complained about because of the absence of a legal definition of *arbitrary firing*).

The measure guaranteeing job stability was defeated to a large extent because of the sharp lobbying response of the business community. The UBE printed an "Alert to the Nation" in the *Folha de São Paulo,* in which it attacked the measure. "Labor market adjustment to the dynamics of the economy is of the essence to private productive activity, especially in the case of small and medium-sized firms. It is imperative to survive."[84] It added that the measure would ultimately hurt workers by forcing firms to lay off employees, raising the unemployment rate, provoking recession, and lowering productivity.[85]

The PNBE went even further in its response to the measure. It committed itself to promoting democratic means of conflict resolution and improving labor–capital relations but saw this measure as a fundamental threat to the interests of small- and medium-size firms. PNBE called for a National Day of Reflection on Stability for November 10, 1987. It sent out telexes to three thousand business organizations asking that debates on the theme be held on that day. One hundred forty complied in what was considered a strong show of opposition to the measure. As one businessperson phrased it, the measure represented one more element of the corporatism and intervention of the state in the economy.[86]

Other lobbying efforts obtained only limited successes. Business lobbies did reverse the stability measure as well as modestly modify nineteen of thirty-eight provisions of articles concerned with social rights (seven and parts of eight, nine, and ten).[87] Ultimately, the business community

---

84. *Folha de São Paulo,* October 10, 1987, p. 3.
85. *Folha de São Paulo,* October 10, 1987, p. 3.
86. *Diário de Comércio e Indústria* (São Paulo), November 11, 1987, p. 5.
87. FIESP, "Evolução do Texto sobre Alguns dos Direitos dos Trabalhadores durante os

viewed the constitution as an antimarket document, especially in its tremendously detailed elaboration of social rights. Many businesspeople believed that those rights should have been left for ordinary law or private
worker-management arrangements or were simply unrealistic given Brazil's state of development.

Overall, as noted above, the business community saw the constitution
as yet another inappropriate encroachment of the state on private initiative—a communism of the right.[88] At a time when high, persistent inflation and wildly fluctuating levels of demand were wreaking havoc with
businesses, the state was blocking businesses' capacity to adjust. One
study calculated that the immediate cost to business as a result of the
constitution would be a 24.1 percent increase in the payroll. The medium-
term effect would be an additional increase of 17.6 percent in total labor
costs.[89] One businessperson summed up the prevailing attitude among
businesspeople by pointing out that the labor victories could well come
in the process of modernization and growth. As constitutional rights in
the context of crisis and underdevelopment, labor's victories would drive
firms into the informal sector.[90] The elaboration of these rights in the
constitution served to confirm business's belief that it needed to remove
the state from private management decisions.

Capital

Four issues about capital dominated business concerns in the new constitution and the debates surrounding it. First, the constitution made new
distinctions between domestic and foreign capital with various limits on
foreign capital. Second, nationalist forces succeeded in nationalizing certain key sectors, such as mining and telecommunications. Third, a number of businesspeople openly declared their concern over the constituent
assembly's transfer of resources without spending obligations to the state
governments. Finally, the constitution set a 12 percent ceiling on annual

Trabalhos Constitueintes" (São Paulo: October 4, 1988). The articles mentioned above relate
to the section of the constitution dealing with social rights.

88. Confidential author interview, as well as relatively common phrasing among businesspeople at the time, e.g., Lawrence Pih interview, *Folha de São Paulo,* October 4, 1987, p. 43.

89. José Pastore and Hélio Zylberstain, in *Senhor* (São Paulo), May 30, 1988, p. 48.

90. Romeu Trussardi Filho, president of the Commercial Association of São Paulo, *Senhor,*
May 30, 1988, p. 59.

interest rates, which could be charged on all transactions (in an economy with 600 percent annual inflation at the time).

The constitution disturbed many businesspeople by defining distinctions between national and foreign capital with special benefits for national capital. National capital, firms owned and controlled directly or indirectly by people whose principal residence is in Brazil, would receive preference in the sale of goods and services and could receive special protection and benefits in areas of strategic interest to the state. Although Brazilian capitalists certainly had gone through a nationalist phase, most notably in the late 1950s and early 1960s,[91] their view changed considerably in the 1980s. Brazilian businesspeople expressed concern that the nationalist tone of the constitution could drive away much-needed foreign investment. Given the financial difficulties of the state and the crucial role of foreign capital in the economy, this measure caused grave concern.[92]

The business community expressed a second concern about the exclusion of foreign capital from the mining sector, large-scale construction, and oil exploration. Specifically, it argued that these areas required large-scale investments that domestic capital could not make. Without the participation of foreign capital, these areas were likely to become new areas of state expansion. Moreover, the constitution enshrined the use of market reserves as a mechanism to protect strategic sectors.[93] Businesspeople saw both these measures as the state's determination to maintain its interventionist role, despite the financial chaos that role had already created.

A third area of concern to businesspeople referred to public finance. In particular, businesspeople objected to the anticentralization sentiment that led to José Serra's measure transferring resources to the states without accompanying spending responsibilities.[94] The idea behind the measure was to restore the federation by weakening the concentration of revenues in the federal government's hands. Prophetically, business critics argued that the measure would further harm the federal government's financial situation. The federal government would then have to increase its taxation of the private sector to finance itself.[95] The introduction of a

91. Jorge Dominguez, "Business Nationalism: Latin American National Business Attitudes and Behavior Towards Multinational Enterprises," in Dominguez, ed., *Economic Issues and Political Conflict: U.S.–Latin American Relations* (London: Butterworth, 1982), 52–58.

92. For example, Jorge Gerdau Johannpeter, *Estado de São Paulo*, July 21, 1988, p. 39.

93. *Senhor*, May 30, 1988, pp. 52–53.

94. Gall, "Floating World," 9–10; Sallum and Kugelmas, "O Leviathan," 18–20, for a discussion of the consequences.

95. *Visão* (São Paulo), June 1987, p. 51.

new set of taxes on wealth and income added fuel to businesses' anger about the state's absorption of private capital at the expense of productive investment.

Finally, the constitution set a limit on interest rates at 12 percent per year. Business critics, as well as economists, regarded the measure as an absurdity. In their view, the ceiling on real interest rates would have a wide range of perverse effects. For one, it would make it impossible for the state to emit debt paper at attractive rates. It would also hinder private lending (including working capital) to industry and commerce, and it would limit consumer credit. Analysts believed it would almost certainly lead to large-scale capital flight. Finally, it would lead to the creation of parallel credit markets.[96]

Ultimately, businesses' lobbying succeeded in modestly modifying a large number of measures that they opposed. Their successes came particularly in the area of labor rights in the second round. For example, business succeeded in overturning the stability measure, introduced a measure permitting it to extend length of work shifts through collective agreements, and shortened paternity leave from eight days to five.[97]

By contrast, on twenty-four points that the business community had declared vital and therefore non-negotiable, it felt it had lost on all but one. The final draft retained the limitation on interest rates with the added clause that individuals who charged more than 12 percent real rates per year would be charged with the crime of usury. It also retained the majority of measures that the business community opposed: nationalizing mining, and other sectors; the extension of the market reserve as an instrument of policy; the sharp distinctions between foreign and domestic capital with all the benefits and restrictions unchanged; the constitutionally mandated transfer of federal revenues to the states and municipalities without the accompanying spending obligations; and multiple taxation of business and individual income. Finally, it still retained an extremely detailed enumeration of labor rights.

INDUSTRIALISTS' TURN AGAINST THE STATE

The constitution confirmed and added to already existing business antagonism to the state over its intervention. Three issues dominated business

96. *Senhor,* May 30, 1988, p. 54.
97. FIESP, "Evolução.

complaints outside the constitutional debates: the state's regulation of prices; the public deficit and its effect on finances and inflation; and the corruption and privileges (particularly in the parastatal sector) of the development model.

Prices

The state's regulation of prices through the CIP became an object of business hostility only in the 1980s. The CIP included representatives from five different government ministries and an advisory council from the private sector.[98] It determined which sectors and which firms in them would have their prices controlled. Firms and sectors with controlled prices submitted cost plans to the CIP for approval of price increases. As long as the economy was expanding, inflation was under control, and each sector could easily pass on costs to its buyers, there was no problem with price regulation.

The severe economic stagnation of the 1980s made regulation much more controversial. Price regulation became more disruptive because it could not match the sharp fluctuations in demand and supply or the rapid pace of inflation.[99] Second, the process became more politicized and conflictual, both because of the CIP's own policies and because firms and sectors used their political access to try to affect the decisions. Finally, regulation itself in an unstable market produced perverse consequences. First, the almost arbitrary selection of firms and sectors to regulate created distortions in the economy's prices.[100] Second, indexation was widely perceived to be itself a cause of inflation even though its intent was to protect economic agents from its effects. Finally, businesspeople perceived it to be damaging to the interests of competitiveness and efficiency because it promoted (in fact inherently caused) collusion.[101]

The chaos of the 1980s led businesspeople to these newly discovered concerns with competitiveness and antistate criticisms. Businesses had profited from the CIP in the past, and many continued to receive the

---

98. Diniz and Lima, *Modernização Autoritaria.*

99. For example, see the criticisms of Antonio Bonamico, president of Brastemp, in *Diário do Comércio e Indústria,* July 10, 1987, p. 3, or of Paulo Francini, director of FIESP, in *Diário Popular,* January 21, 1986, p. 1.

100. Confidential author interview, FIESP official.

101. Confidential author interviews with businesspeople and syndicate representatives.

benefits of artificially low input prices, such as naphtha.[102] The uncertainty of the times coupled with the inadequacies of the CIP's politicized and incoherent regulation, however, began to undermine its potential benefits. The CIP became a principal target of criticism.

Public Deficits

The problem of public deficits probably generated more anger in the business community than any other issue. As I argued earlier, the public deficit drove the state to begin financing itself domestically. That in turn provoked the break between the military and the business community. In the business community's view, the state's dire financial health resulted directly from the developmental model and its fiscal recklessness.[103] The only solution to the disastrous consequences of state growth and state intervention was to force the state to shrink.

In a public address to the UBE, Antônio Ermírio de Moraes, president of the Votorantim Group—the largest private capital group in Brazil—presented a critique typical of the business view.[104] In his address, he blasted the state for its fiscal irresponsibility and its lack of attention to issues of poverty, health, and welfare except during election years: "We are a country that says it is based on free initiative. But our governors insist on intervening in firms. They, who in their majority, never produced anything, never risked an investment, are generally accustomed to paying their payrolls with taxes levied on those who create wealth."[105] Businesspeople felt that they were being unfairly targeted for blame and for sacrifices while the state absorbed huge proportions of the nation's capital and produced nothing. This state of affairs resulted in consistent high interest rates, consistent valuation of financial speculation over production,[106] and poverty conditions comparable to nations like Bangladesh and Gabon.[107]

102. Erber and Vermulm, "Ajuste."
103. Ermírio de Moraes, e.g., *Estado de São Paulo*, November 6, 1987, p. 32.
104. *Estado de São Paulo*, November 6, 1987, p. 32. Ermírio is a member of the *Gazeta Mercantil*'s permanent council of ten leading businessmen in Brazil, a signatory to the Democratic Manifesto of the Bourgeoisie, and a figure of such importance that he was described by one interviewee as the uncrowned king of the business class.
105. *Estado de São Paulo*, November 6, 1987, p. 32.
106. See, for example, Luis Carlos Delben Leite's pointed criticisms while president of SINDIMAQ, in *Diário do Grande ABC* (São Paulo), August 27, 1988, p. 1.
107. Ermírio cited astonishing official government figures on poverty. Twenty-four million Brazilians had no access to hospitals, and forty-six million could not see a doctor; forty-six million were without running water; and sixty million without adequate housing and sanitation; 50 percent of Brazilian children are undernourished; twenty-four million are illiterates.

The perception that the state was demanding sacrifices and exacting them from business while it continued to expand particularly angered businesspeople. In periods of tight price controls, as in 1985, businesspeople complained bitterly that public enterprises were exempt from sacrifice. They received price adjustments above the rate of inflation,[108] continued to expand their payrolls, and took on new debt while private businesses had austerity forced on them.[109]

Businesspeople expressed anger over the state's tremendous concentration of power in the economy and its frequent abuse. They pointed to the overwhelming control of the banking sector by the state through the domination of state-owned banks.[110] The state used control of the financial sector to finance its deficits through a policy of high interest rates, which drew private money back into state hands. The state then funneled much of this money back into parastatals.[111]

Given this view, it is not surprising that businesspeople as a group held a strong preference for privatization of the state productive apparatus. A survey of industrial leaders by the National Confederation of Industry (CNI) reported 67 percent favoring privatization.[112] Business spokespeople argued that privatization was an important cure for the state's operational deficits and promoted a renewal of much-needed investment.[113] In short, businesspeople saw public deficits as the product of a reckless, profligate state. Deficits led to speculation, the undermining of production, the absence of investment in the industrial economy, and the worsening of Brazil's staggering poverty.

Corruption and Privileges

Corruption and the unequal distribution of privileges manifested themselves in the Brazilian model in a number of ways. Businesspeople saw

108. *Gazeta Mercantil*, June 21, 1985, p. 4.

109. *Estado de São Paulo*, August 6, 1985, p. 23.

110. Banco do Brasil, BNDES, the Caixa Econômica Federal, and the Banco Nacional da Habitação—the four largest banks in the country and all federally owned—hold more than 60 percent of the nation's deposits. This, in addition to the regional banks, such as Banco do Nordeste, and the state-level banks, such as Banespa, amounts to an overwhelming dominance of finance. Instituto Roberto Simonsen, "Seminario sobre a Constituinte Abertura" (São Paulo: November 7, 1985): 11.

111. Instituto Roberto Simonsen, "Seminario," 18.

112. CNI 1989, cited in Schneider, "Privatization in the Collor Government: Triumph of Liberalism or Collapse of the Developmental State?" in Chalmers, de Souza, and Boron, eds., *The Right and Democracy in Latin America*, 229.

113. Business figures that appeared in the press repeatedly made this point throughout the period.

corruption and a lack of accountability in public spending and civil service hiring, in the unequal extension of subsidies and privileges throughout the economy—particularly to parastatals—in the nontechnical nature of defining regulatory rules, such as for pricing, as well as in the profiteering from corruption that occurred in both the private and public sectors.

The PNBE, in particular, made a great issue of the lack of transparency and accountability of the budget of the republic. Based on a survey of small- and medium-size business attitudes, the PNBE publicly argued against secrecy over public spending. Fifteen hundred businesspeople were asked to list Brazil's worst problems from a list of seventy-four questions. The PNBE report noted only problems that more than 40 percent of respondents selected. The top-ranked response was corruption with 86.82 percent identifying it. (Corruption was followed by business participation in economic decision making—76.94 percent, privatization—73.2 percent, economic policy for the internal market—67.96 percent, and reducing the public deficit—66.91 percent.)[114]

The PNBE particularly promoted the position that the state had to make transparent its spending practices. Spokespersons from the PNBE joined other prominent businesspeople in condemning the practice of using public-service employment as a reward for friends and political supporters. They condemned the absence of democratic controls on how the state spent money in the republic. In particular, the extensive and ad hoc use of subsidies and the absence of a budgetary-reporting procedure for these subsidies angered them.

Similarly, the conflicts over defining regulatory rules, such as whether a product had a "national similar" (a locally produced good similar to a proposed import) or how to calculate cost increases, produced angry charges and countercharges of favoritism. For example, price negotiations between automakers and their suppliers were charged with accusations of political manipulation.[115] Similar problems became public over charges that the CIP had granted steel, ports, and electricity—all state firms—price adjustments well above the rate of inflation while cement and autos had to accept losses.[116] In an interview in the *Jornal do Comércio*, Lawrence Pih, one of the few outspoken business critics (in a generally cautious community), angrily retorted that "Brazil does not have capitalism, it has a cartorial regime for friends of the king."[117]

---

114. *Diário do Grande ABC*, November 6, 1987, pp. 1–2.
115. SINDIPEÇAS internal letter; interviews in the sector, 1991.
116. *Gazeta Mercantil*, June 21, 1985, p. 23.
117. Lawrence Pih interview noted in note 88 above.

In sum, the concerns of big businesspeople and key business associations in 1989 closely matched Collor's neoliberal rhetoric. Collor promised to reduce the size of the state by reducing many of its roles in the economy. He promised to introduce market regulation of labor and prices. He promoted privatization to remove the state from areas where he and the business community felt it should not operate. He promised to open Brazil to foreign capital and to end discrimination against foreign firms. Most of all, he targeted the state's public deficits as one of his top concerns. Big business may have preferred the more moderate Mario Covas for his conciliatory style or Paulo Maluf for his connections to the business community, but it could not claim that candidates such as Fernando Collor did not stand for the same prescriptions business had been calling for since 1987 and earlier.

LIMITS TO NEOLIBERALISM IN THE BUSINESS COMMUNITY

In this chapter, I have argued that the fiscal crisis of the state undermined both the political and economic bases of the ISI–corporatist model. One consequence of that collapse was that industrialists who had prospered under state guidance and protection for sixty years came to support neoliberalism, but only because it offered to solve particular concrete problems. They were in no way ideologically committed to neoliberalism. In the next chapter, I examine the way that micro-level market factors constrained business support for neoliberalism, but there were ideological and behavioral limits as well.

Limits to business's commitment to neoliberalism came from four sources. First, although all business critics called for a reduction of the role of the state, few claimed that the state should have no role. Despite talk that the state should maintain a productive role, neither the FIESP nor the PNBE nor the UBE had any concrete ideas of what that role should be. Each one frequently noted the basic functions of health, education, and other welfare roles. Otherwise, no well-developed blueprint for reconstructing the economy and the state's role in it existed in business documents or debates.

In fact, the dynamic of this struggle is consistent with the observations of Vogel on American business. Businesspeople actively organized to oppose the state where it interfered in the day-to-day management of firms, but they generally supported state involvement in protecting and nurturing specific firms or sectors.[118] They simply could not determine which sectors and firms should be protected. Businesses did not complain about price control when it effectively protected them from the adverse effects of inflation. They did not complain about the state's regulation of labor issues when the regulations were more repressive than progressive or about state spending when it was producing the miraculous growth of the 1960s and 1970s. In fact, even the heralded campaign against statism of the mid-1970s included few active, business supporters, especially while state investments were driving industrial demand.

The second limit to business neoliberalism came from business's lobbying over the timing of liberalization. These conflicts particularly emerged as Sarney moved toward liberalization in 1988–89 with his new industrial policy.[119] Competing sectors in productive chains argued that they should be opened last because their suppliers caused their lack of competitiveness. For example, bitter disputes arose between electronic component producers and users (such as numerically controlled machine tools).[120] Similar disputes arose between textile and clothing, leather producers and footwear producers,[121] and autos and auto parts.[122] Casting, shoes, and toy makers publicly charged their suppliers with overpricing, which resulted in losses in export competitiveness.[123] Ultimately, a timetable for liberalization emerged under the direction of Heloisa Camargo, the head of CACEX, but not without a great deal of recrimination.[124]

The third limit comes from the small-business community, which on average was far less neoliberal than the big-business community. Aside

118. Vogel, "Why Businessmen Distrust Their State: The Political Consciousness of American Corporate Executives," *British Journal of Political Science* 8 (1997): 45–78.

119. FIESP, "Considerações sobre o Documento 'Política, Industrial, e Diretrizes Setoriais' a que se Refere a Portaria no. 12, de 13.02.87 do Ministério de Indústria e Comércio" (FIESP, 1987).

120. Laplane, "Diagnóstico da Indústria Brasileira de Máquinas-Ferramenta," in Coutinho and Suzigan, eds., *Desenvolvimento Tecnológico,* 53–56.

121. Confidential author interview, ABIMAQ official. October 1991, São Paulo.

122. Confidential author interview, SINDIPEÇAS officials. September 1991, São Paulo.

123. *Gazeta Mercantil,* July 5, 1988.

124. Confidential author interviews, ABIMAQ, SINDIPEÇAS, ANFPC. September/October 1991, São Paulo. Nylen, "Liberalismo," called this period defensive scapegoating and presented it as evidence of the conflict between neoliberal discourse in public and illiberal behavior in private. I believe that the difference does not result from hypocrisy. It is rational and consistent for firms to support liberalization and still wish to open their suppliers' markets before their own.

from its commitment to developmentalism, documented by Nylen,[125] it was far more focused on democratizing the business community. For the small-business community, the specific issues included unequal access to privileges and finances, difficult relations with an increasingly well organized labor movement, high interest rates, and recessionary conditions. These problems made it available for a neoliberal, anti-elite rhetoric, but it did not make it neoliberal.

The last limit to neoliberalism in the business community is that, whatever the discourse, the rules of the game remained the same. Securing financing still required political clout in the National Bank for Social and Economic Development (BNDES). Negotiating price adjustments with the CIP still involved political access and maneuvering. Obtaining import–export licenses still involved political struggles. Obtaining state contracts and winning public bids still required large-scale bribery.[126] Similarly, business leaders spoke of the need to modernize industry, but few actually invested in the process.[127]

Despite their loud protests, many businesspeople and businesses profited by becoming creditors to the desperately broke state. Although production grew increasingly precarious, the rate of return on capital remained healthy. This situation sparked charges that some powerful figures in the FIESP spoke a liberal discourse while working to preserve the status quo.[128] The power struggle between small and big business in the corporative structure particularly provoked this sentiment. The PNBE leaders, especially after their expulsion from the FIESP directorship,[129] charged the FIESP with being *governista* (accommodating any government, any policy) because of the federation's support for the high interest-rates policy.[130]

125. Nylen, "Liberalismo."

126. It is obviously difficult to document this precisely, but it figures very prominently in business complaints in private interviews, as well as the occasional, brave public complaint. The most courageous example is Ricardo Semler, who in 1991 recorded, on two occasions, public officials demanding bribes and who, on being awarded businessman of the year by his peers, lashed out at them for their cooperation in sustaining corruption by public officials.

127. For example, the União pela Modernização and Luis Carlos Delben Leite both conducted unsuccessful campaigns of consciousness raising and encouragement in their respective sectors. See also Erber and Vermulm, "Ajuste."

128. See, for example, Lawrence Pih interview note 88 above. Several interviewees raised this charge, specifically against the Mario Amato administration.

129. This occurred on December 30, 1988, over an internal electoral issue. See *Diário de Comércio e Indústria,* January 3, 1989, p. 3. Although the dispute did not relate to global political issues, it opened the door to much harsher exchanges in the press.

130. *Diário Popular,* August 4, 1989, p. 9.

These limitations aside, the issues driving support for neoliberal solutions remained real for the business community. Some analysts have claimed that businesspeople were hypocritical in their support for neoliberalism, but I believe that explanation does not resolve the business community's apparent contradictions.[131] Rather, I believe that the persistence of the developmentalist rules made neoliberal behavior unlikely. To give up subsidies or political lobbying while a competitor continued to use them was reckless. Furthermore, the enormous difficulties and therefore the organizational costs of lobbying Congress or the executive on broad, encompassing issues made lobbying on narrow, private issues the only means of shaping the reform process. Similarly, observers such as Diniz or Cardoso and Rubens Figueiredo criticized Brazilian businesspeople for their unwillingness to assume risks, but, assuming risks requires some economic certainty or else it is simply accepting losses.

The business community did face a series of real problems that arose from the state's financial crisis and its effect on its participation in the economy. The recession of the early 1980s pushed many more firms to export their production. That experience made clear the need to pursue reform to guarantee that Brazil kept pace with competitive changes abroad. Even the uncompetitive machine tools and equipment sector published an industrial policy proposal that included support for commercial liberalization. Thus, neoliberalism and neoliberal candidates offered prescriptions for industrialists' problems in ways that other models did not. Businesses were virulently antistate because the state's crisis was the root of their difficulties. They expressed anger over the distribution of privilege because the crisis made those privileges more obvious and more unequal. They expressed cynicism about politicians because democracy had not improved the quality of politics—it had merely demilitarized corruption, patronage, and irresponsibility.

Business groups were not naive about the challenges of neoliberalism. Stripping away protective barriers from an economy that had always had them would provoke difficult adjustments. Furthermore, the business community was aware that Chile's and Argentina's radical neoliberal programs had decimated their respective business communities. Nevertheless, it supported neoliberalism as a tactical solution to the crisis of import-substitution's chaotic failure. It did so because it believed that if a credible

---

131. For example, Nylen, "LIberalismo"; Diniz, cited in *Visão,* July 29, 1992, p. 28; and de Souza, "The Contemporary Faces of the Brazilian Right: An Interpretation of Style and Substance," in Chalmers, de Souza, and Boron, eds., *The Right and Democracy in Latin America,* 106–9.

president implemented reforms gradually, business had time to adjust before the tariffs reached their lowest levels. Business believed that unlike its Chilean and Argentine counterparts, it could compete in a global economy. If the president could credibly address the country's severe fiscal problems and relieve business of the high costs imposed on business operations, the benefits could offset the costs.

3

Industrial Adjustment and the Costs and Benefits of Neoliberal Reform

The Micro-Level Bases of Business Preferences

Crises open the possibility of economic reform. In the context of a crisis, politicians try to craft new coalitions by appealing to social actors seeking new solutions, but that process is constrained by the reality of business life at the micro-level. Businesspeople can support only solutions that allow them reasonable opportunities to adjust. The most common accounts of business preferences focus on static characteristics of producers: factor endowments or specific factors, export versus domestic market orientation, size of firms, or origin of capital. These views are insufficient on their own to explain business preferences in a complex and changing economy. Rather, this book focuses on how the political process interacts with the set of problems and adjustment options that firms face. In turn, it examines how this interaction shapes the logic of support or opposition to neoliberal reform. This chapter examines how market structure, sectoral history, and links to the state shaped the ways that firms saw their particular cost/benefit structure and their subsequent adjustment options through 1992—up to and through the initiation of neoliberal reforms.

THE PROBLEM OF INDUSTRIAL ADJUSTMENT

Neoliberal reforms liberalize commerce and remove nonproductive rents, but they also substantially alter the institutional environment for firms.

Markets are embedded in social and political institutions that profoundly shape the experiences and behavior of firms and sectors.[1] Those institutions play a critical role in influencing the relation between the state and individual firms and sectors. They play a critical role in shaping how suppliers and buyers interact, how firms in the same sector interact, as well as how competitors interact. They determine how managers and labor resolve their differences. In turn, all these factors affect critical market decisions such as strategies for investment, production, technological development and capacitation, and even political participation.

The research for this book sought to understand how these "mechanisms of coordination"[2] influenced the possibilities for adjustment and thereby the preferences and behavior of Brazilian firms. In particular, I argue that the fiscal crisis of the state and the breakdown of the state's role caused problems for all sectors. The cost/benefit structure facing individual firms and sectors varied sharply, however. Differences in each sector's market structure, history, and links to the state influenced the problems and the adjustment options that each firm faced.

Market structure and *history* refer to the factors that shaped firm relations in and out of the sector as well as with labor, origin of capital, export/import history (a proxy for international competitiveness), firm size, market concentration, and the use of technology in the sector. *State linkages* refer to the formal (regulatory) and informal (political) ways that the sector linked to the state. By the late 1980s, the crisis led many of those linkages to impose costs on individual firms and sectors, but they still afforded some benefits that businesspeople had to forgo in supporting neoliberal reform. These independent variables yield three hypotheses about industrialists' preferences and behavior:

1. Even the most challenged sectors and many of the most challenged firms could support neoliberal reforms because they could conceive

1. Suzigan and Villela discussed these differences in views, labeling the view that markets are given "neoclassical" and labeling the view that markets are social institutions "neoschumpterian." Their summary analysis of the difference in the two views among economists also admirably captures much of the tension between most economists' views of the market with the large body of work in other social sciences. Suzigan and Villela, *Industrial Policy in Brazil,* 20–25.

2. Hollingsworth and Boyer, *Contemporary Capitalism,* 6–19, used this term to describe the various ways social and political institutions can influence the process of resource allocation. The authors identified the following list of coordination mechanisms: markets, private hierarchies, networks, communities, associations, and the state.

viable adjustment strategies, but their viability depended on the government's delivering on its policy commitments.

2. Because successful adjustments depended on the government's resolving the practical problems of each sector, even the least-threatened firms and sectors could shift into opposition if they believed that the government could not credibly deliver on its policy commitments.

3. Although the potential for support was widely distributed across the industrial community, the strength of support for neoliberal reform varied with the degree to which firms and sectors were internationally competitive and independent of the state.

To test these hypotheses, I examined three industrial sectors: pulp and paper, auto parts, and machine tools and equipment. The technological changes of the third industrial revolution had similar importance for all three. Each had the potential and faced the pressure to make significant changes in production by using numerically controlled machine tools and computer-aided design. All three used continuous-process production and could benefit from new international standards of competitiveness in production techniques, such as just-in-time, total quality control, and quality circles. In addition, the three sectors provided a strong test of production profile explanations.

Each sector differed on several fronts. Pulp and paper was an internationally competitive sector, one of the largest exporting sectors in Brazil's economy and clearly among the best, if not *the* best, prepared industrial sector for import competition. The auto parts sectors occupied a midpoint in the range of preparedness. At the top end were firms that exported regularly and were quality award winners as global suppliers of large multinational corporations (MNC). At the bottom end of the range were low-quality, high-cost producers who stood little chance of surviving the commercial opening. In the large middle were firms with the potential to move in either direction. Machine tools and equipment was one of the more challenged sectors in Brazil. Even the top producers in the sector faced significant uncertainty about their ability to compete in a liberalized market economy.

Other differences included maturity, capital intensity, and links to the state. Auto parts was one of the first sectors targeted for import substitution in the 1950s and as such, one of the most mature sectors in Brazil's industrial economy. Both machine tools and equipment and pulp and paper existed before the 1970s, particularly pulp and paper, but both sectors expanded dramatically in the late 1970s and 1980s under the incentives of the second National Development Plan (1974). All were capital intensive, but labor costs were a much higher percentage for machine tools and equipment than for the other two, and initial capital costs for pulp and paper were on the highest end of the scale. Finally, each of these sectors differed substantially in their linkage to the state. Consequently, the impact of the fiscal crisis differed as did the potential benefits of the state's withdrawal.

MARKET STRUCTURE AND HISTORY

The way that each sector emerged in Brazil played a substantial role in shaping its competitive advantages and disadvantages. For example, the state played an instrumental role in promoting all industrial sectors in Brazil, but its role differed to some extent in each sector. More important, the consequences of state participation differed widely from sector to sector. Thus, as of the 1990 commercial liberalization, the state's participation in pulp and paper helped shape a sector with high degrees of concentration and vertical integration. Both these factors helped the sector's competitive position and helped lure into Brazil the world's foremost producers of capital goods for pulp and paper production. The state's role in the auto parts sector also helped encourage high levels of vertical integration, but here it emerged as a competitive disadvantage—a response to the way in which the state politicized supply relations. As a consequence, the parts sector developed in a skewed fashion, divided between modern firms with better relations with assemblers and technologically backward firms with poorer relations. Finally, the state's presence in the machine tools and equipment sector helped bring the sector into being, but saddled it with tremendous competitive disadvantages, not the least of which was excessive reliance on the state as a consumer.

Pulp and Paper

Pulp and paper is one of the oldest and most competitive sectors in Brazil's industrial economy. One of the major firms in the sector, Indústrias

Klabín, was founded by the Klabín family in 1899. The sector achieved its status as one of Brazil's most important only in the 1970s, however: it grew on average over 18 percent per year through the 1950s and 13 percent per year through the 1960s.[3] In the mid-1970s, the National Bank for Social and Economic Development (BNDES) officials determined that pulp and paper was one of the base industries through which economies captured and developed technology.[4] Thus, along with sectors like machine tools and equipment, the bank targeted the sector for growth by offering a wide range of incentives.

During that period, sectoral leaders, led by one of the industry's pioneers in Brazil, Max Feffer, experimented with eucalyptus fibers, producing a quality pulp at tremendous cost advantage over long fibers used in other major pulp-producing countries. Countries like the United States, Canada, and the Scandinavian countries are among the world's leaders in pulp production based on long-fiber wood. The growth cycle of wood in the north, such as pine, is on average thirty years. The growth cycle for eucalyptus in Brazil is only seven years. Its development as an alternative provided a strong comparative advantage to Brazilian pulp.[5] By 1980, the sector went from a net importer of pulp to a net exporter. With the BNDES's aggressive support, the sector became a world leader.

By 1991, state support had produced a highly successful, widely dispersed, and primarily domestic sector. The sector as of 1991 included 178 firms operating 237 industrial plants across Brazil. Private domestic firms controlled 94 percent of the capital in the sector and were responsible for 95 percent of the production. Paper production was concentrated overwhelmingly in the state of São Paulo and the south, whereas pulp production, especially eucalyptus, took place in the northeastern and central states as well. Overall, production of pulp and paper occurred in seventeen states. In 1991, the sector directly employed 132 thousand employees between industrial and forest workers. It generated U.S.$5.5 billion in receipts and U.S.$650 million in direct taxes.[6]

Despite the number of firms and the wide dispersion, political and economic power remained in the hands of a small number of firms. For example, the degree of concentration in the sector was quite high. Of the 178 firms, 50 were fully integrated (wood, pulp, and paper), 98 produced

3. "Annual Statistical Report" (ANFPC, 1991).
4. Confidential author interview, BNDES official, April 1992, São Paulo.
5. Jaakko Pöyry, "Perspectives e Oportunidades para a Indústria de Papel e Celulose Latino-Americana" (private consulting report, 1991).
6. "Annual Statistical Report" (ANFPC, 1991).

only paper, 25 produced wood pastes, and 5 produced pulp for the market. The nonintegrated firms were mostly small- to medium-size firms. The top seven producers of pulp accounted for 62.4 percent of all production. The top seven paper producers accounted for 42 percent of all production. Private domestic capital accounted for 79 percent of the receipts of the sector's top twenty firms, and the remaining 21 percent was private foreign capital. Of the 178 firms, only three, Champion (United States), Manville (United States) and Rigesa (England) were foreign, and none was a parastatal. The three MNC's were integrated firms, with Rigesa operating largely in the packaging market.[7]

Led by the largest firms, the sector became one of Brazil's most successful exporters. Between 1984 and 1991, the sector exported on average 990,000 tons per year of pulp, reaching a peak of 1,384,021 tons for U.S.\$586,279 million in 1991.[8] The country imported 148,522 tons of pulp in 1991.[9] The sector exported on average over 790,000 tons of paper between 1984 and 1991, reaching a peak of 1,077,346 tons for U.S.\$657,608 million. In turn, it imported 371,588 tons of paper in 1991. These sums corresponded to exports of roughly 25 percent of total pulp production and roughly 20 percent of total paper production. The five firms that produced only pulp exported on average 75 percent of their production. Roughly 60 percent of all pulp produced domestically was sold in integrated firms for paper production. Imports represented roughly 8 percent of total production of paper and only 4 percent of total pulp production.

Export success rested on a series of factors. From 1970 to 1984, the sector, including pulp, paper and board, and paper and board products, experienced rising productivity, a declining share of wages as a percentage of total costs, and rising profitability.[10] During that period, pulp and paper and board products had lower prices domestically than internationally, whereas paper and board had higher prices. During this time, prices were tightly controlled through the CIP. The CIP's pricing policies gave pulp producers a strong incentive to export, as well as effecting a sharp transfer of income from pulp to paper producers. Because most of this

---

7. For a full discussion of the market structure and history, see Sebastião José Martins Soares, Walter Aluisio Morais Rodrigues, and José Clemente de Oliveira, "O Setor Celulose-Papel," in Coutinho and Suzigan, eds., *Desenvolvimento Tecnológico*.

8. Sources, ANFPC and Soares, Rodrigues, and Clemente de Oliveira, "O Setor Celulose-Papel."

9. "Annual Statistical Report" (ANFPC, 1991).

10. Soares, Rodrigues, and Clemente de Oliveira, "O Setor Celulose-Papel."

transfer was internal to integrated firms, it allowed for substantial profit margins.[11] Both the rising productivity and the declining share of wages over the period reflected the large-scale investments made by the sector over the 1970s and early 1980s. Roughly two-thirds of the sector's capacity was installed during that period. The capital requirements for pulp and paper production were extremely high, and the technology was sophisticated. Thus, capital investments over the period further drove down the share of wages while increasing productivity and profitability.

The growing competitiveness of the sector encouraged several multinational producers of machine tools and equipment for pulp and paper to produce locally.[12] Voith S.A. (German), Beloit (English) in conjunction with Rauma (Finnish), and Jaakko Pöyry (Finnish) provided internationally competitive technology to the sector. Several other global leaders, including Asea Brown Boveri (Swedish-Swiss), Fischer (U.S.), and Sunds Defibrator (Swedish), licensed technology to local producers. Thus, the competitiveness of the sector generated a highly competitive supply chain, even in otherwise uncompetitive sectors, such as machine tools and equipment.

Thus, the sector grew on the back of strong profits domestically and a strong performance in exports, despite the chaotic domestic climate of the 1980s. The crisis did drop sectoral growth rates from an average of 14 percent in the 1970s to 5 percent for pulp and 4 percent for paper in the 1980s. Nevertheless, Brazil emerged as the eighth largest producer of pulp in the world and the eleventh largest paper producer by the 1980s. Furthermore, although Latin America represents 9 percent of the world's population, it consumed only 4 percent of the world's pulp and paper.[13] Thus, with expectations of significant growth of demand for pulp and paper in Latin America (estimated at 4 percent per year) coupled with estimates of 2.5 percent growth per year in the developed world, the sector anticipated continued strong growth.

In anticipation of this strong increase in demand, the sector planned investments to double capacity by 1996. The sector in total projected close to U.S.$10 billion from 1990 to 1996, with over U.S.$8 billion in industrial investments, close to U.S.$1 billion in reforestation, and over U.S.$600 million in environmental projects.[14] The sector did not, how-

---

11. Soares, Rodrigues, and Clemente de Oliveira, "O Setor Celulose-Papel," 57.

12. Observations about the competitive strength of local suppliers came in a confidential author interview with a sectoral representative, January 1992, São Paulo.

13. Estimate from Pöyry, "Perspectivas."

14. ANFPC survery, cited in Soares, Rodrigues, and Clemente de Oliveira, "O Setor Celulose-Papel," 67.

ever, anticipate the severity of Collor's 1990 stabilization plan and the resulting recession. In response, most firms reprogrammed their investments, setting the new target date for 2001. The only investments that proceeded during Collor's tenure (1990–92) had already been contracted.[15]

Auto Parts

The history of the auto parts sector led to a mixed picture in which a small number of firms actively participated in exports while the majority remained technologically backward. Overall, the sector was characterized by high-priced inputs and conflictual relations with assemblers. The auto parts sector existed in Brazil on a small scale, even before the automotive sector. It produced for the market in replacement parts to service imported cars. In 1956, auto parts producers, through their *sindicato* (corporatist sectoral association), SINDIPEÇAS, negotiated a deal with the state and MNC auto producers to build an automobile industry in Brazil.[16] The deal stipulated that the MNC producers would receive a market reserve in exchange for producing locally and using almost exclusively locally made parts. The sector grew in the wake of that decision as auto producers entered and began to produce under local content laws requiring that 95 percent of the car, by weight, had to be made in Brazil.

The sector grew substantially throughout the 1970s. The sector invested on average U.S.$250 million per year from 1975 to 1985. Since 1986, investments climbed slowly to over U.S.$1 billion in 1990, primarily in expanding capacity. The effects of the 1990 Collor stabilization plan, including recession and the high cost of capital, however, forestalled most investment plans at least until the recession eased. According to SINDIPEÇAS sources, 80 percent of investments realized in the sector over the course of the 1980s came from the firms' own resources. The sector generated receipts of U.S.$2.5 billion in 1974. By 1990, it generated over U.S.$13 billion, including over U.S.$2 billion in direct and indirect exports. The sector employed over 300,000 employees in 1989, but the 1990–92 recession and competitive restructuring led firms to sharply

15. *Gazeta Mercantil, Balanço anual*, 1991.
16. Discussed in Shapiro, *Engines of Growth*, as well as Caren Addis, *Taking the Wheel: Auto Parts Firms and the Political Economy of Industrialization in Brazil* (University Park: The Pennsylvania State University Press, 1999).

cut their labor forces. By May 1992, the sector employed only 238,900 workers.

By 1992, the sector had around 1,500 firms producing auto parts, most of them relatively small- to mid-size, uncompetitive firms. SINDIPEÇAS represented only 507 firms, and the remainder either claimed membership in other syndicates, such as plastic, rubber, or casting, or were small-scale pirate producers. Pirate producers made parts for the replacement (after-market) market, copying name brands and selling them for much lower prices at much lower quality. Of the 507 firms represented in SINDI-PEÇAS, small- and medium-size firms predominated. Nine firms employed over 4,000 employees. Only 14 percent of the members employed over 1,000 workers, whereas 27 percent employed fewer than 125.[17] Over 700 firms sold directly to the MNC assemblers (General Motors, Autolatina, Fiat, Mercedes-Benz, Scania, Volvo). Roughly 150 firms exported, although the top 10 accounted for 90 percent of the value of all exports.

Auto parts producers sold parts in three basic markets. The original equipment manufacturers (OEM; the MNC assemblers) market, the after market, and the export market. The OEM market claimed a majority of auto parts production (by receipts), but the level declined relatively continuously from over 70 percent in 1977 to only 51 percent in 1990. Exports (direct) rose from roughly 3 percent in the late 1970s to a range of roughly 14 to 16 percent in 1990–92. The after market, which yielded higher returns and demanded less in terms of quality, rose from roughly 18 to 20 percent in the late 1970s to over 30 percent in the early 1990s.

Although domestic private firms numerically dominated the sector, large MNCs dominated the sector by market share. Of the ten largest exporters of parts (both directly and indirectly through the exports of finished vehicles), eight were MNCs. Of the top twenty producers, including assemblers, fifteen were multinational subsidiaries. The degree of concentration overall was not high, however. The largest firms accounted for only 40 percent of sales to the assemblers.[18] Furthermore, at least two or three major producers competed in each category of parts. The same limited competitive structure characterized the parts market outside Brazil as well.[19]

17. SINDIPEÇAS data, monthly reports.
18. Addis, "Auto Parts, Made in Brazil," in Coutinho and Suzigan, eds., *Desenvolvimento Tecnológico*, 19.
19. Booz, Allen, and Hamilton, "Estratégia Setorial para a Indústria Automobilística no Brasil" (private study commissioned by União pela Modernização and SINDIPEÇAS; São Paulo, 1991): 28.

The most important character of the sector reflected a basic conflict in the supply chain of the automotive complex. Both assemblers and the larger parts firms vertically integrated production to high levels. The intensity of the conflicts and the central role of vertical integration in the conflict made accurate data scarce. SINDIPEÇAS officials estimated that the sector (and the assemblers) probably led the world in the degree of verticalization. Estimates from SINDIPEÇAS and private auto parts representatives suggest that the assemblers purchased only about 40 to 45 percent of their components, although with substantial variation among assemblers.[20] Caren Addis, in her report on the sector, recorded levels of vertical integration in the larger firms of most parts categories ranging from 45 to 100 percent. She noted that some firms did their own casting, forging, and stamping of metal products. Of the firms in her sample, some produced their own metal powder, plastic parts, and even rubber parts.[21] One firm in my sample produced its own machine tools.[22]

The level of vertical integration grew from the bitter conflicts over supply and prices characterizing the sector. At first, in the late 1950s, the assemblers depended on local suppliers to achieve the restrictive local content levels, and in turn the suppliers needed the assemblers' production know-how and technology. The turmoil of later years changed the cooperative nature of the relation. Sharp fluctuations in the market along with frequent rule changes and high inflation produced significant uncertainties only partially mitigated by market reserves and price controls. To insulate themselves from the costs of market fluctuations, assemblers followed the Fordist tradition and shifted their costs to their suppliers. They encouraged alternative sources of supply, including relying on imports in the commercially liberal period of military rule. Suppliers responded by shifting the same costs onto the smaller firms of their sector and by withholding supply from assemblers during market upturns. This dynamic led larger firms to continuously increase their level of verticalization to further insulate themselves from the uncertainties of supply relations in the production chain.[23]

One illustration of the volatility of the market came from an analysis of the sector by the consulting firm Booz, Allen, and Hamilton. It conducted a survey measuring changes in assemblers' production programs

20. Confidential author interviews, SINDIPEÇAS and various firms, September 1991, São Paulo; 1991–92, São Paulo.

21. Addis, "Auto Parts," 34–35.

22. Confidential author interview, auto parts representative, January 1992, São Paulo.

23. Addis, "Auto Parts," 23–26.

and the resulting changes in their orders in one month, November 1989. Overall, the survey reported variations in orders from five assemblers resulting in a 6.8 percent total increase in orders and an 8.6 percent decrease over sixty-eight different production programs.[24] Another item of data revealing some of the volatility of the supply relation came from SINDIPEÇAS's monthly report on average lateness of payment in the after market. During the period 1990–92, buyers paid their suppliers from twelve to thirty days late.[25] In a market with 25 percent monthly inflation, lateness represented a severe problem and a conflictual way of shifting costs.

Machine Tools and Equipment

The machine tools and equipment sector grew rapidly with state promotion in the 1970s. Unlike the pulp and paper sector, which expanded at the same time, state promotion helped produce a large, highly fragmented, and differentiated sector, for the most part poorly prepared for commercial liberalization. The machine tool and equipment sector united a wide array of producers in different markets. Examining them together poses certain problems that arise from those differences. For one, the various segments used different technologies, and each segment was further stratified by different levels of technological sophistication. The sector united firms that produced nuclear reactors with firms that produced railway cars with firms that produced ball bearings. Alternative classifications disaggregated the sector in different ways. Some separated the firms into two producer groups: metallurgy and mechanical. Others separated electronic, industrial automation, and transport material. Still others raised the level of aggregation and referred to it simply as capital goods to distinguish it from consumer goods.

I have chosen to treat it as a single sector of machine tools and equipment because that is how the many varied firms aggregated politically. Their association/syndicate, the National Association/Syndicate for Machine Tools and Equipment (ABIMAQ/SINDIMAQ), represented over 1,500 firms from thirty-one distinct groupings. Some producers had a separate syndicate, such as the State Syndicate for Highway and Rail Producers (SIMEFRE), whereas others associated with organizations such as

---

24. Booz, Allen, and Hamilton, "Estratégia Setorial," 31.
25. SINDIPEÇAS *Notícias,* data printed monthly.

the Brazilian Association for Electro-Electronic Producers (ABINEE). Nevertheless, ABIMAQ/SINDIMAQ remained the most critical association for most firms, and its diversity remained an important political issue. Furthermore, despite their differences, the firms had much in common in their response to liberalization.

The machine tools and equipment sector was segmented into different markets based on level of technological sophistication. The highest (and smallest) level included the production of industrial robots, computer-aided design, computer-aided manufacturing, computer-integrated manufacturing, and computer numerically controlled machine tools. The second level produced numerically controlled machinery using sophisticated technology of at least this second level. Finally, the bulk of production in Brazil (and most of its exports) did not use sophisticated technology and produced technologically unsophisticated machinery that benefited from lower wage costs. Small domestic firms numerically dominated this segment of the market.[26] Seventy-two percent of the sector's national production occurred in the state of São Paulo. Small domestic firms numerically dominated the sector. ABIMAQ did not have exact data, but a poll done by the organization among 344 members in 1987 estimated that one-fifth of the firms employed fewer than 50 employees and close to 60 percent employed fewer than 250.[27]

Although MNCs held a strong position in the market, room existed for domestic firms, small and large. Multinational firms accounted for 53 percent of the total receipts of the twenty largest firms in the sector.[28] The sector also included several large domestic firms, most of which were holdings of one of Brazil's large private capital groups (*grupos economicos,* e.g., Votorantim, Villares, Bardella). Furthermore, multinationals, large domestic, and small domestic firms tended to operate in different markets. For example, multinationals predominated in areas requiring the highest levels of technological sophistication, such as equipment for pulp

26. This dependence on wage costs was a particularly important issue as wage settlements were negotiated in the corporatist structure. ABIMAQ was one of nineteen sectors represented in FIESP's *Grupo* 14, which conducted wage negotiations for all metal-bending industries. Sectoral representatives bitterly complained that the auto industry drove the bargaining process. Yet, differences in capital intensity made it much easier for the auto assemblers to absorb wage increases. As a consequence, ABIMAQ was engaged in frequent conflicts with FIESP. This issue is discussed in some detail in McQuerry, "Economic Liberalization in Brazil," 31–55.

27. ABIMAQ, "Política Industrial para a Indústria de Máquinas e Equipamentos no Brasil" (São Paulo: December 1989).

28. *Exame* (São Paulo), *Melhores e Maiores* 1990.

and paper or industrial automation. Large domestic firms predominated in heavy equipment and railroad equipment, areas with large capital requirements and strongly linked to the state. Small firms tended to operate in the least sophisticated, least capital intensive areas, namely, machines without any electronic or microelectronic components.[29]

Production in the sector began around World War I and then increased around World War II as imported supplies grew scarcer. Immigrants, largely Italian, opened most of these firms at this time and later. Most of them had experience with the sector before coming to Brazil, and they based their operations on that existing know-how. Later, under Kubitschek's Five Year Plan (Plano de Metas, 1956–61), state policy actively promoted import substitution of capital goods, and the sector grew again, principally among European immigrants.

Close to 60 percent of the sector emerged after 1961, especially in the 1970s (roughly 35 percent of the sector's firms were founded between 1971 and 1980). In the late 1960s, the military government conducted studies concluding that capital goods needed to be a priority for substitution. Capital goods played an important role in capturing and diffusing technology. They ranked second on Brazil's import list, after oil, and substitution promised to alleviate potential balance-of-payment problems.

As a result, the state, through the BNDES, CACEX, and the Industrial Development Council (CDI), vigorously promoted the sector through the first and second National Development Plans. These plans established heavily subsidized lines of credit, a series of tax incentives, and a strong market reserve for anybody producing in the sector. In response, the number of firms operating in the sector nearly doubled. By 1980, the sector reached its peak. It accounted for roughly 5.5 percent of GDP; equipment made to order (as opposed to serial production) alone accounted for 3 percent.[30] It produced U.S.$17.75 billion worth of goods, of which it exported 6 percent. It directly employed 306,000 workers.

The crisis of the second oil shock hit Brazil hard and the machine tools and equipment sector even harder. Production levels in the sector fluctuated over the decade in response to changes in GDP. The recession of 1981–83 affected the sector badly, but the expansion effect of the 1987 Cruzado Plan restored production to almost its 1980 peak. By 1989, the sector produced U.S.$16.4 billion worth of goods and employed 280,000 workers.

---

29. Erber and Vermulm, "Ajuste," 179.
30. Confidential author interview, ABIMAQ, October 1991, São Paulo.

The sector followed two paths to recovery from the shock of the decade. In the early part of the decade, many firms identified numerically controlled machinery and equipment as the solution. As Brazilian firms sought to keep pace to some extent with changes in global technology, the demand for numerically controlled machinery rose. Local firms invested heavily at that time to produce for the newly expanding market. Later in the decade, the continuing uncertainty and the threat of new stagnation in the domestic market prompted more firms to pursue an export strategy. For their survival, the sector increased the level of exports from an average of 7.5 percent of total production between 1980–85 to an average of 10.5 percent from 1986–90 (over 13 percent in 1989–90).[31]

Nevertheless, the sector continued to fare poorly overall. Throughout the 1980s, the sector's prices averaged as much as three to five times international prices. After Sarney's 1988 moderately liberalizing industrial policy, prices fell to an average of one and a half times international prices (with the most sophisticated production continuing at prices three to five times international levels).[32] By ABIMAQ's estimation, productivity in the sector remained poor in small firms and improved proportionately with the size of the firm.[33]

STATE LINKAGES

By 1990, even the most competitive industrial sectors remained linked to the state in important ways, but the extent to which and the ways in which they linked varied substantially. In turn, those variations played a considerable role in shaping the relative costs and benefits of neoliberal reform. For pulp and paper, the state's decay posed infrastructure problems, particularly in energy. Otherwise, neither the withdrawal nor the decay of the state profoundly affected the sector, particularly because it retained privileged access to capital through the BNDES. For auto parts, the story was more mixed. The sector had benefited from the state's protection of the market, but continued state regulation (particularly price

31. ABIMAQ data.
32. Confidential author interview, ABIMAQ, October 1991, São Paulo. Data come from ABIMAQ 2000, unpublished and uncirculated in 1992. I was allowed to read portions at ABIMAQ.
33. ABIMAQ 2000.

controls) seriously disorganized production. Finally machine tools and equipment faced a particularly difficult situation. On the one hand, the state's fiscal crisis affected it sharply. Declining infrastructure investments, dwindling capital supply for both competitive restructuring and for capital goods sales, and dependence on the state as a consumer all hit the sector hard. On the other hand, its dependence on protection certainly exceeded that of most other Brazilian industrial sectors.

Pulp and Paper

As of 1992, the pulp and paper sector depended less on the state than did many other sectors, but the sector enjoyed state benefits in several ways. First, its massive expansion in the 1970s relied heavily on state financing, often at highly subsidized rates of interest. Second, in some instances, the state helped finance the sector through ownership of shares. Third, price controls had largely beneficial results for the sector. Finally, the sectoral association had been and remained one of the most successful lobbies among industrial associations. Furthermore, it consistently occupied an influential position in the corporative structure, especially in the key corporatist São Paulo federation of industry, FIESP. Its excellent organizational position continued to afford it access to policymakers and state resources through the 1980s and 1990s.

As part of the BNDES's efforts to promote Brazil's industrial expansion, the bank targeted the pulp and paper sector as a key to technological capacitation. The sector in the 1960s included largely small-scale, family enterprises with outdated technology. The BNDES, through the CDI, provided tax incentives for reforestation, massive loans for industrial investments at negative real interest rates, and tax incentives for exportation.[34] Internationally competitive standards of minimum scale far exceeded the average scale in Brazil in the 1960s. Without BNDES support, the sector could not have grown as it did. Even in the 1990s, its strength as an exporter continued to privilege it in receiving state finances. The sector's investment program in the early 1990s, despite the slowdown in investment plans, consumed 50 percent of the BNDES's available funds for industrial investment in 1990.[35]

34. Soares, "O Setor Celulose-Papel," 58–61.
35. Suzigan and Villela, *Industrial Policy in Brazil,* 209. In fact, the sector averaged roughly 25 to 50 percent of the bank's investment resources through the late 1980s and 1990s.

In addition to the highly favorable financing the sector received, some of the largest firms also received financial assistance through state ownership of shares. Although the state did sell most of its shares in the 1980s, the initial infusion of capital was another important source of the sector's growth. Similarly, the state provided subsidized loans to individual share purchasers. These two steps had an important, unintended consequence. The expansion of ownership beyond the founding families resulted in a professionalization of the sector's management. The sector stood out in Brazil both for its recruitment of top managers and the extent to which it used public offerings as a source of capital. Both elements were important factors in its competitiveness.

A third important linkage to the state was price control through the CIP. The state closely regulated the sector's prices through the CIP during its existence from 1967 to 1990. This regulation combined with Brazil's protected market provided two benefits for pulp and paper. First, like many other sectors, price control and protection permitted high profit margins in the domestic market, particularly because the price control structure allowed for substantial collusion. Given that the sector united several large-scale, world-class producers with a large number of small and medium firms with nowhere near the competitive advantages, significant possibilities for abuse existed.[36] Cost plans for the smaller, least efficient producers became the basis of price adjustments, even for the largest firms. Thus, smaller producers may have had reasonable adjustments whereas the most powerful firms in the sector enjoyed substantial margins. A second, related benefit for the sector arose from this combination of price control and protection. The same set of small- to medium-size producers without sufficient scale to invest in modern capital equipment survived because of the system. Thus, whereas giants like Aracruz, Papel Simão, or Indústrias Klabín did not need the system to survive, a majority or plurality of the sector did.

Finally, the sector maintained one more linkage to the state through its influential position in the corporative structure. Members thought particularly well of their association, the Associação Nacional dos Fabricantes de Papel e Celulose (ANFPC). It functioned effectively and professionally as a lobby and technical clearinghouse, but sectoral representatives also held influential positions in the corporative structure. In the executive of FIESP from 1989 to 1992, corresponding roughly to Collor's tenure, representatives held high positions. The sector counted among its repre-

---

36. Confidential author interview in the pulp and paper sector, February 1992, São Paulo.

sentatives Mario Amato, the president of FIESP/CIESP (CIESP is the Center of Industry, the peak industrial association outside, but linked to, the corporatist structure); Hessel Horácio Cherkassky, Indústrias Klabín, president of ANFPC, and vice-president of CIESP; Jamil Nicolau Aun, Papel Simão and vice-president of CIESP; José Ermírio de Moraes Neto, of Indústrias Votorantim and vice-president of CIESP; Roberto Nicolau Jeha, Papel e Papelão São Roberto and second secretary of CIESP; Horácio Lafer Piva, Indústrias Klabín and third secretary of CIESP; and Max Heinz Gunther Schrappe, of Impressora Paranaense and director of CIESP. Given the importance of FIESP/CIESP in the corporative structure and the link between the corporative structure and state benefits, the sector was well placed politically in the old developmental model.

Auto Parts

As a mature industry relative to many sectors of Brazil's economy, the automotive complex had distanced itself from some state benefits. In particular, neither the MNC assemblers nor the auto parts firms relied on the state for financing. Neither sector particularly benefited from the state's subsidized loans of the 1970s (under the aegis of the first and second National Development Plans). As mature sectors, the BNDES did not target them for new expansion. One representative explained that as he had alternatives, he preferred not to make himself vulnerable to the state's potential abuse of power (i.e., virtual monopoly control of finance).[37] Nevertheless, state financing earlier in the 1950s and 1960s and state emphasis on large firms did have lasting consequences for the sector. The policy segmented the market, producing a small minority of large firms with access to state funds and a large majority of small- and mid-size firms without state support.

Despite the distancing from state financial support, the importance of automobile production for Brazil's economy meant that the state kept a watchful eye on the sectors. Specifically, the CIP closely regulated prices for both sectors almost continuously from its creation in 1969. In addition, state policy maintained local content laws at 95 percent of a vehicle's weight until Sarney's liberalizing industrial policy of 1988. Although CACEX played with the law according to its interpretation of Brazil's needs, both the above factors had major consequences for the sector.

37. Confidential author interview, auto parts representative, June 1992, São Paulo.

Government regulation of the sector added further fuel to these conflicts. The price council, the CIP, and the foreign commerce office, CACEX, conducted their policies in ways that alternately favored one of the sectors over the other. The inconsistency of their favoritism provoked well-founded charges by both sectors of political interference by the government against both sectors. Charges that the CIP protected auto parts and CACEX favored the assemblers added fuel to poor relations through the turbulent 1980s. This characteristic of the automotive chain had important consequences for liberalization as relations between the two sectors remained hostile through the 1990s.

The CIP's oversight contributed to hostile relations between parts producers and assemblers. The CIP allowed auto parts firms to form sectoral groups in SINDIPEÇAS to study their cost structures and to submit detailed plans for review. The decision prompted cartel-like arrangements whereby competitors in a market would negotiate through SINDIPEÇAS, ANFAVEA (the automobile association), and the CIP. Agreements on prices and market share stabilized competition and reduced the uncertainty of the relations, but assemblers charged that the CIP authorized higher price adjustments for their suppliers than it did for them. Critics further charged that the program undermined competitiveness by creating de facto cartels.

In turn, the auto parts sector charged the assemblers with disregarding the CIP's decisions and forcing painful costs onto them. The lines of conflict were divided between assemblers and suppliers (whether of domestic or foreign capital control) and between small and large suppliers. Large suppliers, although more successful in organizing cartels against assemblers' economic might, also tended to produce high-value items. For example, a car's suspension system or motor may represent 2 to 4 percent of the cost of the car. A 1 or 2 percent difference in the price increase makes a large difference in the cost of the car. Consequently, price negotiations could be bitter.[38] Conversely, small firms that produced items of little value provoked less resistance from assemblers, but they did not have the protection of cartel arrangements backing them when assemblers did contest their price increases. As a result, some of the most intense conflicts took place in the corporative structure mediated (and probably exacerbated) by the state. At the same time, most small firms believed and claimed that the system's design punished them excessively.

---

38. One interviewed representative, a CEO of a mid-size auto parts firm, reported that the firm lost a contract with an assembler in one such heated price dispute. By report, this was not an uncommon occurrence for auto parts firms.

Another area that produced deep conflict occurred in the state's administration of import controls. In 1973, the assemblers negotiated an export promotion package with the state called Program for Special Financial Incentives to Export (BEFIEX). As the government realized its growing need to earn foreign exchange, it provided tax rebates and allowed U.S.$1.00 for every U.S.$3.00 that assemblers (or auto parts manufacturers) undertook to export. The deal still required that importers pass their requests past CACEX for the examination for national similars. Auto parts producers angrily charged that foreign-exchange-hungry bureaucrats allowed imports without letting suppliers examine the requests for similars.[39]

These mutual recriminations aside, the state contributed to the uncompetitiveness of both sectors through very high effective rates of protection. Average tariffs for auto parts through the 1980s measured 40 percent. Autos could not be imported. These levels of protection, combined with the cartelization of the sectors and the guaranteed minimum prices set by the CIP, had perverse consequences for the sector in addition to engendering conflicts. Critically, it discouraged investment in improving quality and productivity. It eliminated concerns for competitiveness or efficiency as governing principles. In conjunction with the turbulence of the 1980s, it resulted in declining investments (especially in the automotive sector) and declining production.[40] By Collor's inauguration in March 1990, most firms in the auto parts sector had invested little or nothing in technology and process improvements. The assemblers, crucial to the entire productive chain that depended on them, perhaps lagged even farther behind.

Auto parts was well placed politically in the corporatist structure of business representation, but with ambiguous results. Auto parts as a sector occupied an important place in FIESP as well as in the advisory councils of state agencies. During the tenure of Pedro Eberhardt as president of SINDIPEÇAS (1983–92), the sector gained representation on the CIP, the CDI, and CACEX. It also counted among its representatives in FIESP one vice-president of FIESP (José Mindlin—Metal Leve) and two vice-presidents of CIESP (Pedro Eberhardt and Daniel Sahagoff—Pirelli Componentes). Unfortunately, ANFAVEA's much greater power vis-à-vis the government and in FIESP mitigated the influence of auto parts. One representative expressed the view that negotiations between the government

39. Addis, "Auto Parts," 29.
40. ANFAVEA, "Annual Statistical Reports."

and ANFAVEA were dealings between equal powers, not between the state and a business sector.[41] As many of the sector's conflicts concerned ANFAVEA, it is not clear how much benefit the sector derived from its position in the corporative structure. That problem continued to haunt parts producers as the liberalization process left SINDIPEÇAS complaining of preferential treatment for assemblers through 1997.

Machine Tools and Equipment

Machine tools and equipment resembled several other sectors vigorously promoted in the National Development Plans in its deep linking with the state. Much like petrochemicals and computers and not at all like auto parts or pulp and paper, the state profoundly influenced and shaped the sector. The state involved itself with the sector in almost every way possible with the exception of state ownership, which was very limited. On the one hand, the benefit, as Antônio Barros de Castro and Francisco Eduardo Pires de Souza argued,[42] was that the state's policies encouraged and in fact created a mature, diversified, and at times sophisticated industrial park. On the other hand, the state's involvement produced perverse consequences for competitiveness and technological capacitation. From the strict perspective of the sector's preparation for liberalization, the state's influence has to be seen as harmful.

The state was linked to the sector in at least seven different ways. First, it provided financing for the sector, particularly in the 1970s when it did so at highly subsidized rates. Second, the state was the sector's most important customer, particularly of the heavy equipment subsector where the state had at times been the only customer. Third, the state, through the CIP, for the most part allowed the sector to set its own prices, even while the CIP controlled the prices of its customers. Fourth, the sector provided subsidized inputs from state-owned steel companies and through utilities. Fifth, the state provided rigorous market protection, enforced by CACEX in conjunction with SINDIMAQ. At the same time as it zealously guarded the market from imported machinery and equipment, the state also created a range of exemptions for exporters, BEFIEX being the most notable. Thus, state policy neither encouraged competitive re-

41. Confidential author interview, auto parts representative, November 1991, São Paulo.
42. Antônio Barros de Castro and Francisco Eduardo Pires de Souza, *A Ecnonomia Brasileira em Marcha Forçada* (Rio: Paz e Terra, 1985).

structuring nor fully protected local producers. Sixth, the state also passed the computers law, creating a strict market reserve throughout the 1980s for producers of microelectronic and computer products and components. In turn, policymakers actively encouraged large domestic firms to produce in these reserved markets. Finally, as in the auto-parts sector, the chaos of the market with frequent rule and policy changes led many firms to pursue excessive levels of vertical integration to avoid supply problems. This degree of verticalization generated benefits only in the context of a chaotic protected market. For purposes of global competitiveness, verticalization resulted in firms that produced far more components than they could efficiently manufacture. Relatedly, as a rule, most firms produced a wide assortment of products, particularly among the made-to-order firms. Some of these firms reported that they produced as many as forty or fifty different products, even though they may have sold only one or two units per year.[43]

Both excessive verticalization and product diversification stemmed largely from state policies that created strong incentives to produce in the sector, protected firms once they were producing, yet failed to create a market for all the firms producing. The state's highly subsidized financing existed for any firm producing in the sector. Thus, the state did not offer incentives to produce a certain product not produced locally. It offered incentives simply to produce. As a result, firms emerged at a dramatic pace to seek the rents available from the state. Subsequently, to survive, these firms undertook to produce whatever they could.

The problem worsened with the state's significant encouragement of exempted imports under export-promotion programs. These imports undermined the effort to create domestic demand at efficient economies of scale. State failures to develop national standards (or at least to choose among competing foreign ones) for domestic production further segmented the market by splitting it among the various standards of the various national origins of firms. Finally, the state's somewhat schizophrenic policy of restricting imports with one hand while encouraging them with the other hurt the sector. Most important, export firms tended to be at the leading edge technologically in Brazil's economy. Thus, the state's allowance for imports for exporting firms meant that those firms then imported the leading edge of capital goods technology. This tendency, partially checked by the computers market reserve, tended to keep

---

43. ABIMAQ 2000; Erber and Vermulm, "Ajuste," 177–82; and confidential author interviews in the sector, various, 1991–92, São Paulo.

machine tool and equipment producers in lower ends of technological sophistication.

The state helped these firms survive without real concern for questions of competitiveness or efficiency in other ways. The sector's freedom from price controls allowed firms to pass on their high costs with little pressure to contain prices. The tightness of the market reserve for firms not using export promotion exemptions reinforced this power to pass on costs. Subsidized inputs, such as steel, also helped. One additional factor raised by business representatives in interviews was that the sector negotiated with the state during the 1950s and then again in the 1970s to establish the strict local content laws enforced by CACEX and the BNDES. During those negotiations, state agencies never held out the prospect of market liberalization.[44] In the absence of some quid pro quo ("we protect you for X years, then you have to face competition"), the sector did not anticipate the need to improve its competitive position.

The role of the state as a customer raised another critical aspect of the state's impact on the sector and its prices. The state's declining investment throughout the 1980s had an obvious impact on producers, which depended heavily on state investment. Even beyond the scarcity of state investment, the state's unreliability as a customer had its own effect. Sectoral representatives repeatedly reported that the state tended to pay its suppliers late and sometimes not at all. Some firms reported payments delayed over one year. Those payments frequently came without monetary correction or with unfavorable adjustments so that firms lost money on the transaction. In any event, firms adjusted prices to include risk premiums for dealing with the state. On top of the premium, producers had to calculate inflation rates for the period and build that into the price as well. As a result, firms faced problems of chaotic finances, heavy accounting costs, price and cash flow distortions because of late or nonpayment, and at times even bankruptcy. In fact, Latin America's largest railcar producer, Cobrasma, filed for protection from creditors for exactly that reason.[45]

The computers reserve also played a disruptive role for the sector. As mentioned above, the dynamics of sectoral production in the 1970s and

44. This experience, of course, differs dramatically from that of East Asian countries. The notable absence of this quid pro quo is discussed in Suzigan and Villela, *Industrial Policy in Brazil*, 43.

45. *Economist*, December 7, 1991, p. 21. In general, though, firms were able to balance losses in some transactions through high prices in a protected market and through the ample opportunities for financial speculation.

1980s tended to push toward producing goods using electronic or computer components. These included numerically controlled machine tools, as well as computer numerically controlled machine tools, computer-aided design and manufacturing (CAD/CAM), and industrial robots. The market reserve dramatically drove up the prices of these machines—as much as five times world prices. The decision by the state to allow almost no joint ventures further hurt the sector.

Finally, market protection, including the computers reserve and the bitter disputes it raised among producer groups, bred resentment and conflict between the sector and its buyers. Other sectors accused machine tools and equipment, probably more than any other sector, of being the source of their lack of competitiveness. Although hard to measure, public complaints by diverse sectors such as automobiles and textiles as well as statements by sectoral representatives suggest that there was a punitive element to conflicts over liberalization. Certainly the sector faced serious problems with DECEX and the new Commission on Tariffs (CTT). New rules in 1990 allowed for an automatic exemption of duties for capital goods imports, providing no national similar existed. By admission of the CTT itself, the new rule provoked abuses on a grand scale.[46]

COSTS AND BENEFITS OF NEOLIBERAL REFORM

Differences in market structure, history, and state linkages led to widely differing costs and benefits, but all three sectors needed the government to credibly deliver on its promises if they were to realize the full benefits of reform. Collor's economic reform program featured a gradual commercial and financial liberalization, deregulation, and privatization. It also promised, among other things, to contain inflation, address the government's chronic deficits, and reform the tax, civil service, and pension systems. Thus, the program promised several critical elements to facilitate competitive restructuring even while placing competitive pressure on industry. For pulp and paper, producers depended on Collor's fulfilling his program promises to reduce both capital and energy costs. Without that, the trade-off between benefits and costs was much less clear. For auto parts and machine tools and equipment, the situation was clearer: with-

---

46. Confidential author interviews; *Revista SINDIMAQ*, May 1992, São Paulo.

out credible government performance, the negatives threatened to sharply raise the relative costs.

Pulp and Paper

The pulp and paper sector's sources of advantage came from three factors: wood, electrical energy, and labor costs, but low wood costs offered the largest advantage by far. Labor costs were lower per worker, but Brazilian producers used more labor than did Asian, European, or North American producers. Electrical energy provided advantages, but depended on government policies to maintain adequate and cost-efficient supply.[47]

The sector faced challenges from liberalization generally and from Collor's plan specifically. It also faced potential benefits from two sources: the option to buy cheaper imported inputs and Collor's promise to solve macroproblems such as inflation and anticompetitive taxation through his liberalizing program. The commercial opening provided the sector the opportunity to buy cheaper chemicals for use in processing pulp and paper. Similarly, the cost of capital equipment was high in Brazil because of the domestic tax component in equipment prices. Prices were also high because of domestic protection of the computer industry with its consequences for industrial automation, CAD, and computer numerically controlled (CNC) tools. The commercial opening offered the sector the possibility of purchasing imported equipment as well as allowing high-quality domestic equipment producers to import electronic components and computers. Thus, liberalization offered at least these real benefits.

These benefits were doubly real in that environmental concerns assumed great importance. To maintain export markets, Brazilian producers had to meet new global standards of environmental protection, which required both a change in the chemicals used in the production process and specific environmental investments, such as reforestation and specialized machinery. Thus, access to cheaper imported chemicals and specialized, environmentally safe machinery were crucial benefits of the market opening.

The potential costs of liberalization depended on both the reduction of profit margins and the government's ability to resolve critical problems in the economy. One estimate placed the profit margins that large firms ob-

---

47. Soares, "O Setor Celulose-Papel."

tained in the price-controlled domestic market at 40 percent in U.S. dollars.[48] The same source estimated that domestic profit margins in a liberalized market would shrink to something in the area of 6 percent. Naturally, this reduction in profit levels represented a real loss for domestic firms. In particular, this cost of liberalization created two cleavages in the sector: between small firms for whom this reduction in profits threatened survival and between generations. The older generation made enormous wealth off the old system and was therefore less committed to changing the growth model. The younger generation that had not yet earned its fortune faced the possibility of never earning one unless real changes were made to the clearly outdated developmental model.

Second, Collor's plan could become dangerous without government resolution of the macroeconomic problems that Collor had promised to address. These problems included several factors: the high cost of capital and the difficulty of investing in such conditions; the collapsing infrastructure, specifically the internal transportation structure, ports, and especially energy. All these factors threatened the sector's position as a leading exporter. Energy supply became unreliable in some parts of the country, and prices were set by the state and were subject to the whims of the government. Internal transportation costs and port costs were significant competitive disadvantages. These were particularly important as some northern competitors, such as Canada, were making process improvements and reducing Brazil's wood cost advantage.

Finally, liberalization also presented a political problem for the sector by threatening the existence of a large number of small firms, as noted above. Interviews in the sector suggested that this factor had not emerged as a problem because members accepted the inevitability of the situation and sectoral representatives in the ANFPC worked on identifying alternative strategies. Alternatives suggested for those that could not survive a liberalized economy included mergers, sellouts to larger firms, selling off forest stands, and producing for specialty markets.

Auto Parts

Liberalization offered several potential benefits to the auto sector, primarily from those macroeconomic aspects that the program promised to ad-

---

48. Confidential author interview, pulp and paper representative, February 1992, São Paulo.

dress. In turn, it raised several challenges that the sector believed it could realistically overcome. Most challenges concerned how the sector related to the assemblers in the absence of state mediation of conflicts.

At Collor's announcement of the market opening in 1990, the sector ranked poorly in terms of competitiveness. During the 1980s, parts prices averaged above average world prices, but around or below European price levels.[49] By 1988, relative prices rose, hitting as high as 1.2 times European prices and 1.3 times world average prices. According to Booz, Allen, and Hamilton's research, around 65 percent of the parts produced, accounting for 40 percent of the costs of all parts, exceeded European prices. Parts based on iron and steel were more competitive than others.

The principal culprits for the sector's poor competitiveness included the high cost of materials and equipment, the effects of inflation on prices, technology and production process lags, high relative levels of government taxation, and low levels of scale. Liberalization offered alternatives to high-cost inputs including equipment. It also promised to reduce the impact of inflation and to lead to lower tax rates. In turn, it demanded that the sector solve its own problems of insufficient scale and competitive backwardness.

Reducing the price of basic inputs represented an easy-to-reap benefit promised by neoliberal reform. The basic inputs for auto parts ranged from iron to steel, to plastic, glass, rubber, tires, aluminum, lamps, and electronic components. Booz, Allen, and Hamilton's survey of the sector in 1990 revealed the high relative costs of most of these basic inputs. All exceeded world prices by as much as five times, with the exception of long steel, basic plastic resins such as polypropylene, and aluminum, which had prices below world levels. Electronic components and rubber products particularly exceeded world levels. Similarly, by the estimates of its own association, machine tools and equipment prices for transport materials averaged twice world levels.[50] The estimate jumped to five times for CAD/CAM and CNC machine tools.

Another critical issue was the limited scale of the auto sector's production. Booz, Allen, and Hamilton estimated that to reach a minimal scale of world-class efficiency, a plant had to produce 200,000 units per model per year. The United States produced 175,000 units, whereas Brazil produced only 55,000.[51] The 1980s trend of declining production exacer-

49. Booz, Allen, and Hamilton, "Estratégia Setorial." The firm chose European prices as the base for comparison because they offered the clearest comparisons by models.
50. Confidential author interview, ABIMAQ, October 1991, São Paulo.
51. Booz, Allen, and Hamilton, "Estratégia Setorial," 10.

bated the scale problem. The last critical issue for the sector related to technology lags and, more important, process lags. Few firms had invested heavily in numerically controlled machine tools or industrial robots or had used computer-aided design. Clearly, most firms in the sector as well as the assemblers faced a difficult challenge in investing in the new equipment.

The sector perhaps faced a more critical problem than investing in new technology. The latest trends in production techniques promoted productivity, quality, and flexibility. These goals depended on cooperative relations between labor and management and between buyers and suppliers and on streamlined administration of production. All these qualities required fundamentally different approaches to producing than had existed in Brazil. In that sense, whereas commercial liberalization promised to address the state-originated problems of the macroeconomy and to provide access to imported inputs, it also challenged the sector to change the way it operated. The end of price controls challenged the sector to find less destructive ways of apportioning costs throughout the productive chain. The end of state-managed labor negotiations challenged the sector to improve its labor relations.

Taxation, another element contributing to competitiveness problems for the sector, was harder to fix and clearly dependent on government action. According to ANFAVEA, the tax component of the price of a car in 1990 came to 41 percent over the price.[52] The tax level had risen relatively steadily from 35 percent in 1980. In 1986–87, the Cruzado Plan imposed a forced savings in addition to the tax on industrial production (IPI), tax on manufactured goods and services (ICMS), and social security taxes (PIS and Finsocial). The resulting tax load rose as high as 66 percent over the cost of the car. In 1987–88, it fell again only to begin rising back to 42 percent in 1991. The continual increase in the price of a car coupled with a shrinking internal market represented a serious threat to the sector's ability to face a liberalized market.

The stakes were not small. Booz, Allen, and Hamilton estimated that even with tariffs of 20 percent on imported parts, as much as 20 to 30 percent of the parts produced domestically could be substituted for imports.[53] SINDIPEÇAS more optimistically reported an estimated 10 per-

---

52. Booz, Allen, and Hamilton, "Estratégia Setorial"; ANFAVEA, "Annual Statistical Reports."
53. Booz, Allen, and Hamilton, "Estratégia Setorial," 14–16.

cent loss in market share.[54] Labor issues remained difficult as well. SINDIPEÇAS reported that the sector had lost one hundred man-days in strikes through 1990. Although this figure fell sharply in 1991–92, a poor history of relations remained a threat to a hard-pressed sector.

Machine Tools and Equipment

The machine tools and equipment sector, along with computers and consumer electronics, ranked among the most challenged sectors in Brazilian industry in 1990–92. ABIMAQ estimated that Collor's commercial opening schedule would lead to a 40 percent retraction in the market for domestic producers. Others pointed out several mitigating factors that could soften the predicted blow a little. Several business representatives, as well as analysts like Erber and Vermulm, argued that Brazilian businesses had to be adaptive in the past and would adapt quickly in the 1990s.[55] Others observed that the recession controlled the rate of imports, and although capital goods imports had risen sharply between 1988 and 1992, they were still small in quantity.[56] Still other business representatives argued that the sector's security lay in the inevitable balance-of-payment problems that large-scale importing would cause.[57]

In general, all observers, including economists, sectoral representatives, government representatives, and even representatives of other sectors, agreed on the basic challenges facing the sector: technological capacitation and financing. The sector's limited experience in exports (and that experience coming largely in low-technology areas) helped produce this technology lag. To overcome the lag, the sector's firm badly needed financial assistance and/or sufficient demand to amortize the costs of new capital investments. Furthermore, unlike most sectors, export competition in the sector frequently hinged on export financing with the most

54. *Exame,* October 23, 1991. Also confidential author interview, União pela Modernização representative. Both SINDIPEÇAS and União claimed that many firms had substantially improved in the wake of the study, leading to the revised estimate.

55. Erber and Vermulm, "Ajuste"; confidential author interviews, business representatives, Secretariat of Science and Technology, State of São Paulo, various, 1991–92, São Paulo.

56. Hélio Nogueira da Cruz and Marcos Eugênio da Silva, "A Situação de Bens de Capital e Suas Perspectivas," in Coutinho and Suzigan, eds., *Desenvolvimento Tecnológico.*

57. Confidential author interviews in the sector. Several auto parts representatives expressed the same belief vis-à-vis the machine tools and equipment sector, various, 1991–92, São Paulo.

favorable package winning. Finally, subsectors dependent on state consumption, particularly firms that produced for infrastructure work, badly needed new investment if they were to survive.

Thus, the sector hoped for privatization that could restore investments to the country's infrastructure, including its ports, highways, power plants, and railways. For example, the average age of railcars in São Paulo in 1992 was 25 years.[58] Collor's program performed poorly there and failed to pay U.S.$100 million in bills for the private construction of the Ferroeste rail line (under construction by Grupo Itamarati). Similarly, the sector counted on tax reform, which failed to emerge. Export financing for machine tools and equipment resumed under the PROEX program in 1991, but with vastly inadequate funding.[59] Finally, the sector counted on commercial liberalization pressure to increase demand for capital goods, but the depth of the recession and the uncertainty about government policy caused many firms to postpone investment plans.

The last benefit to the sector from liberalization came from access to imported inputs. Like the other two sectors (and indeed like its own critics), machine tools and equipment suffered from expensive, low-quality, and often unreliable supply. A survey conducted by ABIMAQ in 1989 found that firms in the sector rated supply problems as their most serious obstacle to exporting. Indeed, an internal study found that of the principal inputs for machine tools only steel, noniron metals, and electrical motors compared favorably to import prices. Others, such as electrical, electronic, and hydraulic components, ranged from two to three times the prices of imports.[60]

Thus, unlike the previous two sectors, machine tools and equipment could expect benefits from liberalization largely only to the extent that the government lived up to its promises in the program. Machine tool and equipment producers expressed a certain level of preparedness to face import competition in various surveys (ABIMAQ, Nogueira and da Silva, Oliveira, CNI) in 1989–90. That confidence rested on assumptions about the impact of neoliberal reform on the state, which ultimately did not prove reliable.

58. Confidential author interview, National Syndicate for Rail and Highway Materials (SIMEFRE), May 1992, São Paulo.

59. Suzigan in *Carta Política* (São Paulo), Ano II, no. 12, p. 6; *Revista SINDIMAQ;* and confidential author interviews. Interview evidence raised another concern with Proex, namely that the funding was available to exporters who did not compete on the basis of financing packages. Proex seemed more concerned with guarantees of ability to generate foreign reserves than with the mechanics of export competition, May 1992, São Paulo.

60. Cited in Erber and Vermulm, "Ajuste," 226.

The costs were straightforward. The estimates of the impact on the sector noted above, even if imprecise, still suggested great loss. The rush of other sectors to blame machine tools and equipment and to try instead to import fueled concern over costs. By 1992, the list of imports with exemption from duties and 0 percent tariff had grown larger than the list of imports without them. Several businesses reported difficulties with their technology licensers abroad. In one instance, a representative reported that its licenser had decided not to renew a contract because it hoped to directly export to Brazil itself. Another reported that its licenser, a Japanese firm, had begun to export to the firm's Latin American export market because of the recession in Japan.

A second cost of the liberalization resulted from the bitter internal disputes that the commercial opening provoked. Three cleavages divided the sector into separate camps. First, small firms and large firms resolved some of their disputes when a small-firm movement won control of the syndicate in 1985. Their different access to capital, and its consequences for survival, presented difficult political challenges to sectoral representation. Second, multinational and domestic firms were divided over the possible responses to liberalization. To many MNCs, liberalization offered the possibility of greater intrafirm trade and an easy path to deverticalization as well as the possibility to shift fully to imports. Consequently, MNCs took a much weaker position in opposing liberalization once the sector mobilized against the reform process. Finally and perhaps most important, the sector united several distinct steps in its supply chain. For example, ball bearing producers sold to producers of smaller mechanical components, who sold to machine tool producers, who sold to heavy equipment producers. These various subsectors fought among themselves over tariff levels, exemptions from import duties, and state finance policy.

ADJUSTMENT STRATEGIES

Most firms in this interview sample initiated adjustment efforts at the start of the commercial liberalization, regardless of how seriously challenged they were. Two striking conclusions emerged from the research: the vast array of differing solutions businesspeople embraced and the innovativeness of many of their solutions. Perhaps one testament to the creativity of these firms was that most of them were still in operation as of June 1996.

Pulp and Paper

The biggest problem facing firms in the pulp and paper sector was the coincidence of a Brazilian recession with a global one. With the domestic market shrinking and world prices low, large firms faced a cash flow problem. Smaller firms faced more serious problems of long-term survival, which the recession exacerbated.

The sector's adjustment strategies fell into two categories with different dynamics. Large exporting firms faced a different set of issues than did the smaller firms of the sector. Because capital requirements for producing pulp and paper at globally competitive levels were so high, small firms could not reach those standards. One estimate placed the fixed cost of production at U.S.$2,000 per ton produced to operate at a minimally efficient scale.[61] These investments were out of reach of small-size firms, which operated with old, out-of-date machinery.

The large exporters of the sector had been trying to cut costs while they planned investments to increase capacity. As a rule, international competition forced these firms to keep pace with innovations like just-in-time and sophisticated computer-controlled equipment. The firms invested roughly U.S.$5 billion in the late 1980s to expand capacity, to computerize production and administration, and to obtain environmental equipment. These earlier investments responded to estimates of growth in global demand investments rather than anticipation of commercial liberalization.

As a result, by 1990, the large exporting firms of the sector had significantly lowered labor costs and had modernized in pace with global competitors. During Collor's two years, whereas industrial unemployment rose sharply, the largest pulp and paper producers shed hardly any labor.[62] One firm reported making cuts by not filling vacancies, without any layoffs.[63] Another reported an 18 percent reduction in staff, but primarily in management positions.[64]

One interesting observation about the sector was that MNCs and domestic-exporting firms reported no differences in the issues they faced or the strategies for facing them. For all intents and purposes, multinationals in the pulp and paper sector operated like domestic firms. The basic strategies included better cost control, management reorganizations to

61. Confidential author interview, pulp and paper representative, March 1992, São Paulo.
62. *Gazeta Mercantil, Balanço Anual,* 1990, 1991.
63. Confidential author interview, pulp and paper representative, March 1992, São Paulo.
64. Confidential author interview, pulp and paper representative, June 1992, São Paulo.

improve information flows and flexibility, personnel training, and investments.

Smaller firms faced more serious problems. They could not invest in up-to-date technology because it was too expensive and they did not have sufficient scale to operate it. By most accounts, a large percentage of small firms had little chance in a liberalized market if they chose to continue producing in the same market. Among their options were mergers among groups of small firms or alternatively selling any equipment with value (limited among most small firms) or stands of trees, which were inherently valuable.

Interviews among small to medium firms suggested that other options existed. The pulp and paper sector's market was segmented, with much potential for specialization. A brief list of the market segments of pulp and paper includes pulp and various pastes combining pulp and other materials, such as semichemical paste, mechanical pastes, chemical-thermomechnical pastes, thermomechanical, mechanical-chemical, and chemical-mechanical pastes; paper includes white paper, nonwhitened paper, absorbent paper, packaging, cardboard, corrugated board, kraftliner, pasteboard, printing paper, writing paper, newsprint, and special papers such as cigarette papers.

Two examples illustrate the condition of small- and medium-size firms during Collor's tenure. One example comes from one interviewed small businessowner who expressed his belief that he could specialize to survive. He hoped to specialize in a particular shade of packaging board used in some cigarette boxes. He redesigned his assembly line to allow for maximum flexibility and to allow him to introduce an additional layer of clay into his cardboard. This made his board extra durable and cheaper than board using larger ratios of wood to clay. His ability to do this depended on the small size of his operation and the ease and speed with which he could maneuver machinery in his line. Furthermore, he found export opportunities by associating with a large trading company. Because he could not afford the transaction costs of finding and opening new export markets or of assuming the risks of shipping (and nonpayment), he had contracted out. Because smaller markets like Latin America and Africa have higher costs than in Brazil, his products were competitive there. The trading company bought his paper, with taxes (IPI, ICMS, and IR) refunded because the paper was for export, then resold it abroad for a profit. The tax refund allowed him to sell competitively, and the much larger trading company assumed the risks of shipping the paper. Finally, one of the larger firms allowed him to keep one technician in its research labs, which gave him access to research and development (R&D) at the cost of one technician. Through these efforts, he believed that he would survive the liberalization, although he depended on an improvement in the macroeconomic situation.

Another example comes from a medium-size firm. Like many firms in the sector, this firm imported cheap wastepaper, which it then recycled for use in its own finished paper. This firm had obtained BNDES financing and in conjunction with its own resources, was investing to expand capacity. The owner participated in technical exchanges with producers in the United States and Germany to stay technically current. In general, he exported between 30 to 50 percent of his production, allowing him tax refunds and exemptions and thereby improving his price. As a larger firm, he was capable of and was in the process of seeking out new markets. In particular, he believed that China presented a potentially strong market and was seeking distributors there. Ultimately, with both developed export markets in Latin America and BNDES financing, this medium-size firm reported concerns primarily with cash flow and the Collor Plan–induced recession.

Auto Parts

In sharp contrast to the relative uniformity of pulp and paper firms' responses to liberalization, the auto parts sector reported a wide array of strategies. Interviews in firms and in SINDIPEÇAS revealed another sharp distinction. Firms in the pulp and paper sector reported extensive discussion of adjustment issues, technical exchanges, and discussion of the effects on smaller firms. Firms in the auto parts sector reported virtually no knowledge of other firms' strategies and no sharing of information in SINDIPEÇAS.

I visited eight firms between December 1991 and July 1992. The sample is neither random nor statistically significant. I chose firms with the help of experts on the sector, representatives of SINDIPEÇAS, and auto parts representatives themselves. The sample therefore reflects the trends in the sector and accurately represents the range of strategies and difficulties confronted. The firms include four MNCs and four domestic private and range from mid-size (300 employees) to large (4,000 employees). Most used primarily steel or other metal-based inputs, but the sample included firms that used inputs from wood and paper to rubber, glass, and electronic components. The degrees of competitiveness ranged from one firm that reported very little chance of surviving the commercial opening to one that outcompeted its Japanese competitors on global markets.[65]

Several interesting conclusions emerged from these interviews. First, firms were aware of the technology lags in Brazil's economy. In all cases, respondents believed that they could easily identify the technology they specifically needed and could easily obtain it. As a result, it scarcely rated as a concern. Second, all the respondents clearly believed that management issues, particularly labor-management relations, ranked as a key problem to solve. Third, the origin of capital did not predict which firms had prepared the most for foreign competition or which firms exported the most.

Finally, comparing the four MNCs revealed that MNCs cannot be treated monolithically. Only one reported a closer identification with MNC assemblers than with other suppliers. In that case, the MNC supplier reported that price negotiations in Brazil took place in a context of global interactions that mitigated the bitterness of local disputes. The four firms revealed strong differences in the degree of autonomy from their headquarters. They ranged from one that required full approval of every decision to one that had full autonomy. The firms also varied in their relations to the global operations of the company. They ranged from one that saw liberalization as an opportunity to increase imports from other subsidiaries in Latin America to one that competed in global bids against the U.S. branch of the company.

In contrast to the pulp and paper sector, the possible cleavages among firms operated differently. Like pulp and paper, no meaningful cleavage existed between foreign and domestic capital. In the pulp and paper sector, however, the line between large and mid-size and again between mid-size and small overwhelmingly defined differences in preparation and strategies. No such dividing line existed in the auto parts sector. More than anything else, the approach of the specific management seemed to define the differences in outcomes. This fact explains the reasons that firms chose when to modernize their plants and the specific methods they came to use. The following discussion summarizes their strategies by classifying them as labor issues, administration issues, and production issues.

---

65. As of 1996, the firm that reported grave doubts about its survival was still in operation. By contrast, the firm outcompeting its Japanese competitors had closed. The latter firm, a small but very competitive MNC, closed as part of a global restructuring plan having nothing to do with the competitiveness of the local operation. The fates of these two firms offer some indication of how difficult it is to anticipate how a commercial liberalization affects industry.

Labor Issues

Labor relations posed four distinct challenges to auto parts firms. First, managers felt the need to increase the level of trust between themselves and shop-floor managers. Second, almost all made sharp cuts in their labor force. Third, almost all had to confront unions as the metalworkers were among the best organized and most mobilized in Brazil. Fourth, most firms confronted educational lags in their workforce as they contemplated installing new production processes and technology. Finally, several faced labor issues in reorganizing their management and production, which I discuss separately.

Among the different strategies chosen to enhance trust on the workforce, several stand out. One firm actively invested in improving work conditions and instituted several changes. It built a garden for workers to use on breaks and at lunch. It eliminated the separate dining room for management to reduce the sense of distance and privilege. It introduced a suggestion box for shop-floor improvements and instituted formal procedures for recognizing and rewarding suggestions, whether accepted or not. Finally, in 1992, it introduced shop-floor surveys to increase worker feedback on issues of concern. This practice contrasted sharply with another firm's decision to rely on paternalism to increase worker trust (and dependence). The director of this firm encouraged his managers to actively recruit clients on the workforce, through means such as paying for health problems or offering to intercede with the director on shop-floor problems. Both these firms contrast sharply with two others, which successfully and thoroughly implemented total quality management. In these firms, management earned workers' trust through incorporation of the workforce into the administration of the plant. One firm stands out for having created work teams for each area of production, which met every day with mixed administrative and worker representation. In the work group, individuals did not use titles, and leadership of the group was chosen based on consensus-building skill, not hierarchy.

On cutting the workforce, reductions ranged from as little as 0 to as many as 1,200. All firms reported that they had cut primarily from management, then indirect labor, and finally direct labor. For the most part, the firms reported that they tried to make cuts by not filling vacancies, but the recession and the Collor shocks forced some layoffs. In all cases, the cuts were permanent, and firms reported that they would not expand employment even in the event of an economic upturn. Most firms reported that the way in which they made the cuts helped them with respect to strikes and the influence of the unions. In all cases, firms reported reluctance to deal with the unions (labor centrals, to be more precise), and made side deals either with their workforce or with the central. Several reported frustration with the persistence of collective negotiations between the union and the FIESP negotiating group for all metal-bending industries (*Grupo* 14—named for the fourteen original sectors of the group), particularly because they did not have a firm representative in the group.

Finally, four firms reported that they overcame education problems by teaching their workers in the plant, in two of the smallest firms in the sample, as well as in two of the largest. In the case of the largest, the firm actually built a school and hired a teacher from the São Paulo school system to run it. All four firms reported that methods such as statistical process control or use of CNC machinery required a level of numeracy and literacy beyond most workers' educational levels.

Administration Issues

With the exception of two MNCs, the other firms reported that administration represented a significant problem. All six reported that their managements were too large. As noted above, administrative staff reductions figured prominently in workforce reductions. Several reported that their administrations were too complicated and impeded information flows and decision making. Besides cutting staff, two firms reorganized their administrations around different divisions and operated them as separate entities. In one firm, the director opened the different divisions to outside competition to force them to cut costs. Several firms reported problems in the training and/or attitudes of managers. In several firms, directors reported that lower levels of management either opposed or did not understand the imperatives of competitive modernization. The strategies differed from simple layoffs to internal competition to management retraining courses. Finally, the domestic capital firms reported difficulty with a lack of professionalization, particularly because of the large-scale participation of family members. Aside from management training courses, none of the firms I interviewed reported any notable success with this issue.

Production Issues

Two of the eight firms reported that their overwhelming principal concern was insufficient scale. Of the two, one planned investments in expanding capacity using its own resources—the only firm of my sample to report any sizable investments. In addition to scale investments, this firm reported new marketing strategies and diversifying its holdings into shopping centers and parking lots.[66] The other firm reported that it could not make any investments because it had already assumed debts before 1990 and capital costs under Collor's plan made further investment prohibitive. In fact, the increase in costs of servicing its old debt threatened to bankrupt the firm unless the recession ended.

The other firms reported more concern with issues of work organization, administrative control, and production techniques. Three firms in the sample had fully implemented an internal just-in-time. All three reported that the poor relations between assemblers and suppliers made just-in-time very difficult between firms, but just-in-time principles still allowed for effective internal control of merchandise. In particular, given the vagaries of the Brazilian supply chain, firms maintained stocks of basic inputs while carefully controlling stocks of finished goods. One firm began implementing just-in-time and total quality management in the early 1980s. The director of another studied the two management approaches in the United States and in Germany and began implementing them in 1989, with dramatic results.

Several firms conducted substantial reorganizations of their shop floors. The stated goals included facilitating and streamlining the production process; reorganizing workers and machinery around specific sets of tasks (referred to alternatively as technology groups or quality circles); improving work conditions, especially cleanliness; and more efficient use of space. Several firms began investing in machinery capable of performing multiple tasks and reorganized work and training around these machines. Several firms implemented measures to improve productivity by eliminating distance between the design of tools and the workers who used them. For example, two firms reported directly involving workers in the design of new tools. One firm went so far as to film its workers and then ask the workers to suggest ways that they could improve the productivity of their performance. Three firms reported eliminating separate quality control

---

66. In fact, according to Addis and representatives of SINDIPEÇAS, a common strategy for smaller firms without access to capital was to diversify their holdings into ranches, luxury boats, apartments, and phone lines—anything to protect their assets in case of the firms' not surviving the twin perils of recession and commercial opening. Interestingly, an interview with a large domestic producer identified by others in the sector as a probable loser in the reform process reported the same strategy. As of 1997, the firm retained highly diversified holdings, yet had also entered into a joint venture with a large multinational.

and incorporating it into the production process. Thus, for each production task, workers were responsible for quality control. In each case, firms reported large increases in quality and sharp drops in rejects.

Finally, every firm sampled reported that the answer for Brazil lay in the domestic market, but the ideal mix of domestic and exports placed exports at 30 to 50 percent of production. Firms in this mix reported different strategies and motives. Several believed that the assemblers had no commitment to their local suppliers and therefore exports represented a survival tactic. One firm increased its exports from virtually none to 40 percent of production in three years. Another firm reported that it concentrated on the smaller markets of Latin America because the bigger firms tended to devote little effort to those markets. Two firms reported that they specifically targeted smaller domestic competitors to squeeze them out of the marketplace.

Problems

Despite the extensive efforts made by these firms, all reported grave concern with the condition of the economy and the performance of the government in addressing it. Overwhelmingly, these firms reported that the economy desperately needed fiscal reform and successful stabilization. Two firms blamed inflation for the existence of the corporatist business structure and the corruption associated with it. They saw the desire to obtain protection from inflation as the driving force behind the politics of the Brazilian development model. Another representative observed that inflation was one of the primary tools of government financing in that it effected transfers of income through taxes and interest rates. All the firms agreed that cost planning and long-term thinking were virtually impossible. As one representative observed, no computer model in existence could track Brazilian inflation.

Similarly, the tax system unfairly burdened private enterprise, particularly in that its high levels drove many firms into the informal sector, increasing the load for others. Of the eight, only one reported no difficulty with the tax structure. It, like the pulp and paper producers, exported roughly 50 percent of production on a weekly basis. Therefore, it used tax refunds from earlier shipments to pay the taxes on new production, which then received export refunds to be used for later production. The other firms did not export, exported on a seasonal basis, or exported less than 20 percent of their production.

Finally, all the representatives reported concern with the government's credibility, particularly concern that their adjustment strategies would be undermined by government inaction, reversals, or insincerity. Later interviews, conducted after the corruption scandal emerged, revealed their deep concern with the impact of corruption on the economy.

Machine Tools and Equipment

In some respects, the machine tools and equipment sector resembled the pulp and paper sector. Like the latter, SINDIMAQ offered a wide array of technical courses, created working groups in each subsector, and generally provided a clearinghouse for ideas about adjustment. Similarly, the responses to liberalization were more narrowly circumscribed because, like pulp and paper, the sector faced a limited set of important questions—primarily how to advance technology and improve scale. Ultimately, two issues distinguished firms in the sector: access to capital and timing of adjustment efforts.

Erber and Vermulm, in their study on the machine tools subsector, defined an informal typology of firms: leaders, followers, and passive survivors. Leader firms anticipated changes in competitive technological standards and began new capital investment early in the 1980s. These firms learned about management strategies like just-in-time and total quality control and tried to implement them. Followers saw the path, but waited until Collor's program or just before and as a result faced greater challenges. These firms invested less in new technology and paid less attention to new competitive production techniques. Finally, the passive survivors neither invested in the past nor invested in response ro the initiation of neoliberal reform. They paid no attention to new competitive processes and quality and in general had limited access to financing. These firms tried to simply sit out the crisis by cutting costs as sharply as possible, especially by drastically reducing their workforce.

Erber and Vermulm conducted their study roughly in the same period as I conducted mine, with only one overlapping firm. They interviewed in thirteen firms of which eight were domestic capital, four MNC's, and one joint venture. The firms in their sample ranged in size from one under 100 employees to two firms with over 1,000 employees, among the biggest in the sector. In their typology, leader firms numbered four companies from among the six largest in the sample; one domestic capital, one joint venture, and two MNCs. The follower category numbered five firms, four domestic capital and one MNC, all mid-size firms between 200 and 650 employees. Finally, the last category included four firms, three domestic capital and one MNC, and all among the smallest in the sample. I interviewed in ten firms in the sector, in several subsectors. These firms, two MNCs, seven domestic capital, and one joint venture, ranged in size from under 100 employees to over 3,000. In Erber and Vermulm's typology, the leader category numbered three firms, including both MNC's, the follower category included four firms, three domestic capital and one joint venture, and the passive survivors included three firms, all small domestic capital.

One characteristic that described all three segments was their attitude to labor questions, which differed markedly from the other two sectors in this comparison. With very few exceptions, firms in this sector expressed more concern with collective bargaining than with shop-floor relations. The collective bargaining with the Metal Workers' Union takes place in what is called *Grupo* 14. *Grupo* 14 unites nineteen metal-mechanical sectors and is a vestige of pre-1988 Constitution corporatist law. The auto assemblers set the standard for all the others in *Grupo* 14. Labor costs represented 8 percent of total costs for autos, but averaged 40 percent for machine tools and equipment. This strain on the sector posed much more concern than do shop-floor questions, especially because union tactics hindered the sector's efforts to negotiate separately.

Leader Firms

As Erber and Vermulm defined the category, leader firms were trying to become or remain leaders in their particular markets. Consequently, they invested over the course of the decade in new technologies, they invested portions of the revenue in R&D (either in their own firms or in conjunction with outside laboratories), they sought technical exchanges, and in general they developed their know-how through participation in the export market. Without exception, both in my sample and in Erber and Vermulm's, these firms approached the 1981–83 recession aggressively, investing in numerically controlled machinery and expanding exports slightly in response to the retraction in the domestic market. These firms subsequently invested heavily again in microelectronic technology in the late 1980s and rapidly expanded their exports. All these firms reported significant efforts to implement just-in-time in their own factories, as well as reorganization of the shop floor to improve the flexibility and efficiency of the production process. Finally, all these firms reported awareness or concern with excessive levels of verticalization and product diversification. Of the firms in my sample, one, a producer of numerically controlled and computer numerically controlled machine tools, already decided in 1988 to strictly specialize and narrow its range of products. The two MNCs reported originally having more limited diversification.

Despite their timely adjustment efforts, the Collor Plan-induced crisis hit these firms hard. Although all these firms reported sharp increases in exports, as much as 40 to 50 percent for most firms, the domestic recession hurt them all. Exports, largely to Latin America although increasingly to the United States as well, rendered much smaller margins than the domestic economy, on the order of a 2 percent return. Although several firms reported that 40 to 50 percent exports represented their ideal mix, improvement in the domestic market was necessary. One firm reported that it would need to export over 80 percent of its production to survive if the domestic market did not improve by 1994–95.

Another firm, a large MNC, reported no export problems as it exported regularly to its head branch in the United States (90 percent in one division, 20 percent overall), but worked out a strategy for improving its domestic position. This firm reported barriers to improving the production process as a result of the slowdown. The recession skewed its production cycles and in some periods, no actual production occurred. This fact also contributed to its scale problem. Consequently, the firm entered into a joint venture with another major producer in its subsector. Although it had not yet begun operating at the time of the interview in 1992, it anticipated competitive improvements on the scale and production flexibility and efficiency fronts.[67] The BNDES supported the merger and acquisition strategy in the sector and defined it as one of its priorities for funding. One such merger received a great deal of attention as it involved two of the most competitive firms of the sector, Nardini and Zanini.

At least one firm in this sample (the producer of machine tools noted above) reported a serious threat to its survival from the commercial opening. It decided to narrowly produce this machinery and limit the diversity of its production in response to government incentives to produce microelectronic based goods. The cost of microelectronics in Brazil was still much higher than competitive foreign goods, rendering the final price higher as well. The legislation ending the computers reserve promised

67. It is interesting to note that when this firm was reinterviewed in 1996, the joint venture had still not been completed. Policy changes under Itamar Franco discouraged the two firms from entering into the joint venture, and it was not until BNDES policy changed again under Cardoso that the two firms re-entered negotiations. As of 1996, the joint venture was slated to commence operations only in 1997. As of this writing, I am not aware of its status.

help in access to imported microelectronic components, but the rate of protection on machine tools was dropping much faster than for computers.[68]

Overall, the leadership firms had positioned themselves to face import competition better than the rest of the sector. All kept pace with changes in the technology of their competitors. All moved to implement new competitive production practices with varying degrees of success. All were either better capitalized than the average in the sector or were large enough to benefit from the BNDES financing (as state financing overwhelmingly benefited large firms). Nevertheless, the domestic recession had a real impact that limited the success of their reforms and threatened the health of even these firms over the medium term.

Follower Firms

Follower firms had begun adjusting to the pace of technological change by the early 1990s and as a result encountered more difficulty in responding. Erber and Vermulm reported that the five firms in their sample had not computerized their companies until after 1989. Thus, not only were their products behind electronically, but their administration lagged as well.[69] These firms began to invest in numerically controlled machinery and equipment in the late 1980s. The lateness of these investments meant that they played catchup in a recessionary market, and at least two of them entered into the 1990s with a sizable debt load.

Technologically, these firms did not conduct their own research or invest in R&D. They were completely dependent on foreign licensers for technology and product innovations, which had become riskier. Nor did these firms report significant efforts to implement new competitive production processes. One firm just began to work with total quality control management as of 1992. At that stage, the firm entered into the "conscientization" stage of the program and anticipated seven more years for the administration to operate fully under total quality management (TQM). Another firm reported that TQM and just-in-time violated the norms of Brazilian culture and therefore could not be implemented in the foreseeable future.

68. As of 1996, this firm was still operating, but it concluded that the policy environment would not permit it to continue producing high-technology tools. As a consequence, the firm maintained production of lower technology machinery and imported and distributed the CNC machines it had previously produced.

69. Erber and Vermulm, "Ajuste," 237.

The firms in this category also tended to have much more diversified production and more pronounced scale problems, both of which also hurt technological capacitation. For example, one firm in Erber and Vermulm's sample produced machine tools in four distinct families of tools; one firm in my sample produced forty different products for markets as diverse as pulp and paper, petrochemicals, and nuclear power plants. The degree of concern over this diversity varied in the two samples from actively diversifying to not believing that diversity was an issue.

These firms did report an awareness of excessive verticalization and reported an increase in subcontracting as they assessed what they could and could not produce efficiently. The firms in these samples also varied in their use of exports as a strategy, from one that actually stopped exporting because it lost its competitive position in Latin America to several that increased their exports to as much as 30 percent of production. All suffered financial setbacks, in some cases of severe proportions, as a result of the recession and high interest-rate policies. Without an expansion of the domestic market, most of these firms did not have the ability to fully implement technological improvements, finance new technology investments, or lower the rates of verticalization and product diversity.

One firm in the sample reported an innovative response to the crisis. It formed an association with another small firm to expand production to the United States. These two firms pooled their capital resources to have sufficient capital to build a plant in the United States. They planned to produce the mechanical part in Brazil where labor costs gave them an advantage, purchase technology from Fujitsu-GE, and assemble the machine in the United States. The United States offered several advantages. The firms could overcome Brazil's limits in technical skills by hiring U.S. engineers there to develop an internal capacity to innovate from their licensed technology. Several U.S. states offered incentives to foreign capital to invest, and they planned to do so near a center of technology research. Finally, in assessing the growing regionalization of the global economy, they concluded that the U.S. market remained far more open to their scheme than the European or East Asian markets.

Overall, these firms faced serious challenges and remained much more vulnerable to macroeconomic conditions than did the leader firms. Despite the innovations of the firms noted above, most depended on macroeconomic improvements to survive and adjust. Without those improvements, it was unlikely that many of these firms could successfully absorb new technologies.

Passive Survivors

Firms classified as passive survivors made the least efforts to modernize. Unlike firms in the other two categories, these firms depended completely on macroeconomic conditions and had no means of accomplishing technological changes on their own. In my sample of four firms, two simply did not think in terms of technological capacitation, and two did not have the means to do so. In these latter cases, one firm declared bankruptcy under a crippling debt load, and the other, a small firm, had no access to financing.

These firms practiced whatever cost cutting they could, primarily through shedding labor. They operated on the lowest level of technology, producing unsophisticated goods. These firms had not computerized their administrations. They produced a wide array of goods and had no plans to reduce the number because of the tenuousness of their survival. Even firms that reported awareness of the number of products they produced as a problem had no alternative but to continue to produce and sell whatever they could. Three of the four in Erber and Vermulm's sample and one of the four in mine reported high levels of verticalization, although they had few plans to lower it.[70]

None of the firms in Erber and Vermulm's sample exported, although one had in the early 1980s and then reached 30 percent of its receipts.[71] Two of the four in my sample exported small amounts although both faced tremendous competitive pressure because of a lack of export financing. Naturally, the domestic recession hit these firms hard. Although the size of Brazil's unsophisticated market was large enough to continue supporting these firms for some time, the Collor Plan-induced crisis increased their technological lag. The growing pace of subcontracting in larger firms offered possibilities for these firms, but this segment faced considerable threat to survival from technologically unsophisticated machinery from South Korea and China and from other Latin American producers with lower labor costs. Overall, the commercial opening without conditions for technological modernization hurt this segment most of all.

CONCLUSION

The fiscal crisis of the state broke the basis of business-state cooperation under the ISI-corporatist model. That crisis filtered down to the micro-

---

70. Erber and Vermulm, "Ajuste," 243.
71. Erber and Vermulm, "Ajuste."

level in ways that differed depending on the history of the sector and how its market evolved over that time, as well as on the ways the sector remained tied to the state. Those differences led to varying challenges and solutions particular to each firm and sector. Most firms could support neoliberal reforms because the fiscal crisis created very real problems and very real adjustments options existed. Even the most competitive firms and sectors depended on the government to solve key macroeconomic problems if they were to realize the full benefits of reform.

Interviews, surveys, and public statements point to initial acceptance of neoliberal reform at the least and to active support at the most. This evidence is documented in Chapters 5 and 6. The most effective expressions of political support or opposition depend on how interests are aggregated and represented. In the late 1980s, the business community lacked an effective peak representative, and defenders of the ISI-corporatist model dominated many sectoral associations. By 1990, that situation began to change rapidly.

4

Business Modernizers and the Challenge of Economic Reform

The Organizational Bases of Opposition and Support

Through the 1980s, the corporatist organizations representing industrialists tended to limit their ability to address issues of collective concern. Instead, the corporatist system encouraged fragmentation of the industrial community and gains for individual sectors and firms. As a consequence, the industrial community was poorly prepared to participate in democratic politics, but pressures stemming from above and below led to a flurry of reforms through the late 1980s and 1990s. From above, the state's fiscal crisis eliminated many rents once available, thus rendering obsolete many functions of the corporatist system. From below, business modernizers challenged the leadership of their organizations to become more democratic, more professional, and more focused on issues of collective concern. As of 1997, there remained considerable constraints on effective interest representation, but reform efforts led to two outcomes: marked improvements in the ability of sectoral associations to represent member interests and a marked improvement in the performance of encompassing associations (notably the Federation of Industry of the State of São Paulo [FIESP] and the National Confederation of Industry [CNI]) to address issues of collective concern.[1] As a consequence, the Brazilian industrial community could better participate in the politics of neoliberal reform.

---

1. The extensive improvements in the performance of peak business organizations are discussed in Schneider, "Organized Business Politics."

CORPORATIST BUSINESS ORGANIZATION AND THE RISE OF BUSINESS MODERNIZERS

Business groups began autonomously organizing themselves as early as the mid-1800s, but business's modern organizational structure emerged in the Vargas period in negotiations over the character of the corporatist state. At the time, the most influential business organization was the Centro da Indústria do Estado de São Paulo (CIESP), a voluntary organization of firms. Representatives of the textile, shoe, and food industries dominated the organization.

Vargas's labor legislation (the CLT)[2] forced the closure of CIESP in 1937 as a noncorporatist, and therefore illegal, organization. The business community grudgingly complied, forming FIESP, a corporatist federation of syndicates, in its place. Continued business resistance to the law, led by Vargas's adviser and the most prominent businessman of his day, Roberto Simonsen, finally allowed some flexibility. The modified law permitted a parallel, voluntary business structure to exist alongside the corporatist one. Under the new law, CIESP reopened as a voluntary organization of firms, existing side by side with FIESP. This dual structure of business representation continued to exist as of 1998.

The corporatist system severely curtailed effective business representation by limiting horizontal and national linkages. Instead, it permitted one syndicate to form per category of production per region. The syndicates of a state then collected in one federation (such as FIESP, FIERGS (Rio Grande do Sul), FIRJAN (Rio de Janeiro), and so on, under the principle of one syndicate, one vote. Finally, under the same principle, all the state federations united in the national-level National Confederation of Industry (Confederação Nacional da Indústria—CNI). Corporatist law supported this structure through a compulsory syndical tax (*imposto sindical*) although membership was not obligatory. Each organization in this structure, from syndicates up to the CNI, elected a president under rules defined by corporatist law. Every three years, elections under the principle of one member, one vote, select presidents for three-year terms.[3] The law did not restrict the number of terms a president could serve, although

2. See Erickson, *Brazilian Corporative State,* 27–46, for a detailed discussion of the CLT. Although he discussed it in the context of the labor movement, the same law governed business organization.

3. More extended discussions of the origins and functioning of Brazilian business organizations, especially FIESP and the CNI, can be found in Schmitter, *Interest Conflict and Political Change in Brazil*; and Maria Antoinetta Leopoldi, "Industrial Associations."

some organizations did pass internal term limits, as FIESP did in 1980. In general, the corporatist structure was characterized by significant *continuismo,* that is to say, low turnover in leadership (even more common in states other than São Paulo).

This structure placed serious limits on business mobilization. It favored the small and powerless over the large and powerful firms and federations of the structure. The equal weighting of enormous and smallest firms in a syndicate limited the influence of the small number of very large firms. In addition to this distribution of voting power, syndicates derived most of their budgets from the syndical tax contributions of large firms. Because these large firms tended to have more ability to influence the government than did small firms, they tended not to depend on the syndicate. Similarly, the equal weighting of São Paulo's federation with Rio Grande do Norte's weakened FIESP's participation in the CNI.[4] Thus, the corporatist structure suffered somewhat by discouraging the most powerful firms from putting their influence behind the syndicate.

Another important limitation arose from the syndical law, which prohibited syndicates from participating in politics, including making public pronouncements about policy decisions and lobbying. It also prohibited syndicates from forming associations with foreign business or producer association. Under the law, the state could dissolve any syndicate for violating these rules and could expropriate its assets. Internal decisions about the constitution or functioning of a syndicate required state approval. Although in practice many sectoral syndicates came to act more independently, the structure built a degree of state dependence into business organization.

The function of these organizations further reinforced the dependent, paternalistic, and at times even passive character of the structure. These organizations existed to validate government regulations, facilitate government communication with business sectors, and facilitate the flow of benefits and rents to business sectors. Corporatist leaders built relations with specific ministers and bureaucratic agencies to obtain the rents that the state provided in such abundance. This character reinforced the clien-

---

4. See Steven Krasner, *Structural Conflict: The Third World Against Global Liberalism* (Berkeley and Los Angeles: University of California Press, 1985), 75–81, for a discussion of the relation between regimes and underlying power structures. This case roughly fits into what Krasner described as "dynamic instability" where divergent interests in a regime undermine the existing power structure and thus generate an unstable dynamic. Here, however, the state's conferring of legal monopoly status preserves the system despite its tendency to collapse if the state's legal sanction disappears.

telistic, personalistic, and often corrupt quality of the corporatist structure. It also limited horizontal linkages among business sectors and thus
helped define business mobilization in terms of particularist rather than
collective interests.

Two unusual results arose from the limits of the corporatist structure.
First, despite the CNI's existence as the nation's peak organization, FIESP
in fact assumed that role. In 1988, FIESP represented over 50 percent of
Brazil's industrial GNP, even after a ten-year secular decline. In the CNI,
it had one vote among many industrially irrelevant states. On its own,
FIESP could speak for Brazilian industry (and business in general). In a
1991 poll conducted by the CNI, FIESP had substantially higher rates of
recognition than the CNI in every state in Brazil. Moreover, FIESP out-
scored by high margins even the local state federation in every state in
Brazil.[5]

Second, as a result of the limits on the corporatist structure, the business community moved much of its organizing energy into the voluntary
structure, referred to as class associations. Voluntary associations escaped
corporatist limitations in that they were voluntary, member supported,
competitive, self-created, and protected from state intervention.[6] The
most important distinction was that *big* firms in *modern* sectors played
the principal role in creating them and tended to dominate them as well.[7]

Surveys by Diniz and Boschi in 1979 confirmed that class associations
differed from syndicates largely by their date of foundation and by the
participation of big firms. In 1979, 65 percent of all associations had
formed between 1964 and 1979 (as opposed to only 18 percent of syndicates).[8] Furthermore, 63 percent of class associations operated in modern
sectors (capital goods, chemicals, transport material) versus traditional
sectors (textiles, umbrellas, wine, food products). In contrast, 57 percent
of syndicates operated in traditional sectors.[9] Finally, class associations
on the whole tended to count large firms and multinationals among their
members more than syndicates did on the whole.

Nevertheless, most important class associations either existed side by
side with the sector's syndicate or included several associated syndicates.

---

5. CNI survey, cited in Rubens Figueiredo, unfinished master's thesis (Universidade de São
Paulo, 1992), 2.

6. See Schmitter, "Modes of Interest," 7–38. Schmitter's basic distinction between the two
modes of interest representation continues to drive debates about the business structure today.

7. Diniz and Boschi, *Agregação e Representação*.

8. Diniz and Boschi, *Agregação e Representação*, 33.

9. Diniz and Boschi, *Agregação e Representação*, 41.

For example, the executive of the machine tools and equipment syndicate, SINDIMAQ, ran the association ABIMAQ as well. The same was true for the National Syndicate for Electro-Electronic and Similars/National Association for Electro-Electronics (SINAEES/ABINEE), the National Syndicate for Auto Parts/National Association for Auto Parts (SINDI-PEÇAS/ABIPEÇAS), and the National Syndicate/Association for Automotive Producers (SINFAVEA/ANFAVEA). Alternatively, the pulp and paper sector's influential National Association for Pulp and Paper Producers (ANFPC) represented all the producers in five distinct syndicates. The same holds true for the Brazilian Association for the Development of Base Industries (ABDIB), which aggregated all producers of capital goods despite the existence of several syndicates and associations operating in these sectors.

Where associations existed side by side with syndicates, members elected one executive for the two organizations in a single election. In these organizations, the syndicate participated in collective labor negotiations, and the association conducted all other business.[10] The formation of associations enhanced the influence of big business in the structure, but it did not truly transcend the corporatist structure. The associations did not lead to business's overcoming the particularism, clientelism, or paternalism of the state-business relations. For that reason, they remained fundamental parts of the ISI-corporatist model.

With the advent of military rule, the government strengthened the incentives to participate in sectoral associations. The concentration of power under military rule facilitated pressure-group politics. All the state's benefits came from a set number of bureaucratic agencies and certain powerful ministries. The absence of legislative oversight made lobbying and negotiating much easier for business than either before or after military rule. The military's ambitious developmental strategy provided a sharp increase in the number of benefits. The structure of the system encouraged businesses to mobilize to maximize their access to those resources. Thus, businesses formed new associations to enhance their lobbying capacity vis-à-vis the state.

This tendency accentuated the cleavages forming in the business structure. As the state provided largely private benefits rather than public goods[11] (such as subsidized financing and ad hoc tax exemptions), those

10. Confidential author interviews, ANFPC, ABINEE, SINDIPEÇAS, ABIMAQ.
11. See Mancur Olson, *The Logic of Collective Action: Public Goods and the Theory of Groups* (Cambridge: Harvard University Press, 1971), 51, for the differences between the two and their consequences for collective action.

with less influence lost out more and more. The state's development priorities clearly favored the modern segments of industry.[12] This favoritism, coupled with modern industrialists' tendency to mobilize more effectively, meant sharp disparities in the flow of resources, which increased the gap between modern and traditional sectors.

When the state's financial crisis hit, these selective benefits grew even scarcer. For small firms, the disparity in the benefits of participating in business organizations grew even more striking. Lip service from the government aside, the availability of benefits increasingly depended on political influence—the exclusive domain of big firms and business organization leaders. For industrialists concerned about competitiveness, the growing disparity between what global economic competitiveness demanded and what the ISI-corporatist model provided provoked increasing dissatisfaction. For industrialists concerned about effective business representation, the issue of weak capacity for collective action also remained. Whereas modern sectors had formed business associations to escape the limits of the CLT, FIESP continued as virtually the only option for collective action but remained dominated by backward sectors of the economy.

Thus, during the 1980s, three active movements emerged in the business structure: democratic modernizers, mostly small businesses, angered over the disparity in influence between them and large firms; professional modernizers, concerned about their associations' corrupt practices and emphasis on rent seeking; and collective action modernizers, concerned about business's inability to address vital issues of collective importance. For this last group, the influence of backward sectors in the corporatist structure limited its efforts to mobilize business around "modern" concerns.

The syndical structure came under increasing attack for failing to serve its smaller members. The continuing economic and political crisis continued to undermine the number and quality of collective benefits that the association structure provided them. Similarly, the selective benefits of business organizations tended to become even more selective, prompting widespread charges of authoritarianism and corruption in the leadership.

---

12. Discussed in Chapter 2 in reference to Frieden's (*Debt, Development, and Democracy*) argument that state policies arose from the organizational strength of specific sectors. The weakness of Frieden's argument is that state priorities created incentives and opportunities to organize. Thus, state decisions shaped business organizational strength, not the other way around.

The highly uneven impact of the crisis on small firms enhanced their feeling that their associations ignored them.

On the professional front, firms with a concern about the condition of Brazilian industry charged the association structure with placing too much emphasis on rent seeking. They charged that business organizations had an obligation to promote consciousness of global economic and competitive changes.[13] They criticized their association leaders for getting too involved in *jogos dos interesses* (literally "game of interests," maneuvering for personal gain). They demanded that their associations instead provide more technical services relevant to a rapidly changing global economy.

Collective action modernizers expressed their frustration with FIESP's leadership shortcomings. The crisis of the 1980s made clear to these business leaders that the business community had to end its paternalistic, passive relation to the state. FIESP's apparent inability to move from its passive stance to a more aggressive position on crucial issues such as inflation and taxes provoked angry responses. The advent of Collor's liberalization reinforced these dynamics and the perceived importance of reform.

Through the late 1980s and into the 1990s, professional modernizers and collective action modernizers formed alliances with democratic modernizers in a series of challenges to the existing leadership. These challenges led to a wave of renovation at the sectoral level, to a series of revolts in and against FIESP, and ultimately to a limited, but effective renovation in FIESP itself. In turn, these renovations, discussed at greater length next, enhanced industrialists' ability to shape the course of neoliberal reform.

RENOVATION OF SECTORAL ASSOCIATIONS

Sectoral business organizations began experiencing significant pressure for reform in the mid-1980s. The pressure sharply increased again in the face of the challenge of liberalization. Privately, many businesspeople complained that the problem in business leadership was generational. New times called for new leaders, but many syndicates and associations

13. Confidential author interview, União pela Modernização do Setor de Auto Peças, ABIMAQ, Secretária de Ciencia e Tecnologia (São Paulo State).

had the same leaders throughout the 1980s. The demands for change had their effect. By July 1992, 65 percent of all syndicates in São Paulo had elections,[14] with leadership changes (or at least serious challenges) in some.

An alliance of democratic and professional modernizers drove the direction of change in the sectoral associations. That "professional modernization" reflected the associations' efforts to reconstruct their relations with the state and with their members. Professional modernization did not imply dismantling the corporatist structure (i.e., division of business into sectors represented by a single association or combination syndicate and class association). Rather, it implied professionalizing the association to better serve its members in a competitive economy, globally and domestically.

Associations had to respond to several threats to their functioning. First, the increasing scarcity of state benefits during the 1980s made the associations' existence less and less legitimate. At the same time, the large firms that still benefited did not need the associations' help. Furthermore, these firms expressed concern over the lack of leadership on issues of collective importance, such as the tax system. Second, Collor's liberalization program eliminated many remaining benefits that the associations provided. For example, with the closing of councils like the Interministerial Price Council (CIP) and the Industrial Development Council (CDI), the reform of CACEX, and the ending of almost all tax exemptions, associations lost most of their primary functions. Finally, new demands to negotiate in new contexts, such as in sectoral chambers or in the regional trading bloc Mercosur, challenged the mentality typical of older leaders and the weak history of horizontal bargaining.

As a result of these challenges, many associations experienced both a crisis of identity and a crisis of members' participation. As one prominent business leader explained, in crisis times businesspeople had tended in the past to race to their associations to complain about the state and to ask for help. In the crisis of the late 1980s and into the 1990s, they stayed away and complained about their associations.[15] Those complaints translated into demands for changes.

In some major associations, business leaders heeded those demands. Several associations experienced leadership turnovers that brought in new leaders, less associated with the old corporatist developmental model. For

14. *Estado de São Paulo,* January 25, 1992, p. 5.
15. Confidential author interview, February 1992.

example, the critically important National Association/National Syndicate of Automobile Producers (ANFAVEA/SINFAVEA) replaced the combative, traditional leader Jacy Mendonça with the younger Luiz Adelauer Scheuer. Participants in the historic 1992 auto accord agreed that the deal could not have emerged with Mendonça (or with Pedro Eberhardt of SINDIPEÇAS). The Brazilian Association/National Syndicate of Electro-Electronics (ABINEE/SINAEES) elected Nelson Freyre to the same end. A unified slate combining representatives from the auto parts modernizers' protest movement, União Pela Modernização (Union for Modernization), and SINDIPEÇAS representatives replaced Pedro Eberhardt with Claudio Vaz, a young modernizing candidate.

In addition, sectoral associations turned their attention from the state to their members. With almost no traditional ISI–corporatist functions left to them, associations had to find new services to provide their members to justify their existence. In this area, the developed world offered a model for business associations corresponding well to the needs of their members.

Associations renewed themselves by improving their technical services to help firms adjust to liberalization pressures. To that end, they improved their statistical data gathering and reporting. They organized technology fairs in which they presented state-of-the-art technology in their sectors. They offered technical courses on new technology and new management and production techniques. They formed associations with international and foreign sectoral associations to facilitate dissemination of market and technical information. They sought information on new markets and acted as clearinghouses for information on joint ventures and other market arrangements with foreign firms. They also continued to lobby the BNDES for sectoral financing, and they continued sectoral-level negotiations, whether intersectoral, international, or with labor.

This review of adjustment efforts does not imply uniform success or even uniform or universal efforts, but it does describe the tendency in associations at the sectoral level. Interviews in associations representing machine tools and equipment, pulp and paper, auto parts, electrical and electronic goods, capital goods, men's clothing, autos, toys, and rail and highway material revealed that almost all initiated some reforms. Furthermore, almost all experienced some degree of frustration and participation crises.

The associations still faced some distinct limits. First, they had little to offer firms that could not survive the commercial liberalization (and intense recession). Second, some associations faced difficult conflicts among diverse interests grouped in the same association. This is the case, for example, with SINDIMAQ and ABINEE.[16] In fact, some firms formed new associations to better serve the interests of a smaller, less diverse population (such as Agribusiness or Eletros, primarily representing consumer electronics producers with operations in Manaus). Interviews in SINDIMAQ, ABINEE, and SIMEFRE raised the possibility of splintering in these associations, but the corporatist organization of sectoral interests generally remained intact.

To get a clearer picture of the issues facing the associations, I briefly review the sectoral associations of the three sectors compared in Chapter 3. The pulp and paper sector had three syndicates in the state of São Paulo, but the National Association of Pulp and Paper Producers (ANFPC) played the most critical role in representing sectoral interests. In addition to the three syndicates, the ANFPC also represented two additional syndicates in the graphics sector. By universal testimony, the ANFPC was throughout the 1980s and 1990s among the most modern, professionalized associations in Brazil. It provided thorough statistical data gathering, which it compiled and reported annually. It maintained several effective technology groups where members could address technical and technological problems. It successfully disseminated technical norms throughout the sector. Interviewed members reported that it was an effective lobby on behalf of the sector. In fact, the ANFPC's success in obtaining special lines of credit from the BNDES continued through 1997. The ANFPC also ran a highly regarded, full-service free hospital for all members of the sector, including employees and their families.

Another indicator of the competitiveness orientation of the association came from the association's participation in Collor's Brazilian Program for Quality and Productivity (PBQP). By the first collective meeting to present results in October 1991, the sector had developed over thirty programs through six working groups. These included work in consciousness raising, quality management training, improvement of technical services, human resource training, investment in employee and community social services, and investments, training, and certification in the International Organization for Standardization (ISO)-9000 quality standard. Interviewed firms and staff members reported that members actively discussed the competitive issues facing the sector, especially small firms. This situa-

---

16. Confidential author interviews, SINDIMAQ, ABINEE, November 1991, May–June 1992.

tion starkly contrasted with interviews in other associations. The easier relations and fuller participation of small firms in the association facilitated managing the cleavage between the large, powerful firms and the smaller, more threatened ones. Finally, association leaders participated heavily in the industrial community's leading organizations. ANFPC representatives figured prominently in the efforts to publicly support the turn to neoliberal reform under Collor. They also actively participated in the efforts to oppose the process by 1992. In particular, leading members of the association played important roles in FIESP during the Federation's open criticism of the neoliberal reform process and during its later renewal as a community leader. They also played a lead role in the Institute for the Industrial Development Studies (IEDI) as both an interlocutor with Fernando Collor and ultimately an opponent of his.

The associations for machinery and equipment and auto parts both faced more difficult challenges. SINDIMAQ/ABIMAQ faced a revolt of small businesses in 1985. Charging that the association primarily concerned itself with big businesses and their privileges, Luis Carlos Delben Leite successfully mounted a campaign against Walter Sacca, of Holstein Kappert Industries, who followed the presidency of Einar Kok, of Indústrias Romi. Both these predecessors came from large firms in the capital equipment sector, and both were prominent figures in the peak organizations of the business corporatist structure. Delben Leite's primary goal was to improve small firms' access to the benefits of the ISI–corporatist model.

He also hoped to encourage member firms to competitively modernize their firms in the face of global economic changes. He and his staff believed that the global economy was dividing into regional economies and peripheral countries such as Brazil would have to integrate or be left out. Thus, he both anticipated and supported an eventual commercial opening and the need for the sector to improve its competitive position.

Delben Leite's staff promoted several reforms. It conducted a membership drive, substantially increasing membership from 750 to 1,300 firms.[17] It promoted active participation of members in sectoral diagnoses and technical exchanges through the many subsectoral working groups. It initiated in-depth studies for the sector intended to inform the members and to serve as a base for future political action. These studies included detailed surveys of the level of technical and technological preparedness,

17. Nylen, "Small Business Owners Fight Back," 257.

a proposal for an industrial policy for the sector, and an evaluation of the likely impact of a commercial opening on the sector.[18]

Delben Leite left in 1991, with his staff, to become the São Paulo state secretary for science and technology. He left behind him an association that continued to face difficulties. Commercial liberalization weakened participation in the association as well as sharpening internal conflicts, such as between machine tool producers and their many users. Not only had state benefits largely disappeared, but the sector had become one of the primary targets of the commercial opening. The association had little to offer firms facing bankruptcy.

Nevertheless, under the new president, Luis Pericles Michielin, the association continued to make adjustment efforts. It had begun to improve its statistical data gathering, a problem that had arisen from the association's use of surveys with widely varying samples over the 1980s.[19] It also increased the number of technical courses it offered and organized a large technology fair late in 1991. The association increased its activity in developing foreign contacts and acting as an agent for the sector in arranging joint ventures and international marketing agreements. The sector participated in the PBQP, planning a series of new quality training programs under the aegis of the government initiative. As of the October 1991 meeting, the association had defined some twenty programs, most of which consisted of lectures and none of which had begun. The sector also emerged as one of the most vocal critics of Collor's neoliberal reform process by late 1991. Facing increasing pressure from commercial liberalization under terrible macroeconomic conditions, the association became one of the first to publicly criticize the reform process.

By the mid 1990s, SINDIMAQ had substantially improved its performance. Interviews in the sector suggested widespread approval of the association's performance in Mercosur negotiations.[20] Furthermore, the

18. ABIMAQ, 2000. At the time of this research, the report had not been published and was not available for public review. By 1996, the association had concluded that the findings and proposals contained in the report were outdated, and therefore the report was shelved. No association representative was willing to discuss the decision not to publish the report, but several members hinted at significant internal political struggles over the decision. At root, the issue seemed to be how aggressively the association should present its concerns about the reform process. By 1996–97, the issue had been rendered moot by the speed with which the reform process effected change in the sector. The issue of change in the sector is explored further in Chapters 6 and 7.

19. Confidential author interviews, June 1992.

20. I interviewed one of the high-ranking members of the AMBIMAQ executive and one of the leading negotiators on Mercosur issues. At the interview, I asked him how he managed the conflicts inherent in the process. After all, these negotiations had the potential to determine the

association, under its new president Sergio Magalhães, improved its leadership on issues of sectoral and collective concern. For example, SINDIMAQ worked with the BNDES to redefine lending rules for Finame—the BNDES financing program for capital goods purchases. The association's executive was also in the forefront of industrialists' efforts to mobilize in support of Fernando Henrique Cardoso's constitutional reforms. Nevertheless, despite their best efforts, constitutional reforms did not pass. The country's fiscal problems continued to undermine the sector's adjustment efforts while government policy favored capital goods consumers over producers. Thus, by 1997, ABIMAQ's leadership was forced into lobbying for defensive measures.

In 1989, a group calling itself the Union for the Modernization of the Auto Parts Sector (União pela Modernização do Setor de Auto Peças) led a campaign for leadership of the auto parts association. This group, mostly from small businesses, challenged the leadership of Pedro Eberhardt of Arteb, one of the largest firms in the sector. Although the challenge started as a complaint about the privileges of the leadership group, it changed over the course of the two-month campaign. In the course of the campaign, members of the union added concerns about competitiveness and the priorities of the association. Thus, modernization took on two meanings: it referred to issues of competitiveness and productivity and to democratizing the association. The union lost by a margin of 250 to 225 votes in a hotly contested, closely watched, and emotionally charged election.[21]

The union responded to its loss by creating a parallel organization. From that new base, it continued the critical debate with the association, eventually forming a more cooperative relation with the Eberhardt staff. The result of that cooperation was a study on the competitiveness of the sector conducted by the consulting firm of Booz, Allen, and Hamilton. The study reflected the union's concerns. Although there were observa-

---

line between survivors and losers. His response was to quote Julius Caesar's exhortation to his wife that she must not only be scrupulously honest, but must appear honest as well. He elaborated on this by observing that the process required him to avoid even the slightest hint of favoritism, or *jogos dos interesses*. When I pressed him on how successfully he thought he had performed, he noted that he had been re-elected to the association executive, which to him constituted evidence of his success. Further interviews in the sector suggested that members of the association did believe that the negotiations were well handled. This story is a clear indication of how much commercial liberalization had pushed the association to reform itself into a technical, member-oriented association and away from the politicized, rent-seeking organization most syndicates represented before the onset of reforms.

21. SINDIPEÇAS, *Notícias*, 1989.

tions about government policy (such as taxation and port costs), the study placed its emphasis on the individual firms. Finally, in 1992, rather than face a divisive election, Eberhardt's staff agreed to a compromise with the union. Together, they presented a unified slate with representatives from both sides, but with the presidency in the hands of the union's Claudio Vaz.

Members of SINDIPEÇAS voiced serious complaints against the association. Even members of Eberhardt's executive admitted that the syndicate did little work in modernizing or promoting competitiveness and that it played the political games associated with the ISI-corporatist model. For the most part, the syndicate worked on regulation of prices and tariffs in a centralized decision-making process that provoked charges of self-interested administration. Interviews in the sector revealed that firms did not actively participate in working groups and that those that did withheld information about their own competitive adjustment efforts.

In general, the syndicate tied itself significantly to ANFAVEA. Although it often confronted the automotive sector in negotiations, its orientation lay heavily toward the automotive sector. Even its statistical reports relied largely on ANFAVEA data. For example, SINDIPEÇAS used ANFAVEA data for production, exports, imports, and sales. In the PBQP, the sector operated its programs in conjunction with ANFAVEA.

Vaz offered two kinds of solutions to SINDIPEÇAS's perceived problems. First, in response to the competitive modernizers in the union, he offered several technical improvements, including increasing the number of technical courses, enhancing the association's linkages with foreign associations, and helping to identify new markets and new business associates. Second, he promised to decentralize decision making in the association so that all members could have an opportunity to voice their concerns and to participate in decisions. Indeed, shortly after assuming office in March 1992, he began opening association meetings to any interested member.

SINDIPEÇAS's work on behalf of the sector continued into the mid-1990s, first under Claudio Vaz and then under Paulo Butori. By the mid-1990s, the sector faced an extraordinary challenge at the micro-level. A combination of a significant shift in the auto assemblers' strategy coupled with the Cardoso's government's auto industry policy provoked a wave of mergers, acquisitions, and bankruptcies. Butori and SINDIPEÇAS particularly opposed the auto policy that drastically reduced auto parts tariffs while increasing protection for the assemblers. By 1996, the syndicate successfully made the case that the policy was unnecessarily punitive, and it secured new lines of credit and some increased tariff protection. Nevertheless, the sector remained challenged by commercial liberalization as of 1997. As a consequence, Butori and SINDIPEÇAS continued to charge the government with favoring the assemblers and pressed for further policy relief. The problem for the sector was aggravated by declining domestic demand for autos through 1997.

Overall, the changes at the sectoral level did not follow a uniform path or emerge from identical forces in all associations, but the basic direction and impetus were similar for all of them. Alliances between democratizers seeking decentralization of decision making and competitive modernizers seeking professionalization forced leadership changes or reforms in many of industry's important associations. In turn, these changes permitted association leaders to effectively participate in political efforts to support and oppose the reform process. Although the change was not complete, decisive, or irreversible, the trend was toward more professional associations that provided a wider array of member services.

FIESP AND THE CHALLENGE OF COLLECTIVE ACTION

Although reform movements at the sectoral level united democratizing and professional modernizers, reform movements at the peak level brought collective action modernizers into play as well. FIESP's performance as the lead organization of the business community had provoked increasing frustration among all three branches of the reform movement, culminating in a series of defections and challenges through the late 1980s and early 1990s. The organization was charged with having an authoritarian and big business bias, a lack of attention to issues of competitiveness, and an inability to take leadership positions on political and economic issues of vital concern to business.

The challenges arose as it became increasingly apparent to business reformers that FIESP would not make the adjustments itself and that the CNI did not represent an alternative. Consequently, several prominent businesspeople founded the Liberal Institute in 1983 to disseminate liberal ideas throughout the business, academic, and political world.[22] In

22. Gros, "Empresariado."

1987, a group of dissident syndicate presidents formed a protest bloc in FIESP, calling itself the National Thought of the Business Bases (PNBE).[23] After a series of struggles with the executive, the PNBE finally institutionalized its movement in 1989. Shortly thereafter, Joseph Couri broke away from PNBE and formed the National Syndicate for Small and Micro Industries (SIMPI). Claiming to speak for all micro- and small firms, Couri entered into a series of legal battles with Mario Amato and FIESP. In 1990, just before Collor assumed the presidency of Brazil, a group of the nation's leading industrialists abandoned FIESP to form the Institute for Industrial Development Studies (IEDI).[24] Finally, in 1992, several powerful members of IEDI combined to bankroll an electoral challenge to FIESP's presidency, led by the PNBE's Emerson Kapaz. To understand this substantial level of reform activity, it is necessary to further examine FIESP itself.

FIESP: A BRIEF REVIEW

FIESP is more than a peak business organization. Business peak organizations in the developed world, such as the Business Roundtable or the National Association of Manufacturers in the United States or the Business Council on National Issues in Canada, do not compare with FIESP.

FIESP is a ministate in the Brazilian republic. From its headquarters on Avenida Paulista in São Paulo, FIESP runs schools, parks, recreation centers, hospitals, health clinics, a vast array of technical, archival, and consulting services, a think tank, Brazil's most complete library on business and economic issues, a host of government services, in addition to all its political and corporatist functions. FIESP also served as Fernando Collor's most important symbol of corruption and privilege, both in his electoral campaign and later while he was in office.

As of 1990, FIESP had 121 member syndicates from the city of São Paulo and from smaller cities throughout the state as well as several national syndicates. CIESP, the parallel voluntary organization administered by the same executive, counted over 9,000 individual firms as members.

23. See Nylen, "Small Business Owners Fight Back," 254–60, for discussion of origins of the PNBE.

24. See Diniz and Boschi, "Brasil," 12–18, for discussion of the structure, membership, and goals of IEDI and the PNBE.

In this broad division, FIESP had an additional thirteen departments, twenty divisions and directorates, and four centers.[25] Aside from these, FIESP maintained the Instituto Roberto Simonsen think tank and the associated Roberto Simonsen Library, the Industry Social Service (SESI), and the organization's educational service, SENAI. In 1992, FIESP represented one hundred thousand firms, employing two million workers. Through SESI alone, FIESP trained over one million workers. To manage everything, FIESP maintained an annual budget of over U.S.$15 million, drawn from the syndical tax (5 percent), CIESP fees, and user fees on its many services.

To its executive, FIESP's primary function was to act as an agent to firms and syndicates that were too small to influence or gain access to the government on their own. As they describe it, FIESP was a giant *despachante*.[26] In Brazil's densely regulated society, people commonly hired agents, *despachantes*, to stand in lines, argue with bureaucrats, fill out interminable numbers of documents, and slip bribes where needed for expediting anything from registering a car to firing or hiring a worker to exporting a good or opening a business. FIESP existed to ease the life of the less influential members of the business community in an economy that complicates virtually all activity.

Popular perceptions in the business community differed. In a 1992 survey conducted by the public opinion research firm Ibope, 60 percent of all business respondents said that FIESP/CIESP represented only big business interests. For firms of less than one hundred employees, 64 percent of respondents agreed with the statement, and even 51 percent of large firms agreed. Despite this response, 72 percent of respondents still believed that FIESP played an important role in the national political and economic scene.[27]

This perception of a big business bias arose from two aspects of the federation. First, the prominence of the organization placed its president among the ranks of the most noticeable and influential figures in the public sphere. Even if FIESP lacked a degree of legitimacy among many members, any utterance by the president became national news. This was not always for the best in business eyes. Mario Amato's claim that the 1986 Cruzado Plan was pushing business toward civil disobedience and his

25. FIESP, "A Serviço da Indústria," February 1990.

26. Confidential author interviews, January and March 1992. Former president of FIESP Luis Eulalio de Bueno Vidigal Filho has stated this publicly several times, most recently in an interview with *Playboy* (Brazilian edition), December 1991.

27. Ibope survey reported in the *Diário de Comércio e Indústria*, January 28, 1992, p. 18.

1992 comment that the tax system was making all businesspeople into criminals did not find hearty approval in the business community when they made front-page headlines.

Second, the heart of FIESP's power lay in its backrooms and corridors, not in its service departments. Even more than the president of the republic, FIESP's president wielded vast powers with few limits. Industrialists held all executive and top management positions at the president's discretion. Although the president needed approval of some decisions (mostly constitutional issues) from CIESP's general assembly or FIESP's council of representatives (made up of the 121 syndical presidents), he could otherwise act on his own initiative. To that extent, decision making in the organization was extremely centralized.

The traditional electoral process gives one indication of the somewhat undemocratic character of the federation. Historically, the choice of successor lay in the hands of the past president and the syndical presidents. Thus, in 1985, Luis Eulalio de Bueno Vidigal Filho coordinated the peaceful succession by Mario Amato. The election involved Vidigal's personally calling on all the eligible voters, the syndicate presidents, as well as conferring with the past presidents of the federation and the rest of the administration. On confirming these various members of FIESP's administration's preferences, Vidigal announced the successor.

The preference turned largely on who had most actively participated in the federation and had most actively curried favor among the syndical presidents. The principal means of currying favor among syndicate heads was to offer them positions in the executive of FIESP. In 1985, Mario Amato, known for his extensive participation and effective networking in FIESP, emerged as the four to one preference over his alternative, Carlos Eduardo Moreira Ferreira.[28] Two days later, Amato silenced Moreira Ferreira's opposition by making him first vice-president and thus the front-runner for the 1992 transition.[29] Paulo Francini, a prominent industrialist and another presidential contender, began a long public campaign of criticizing the electoral process in FIESP with his statement that the electoral process in FIESP was closed.[30]

28. *Diário Popular,* October 27, 1985, p. 10.
29. *Folha da Tarde,* October 30, 1985, p. 21.
30. *Gazeta Mercantil,* October 30, 1985, p. 3. In private, other distinguished members criticized the federation as well. For example, private documents obtained at FIESP revealed Ricardo Semler's repeated efforts (some of which became public) to diagnose problems and identify solutions to the lack of accountability and weakness of leadership in FIESP. Semler's critiques predate the foundation of IEDI. Not surprisingly, interviewed members of IEDI expressed criticisms similar to Semler's private written accounts.

Both candidates openly expressed the views of a modernizing segment that had been more and more active in the federation. Luis Eulalio de Bueno Vidigal Filho's election in 1980 had mobilized the support and hopes of these same modernizers. Despite receiving high marks as president (for example, from Francini himself), Vidigal had not accomplished the modernizers' goals. Mario Amato held even less promise to do so than had Vidigal.

This modernizing segment had begun to emerge among a narrow stratum of business leaders in the late 1970s. Issues like the Democratic Manifesto, business concern over the military's mildly orthodox policies under Mario Simonsen (economy minister from 1977–79), and business concern over the rising labor movement prompted concerns that FIESP did not play an aggressive enough role on behalf of business. This small group of modernizers supported Vidigal in his campaign against the long-standing incumbent president of FIESP, Theobaldis de Nigris.

Luis Eulalio de Bueno Vidigal Filho emerged as a noteworthy member of this group when, as president of SINDIPEÇAS, he publicly joined the campaign against the state's expansion—one of very few businesspeople to do so.[31] His record of public criticism of the military's policies provoked opposition from the military's economy minister, Delfim Netto, as well as from São Paulo's governor, Paulo Maluf.[32] To the modernizers who sought a change in FIESP's stance vis-à-vis the government, Vidigal held out the promise of reform.[33]

For many would-be reformers, FIESP's governing structure did not give sufficient weight or voice to the most modern segments of industry. FIESP's structure had not kept pace with the changes in the structure of industry. The constitution protected the syndicates' monopoly rights to represent a single category in a single municipal area. Although some modern sectors, such as auto parts, machine tools and equipment, and electroelectronics, elected to have a single national syndicate represent their sectors, the law protected the exclusive rights of any existing syndicate, no matter how few the firms in the category and/or region. As a consequence, sectors such as food industries, clothing, and construction were highly overrepresented, while the critical metal-bending and electronic industries were highly under-represented (Table 4.1).[34]

This imbalance also stemmed from the military's expansionist policies

---

31. Vidigal's participation is discussed at some length in Velasco e Cruz, "Os Empresários."
32. *Senhor,* August 1985, 28–32.
33. Confidential author interview, July 1992.
34. Figueiredo, unfinished master's thesis, 93.

Table 4.1. The structure of FIESP compared with the structure of industry in São Paulo

FIESP Sectoral Group	No. of Syndicates and % in FIESP		Industrial Value Added (%)
	No.	Percentage	
1. Food industry	23	19.49	9.66
2. Clothing	11	9.32	4.04
3. Construction and furniture	18	15.25	1.81
4. Refiners	01	0.84	N.A.
5. Mineral extraction	04	3.36	3.64
6. Spinning and weaving	04	3.36	5.73
7. Leather goods	01	0.84	0.30
8. Rubber goods	02	1.69	2.65
9. Jewelers and cutters	02	1.69	N.A.
10. Chemicals and pharmaceuticals	17	14.40	22.90
11. Paper and cardboard	03	2.52	3.25
12. Graphics	02	1.69	1.92
13. Glass, crystals, mirrors	04	3.36	N.A.
14. Musical instruments and toys	01	0.84	N.A.
15. Cinematographers	01	0.84	N.A.
16. Metal-mechanical and electrical material	24	20.33	40.64

SOURCE: Rubens Figueiredo (unfinished master's thesis, Universidade de São Paulo).
N.A. = Not available.

in the 1970s. The first and second National Development Plans had produced several notable changes in the economy. They had promoted the massive growth of modern sectors, such as metallurgy, electroelectronics, petrochemicals, and paper, at the expense of traditional sectors. Their priorities encouraged the rapid vitalization of those sectors' associations through the organization of class associations parallel to the syndical structure. As noted above, 65 percent of all class associations in existence in 1979 had formed after 1964.[35] In contrast, roughly two-thirds of all of FIESP's syndicates joined the federation before 1960. In fact, more than one-half joined between 1942 and 1945 (Table 4.2).[36]

The consequence of this split was that one segment of industry had grown more and more sophisticated while the other segment remained backward and state-focused. Thus, Vidigal and other modernizers' goal

35. Diniz and Boschi, *Agregação e Representação.*
36. Figueiredo, unfinished master's thesis, 98.

Table 4.2. Dates and numbers of syndicates affiliated with FIESP

1942–1945	66
1946–1950	03
1951–1955	05
1956–1960	09
1961–1965	05
1966–1970	09
1971–1975	07
1976–1980	04
1981–1985	02
1986–1990	10

SOURCE: Rubens Figueiredo (unfinished master's thesis, Universidade de São Paulo).

was to reform the structure of FIESP to more adequately reflect the structure and power of industry. Vidigal's method was to encourage syndicates to merge, thereby reducing the total number and modifying the sectoral distribution of syndicates. The syndicates refused to back him, leaving FIESP's elections in the hands of the backward syndicates. For collective action modernizers, the rift and the traditional sectors' weight in FIESP prevented any meaningful debate or action in FIESP. To the federation's modernizers, effective collective action in FIESP would remain impossible as long as FIESP's structure remained unchanged.

Mario Amato's election in 1986 presaged a sharp rise in internal pressure for reform. The combination of the economy's worsening condition and Amato's leadership style fueled the intensity of the internal struggles. The collective action modernizers' agenda had not progressed under Vidigal and had little promise of doing so. In addition, democratic modernizers in FIESP challenged the closed nature of the federation, especially the election process. Finally, both movements included professional modernizers whose concern over the direction of the economy manifested itself in a concern over FIESP's failure to lead the business community in modernizing itself. Over the course of Amato's tenure, these movements increasingly fought for reforms in, and then without, FIESP. Sometimes they acted in conjunction with one another as their concerns and criticisms overlapped. Sometimes they acted separately. In either event, these business modernizers emerged as new business interlocutors, both in support of Collor and later in opposition to Collor and commercial liberalization.

THE RISE OF THE PNBE AND THE REVOLT OF THE DEMOCRATIC MODERNIZERS

The National Thought of the Business Bases (PNBE) appeared in 1987 as a revolt of small businesspeople, a cross between democratic and collective action modernizers. From 1987, it played a siginficant role in the business community at the national political level until 1992, when internal conflicts over Emerson Kapaz's candidacy for the presidency of FIESP weakened the organization. During that time, the PNBE captured the attention of the press, politicians, and academics as it attempted to offer an alternative model of business collective action, business-labor, and business-state relations.

The PNBE emerged informally in the lower ranks of FIESP among a small group of new syndicate leaders and CIESP representatives. Its six originators came from modern sectors (specifically machine tools and equipment, musical instruments and toys, and casting), but they themselves represented smaller firms and a younger generation of businesspeople. Amato had largely left them out of his executive, preferring, for example, the defeated past-president of SINDIMAQ, Walter Sacca of Holstein-Kappert Industries, over the new democratic modernizer, Luis Carlos Delben Leite.

This small group of democratic modernizers, numbering only six members initially, met in FIESP regularly and informally to discuss common concerns: the lack of opportunities for the syndicates to participate in decision making, the lack of leadership concern for the base of small- and medium-size firms, and the lack of FIESP leadership on crucial economic questions. The six members—Emerson Kapaz, Fabio Starace Fonseca, Luis Carlos Delben Leite, Oded Grajew, Paulo Roberto Butori, and Joseph Couri—eventually transformed themselves from an informal grievance session into a formal opposition in the federation.

In a dramatic display of mobilizing ability, the PNBE's first public act was to organize a public protest of 2,000 small businesspeople in Anhembi Stadium in São Paulo. At this inaugural event, the coordinators of the PNBE announced three basic goals: first, to democratize FIESP by forcing the leadership to pay more attention to the concerns of the base of industry, overwhelmingly made up of firms with 200 or fewer employees;[37] second, to oppose the government on several fronts, including inter-

---

37. See Nylen, "Small Business Owners Fight Back," for data on industry breakdown by size.

est-rate policy, state regulation and ownership of the economy, wage policies, and various measures in the constitutional debates of 1987–88; third, to improve labor relations and business-society relations in general by promoting democratic, negotiated approaches to social issues.[38]

From June 1987 when it formally constituted itself to 1988 when Amato threw it out of FIESP, the PNBE made a significant mark on business politics and FIESP. During the period, the PNBE carried out several visible and successful actions. It conducted a survey among small businesspeople, which results led to the PNBE's submitting a proposal to the constituent assembly. The proposal endorsed a liberalization of the economy and an end to corruption. Members of the PNBE, which had grown substantially over a short time (including the vocal businessman Lawrence Pih), frequently appeared in the press to reinforce these views.

In October 1987, the PNBE organized a meeting of 1,500 businesspeople with Finance Minister Luis Carlos Bresser Pereira. Later in November, it publicly criticized FIESP for forming a lobby to try to obtain a legislative majority in the constituent assembly through massive expenditures. Again in November, it organized a successful day of reflection on the proposed constitutional article guaranteeing employment stability. One hundred forty business organizations held debates internally, while the PNBE publicly debated the issue with the General Workers' Central (CGT) labor leader, Luis Antonio Medeiros.

On the labor front, the PNBE actively sought out the CGT, the United Workers' Central (CUT), and the Workers' Party (PT) to debate and explore themes of common interests. The PNBE actively and aggressively argued publicly for redistribution of income and support for real wage levels against inflationary erosions. In December 1988, coordinators of the PNBE traveled to Israel with leaders of CUT to jointly study Israel's inflationary experience and success in combating it. Using its links with labor and its contact with business bases, the PNBE played an instrumental role in trying to form a social pact against inflation.

---

38. It is interesting to compare the views articulated by the PNBE, a group of small- and medium-size entrepreneurs with pronounced left or social democratic leanings, with the Democratic Manifesto of the Bourgeoisie. The latter document, published in the *Gazeta Mercantil* in 1978, was signed by eight of the most prominent big businessmen in the country. Nevertheless, the essential goals and concerns match closely. The Democratic Manifesto (and the lesser known and less discussed followup in 1983) insisted on the need for an inclusive debate on future development goals. In fact, the Manifesto opposed military rule specifically on the grounds that the military could not be inclusive. The similarity in views between these near-polar opposites in the industrial community highlights the extent to which there existed broad agreement on the policy direction for the country.

Despite its successes and growing fame outside FIESP, inside, the story was different. The PNBE's most difficult struggles were inside FIESP where its efforts to reform FIESP's electoral process ultimately led Amato to expel it from the federation. The PNBE tried to end FIESP's closed system by attacking the clientelism of the president's relation with the numeric majority of traditional syndicates. It proposed reversing the traditional order of elections in FIESP and CIESP, thus holding CIESP's election first. In that scheme, CIESP's 9,000-odd members, who looked much more like the base of industry than FIESP did, would choose the president in their election. FIESP's vote, then, would simply ratify that choice. Amato countered by proposing ending direct elections in CIESP and creating an electoral college for CIESP as well. At the end of this publicly waged battle, the two sides reached a compromise to hold elections simultaneously. Shortly afterward, on December 30, 1988, Amato expelled the three PNBE members who held positions in FIESP's management. The PNBE left FIESP and became a true opposition organization.

Amato laid out his basic reasoning for expelling the members of the PNBE in an internal letter sent to syndicate presidents and CIESP delegates in 1987. In his letter, he encouraged the PNBE's members in their efforts, but expressed concern about the "dispersion" of business force. In particular, he claimed that only FIESP/CIESP and its syndical structure had the legitimacy to speak for business. The PNBE, he charged, had to work in FIESP.[39] In acting as an opposition, Amato charged the PNBE with betraying FIESP,[40] but, in throwing out PNBE, he only made it stronger.

Freed from the constraints of FIESP, the members of the PNBE openly and vocally criticized FIESP, both for its lack of representatives and for its lack of leadership. The PNBE members accused FIESP of compromising business interests by passively supporting government policies regardless of their impact. In particular, the PNBE leaders harshly criticized Mario Amato for supporting the high interest-rate policy despite its brutal impact on businesses, especially small businesses (in private, some individuals charged that Amato's workers' team supported the policy because they were earning high rates of return on their own capital).[41]

As the 1989 FIESP/CIESP presidential election approached, the fight between Amato and the PNBE broke out again. The PNBE syndicate

39. FIESP, internal letter from Mario Amato, dated July 22, 1987.
40. *Diário de Comércio e Indústria,* January 3, 1989, p. 3.
41. *Diário Popular,* August 4, 1989, p. 9.

heads held consultations with their members over whether to vote for Amato's slate or to vote against it (despite Amato's having run unopposed). Although the three sectors (machine tools and equipment, musical instruments and toys, and casting) voted for Amato, large minorities favored opposing him. Amato responded with harsh criticisms of the three presidents, charging their incompetence to lead their sectors. Amato's attack provoked a counterattack in which the press widely reported the PNBE's views that FIESP was incapable of modernizing itself, the business community, or Brazil.[42]

The PNBE did not level idle or hypocritical criticisms at FIESP. In its goals, vision of society and business, and actual structure, it truly did offer an alternative model of business organization. As opposed to FIESP, membership was open to all businesspeople as individuals (or as "citizens" in PNBE terms), regardless of region, category, or firm size. That the members came largely from younger businesspeople (35–45), from small- to medium-size firms, and from the three original sectors did not change that orientation. Furthermore, as opposed to FIESP and the syndical structure, the PNBE thought of long-term projects, not immediate interests. Thus, the PNBE did not promote or defend particular firm or sectoral interests or think of its goals in terms of immediate results.

Unlike FIESP, the PNBE publicly and privately committed itself to democracy, negotiation, and consensus building from the bottom up. Thus, it believed in negotiation among conflicting parties to achieve an equitable distribution of costs in any public policy. It actively rejected the syndical structure's emphasis on fighting by sector or by firm to preserve gains and impose costs on others. Contrary to FIESP, it held this view not only with respect to collective action among businesses, but with reference to labor relations as well.

To further its agenda, the PNBE's organization reflected the democratic, open decision-making process promoted in its public acts. Each year, the PNBE chose twenty coordinators by direct election; they met once a week to debate and discuss priorities, positions, and projects. Among them, two general coordinators had responsibility to ensure implementation of PNBE policy. Members stayed informed and presented their views by faxing responses and viewpoints to the coordinators for inclusion in policy discussions. As of 1992, the group had 260 members in São Paulo and had also spread to Rio de Janeiro, Recife, and Fortaleza.

---

42. See, for example, the *Diário de Comércio e Indústria, Diário Popular, Isto É Senhor,* and *Folha de São Paulo* throughout September 1989.

Although the membership remained limited, its high visibility in the press as a dynamic business modernizer allowed it a disproportionate role in national politics. With Collor's election in 1989, the PNBE's modernizing agenda was matched by an apparently modernizing president. Although some members voted for Lula (such as Emerson Kapaz or Oded Grajew), the PNBE's agenda and its opposition to FIESP made it Collor's preferred business interlocutors. However, that situation quickly ended.

Collor's communications channels with business never opened even close to the extent that they had been open under past presidents. Initially at least, he worked more closely with the PNBE than with any other business group. The PNBE openly expressed support for Zelia Cardoso de Mello as economy minister against a lobby working for Mario Henrique Simonsen. Her leftist background, along with the secretary for economic policy, the economist Antonio Kandir, agreed with the PNBE's belief that business should bear the cost of adjustment, that monopolies and cartels should be broken, and that salaries should be protected. Thus, from early on, the PNBE had a sympathetic ear in Zelia and Kandir.[43]

Later, with Collor in power, the PNBE played the lead role as Collor's business interlocutor in the effort to work out a social pact (discussed in the next chapter). On two separate occasions, in mid-1990 and again in late 1990, the PNBE worked out the basic proposals, secured FIESP's government, negotiated with the CUT and the Força Sindical, and brought an essentially done deal to Collor. In both cases, Collor's unwillingness to negotiate undermined the deal and eventually the PNBE's willingness to work with him.[44]

From early 1991 on, the PNBE more and more openly criticized the Collor government for what it saw as his principal abuses: his unwillingness to talk seriously to business groups; his continuation of the recessionary program despite its impact on businesses, especially smaller, less capitalized firms, and its exacerbating effect on the distribution of income; his maintenance of the pace of the commercial opening despite the recession and continuing high inflation; and his apparent lack of support for democratic principles of negotiation. It openly criticized his proposed constitutional amendments, offered in late 1991. It opposed his tax proposal of December 1991 and criticized his wage policies throughout the year. Finally, PNBE publicly joined the CUT and São Paulo State Gover

43. See, for example, *Folha de São Paulo,* January 24, 1990, p. 5.
44. Diniz and Boschi, "Brasil," 22–24.

nor Luis Antônio Fleury in a candlelight vigil against Collor's policies as Fleury emerged as a focal point of antiliberalization mobilization.[45]

In response to its critical posture, Collor replaced the PNBE with IEDI as his new preferred business interlocutor (although not for long). Nevertheless, the PNBE continued to play an important role as the only business organization actively and publicly opposing Collor's recessionary policy and the commercial opening. To that extent, the PNBE challenged FIESP's legitimacy by voicing the concerns of a large proportion of businesses while FIESP sat silently. Furthermore, in taking its aggressive public role, the PNBE probably had more influence in forcing FIESP to change its policies than did any other source.

Unfortunately, despite its accomplishments, the PNBE faced serious limits as an alternative model for business representation. Although it grew substantially between 1992 and 1997, its membership numbered only several hundred, drawn primarily from small industry and professionals. Internal differences weakened the organization, particularly between industrialists and professionals and especially after the 1992 FIESP election (which provoked a sharp internal battle over the organization's purpose).[46] Since 1992, the changing profile of the organization led it to focus on citizenship issues, such as hunger, child poverty, and land reform.

Support from the press, academics, links to the Collor government initially, and the party of President Cardoso and São Paulo Governor Mario Covas (PSDB) all afforded the PNBE disproportionate influence. In the final analysis, however, both businesses and politicians pay more attention to a giant such as José Mindlin or Antônio Ermírio de Moraes than they do to small businesspeople. This limits the mobilizing power of the PNBE.

The PNBE's weak impact on the business community was evident in a poll that Ibope conducted among businesspeople in 1992. Only 11 percent of business respondents in São Paulo claimed to know alot about the PNBE. Forty-four percent claimed to know a little, while 43 percent claimed never to have heard of it. Among small businesses, the figures

---

45. Fleury's alternative coalition building fell as large-scale corruption charges caught both Fleury and his mentor, Orestes Quercia, in 1992–93. Before his downfall, one executive of a small but competitive domestic consulting firm detailed Fleury's public contract kickback scheme, which involved leaving cash payments at a five-star downtown hotel. Like Collor (and Paulo Maluf and Celso Pitta—Fernando Henrique Cardoso rivals discussed in Chapter 6), the downfall came because of much bigger ticket items.

46. Discussed in McQuerry, "Economic Liberalization in Brazil."

changed to 9 percent knew well, 38 percent knew a little, and 50 percent never heard of it. Although IEDI performed even worse on this survey (2 percent, 11 percent, and 82 percent, respectively), it formed later than PNBE and operated exclusively out of the public eye. If the PNBE never represented a future path for business collective action, IEDI held out that possibility.

IEDI AND THE REVOLT OF BIG BUSINESS

The Institute for Studies of Industrial Development (IEDI), formed in 1990, offered yet another alternative to FIESP's model of business leadership. Whereas the PNBE's alternative model resulted from a combination of democratic and collective action modernizers, IEDI's alternative resulted from an alliance of competitive and collective action modernizers. Thirty of the most powerful businesspeople in Brazil, almost all members of FIESP's executive, joined together in 1989 to address their concern with FIESP's lack of leadership on business issues. IEDI ostensibly began as a think tank run by professional economists. In reality, it was an organization that acquired tremendous political power and eventually became business's most important center of opposition.

IEDI emerged from the frustration of several prominent FIESP members with the federation's ability to act effectively on business's behalf. Convinced that the federation would not or could not reform itself,[47] these FIESP members withdrew to form a new organization where topics of vital concern to business as a whole could be debated. In this, IEDI was similar to the PNBE. Its aim was to escape the particularism, short-term emphasis, and lack of professionalism of FIESP's outmoded corporatist structure. Its principal goal was to develop studies on key issues of industrial policy to inform the debate on Brazil's competitive modernization and integration into the global economy.[48]

47. One of its originators, Ricardo Semler, a young, Harvard-educated businessman who had become renowned throughout the business community, conducted a serious study on reforms in FIESP in 1989, a study widely reported in the press. Amato ultimately ignored the entire proposal.

48. In fact, IEDI's efforts and tactics conform to the goals and means to achieve those goals laid out in the Democratic Manifesto and its followup in 1983. Not coincidentally, almost all the signatories of the two documents were founding members of IEDI (the notable exception was José Mindlin of Metal Leve). It was not clear to me in my research why Mindlin was not a member, no interviewee or written record gave any hint. It is worth recording, however, that Metal Leve was represented by Celso Lafer; Mindlin's son, Sergio Mindlin, was a member of the PNBE and was on the coordinating council of the association.

In structure, it differed sharply from PNBE. The originators limited membership to thirty businesspeople, representing a regional cross-section and broad sweep of industry's modern sector. It restricted membership to younger businesspeople, representing the largest industrial groups and firms. In that sense, each individual member of IEDI could capture as much press attention on his or her own as almost any business group in Brazil. In fact, as individuals, members such as José Ermirio de Moraes Filho, Ricardo Semler, Abraham Kasinsky, Claudio Bardella, Paulo Villares, and Jorge Gerdau Johannpeter ranked among the most cited, quoted, and discussed businesspeople in Brazil.

IEDI solved the business community's collective action problem in ways suggested by Mancur Olson in reference to the Business Roundtable in the United States or by Russell Hardin.[49] Both analysts argued that the profound obstacles to large-group collective action can be overcome when a small subgroup is willing to pay the costs to provide the good. In this case, thirty business giants undertook the task of confronting Collor and of trying to create an alternative economic strategy. Rather than following the PNBE's democratic mobilization strategy, IEDI relied on pure economic muscle.

IEDI's means of operation was through disseminating the studies that it developed through its professional staff. Thus, from 1990 to 1992, the institute published a series of studies entitled "Changing to Compete" on education, taxation, and industrial policy, based on technical research and on internal debates over the content. The members then sent out their studies to other businesspeople, academics, labor leaders, and politicians to disseminate the results and to generate discussions. The institute itself had no formal, institutionalized mechanisms for holding or recording such discussions.

IEDI's members initially expressed support for Collor's program and his basic goals. They acknowledged the urgent need for macrostabilizing adjustments and expressed support for his efforts.[50] Underlining that support, they also expressed a concern for an industrial policy that would guide business decisions through the uncertainty of the transition period. Ultimately, Collor's lack of response to this concern led IEDI to upgrade its political activity as a new source of opposition to the commercial opening.

IEDI's opening statement, dated June 29, 1990, and its three studies

---

49. Olson, *Logic of Collective Action*. Russell Hardin, *Collective Action* (Baltimore: Johns Hopkins University Press, 1982).

50. IEDI, "Modernização Competitiva, Democracia, e Justiça Social" (São Paulo, 1992), 1.

(taxation—August 1991, education—January 1992, and industrial policy—June 1992) explicitly laid out IEDI's vision. As observed in the opening statement, Brazil had taken ISI to its limits at a time when integration into the global economy clearly presented itself as the new path to growth and wealth. Because global competitiveness depended on more than just private initiative, Brazil needed a policy that promoted systematic competitiveness. The problem lay in the twin tasks of macroadjustment and promoting new growth. The two could not occur at the same time, and the former could be extremely painful; therefore, the government had to manage the uncertainty of the adjustment period. Managing uncertainty depended on the government's sending clear signals through an industrial policy that laid out the government's intentions and priorities after stabilization. The IEDI members observed that without clear signals from the government, businesses would avoid investments and would be forced into speculative activities to protect their assets.[51] In that statement at least, they were prophetic. Their proposal was similar to Collor's program for industrial competitiveness, which never really took effect because of Collor's failure to manage stabilization.

Over the following two years, IEDI disseminated two documents examining the anticompetitive character of the tax system and the dreadful state of Brazil's educational system. Both documents sprang from careful technical analyses, and IEDI presented them as technical documents, but as Collor's program of stabilization continued to make no progress, IEDI shifted its course. In early 1992, IEDI members began to quietly criticize the Collor government's program, charging that it was leading to deindustrialization *(sucateamento)*. In a draft version of what would come to be their industrial policy proposal, they criticized Collor for the recessionary policy, tight money policy, pace of the commercial opening, and lack of tax and finance reform. Otherwise, IEDI's industrial policy proposal, released in June 1992, differed little in substance from Collor's earlier proposal.

Primarily, IEDI's proposal differed in its emphasis on the possible negative outcomes if the commercial opening continued and on its opposition to continuing the recession. It also differed from IEDI's inaugural statements. First, its initial statements were more supportive of commercial liberalization as a policy. Second, in 1990, IEDI clearly stated that "adjustment and renewed growth cannot be accomplished at the same time. They demand distinct decisions and priorities, both on the part of busi-

51. IEDI, "Modernização," 1–2.

ness people as well as on the part of government."[52] Two years later and facing the economic difficulty of the recession and the political difficulties of stabilization, IEDI backed off.

Collor's reaction to IEDI's quiet but meaningful move into opposition came even before the public release of the proposal. In May 1992, in a private note widely discussed among businesspeople and academics with contacts in IEDI, Economy Minister Marcílio Marques Moreira accused IEDI of being the principal opponent of liberalization.[53] Marcilio was angry with more than just IEDI's industrial policy proposal. In early 1992, IEDI shifted its tactics from simple dissemination of ideas to promoting debates to coalition building around those ideas. Working quietly outside the press and public arenas, IEDI invited representatives of the labor centrals and several political parties to discuss its proposal.[54] The hope was to generate a consensual position around the need to slow the pace of the commercial opening and to end the recession. IEDI members found sympathetic ears among their audience composed of high-ranking representatives of CUT, Força Sindical, the Workers' Party (PT), the Brazilian Social Democratic Party (PSDB), and the Brazilian Democratic Movement Party (PMDB).

Ultimately, IEDI's coalition-building efforts became moot as the Collor corruption scandal grew. Members of IEDI in mid-1992 observed that the scandal granted new room to pressure the government. Thus, coalition building gave way to more aggressive tactics. Businesspeople played a critical role in helping bring down the Collor government. In interviews in mid-1992, IEDI members suggested that they were participating in the effort. This was the high point of IEDI's influence.

Three factors led to IEDI's declining influence. First, several members suggested that the Franco government had made an offer to Paulo Cunha to join the cabinet, which he declined. Once that opportunity passed, these members felt that IEDI had wasted its best opportunity to influence policy. Second, despite their efforts to produce broad proposals for an industrial policy, there were sharp disagreements about concrete details. When it came to broad conceptual issues, IEDI could take a position, but its effectiveness as a lobbying organization was practically nonexistent on concrete policy questions. Finally, and perhaps most critically, the course of commercial liberalization imposed its own logic, rendering much of

---

52. IEDI, *Mudar Para Competir* (São Paulo, June 1990), 1.
53. Confidential author interviews, May, June 1992.
54. Confidential author interview, July 1992.

IEDI's platform moot and forcing many IEDI members to defend their own positions. By 1997, IEDI's commitment to a dialogue on industrial policy made little sense. IEDI members themselves reported that the organization had become irrelevant.

THE 1992 FIESP ELECTIONS:
THE TRIUMPH OF CORPORATISM

FIESP's 1992 presidential elections became the event of the year in the business community as all three aspects of business modernization came into play. FIESP's statutes prohibited Mario Amato from running again, leaving the presidency vacant. As interest peaked and names of Amato's successor began to surface, it became clear by late 1991 that the elections would not follow the tradition of a unified, unopposed slate. Notwithstanding all the modernization rhetoric on both sides, the election on July 29, 1992, reinforced the durable corporatist logic of the federation.

Mario Amato designated his first vice-president and one-time opponent Carlos Eduardo Moreira Ferreira as his successor. The context of crisis provoked a flurry of alternative names as businesspeople offered themselves as candidates or promoted other prominent figures. One group, calling itself the Movement for Institutional Renovation (MRI), formed to promote a modernizing candidate to contest the election. Prominent names like Claudio Bardella and Nildo Masini came up and disappeared. By January 1992, the MRI had settled on a candidate: the coordinator and co-founder of the PNBE, Emerson Kapaz.

The two candidates had little in common. Moreira Ferreira was an executive in the Companhia Paulista da Energia Elétrica, a private concession of the state's electricity utility, CESP. He was also the president of the Electrical Energy Industry Syndicate of São Paulo. As such, his business dealings tied him closely to the state. His close dealings with the state and its abusive power taught him the necessity of an active, independent FIESP. For that reason Moreira Ferreira had joined Luis Eulalio de Bueno Vidigal Filho's modernizing campaign in 1980 and had served in FIESP ever since. As a member of FIESP, Moreira Ferreira had occupied numerous roles, from first vice-president of FIESP and third vice-president of CIESP to director of two departments, vice-president of six superior councils, member of ten commissions, acting director of SENAI, representative to the CNI, and representative of FIESP in a wide range of government agencies. As such, Moreira Ferreira was the consumate insider.

Emerson Kapaz served as president of the Syndicate for the Musical Instrument and Toys Industry of São Paulo, which is where his service in FIESP ended. When in 1989 Amato offered him a position on the administration in an effort to lure him back, Kapaz refused. Kapaz owned a small toy factory, Elka Plasticos, a member of a modern, competitive, and fully private sector. His political history differed markedly from Moreira Ferreira's. An original founder of the PNBE, Kapaz had emerged as probably its best-known member by 1992. Kapaz's orientation revealed itself in his publicly disclosed vote for Lula in the second round of the 1989 presidential election, his well-publicized visit to Israel with labor leaders, and his participation in actions like the creation of a cross-societal pressure movement, the Brazil Option Movement (Movimento Opção Brasil), which united segments of industry, labor, and the growing lawyers' association, among others. Kapaz was the consumate outsider.

The election turned on high-stakes issues. The Collor government had maintained the pace of the commercial opening at the same time as it had maintained the worst recession in history. Rather than reforming the tax structure, Collor's government simply raised taxes three times. Small firms suffered disproportionately in this crisis yet had a limited voice in the decision-making process of FIESP. All the while, FIESP barely managed any action on behalf of small businesses, or even of the business community as a whole. Both candidates declared that they could modernize FIESP and could unite the business community behind a collective action project to defend its interests against an increasingly abusive and dangerous government.

To do this, both candidates promised to address all three issues of business modernization. Both played their campaigns heavily to the smaller firms that made up over 90 percent of the state's industry and numerically dominated CIESP. Both candidates promised to ensure FIESP's leadership role in encouraging and promoting competitive adjustments. Both candidates claimed that only they could lead the federation in collective action on behalf of business.

Carlos Eduardo Moreira Ferreira followed the traditional path of succession. He claimed many of Amato's prominent administration members as his backers—individuals like José Mindlin (auto parts), Roberto Nicolau Jeha (pulp and paper), and Ruy Martins Altenfelder Silva (agribusiness). He and his supporters argued that he had worked hard in the federation; he had occupied numerous important positions, and thus only he knew what FIESP needed to modernize. Behind his campaign, he could claim the ample resources of the federation itself. For example, much as a political campaign uses public works, Moreira Ferreira presided over the televised openings of new SESI recreation centers throughout São Paulo state.

Emerson Kapaz represented the marriage of the PNBE and IEDI. Although not a formal alliance (significant parts of both supported Moreira Ferreira—which caused a crisis in the PNBE, but not in IEDI, where members explicitly agreed not to formally endorse either candidate), members of IEDI acted as campaign advisers and financial backers. Kapaz substantially broke with tradition and extensively relied on the media, including paid television programs to promote himself and his campaign. He began touring regional CIESP headquarters and spoke in syndicates to promote his ideas. In both these approaches, he forced Moreira Ferreira to do the same (although Moreira Ferreira did not use television). He and his supporters in the PNBE aggressively called for syndicate presidents to hold consultations with their members before voting. Finally, and most important, he explicitly targeted CIESP as the more likely organization for him to win. As victory in FIESP appeared more and more likely for Moreira Ferreira, Kapaz sought to create an unprecedented split between the two organizations.

Although their electoral tactics differed, their campaign discourse was similar. Both candidates guaranteed that small firms would have a voice in the new administration and that FIESP/CIESP would better serve them. Moreira Ferreira assured voters that his plan of action would expand the representativeness of small firms and that any industrial policy that FIESP fought for would consider their needs. Kapaz countered with the assurance that his support for small firms would not simply be the talk of "FIESPocrats." His campaign cited Ibope findings that 87 percent of CIESP members used its services at most only from time to time as a criticism of Moreira Ferreira's performance as an insider.

Both candidates promoted themselves as professional modernizers who would expand the educational and technical resources available to Paulista industry. Both candidates argued in favor of developing closer ties to universities to promote technological research and development and dessemination of new ideas. Both candidates argued that labor–capital relations needed to be modernized and that labor's share of the national income urgently needed to increase. Both argued that FIESP had to address the high social taxes on payrolls, which caused the "paradox" of low wages and high labor costs, coupled with poor social services.

Finally, both candidates argued that the country needed an industrial policy (as IEDI had already begun promoting) and that FIESP needed to lead the business community in its development. Both opposed the existing tax and finance system and argued for the need to reform it. Both opposed commercial opening, arguing that the pace had to follow the pace of industry's capacity to competitively adjust. Both argued that the developed countries had entered a stage of "neoprotectionism" and that Brazil could not indiscriminately open its borders without reciprocity. Both candidates attacked the government's tight money policy and its effect on financing the state at the expense of business. Both candidates called for the state to balance its finances and for an end to state discrimination against foreign firms. In short, both candidates mirrored the list of concerns and frustrations growing at the micro-level throughout 1991 and 1992.

The candidates did differ in one critical area: how to reform FIESP/CIESP functions. Moreira Ferreira's response was the response of the consumate insider: "The profound understanding we have of the FIESP/CIESP/SESI/SENAI/IRS system enables us to assume the promise of promoting an ample reform of its structures and programs, in order to strengthen the entities, increase its representativeness and credibility and turn them more and more participative, influential, and modern."

Kapaz, true to his democratic modernizing agenda and his PNBE past, offered a different solution. In essence, Kapaz proposed a full-scale assault on what he called the "FIESPocrats"—the narrow group of insider businesspeople who made most decisions without any consultation. He proposed creating constituent councils of directly elected industrialists to act as debating forums and clearinghouses for proposals on how to reform the statues of CIESP and FIESP. Kapaz suggested computerizing the federation and creating electronic communications channels (primarily faxes) to record and disseminate the ideas of the bases. Kapaz's ideas actually went further than what he openly proposed. In private interviews, members of his campaign explained that the deeper intent was to end the institution of FIESP's presidency. Directly elected councils of businesspeople would sit atop the federation in an advisory or consultative capacity, but the rest of the functions would be professionalized after the IEDI, or the U.S. Business Roundtable model. Furthermore, FIESP and CIESP would be more thoroughly split, with CIESP providing only services to members and FIESP assuming the collective action role. In these proposals, Kapaz was certainly far more radical than Moreira Ferreira and far more threatening to entrenched interests, primarily the syndicates.

Ultimately, the corporatist logic of FIESP worked against Kapaz. Syndicates' influence in FIESP largely varied by the presence of their members in the administration. Voting for the loser would hurt a syndicate's position in the federation. Moreover, Kapaz's plan of action threatened syndicate influence with the participation of the bases. Moreira Ferreira cemented the corporatist barrier facing Kapaz by incorporating sixty-two syndicates into his slate. Forty-seven members of his administration were syndicate presidents with the voting rights of their syndicates. One was a vice-president of his syndicate, and fourteen were their syndicates' delegates to FIESP. With that distribution of positions, Moreira Ferreira locked up the majority of FIESP's 121 syndical votes. On July 29, 1992, Moreira Ferreira won FIESP with 113 votes (eleven syndicates held plebiscites among the members, of which eight picked Kapaz). He also won a plurality of CIESP with a margin of 42 percent to 35 percent for Kapaz. With less support than he expected, Kapaz conceded rather than pushing the election to a second round (for one candidate to get 50 percent).[55]

THE 1992 ELECTIONS: POSTSCRIPT

After the election, FIESP did not substantially reform. Shortly after the election, tensions again emerged in the federation as reformers who backed Moreira Ferreira criticized him for not pursuing reforms.[56] Calls for direct election of the president surfaced again as did rumors of another contested election in 1995.[57]

On the collective action front, not much changed either. The criticisms intensified with FIESP's failure to mount an effective lobbying campaign for the constitutional review of 1993. In parallel fashion to the 1987–88 debates, FIESP's failure left business without an effective voice to support the reforms it cared most about.[58] In a similar vein, despite the prominence of the commercial liberalization as a campaign issue, FIESP under

---

55. Rubens Figueiredo left his master's thesis incomplete for more lucrative work as a private consultant. One testament to his skill came in 1992 when he did private polling and analysis for the Moreira Ferreira campaign. Figueiredo observed that Emerson Kapaz's support in CIESP came from those least informed, least involved, and least likely to vote. In contrast to all the opinion polls routinely published in the press, Figueiredo's work pointed to a plurality, first-round victory for Moreira Ferreira. (Private polling work, São Paulo, 1992.)

56. *Estado de São Paulo,* August 4, 1994, p. 8B.

57. *Jornal do Brasil* (Rio de Janeiro), August 3, 1994, p. 1.

58. *Isto É* (São Paulo), October 13, 1993, pp. 40–42.

Moreira Ferreira backed away from opposing the government.[59] Again, FIESP's timidity on crucial economic issues, such as the pace of liberalization or the real rate of interest under Cardoso's *Plano real* (Real Plan), provoked charges that the FIESP executive was more interested in maintaining good relations with government than in defending business concerns.[60]

By 1995–96, however, FIESP's performance began to improve. The reasons for the improvement had more to do with Carlos Eduardo Moreira Ferreira's style than with actual changes in the federation. Moreira Ferreira commited himself to a participatory form of decision making. All public positions emerged from internal debates and formal approval from the council of representatives. With this backing, Moreira Ferreira assumed a vigorous public role by staking out the positions of national industry. He repeatedly defended the importance of constitutional reforms as a necessary complement to commercial liberalization. He also repeatedly defended democracy and democratic means of resolving disputes. As part of his defense of democracy, Moreira Ferreira and his executive actively encouraged FIESP members to join political parties.

FIESP aggressively addressed what it saw as weaknesses in Fernando Henrique Cardoso's approach to the reform process. In April 1996, Moreira Ferreira presented Cardoso with a set of proposals that would support competitiveness but did not need constitutional reform. FIESP played a leading role in organizing a march of over 2,000 businesspeople to Brasília to lobby in favor of constitutional reforms. Finally, when Cardoso announced his intention to run for re-election, FIESP immediately rallied publicly to his side.

Thus, by 1997, FIESP still suffered from an outdated corporatist logic, but Moreira Ferreira had profited from the criticism and challenges that FIESP had faced through the 1980s and 1990s. Thus, FIESP could still have benefited from institutional reform, but Moreira Ferreira's efforts had allowed FIESP to play a far more effective role in politics.

CONCLUSION

In the early 1980s, Brazilian industrialists were unable to represent themselves effectively. As a consequence, they were incapable of effectively

59. *Folha de São Paulo,* October 16, 1994, p. 5.
60. *Isto É,* October 13, 1993, pp. 40–42.

influencing the writing of the 1988 Constitution. Instead, they watched as their most dire predictions came true. In that context, modernizing revolts emerged throughout the corporatist structure of representation. By the mid-1990s, sectoral associations were much better placed to serve their members in the context of a rapidly changing economy. At the peak level, two experiments emerged, succeeded for a while, then dissipated, but their efforts helped produce a far more effective FIESP.

As a consequence of these changes, the industrial community was in a much better position to participate in the politics of economic reform. It could offer effective articulation and mobilization in support of and in opposition to goverment policy as well as negotiation over specific policy matters. Indirectly, these changes also contributed to neoliberal reform in that business organizations worked much harder to improve member services. The renovation of sectoral associations led to technical changes that supported micro-level efforts of member firms and consequently formed part of the supportive base for the neoliberal reform program. The pattern of response is addressed in the following chapters.

5

Crafting the Coalition

The Rise and Fall of Fernando Collor's Neoliberal Reform

Fernando Collor's 1989 presidential election campaign crafted the first successful economic reform coalition in the New Republic, but the coalition was weak and linked poor voters with a mistrustful business community. Although industrialists were concerned about Collor's "neopopulist" style[1] and his attacks on elites, his program was consistent with their policy demands through the 1980s. Consequently, their initial response to his aggressive tactics was guarded but positive. Collor's tactics rapidly changed, however, as they proved inadequate to overcome the combination of economic crisis and ungovernable constitutional design. As Collor looked increasingly incapable of providing the policy benefits that business needed to successfully adjust, business mobilized against him and commercial liberalization. The varying mobilization strategies benefited from the organizational renovations discussed in the previous chapter. This chapter examines Collor's tactical decisions and the accompanying rise and fall of his neoliberal coalition.

---

1. A number of scholars have discussed the relationship between populist political styles and neoliberal reform. Populist politics features direct appeals from charismatic leaders to the masses without intervening organizations. As a political form, it has been adaptable to neoliberal appeals, especially in combination with anti-elite messages and/or targeted but limited social spending. For fuller discussions of neopopulism, see Denise Dresser, "Neopopulist Solutions to Neoliberal Problems," *Current Issue Brief* 3 (Center for U.S.-Mexican Studies, University of California, San Diego, 1991); Weyland, "Neo-Populism and Neo-Liberalism in Latin America," *Studies in Comparative International Development* 31 (Fall 1996): 3–31; and Kenneth M. Roberts, "Neoliberalism and the Transformation of Populism in Latin America: The Peruvian Case," *World Politics* 48 (October 1995): 82–116.

COLLOR'S CAMPAIGN RHETORIC
AND PROPOSALS

Collor's election has been described as the triumph of style over substance.[2] Some observers have argued that his campaign had no real content,[3] no developed ideological framework, and no clear blueprint for the future.[4] Whatever the specific charge, Collor's campaign aggravated most observers.[5] It was a campaign laced with sharp anti-elite criticisms, right-wing demagoguery, and savvy television self-promotion and was supported by the ignorant, the uneducated, and the brutally poor.[6]

Beneath Collor's superior use of sophisticated images and telemarketing, however, lay considerable substance. The business community had a fair idea of where Collor was going. Before his inauguration, FIESP prepared an internal aide-mémoire for president Mario Amato, which showed that Collor's program had few surprises and generally conformed to business's policy preferences.[7] Collor's intentions on commercial, fiscal, finance, debt, income, agricultural, and foreign capital policy were basically known. The only questions were who would be economy minister, what stabilization strategy would he or she follow, and what impact would that policy have.

Aside from his appeals to poor voters through his attacks on elites, Collor differed little from several of the leading contenders who promoted neoliberal reforms. Leading center and center-right candidates Guilherme Afif (Liberal Party—PL), Paulo Maluf (Democratic Social Party—PDS), and Mario Covas (Brazilian Social Democratic Party—PSDB) all played to business community audiences with mildly liberalizing and antistate appeals, and all three drew substantial business support in the first round, but Collor outperformed these politicians tactically. In a polarized runoff election, the right-wing candidate holds business votes captive. Collor

2. Schneider, "Brazil Under Collor: Anatomy of a Crisis," *World Policy Journal* 8 (Spring 1991): 321–47; Soares, "Governo Collor: Autonomia da Conjuntura Política" (IUPERJ, Cadernos de Conjuntura, no. 34/35; November–December 1990).

3. For example, *Veja*'s coverage throughout 1989.

4. Such as de Souza, "The Contemporary Faces of the Brazilian Right: An Interpretation of Style and Substance," in Chalmers, de Souza, and Boron, eds., *The Right and Democracy in Latin America*.

5. Until his victory in the first round, which then set him up as the opponent to the extreme left, virtually no major press supported or liked his candidacy after his initial highly touted entry. Even the conservative *O Globo* did not support his candidacy until the second round.

6. This style of campaign has been dubbed "neopopulism." See note 1 above.

7. FIESP, Aide-mémoire, no. 177, December 22, 1989.

outflanked his neoliberal competitors by ignoring business groups, avoiding business endorsements, and trying to capture the votes of the majority of the electorate.

Collor began to acquire some measure of fame before he declared his candidacy. As governor of the tiny state of Alagoas, he set out to find and fire bureaucrats who received one or more salaries without ever showing up for work. This practice was common in Brazil as a traditional form of patronage. Collor, the self-proclaimed *caçador das marajás* (literally "hunter of the maharajas"), fired thousands of civil servants to much public fanfare and acclaim. He also positioned himself as a vocal and frequent critic of the unpopular incumbent president, José Sarney, for his mediocrity and the corruption in his government.

When Collor entered the race, he was a little-known figure in the country. Within one month, he led all other candidates by a large margin by framing his candidacy against the corruption of all other parties, the professional class, and the elite. In short, he offered himself as an antisystem candidate.[8] He emphasized his outsider status by rejecting any link to existing parties and running on the newly created Partido Renovação Nacional (National Reconstruction Party—PRN). He further made his case as an outsider to the established political class by repeatedly attacking Sarney, referring to him as "weak," "irresponsible," and a "second-class politician." He also attacked FIESP, using it as a symbol of corruption, privilege, and backwardness.[9]

Collor claimed that he intended to moralize Brazil: "to reestablish honor, dignity, and character in public life."[10] Copying President Janio Quadros's (1960–61) successful populist campaign thirty years earlier, he carried a broom with him to symbolize his intention to sweep away the dirt. Going into poor neighborhoods, he declared that his program would be paid for by the elites who had got rich off the backs of the poor without giving anything back. Passionately rejecting everything to do with Sarney's government and the political system in general, he introduced a new theme: corruption.

He forced every other candidate to respond to him. For example, Afif,

---

8. Although Collor's style fits what some Latin Americanists have called "neopopulism," it also fits a much wider phenomenon of outsider politicians attacking the system. This phenomenon is explored by Andreas Schedler, who has noted that these antisystem politicians have become prevalent in the 1980s–90s. Schedler, "Anti-Political-Establishment Parties," *Party Politics* 2 (July 1996: 291–312).

9. Figueiredo, unfinished master's thesis, 1.

10. *Veja* (São Paulo), April 19, 1989, p. 37.

the voice of small businesspeople, turned populist and announced that Collor had shown that the people wanted Coca-Cola, so he would offer them Pepsi.[11] Mario Covas claimed to be the real Collor as he and the other candidates strove to prove that they were truly something new. They failed. When free television coverage began in September, most candidates explicitly attacked Collor. Although he lost some ground between September and the November vote, he still won by virtually a two to one margin over his nearest competitor, Luís Inácio Lula da Silva.

Collor directed his rhetoric primarily to the poorest segment of the population. In a context of resentment and distrust, his antisystem campaign found fertile soil. He won the votes of the poorest and the least educated by margins of two and three to one over his nearest competitors in the first round in November 1989.[12] In the second round, he beat his competitor, Lula, by a 10 percent margin among the poorest segment and by 17 percent among the least educated.[13] In fact, he beat Lula in every electoral district but one in the city of São Paulo. This record is striking because Lula was from São Paulo, his base constituency was in the Paulista working class, and Collor was a *nordestino* (northeasterner) completely unknown in the city a year before the election.[14]

In contrast, Collor did not perform nearly as well among higher income groups. In the first round, he received roughly the same share of middle-class votes as the other four leading contenders, Luís Inácio Lula da Silva, Mario Covas, Leonel Brizola, and Paulo Maluf.[15] In the second round, Lula defeated Collor in every wage category but the lowest (up to two minimum salaries annually).[16] Among higher income groups, business supported Collor, but only as the nonleftist, nonlabor option between two evils.[17]

Fernando Collor was not the business community's first choice for president of the republic. In the first round, business preferred Mario Covas, Paulo Maluf, and, among small businesspeople, Guilherme Afif Domingos. Although Collor's promarket, antistate rhetoric conformed to the

11. *Veja*, September 13, 1989, p. 56.

12. André Singer, "Collor na Periferia: A Volta por Cima do Populismo?" in Lamounier, ed., *De Geisel a Collor: O Balanço da Transição* (São Paulo: Editora Sumaré, 1990), 137.

13. Singer, "Collor na Periferia," 138.

14. Singer, "Collor na Periferia," 142.

15. Singer, "Collor na Periferia," 137–39.

16. Singer, "Collor na Periferia," 137. Seventy-five percent of the electorate earned two minimum salaries or less in Brazil.

17. Schneider, "Brazil Under Collor"; Roxborough, "Neo-Liberalism in Latin America: Limits and Alternatives," *Third World Quarterly* 13, no. 3 (1992): 421–40.

business community's demands, his demonizing business made that community nervous. In interviews, many reported that he appeared rash and unpredictable.[18] It is not surprising that many opted for promarket candidates who did not paint businesspeople as the villains of society.

In the second round, Collor was the clear preference over Lula, one of the founders and former head of the São Bernardo Metalworkers' Union. Lula represented the threat of greater state involvement in the economy, and even possible extensive nationalizations. Collor demonized the business community, but he did so in the name of the market. He promised to transform Brazil into "Brazil Inc.," a sleek, competitive country without the domination of cartels, monopolies, and the state.

The business community poured money into his campaign, offered endorsements (which Collor publicly and dramatically rejected),[19] and ultimately gave him their votes.[20] Nevertheless, as a captive community, Collor did not owe business anything, and he did not decrease his attacks on the business community after he won the 1989 election, or even after he assumed office. After his victory, Collor called FIESP the most backward institution in Brazilian society.[21] True to his pledge to end corruption and to attack privilege, Collor closed the door on business lobbies. Ultimately, this tactic proved part of Collor's anti-institutional approach to pushing economic reform.

INSTITUTIONS OF POLITICS AND THE BASES OF FISCAL CHAOS

The organization of Brazil's political system has played a considerable role in driving fiscal imbalances and in preventing actions to restore the state's fiscal health. In a continent of nations with fragmented, poorly

18. Confidential author interviews conducted August 1991–August 1992.

19. Mario Amato, president of FIESP, publicly endorsed Collor before the election. Collor equally publicly announced his lack of interest in FIESP's support. Privately, he accepted FIESP's money.

20. There were a few notable exceptions to the tendency to vote for Collor. Emerson Kapaz, the coordinator of PNBE, announced his vote for Lula. This choice and its public airing came to haunt him somewhat during his campaign for the presidency of FIESP in 1992. This was particularly true among small businessmen who had voted overwhelmingly for Collor against Lula.

21. *Estado de São Paulo,* December 1989.

institutionalized political systems, Brazil has consistently ranked among the worst.[22] Four problems stem from the fragmentation and fragility of Brazil's democratic institutions: first, electoral rules and the constitutional design fragmented political power into several poles; second, this fragmentation weakened parties and encouraged particularistic tendencies; third, as a consequence, patronage was the principal motivator in the political system; finally, these qualities made it hard for politicians of any stripe to craft stable legislative coalitions or pursue any coherent developmental program. These problems arose primarily from the character of Brazil's multiparty presidentialism, proportional representation, and weak political parties.[23]

Presidentialism

Brazil's president theoretically and in practice concentrated significant political power in the office of the executive. Most of that power lay in what the president could do without congressional oversight. Primarily, the president could issue and reissue provisional decrees (*medidas provisórias*) that had the status of law until voted on by the Congress. Although the constitution intended the measures for emergency purposes, it did not legally limit the president's use of them.[24] The other crucial area of presidential power came from the extensive off-budget spending available to the executive. Although the Congress maintained the right to approve or reject the president's budget, the constitution allowed ample room for the president to make off-budget deals that were not subject to any oversight. This right granted the president extensive patronage resources, even if they required public-sector borrowing.[25]

Brazilian presidentialism also worked through patronage-driven bar-

22. Mainwaring and Scully, *Building Democratic Institutions*.

23. Brazil's political system has engendered a mini-industry of studies of its problems. A few excellent exemplars are Power, "The Pen Is Mightier Than the Congress"; Mainwaring, "Presidentialism"; Ames, "Electoral Rules," "Electoral Strategy," and "The Reverse Coattails Effect: Local Party Organization in the 1989 Presidential Election," *American Political Science Review* 88, no. 1 (1994): 95–111. Also Mainwaring, "Brazil."

24. Power, "The Pen Is Mightier Than the Congress."

25. For excellent discussions of Brazilian presidentialism in comparative perspective, see Matthew S. Shugart and John M. Carey, *Presidents and Assemblies: Constitutional Design and Electoral Dynamics* (New York: Cambridge University Press, 1992); and Scott Mainwaring and Matthew S. Shugart, *Presidentialism and Democracy in Latin America* (New York: Cambridge University Press, 1997).

gains with state governors.[26] Governors exerted some influence over their states' caucuses in Congress. Again, the link between the two was patronage. Governors had been able to provide patronage resources for members of Congress, and in turn, members of Congress consistently defended state interests against the federal government. This link between state governors and members of the federal Congress forced the president to court the governors in exchange for votes. Thus, on the one hand, the president could exert some leverage against governors through the states' dependence on federal banks. On the other, the governors and their links to Congress could force presidents to make concessions in exchange for legislative support.

The Rules of Proportional Representation in Brazil

The political system's problems extended to the constitutional and legislative rules that govern the electoral system. Jairo César Marconi Nicolau argued that proportional representation (PR), another frequent target of criticism, was not Brazil's problem. Rather, the specific rules that governed Brazil's PR system were at fault.[27] First, the constitution allowed free organization of parties without a requirement that parties demonstrate any national representativeness. Thus, all registered entities received the benefits available to political parties, including access to financial resources, free television time, and seats in Congress. Unlike other proportional representation systems, parties did not need a minimum number of signatures to register or a minimum percentage of the national vote. Furthermore, the minimum threshold of votes was simply the electoral quotient (number of votes divided by number of seats, yielding a very low threshold, e.g., only 1.67 percent of the vote in São Paulo).[28] Consequently, thirty-three parties competed in the 1990 elections. As of 1990, nineteen parties held seats in the Chamber of Deputies and seventeen held seats in the Senate.

Second, Brazil featured a unique electoral rule providing free television time to all parties, again without restriction. Before an election, every

26. For an excellent analysis of the role of the governors in Brazilian politics, see Luiz Fernando Abrucio, "Os Barões da Federação: O Poder dos Governadores no Brasil Pos-Autoritário" (master's thesis, Universidade de São Paulo, 1994).

27. Jairo Nicolau, "Representatação Proporcional: É Preciso Mudar?" in *Regimes Eleitorais e Sistemas Partidários* (IUPERJ, Cadernos de Conjunto, no. 43, August 1991): 21–23.

28. Mainwaring, "Politicians, Parties, and Electoral Systems," 22.

registered party regardless of its size or representativeness had access to free one-hour political programs. Parties could then "rent out" their free time to larger parties by forming coalitions. Unfortunately, this practice encouraged parties to form solely for the purpose of renting out their free television time. Third, the legal limit to the number of candidates that a party could field in an election was permissive—1.5 candidates per available seat in federal and state elections and up to three times as many in lower level elections.[29] This rule permitted a vast proliferation of congressional candidates, increasing political fragmentation, voter confusion, and apathy.[30]

Parties Versus Politicians in Brazil

The nature of political parties in Brazil further worsened the situation. The Workers' Party (PT) was widely viewed as the only effective political party in Brazil. Unlike all other parties, the PT had a strong, mobilized grass roots that actively participated in the party and in elections.[31] No other party could make the same claim. Some, like the PRN or to a lesser extent the Democratic Workers' Party (PDT), were primarily vehicles for their leaders—Collor and Leonel Brizola, respectively. Others were notorious patronage machines that opportunists of all stripes could join, such as the Liberal Front Party (PFL) and the Brazilian Democratic Movement Party (PMDB)—as of 1990 by far the two largest parties. After the 1994 Cardoso election, the PSDB lost some of its coherence as opportunistic politicians joined the party.

The parties' weakness derived from their lack of control over their candidates and members of Congress.[32] Several electoral system rules eroded party control over candidates. First, parties exerted little or no control over candidates. National party headquarters often had little influence

29. Mainwaring, "Politicians, Parties, and Electoral Systems," 25.

30. Power, "Politicized Democracy: Competition, Institutions, and 'Civic-Fatigue' in Brazil," *Journal of Interamerican Studies and World Affairs* 33 (Fall 1991): 75–112.

31. The PT is noted for dramatic end runs during electoral campaigns, such as in the city elections in São Paulo in 1988 where Luiza Erundina pulled ahead with the support of massive grassroots mobilizing in the city in the final weeks as workers with little free time to mobilize otherwise took to the streets in her support.

32. Mainwaring, "Presidentialism," 11. The magazine *Exame* reported another indicator in which members of leading parties, such as the PFL, PMDB, and the PSDB, supplied both the principal proponents and opponents of all major legislation in 1991. *Exame,* August 1991.

over local branches.[33] The *candidato nato* rule, in which representatives automatically had the right to be on the ballot, and the lack of restrictions on party switching also reinforced candidate autonomy over parties. Furthermore, parties had limited access to funds, forcing candidates to supply their own. The strict legal limits on private donations to campaigns meant that candidates either obtained help from governors' war machines and/ or received substantial amounts of illegal private funding.[34] In either event, candidates were not beholden to their parties.

Statewide, open-list elections exacerbated the already weak link between parties and candidates. As parties needed to maximize their votes across the state to maximize their seat total, they tended to court well-known figures who could bring their own votes.[35] The individuals they drew to the party brought with them well-defined support groups, usually through narrow functional or geographical constituencies. These individuals could move among parties when it was convenient for them, bringing their votes along. Thus, the parties depended on the candidates and their reputations or interest-group connections rather than the reverse.[36] This system of politicians' protecting well-defined client groups, referred to in Brazil as *corporativismo*,[37] created strong particularistic tendencies in Congress. Members concerned themselves with obtaining benefits for their corporate clienteles without any centripetal forces checking their behavior.[38]

This system produced several disheartening tendencies. First, party leaders exercised very little control over member votes. Thus, deal mak-

33. A striking example is when the local PFL rejected the national office's efforts to run popular television personality Silvio Santos for the 1992 mayoral race. The local office rejected its efforts even though Santos immediately assumed the lead in the polls by virtue of his popularity. The local branch did not want the national branch to compromise its autonomy.

34. As the Collor scandal developed, charges of illegal campaign contributions from prominent businessmen arose. Interestingly, they receded after television cameras caught on film angry responses of businessmen who demanded that Lula's accounts be studied to show how much he had received from them as well.

35. Silvio Santos and the São Paulo mayoral elections is a good example.

36. Roberto Macedo's talk at Instituto Fernand Braudel, cited in William Hinchberger, "Coalition Quandary: Collor, Liberalization, and Brazilian Political Elites" (master's thesis, Berkeley: University of California at Berkeley, 1992), p. 103.

37. Distinct from the term *corporatism* as discussed in Chapter 1.

38. José Luciano de Mattos Dias confirmed the localized nature of the candidates' support in his research on Paraná and Rio de Janeiro states. In both states, a majority of the municipalities featured competition among no more than three candidates. Furthermore, sizable minorities of candidates drew over 60 percent of their votes from no more than one or two neighborhoods. Dias, "Legislação Eleitoral: Situação e Perspectiva de Reforma," in *Regimes Eleitorais e Sistemas Partidários* (IUPERJ, Cadernos de Conjunto, no. 43, August 1991): 16–17.

ing, pact making, and negotiations in general were complex, costly, and unstable. The frequency with which members (aside from the Workers' Party—PT) voted against their leaders routinely weakened collective agreements or deals. Second, as a consequence, executives and their oppositions found it virtually impossible to construct any stable coalition behind any long-term program.[39] Congressional coalitions formed on an ad hoc basis behind single issues or in semiformal single issue blocs (although not by party). Third, as a consequence of these factors, executives had to reconstruct new coalitions for each new initiative they sent to Congress. As coalitional support usually depended on patronage,[40] two results ensued: policymaking as a rule cost a great deal in federal resources and executives found it difficult to build coalitions that threatened major sources of patronage.

These points help explain Collor's political dilemma and strategy. Collor faced a dense network of patronage alliances in a context of near hyperinflation, substantial budget deficits, and generally poor financial conditions. To address the economic crisis, he had to attack the set of political interests supporting fiscal instability. Collor chose to try to resolve the zero-sum political stalemate by hitting all organized groups, but he faced several problems. First, as Kugelmas and Sallum have argued, the fragmentation of political power forced a reliance on shock-package strategies,[41] which have limited effectiveness in Brazil's too frequently shocked polity. Second, Collor tried to rule without Congress, but eventually both Congress and the governors forced him to play patronage ball. Third, Collor's style and his failures provoked growing business opposition and helped fuel congressional resistance to him.

39. This view is strongly contested by Argelina Figueiredo and Fernando Limongi, "Presidencialismo e Apoio no Congresso," *Monitor Público* 3 (January–March, 1996): 27–36. The authors argued that Brazilian parties are in fact much more disciplined and as a consequence executives have an easier time constructing coalitions than the prevailing view suggests. Although their argument is provocative, Figueiredo and Limongi overstated their case by using only aggregate voting results. Looking at the outcome of policy voting can give rise to several errors in estimating executives' strength. First, this method does not differentiate among policies, so that there is no way to distinguish between crucial and controversial legislation and more mundane issues. Second, the method does not measure the extent to which executives' policy proposals suffer significant alterations in the course of negotiations. Finally, the method does not recognize that party leaders have at times killed proposals before voting because it was clear that party members would not support them. For a fuller critique, see Power, "Political Institutions in Democratic Brazil: Politics as a Permanent Constitutional Convention," in Peter R. Kingstone and Timothy J. Power, eds., *Democratic Brazil: Institutions, Actors, and Processes* (Pittsburgh: University of Pittsburgh Press, 1999).

40. Ames, *Political Survival*; Kugelmas and Sallum, "O Leviathan," 15–17.

41. Kugelmas and Sallum, "O Leviathan," 19.

As José Luis Fiori has argued, Collor faced two choices in pursuing liberalization: the top-down strategy (the Thatcher model) or the social concertation strategy (the Spanish Moncloa Pacts model).[42] Collor's dilemma was that to pursue the Thatcher model, he needed the kind of legislative dominance that Thatcher herself possessed. On the opposite side, the combination of economic crisis and the patronage basis of politics afforded little possibility for serious social pact negotiations. Nevertheless, Collor attempted both.

MARCH–OCTOBER 1990: STABILIZATION AND THE WAR ON CONGRESS

The period from Collor's inauguration to the October legislative elections saw the new president implement a dramatic reform program.[43] Collor's brash style initially put off business leaders, but his apparent successes in this period eventually won significant business support. Yet, by the end of the period, new doubts arose, and these foreshadowed the eventual breakdown of business confidence in Collor's capacity to deliver on his promises.

Collor's initial strategy relied on three tactics.[44] First, he used his high popular approval ratings, particularly among the numerous but disorganized poor, as a weapon against the Congress. He repeatedly reminded politicians and political observers that he had won 35 million direct votes, which granted him greater legitimacy than the members of Congress. Sec-

---

42. José Luis Fiori, "Dezembro 1990: O Impasse Político da Razão Tecnocrática," 66. The models are from Colin Crouch, cited in José Luis Fiori, "Dezembro 1990: O Impasse Político da Razão Tecnocrática" (UPERJ, Cadernos de Conjuntura, no. 34/35; November–December 1990). Another excellent analysis is in Weyland, "Brazilian State."

43. For additional discussion of Collor's reform program, see Weyland, "Brazilian State"; Baer, *Brazilian Economy,* 262–65, 182–91; Bresser Pereira, *Economic Crisis and State Reform,* chap. 14.

44. A number of works analyze Fernando Collor's government. Among them, Bresser Pereira, *Economic Crisis and State Reform,* stands out for its defense of the Collor government. Although Bresser Pereira does not deny Collor's corruption, he also makes a case for Collor's having made a number of critical reforms and having had a coherent agenda. For an argument that parallels this one, see Lamounier, "Brazil: The Hyperactive Paralysis Syndrome," in Dominguez and Abraham F. Lowenthal, eds., *Constructing Democratic Governance: Latin America and the Caribbean in the 1990s* (Baltimore: Johns Hopkins University Press, 1996). In particular, Lamounier (p. 174) suggested that Collor's collapse gave new life to statism.

ond, Collor sidestepped Congress as much as he could. In his first year of office, Collor used the legal, although unorthodox and undemocratic, provisional decree. Under this constitutional mechanism, the president issued executive orders that acted as law pending congressional approval. Flooding the legislature with decrees, Collor bludgeoned the Congress into stunned complacency. Overall, Collor resorted to this mechanism 250 times in 1990 alone.

Finally, Collor used his eclectic political program to throw the Congress off balance.[45] Collor's policy positions jumped from the left to the right, which prevented any effective opposition from forming. Policies like privatization attracted the right, whereas his highly public acts against the military drew the left (e.g., ending the nuclear power program or closing the military intelligence office [SNI]). Soares has dubbed this strategy "the *sarneyzação* of the opposition."[46] The term *sarneyzação* refers to Sarney's political immobility because of the number of cleavages in his own cabinet. In essence, Collor's political manipulation of cleavages in Congress immobilized opposition parties' efforts to mount a campaign against him.

It is difficult to understate the dramatic impact of Collor's first one hundred days in office. One day after his inauguration on March 15, 1990, Collor implemented the most drastic anti-inflation plan the country had ever seen. In addition, he set in motion an enormous reform program involving changes to the fiscal, trade, and administrative frameworks of the country. The initial response to his program was extremely positive, winning an 80 percent national approval rating. The country appeared to be on the road to modernization.

Collor's economic program in the opening days of his tenure had several parts. First and foremost, his dramatic plan to counter inflation involved freezing 80 percent of the nation's liquid assets. Second, he instituted a temporary global price freeze and a new wage indexation mechanism aimed at eventual free wage negotiations. Third, he announced his intention to begin reducing tariffs as part of a new commercial policy. He left the schedule to be resolved and announced later. Finally, he instituted the Special Commission for the Federal Deregulation Program (Comissão Especial do Programa Federal de Desregulamentação) to study and implement deregulation decisions.

45. Schneider, "Collor's First Year: The Stalled Revival of Capitalist Development in Brazil" (IUPERJ, Cadernos de Conjuntura, no. 34/35; November–December 1990): 93; Soares, "Governo Collor," 33–34.

46. Soares, "Governo Collor," 33–34.

The stabilization plan was the linchpin of the whole program. Without successful stabilization, no other program would reap returns. At the time of Collor's inauguration, high inflation presented three problems. First, it drove constant and rapid expansion of the monetary base, which helped fuel further inflation. Second, the persistence of such high inflation eroded public confidence in the state's solvency and in the financial instruments of the state. As a result, Sarney's government had to continuously increase the interest rate offered on government paper to induce private investors to lend to the state. Third, this need to offer higher and higher rates itself exacerbated budget deficits, further driving inflation and further eroding public confidence. In response to what was clearly a dangerous hyperinflationary situation, Collor had to restore public confidence, rein in budget deficits, and limit monetary expansion. Collor's restructuring and stabilization plan involving tax and administrative reforms, commercial liberalization, and privatization required that he accomplish these tasks.

To correct such a dire situation and implement an orthodox solution, Collor had to rely on an unorthodox tactic. On March 13, two days before Collor's inauguration, President Sarney declared a three-day bank holiday. On March 16, 1990, Collor announced his dramatic, unorthodox solution. First, he changed Brazil's currency from *cruzados nôvos* to *cruzeiros* (the name of the currency before the Cruzado Plan of 1986), with no change in face value. Second, he blocked all deposits in banks, allowing only the equivalent of $1,000 to be withdrawn from regular accounts and only 20 percent of the balance of accounts in overnight accounts (where, for example, most corporate payrolls were deposited). The block was to continue for eighteen months, at which point the government would begin to release it in parcels. Finally, he freed the exchange rate from Central Bank control although strict restrictions on foreign currency exchanges remained in place.

The plan aimed at providing relief from mounting debt at ever-higher rates of interest while Collor's government put a more orthodox program in motion. The block had several effects. It constituted a progressive, forced-lending program on a massive scale, freeing the state from the need to incur higher debts at high interest rates. Furthermore, the new debt had very low, and even negative interest rates, providing a second important source of debt relief. Collor's plan obtained even further debt relief in that almost 80 percent of the assets frozen were public debt paper (now earning the same low or negative interest rates), freeing the state from payment obligations. The block also attacked the inflationary crisis by drastically cutting liquidity (by as much as 80 percent). Finally, outrageous though it was, it actually restored public confidence in the state's solvency, at least temporarily.

In addition to the stabilization, commonly referred to as the Collor Plan, Collor passed a series of other measures. First, he implemented the beginning of an administrative reform that by June 1990 had already produced significant results. He eliminated eleven ministries, merging those with overlapping functions to produce a more streamlined cabinet. The most significant streamlining merged the former ministries of Industry and Commerce, Finance, and Planning into a single Economy Ministry. In addition, he closed a large number of agencies and companies, including the politically influential Coffee Institute and the Institute for Alcohol and Sugar. He also closed a series of politically important holding companies, including Portobras, the port holding company, Interbras, Petrobras's international trade company, and Siderbras, the large steel holding company.

In Brasília, Collor continued his administrative reforms by chopping away at a number of the benefits to government there. He restricted use of state-owned vehicles to the president and his ministers. He rounded up four thousand other cars, which he then auctioned off. He prohibited his ministers and top secretaries from living in any of the mansions owned by the federal government, and he himself converted the presidential mansion into guest lodgings for foreign dignitaries. He stripped Brasília bureaucrats of the benefit of free housing and cut free lunches and coffee breaks as well. He projected cutting 300,000 federal bureaucratic jobs. He ordered all federal ministries to cut their staffs by 20 percent. Because the 1988 Constitution prevented firing civil servants with five or more years of service, he placed those bureaucrats in a pool of available labor to be transferred to locations with demand for labor (such as remote Amazon posts).[47]

He made, as well, a number of sweeping changes at the administrative level regarding foreign trade. Most important, he closed CACEX, the foreign trade center, the center of Brazil's market reserve and import-substituting strategy. In its place, he created DECEX (Departamento de Comércio Exterior). The new department differed dramatically from CACEX. It had far fewer personnel as well as vastly reduced powers, and its control was removed from the Bank of Brazil (from which CACEX

47. Weyland, "The Brazilian State in the New Democracy," *Journal of Interamerican Studies and World Affairs* 39, no. 4 (1997): 63–94.

had operated).[48] Similarly, another crucial agency in the foreign trade and protectionist pantheon, the Customs Policy Commission (CPA), was eliminated. The CPA had maintained close contacts with the private sector and had administered a strongly protectionist policy. The new commission, the Customs and Tariffs Coordinator (CTA), moved to DECEX from the Revenue Service with new rule changes as well. Those changes consisted primarily in keeping customs open twenty-four hours a day as opposed to the work schedule of the revenue office. Second, the transfer placed the office under the authority of the economics ministry via DECEX and subjected it more clearly to government trade policy.

The changes at CACEX had a profound impact on foreign trade. CACEX had the authority to conduct searches for national similars to either prevent their import by withholding licenses or to set the appropriate duties for import. CACEX was ideologically committed to import substitution and, in conjunction with certain business associations, effectively maintained a firm border against imports. It was also the guardian of the country's market reserves, which it carefully protected with reference to a list of about 1,500 products that could not be imported.

DECEX operated on much simpler guidelines. Collor removed any discretionary authority to issue export or import licenses. Under new rules, an importer or exporter need show only a line of credit to obtain a license. The list of suspended imports, Annex C, was effectively suspended, putting an end to almost all market reserves in Brazil. Similarly, Collor eliminated virtually all exemptions and reductions of import duties and taxes, excepting government agencies, the Manaus Free Trade Zone, and a small number of others. This move effectively eliminated any of DECEX's discretionary authority under the national similars law. Finally, to mark the seriousness of the steps, Collor also reduced the tariff to zero on dozens of products not made in Brazil.

Overall, these steps substantially liberalized the economy. The removal of DECEX from the Banco do Brasil, the elimination of licensing controls, the abolishing of Annex C, and the effective cancellation of the national similars law with its concomitant bureaucratic controls and obstacles effectively opened the Brazilian market to an unprecedented degree. The

---

48. The significance of this one act, removing control from the Bank of Brazil, is hard to overstate. The Bank of Brazil operated as a state within a state, controlling a large network of congress members and pursuing its own policies at will. CACEX was long charged with pursuing its own agenda regardless of government priorities. Shifting DECEX away from the bank removed a powerful policy tool from an institution that was often a rival to the elected government.

substitution of all controls for a simple tariff system with the pledge to begin gradually reducing tariffs is perhaps the most striking element of Collor's program. Because so much of the business-bureaucracy relation revolved around granting benefits on ISI issues in agencies like the CPA and CACEX, this reform had real meaning.

Collor's final significant step in the opening weeks of his program regarded tax changes. Collor indicated that Brazil needed a serious reform of its fiscal structure. In general, Brazilians had to cope with too many taxes (around sixty-three), which made the structure too complex, encouraged evasion, and disproportionately allocated the tax burden on those who could not evade it (principally salaried workers and large businesses). The task of tax reform was a medium-term project; in the short term, the state needed to increase revenues.

To meet the state's short-term revenue needs, Collor raised corporate tax rates, eliminated virtually all incentives and exemptions, and strengthened the enforcement of tax collection. The incentives eliminated included income tax exemptions for exports and agriculture, all trade (except Manaus) incentives and regional investment incentives, and deductions for investment in computers, among many others. Collor also decreed a one-time tax on all financial operations, which was later passed by Congress but which the courts ultimately ruled unconstitutional.

All told, Collor's policy initiatives contributed to an immediate improvement in inflation and fiscal performance. Collor's various efforts at stabilization, administrative reform, and tax and trade reforms contributed to an estimated budget surplus of 1.2 percent of GDP for 1990. This surplus contrasted sharply with the 1989 budget deficit of 8 percent of GDP. Collor's stabilization plan sharply reduced the deficit by manipulating debt payments, but it produced only a transitory surplus. Permanently reducing the deficit depended on constitutional reforms passing Congress.

The business community's reaction increasingly warmed up as the positive effects of the Collor Plan began to appear. The business community, like the rest of Brazilian society, spent much of the pre-inauguration period speculating on the stabilization program that Collor was likely to implement. Much like the rest of society, business anticipated a shock of some sort. In anticipation of the shock, it raised prices dramatically, thereby fueling the worst rate of inflation the country had ever seen. These speculative price increases were abetted by the president-elect's rhetorical campaign.

The initial shock of the Collor Plan provoked sharp resistance. Although the public expressed high levels of support, the business community watched the economy grind to a halt as idle capacity increased to 80 percent.[49] Business representatives such as Paulo Francini (FIESP and Coldex Frigor) and Mario Amato openly challenged the president on the block of funds for payrolls. Collor not only conceded little at that time, but he visibly closed the door to Mario Amato and FIESP. On the positive side, Collor's administrative and trade reforms received high marks from business.[50]

As inflation fell and Collor increasingly facilitated the release of seized assets, business enthusiastically moved to support Collor's program. With inflation down and industrial production resuming, the prospects seemed much brighter, even if the president was no friendlier. Business attitudes certainly improved as nearly all blocked corporate money found its way back into business pockets. In a survey conducted by the Estado de São Paulo with forty big and medium-size businesses in seven cities, the over-whelming majority voiced optimism about the plan. Only two thought that the plan had not worked, while thirty-three believed that it had, with inflation returning only at moderate levels. Nevertheless, many reported a sharp, negative impact on sales.[51]

Mario Amato joined the chorus, along with other influential members of FIESP's Economic Council. He emphatically endorsed the Collor Plan, arguing that the May inflation rate of 8.5 percent did not suggest its fail-ure, but he too expressed concern about the need for "concrete measures to eliminate the structural causes of inflation, among them the public deficit."[52] Amato repeated business opposition to a return to indexation and called for public information on the real size of the deficit.

Although business optimism continued through the middle of the year, concerns began to surface as well. A survey of 912 firms conducted by DECON (FIESP's Department of the Economy) in July 1990 found con-tinued support for Collor's Plan (33 percent believed the plan had suc-ceeded and 25 percent believed it had failed). Yet, 42 percent of respondents hoped that the plan had worked, but worried about projec-tions of a sharp drop in both industrial (-40 percent) and commercial (-34 percent) sales over the next two months. Overall, 92 percent of the firms in the survey reported drops in sales since March 16. Seventy-one percent faced cost pressures, 81 percent faced wage demands (although

49. *Isto É Senhor,* April 4, 1990, p. 23.
50. *Gazeta Mercantil,* March 17, 1990, p. 6.
51. *Estado de São Paulo,* May 27, 1990, pp. 1, 8.
52. Mario Amato, quoted in *Estado de São Paulo,* May 31, 1990, p. 5.

only 40 percent had granted concessions), and 56 percent of firms were using less than 70 percent of installed capacity.[53]

In August, Collor addressed a gathering of two thousand businesspeople on the occasion of the magazine *Exame*'s (Brazil's leading business magazine) announcement of its two thousand top businesses. He expressed concern about rising inflation and revealed the government's preoccupation with short-term problems. He repeated his modernization theme, stressing that he was constructing a new relation with business. The state would no longer rush to the rescue of firms, but would provide only those services to which each citizen had a right. The business reaction was enthusiastically favorable and supportive.[54]

One reason for business's enthusiasm was its approval of Collor's overall policy direction (despite numerous criticisms about implementation) and its confidence in its ability to adjust. One source confirming business support for liberalization comes from research by Gesner Oliveira of CEBRAP in São Paulo.[55] Oliveira's research, conducted with 133 firms during 1990, confirms public statements from business representatives, both on the level of support and on the identification of problems (Table 5.1). One year into the program, only 25 percent of respondents thought that the commercial opening would seriously hurt their sector; 22.4 percent believed that their adjustment would take longer than three years, and only 5.4 percent believed that they could not adjust at all; only 10.7 percent of respondents thought that the program was wrong. That large majorities believed that the market would genuinely be more open in 1992 supports the basic credibility of the program at the time. Similarly, the large majority (72.3 percent) of respondents who said that the program was encouraging investments points to the same conclusion.

Another interesting element in Oliveira's findings are the obstacles to successful implementation of the program, which businesspeople identified. Among the top responses were the absence of investment in Brazil's infrastructure, the recession (a product of the all-out attack on inflation), the continued size of the bureaucracy, and political blocks to Collor's passing reform legislation. The least troublesome points included lags in technology, the credibility of the program, the absence of a guiding industrial policy, and the speed of the opening.

53. *Estado de São Paulo*, p. 5.

54. The meeting was reported in the *Gazeta Mercantil*, August 31, 1990, p. 6.

55. Gesner Oliveira, "Condicionantes e Diretrizes de Política para a Abertura Comercial Brasileira" (IPEA Texto para Discussão, no. 3 (September 1993).

Table 5.1. Evaluation of commercial liberalization, 1991

Belief That Market Will Be Open in:		
	1992	1994
Yes	70.5%	80.4%
No	16.1	3.6
Don't know	12.5	14.3

Effect of Opening on Investments (%)		Evaluation of Policy (%)	
Encourages	72.3	Correct, well done	27.7
Discourages	11.6	Correct, poorly done	51.8
Don't know	11.6	Wrong	10.7

Time Needed to Adjust (%)		Impact on Sector of Tariff Reduction (%)	
Already adjusted	36.6	Compromises seriously	25.0
Up to 1 year	5.4	Compromises a little	26.8
1 to 3 years	28.6	No change	11.5
3 to 5 years	17.0	Improves	35.7
5 and more	5.4		
Can't adjust	5.4		

Obstacles to Effective Implementation of the Policy (% of Respondents)			
Infrastructure	67	Technology lags	36
Recession	49	Credibility	35
Exchange rate	48	No industrial policy	35
Excess bureaucracy	42	Import financing	25
Political resistance	40	Pace of policy too slow	14
Export financing	40	Pace of policy too fast	9

SOURCE: Oliveira 1993.

These responses in 1990 point to the credibility of Collor's program at that time, the widespread acceptance of the commercial opening, and the awareness that investments were necessary to prepare for an open market. They also point to the concerns that depended on Collor's performance, concerns both about the financial crisis of the state and the political paralysis that had undermined José Sarney and that threatened Collor. As in their earlier initial support for the Cruzado Plan of 1986, the business community accepted sacrifice as long as the state fulfilled its obligations. More than anything else, business respondents expressed concern about the need for permanent deficit-reducing measures. One respondent observed that interest rates had risen from 8 percent per month to 20 percent per month, revealing the government's worrying return to borrowing from the private sector.[56] Relatedly, respondents pointed to the need for credit, particularly for capital goods.[57]

Collor worked to maintain business confidence by indicating that he shared the same concerns. In response to rising inflation, Collor made his first effort to work out a social pact in June 1990. This effort differed from earlier Brazilian efforts in that it happened quickly and informally. Although the bargaining took place in a quiet backroom, the Brazilian press covered the effort and its unraveling extensively.[58] The idea for the pact arose informally in discussions between Zelia Cardoso de Mello and Luis Antonio Medeiros, the leader of the Força Sindical. The PNBE came in through Emerson Kapaz, who acted as principal intermediator, bringing both FIESP and the CUT into the bargain. On June 18, representatives of all these groups met to negotiate the terms. Soon the group had hammered out the basic terms of the pact, actually only a thirty-day truce. Business promised to freeze its prices voluntarily for thirty days. Workers promised to stop their strikes for wage adjustments. The government promised that it would not raise utility rates and would suspend its public-sector dismissal program. Furthermore, the government proposed to develop a wage policy based on free negotiations and a policy to encourage employee profit sharing. A deal appeared to be in the works.

The deal unraveled, however, as the government stuck to critical aspects of its program. Notably, the government refused to rescind existing orders to dismiss 10,000 public-sector workers. Jaír Meneguelli, leader of the CUT, made it clear that he would not sign any agreement that did not rescind those orders. After a flurry of phone calls, proposals and counterproposals, charges and countercharges, the CUT backed out of the agreement. Cardoso publicly condemned the CUT for torpedoing the *entendimento nacional* (national agreement), especially in view of Collor's willingness to negotiate on crucial policy planks like reducing the federal payroll. The CUT was not the only member unwilling to accept losses. FIESP's 121 syndicates also voted to reject the pact because they refused to accept a limit to their passing cost increases on to prices.[59] In the wake of the negotiations, bargaining descended into a public blamefest. The only productive outcome of the effort was the creation of a

56. Keizo Assahida (Yok Equipamentos), cited in *Estado de São Paulo*, May 27, 1990, p. 8.
57. *Estado de São Paulo*, May 27, 1990, p. 8.
58. See, for example, *Veja*, June 27, 1990, p. 68, and *Isto É Senhor*, June 27, 1990, p. 16, for a detailed accounting of the comings and goings, secret phone calls, rounds of accusations, positions and counterpositions that characterized the ten hours of negotiations.
59. *Folha de São Paulo*, June 26, 1990, p. 4.

tripartite commission with a broad mandate to negotiate terms for a new social pact covering labor–capital relations, deregulation of the economy, private-sector participation in infrastructure investments, definition of priority sectors for investment, and measures attacking poverty and improving education.

With the failure of a social pact, Collor targeted the October 1990 elections to seize control of the Congress. In anticipation of the elections, Collor maintained inflation until shortly before the election when he released large amounts of money for public works projects. Collor's tight hold on inflation stemmed from an accurate assessment of its importance to voters. A survey of voter opinions of Collor's plan in October 1990 found that voters by far supported or opposed him based on their views of inflation's progress.[60] With inflation resurgent and electoral politics on a patronage as opposed to a programmatic axis, Collor emerged from the election without clear support or opposition.

NOVEMBER 1990–APRIL 1991: THE RISE OF BUSINESS–COLLOR CONFLICT

Following Collor's several political and policy failures, his tactical decisions led to a hostile and volatile relation with the business community. By October, the economic situation had deteriorated further. Several business representatives expressed concern over the continuation of the recession and the tightness of the money supply. Prophetically, Emerson Kapaz pointed out that the situation would only worsen as the seasonal cycle slowed down in the beginning of 1991.[61] Business representatives also reiterated their concern that Collor had not addressed long-term anti-inflation measures, such as dealing with the states' debt and fiscal reform.

The need to pass long-lasting reforms became apparent as the one-time shock attack on inflation began to lose force. At the start of his program, Collor had announced that he had one bullet to kill inflation, but the resurgence of inflationary pressure through late 1990 revealed that the bullet had missed. As one businessman noted, Collor's bullet to contain

60. Reported in *Diário de Comércio e Indústria,* November 5, 1990, p. 2.
61. Quoted in *Estado de São Paulo,* October 7, 1990, p. 1.

inflation was enough to have killed an elephant, but it could not kill inflation.[62]

The problem stemmed largely from the unintended effects of the block of *cruzados nôvos* and the subsequent adjustments to the Collor Plan. Wholesale confiscation of a nation's assets had been tried before in Weimar Germany. Otherwise, the measure had few precedents, and little guidance was available from other experiences. As a result, Collor's economic team found themselves making numerous and frequent adjustments to the original plan to permit the economy even to function. Most important, the plan had blocked almost all the private sector's working capital and payrolls. Without it, the basic economic activities of paying suppliers and workers could not continue. By May 1990, Collor's team had permitted forty-eight different exceptions to the blockage. These included measures to free working capital and payrolls, funds for unemployment (the Fundo de Garantia por Tempo de Serviço [FGTS], a specific employment severance fund), retired people, as well as municipalities, donations, and numerous other organizations. In mid-March, total *cruzeiros* in circulation amounted to 9.6 percent of GDP. By mid-April the figure had risen to 14.1 percent by official figures and 20 percent of GDP by private estimates. By mid-June, the Central Bank reported that only 25 percent of the original blocked funds remained in banks.

The large number of exceptions that Collor's government allowed also opened the door to widespread fraud. Although the Central Bank tightened the rules on release of blocked funds, reducing the exemptions from forty-eight to twelve, it had little effect. By private estimates, almost all corporate funds blocked on March 16 had been converted to *cruzeiros* by June 1990.[63] Thus, halfway through the year, Collor's initially tight monetary squeeze had dramatically relaxed. The lifting of virtually all price controls through the course of May, June, and July 1990 added to inflationary pressure. Although removing controls did not lead to a price explosion as businesses tried to recuperate losses, prices still rose faster than Collor's announced inflation goal of 1 percent per month.

This situation continued to deteriorate through the October legislative elections. Inflation passed 10 percent per month by August, and by December it registered 19 percent per month. Greater liquidity, wage adjustments, and price increases all drove inflation up again. The most

62. Confidential author interview, November 1991.

63. Business International, "Coping with Crisis in Brazil: Business Under Collor" (New York, June 1990): 11.

damaging blow to Collor's inflation management efforts came from the October gubernatorial and midterm congressional elections. The states, free to issue debt paper, took advantage of debt financing to spend their way into elections. By the end of elections, states and municipalities had generated, between old and new debt, some U.S.$70 billion. Collor's target of 9 percent annual growth of the money supply gave way to a 116 percent monetary expansion. Inflation seemed out of control once again.

Businesses' concerns began to mount, although most business leaders publicly counseled patience. When in November Mario Amato turned on Collor and the plan, calling it treachery, his remarks sparked a new round of charges and countercharges. As Kandir responded angrily, blaming rising inflation on businesses and workers, the business community denounced Amato. Abram Szajman, president of the São Paulo Federation of Commerce, criticized Amato for failing to take the plan seriously and failing to make the necessary adjustments. He charged Amato with being opposed to modernization.[64] Even Amato's colleagues in the upper echelons of FIESP went out of their way to distance themselves from Amato's critiques. One director anonymously observed that Amato was simply responding to the frustration of having been shut out by the Collor government.[65] Ricardo Semler, one of the country's most influential young businesspeople (Semco, Director of FIESP, and member of IEDI), observed that recession was the route that Collor had chosen and there was nothing to do but patiently wait for the results.[66] Nevertheless, Amato and other business representatives complained about the lack of dialogue and claimed that recession would be easier to accept if they knew what the government planned for the next step.[67]

Faced with the deteriorating economic condition, Collor made tactical choices that heightened business antagonism. The president returned to his favorite villain: the business community. He publicly blamed business speculation for the rising wave of inflation. In separate attacks, members of his staff charged the auto and pharmaceuticals industries with abusive price adjustments. In this context of parceling out blame, Collor issued a decree, *Portaría 852*, demanding information from over seven hundred of the largest firms in the country. The decree sparked a new fight with the business community. Collor's economic team insisted that the information was necessary to better understand the impact of policies on different

64. Quoted in *Diário de Comércio e Indústria,* November 8, 1990, p. 1.
65. *Diário de Comércio e Indústria,* November 8, 1990, p. 1.
66. Quoted in *Estado de São Paulo,* November 18, 1990, p. 4.
67. *Estado de São Paulo,* November 18, 1990, p. 4.

sectors. The business community charged government with being schizophrenic—on the one hand liberalizing, on the other intervening more than any government in the history of Brazil. At issue was the extraordinary amount of detail that the government demanded. It involved over 250 separate pieces of information, including items that firms had already registered once or even more often with other government agencies, items requiring detailed projections of future business, and items such as the name, address, and phone number of every partner of the business. Business representatives charged that the information would be of no use to the government and would simply hurt businesses by driving up administrative costs. In defiance, FIESP counseled outright refusal to comply, but after several days of charges and countercharges, the federation reversed its position and counseled compliance.

Despite FIESP's cooperation, the government unleashed a new shock plan in late January 1991: the so-called Collor Plan II. The second Collor plan amounted to little more than a price freeze, a new set of restrictive rules on wage adjustments, and a freeze on state-level debt paper. The economic team intended to finally remove any indexation from the economy and move toward a total liberation of prices and salaries. It argued that one more shock was necessary to rid the economy of inflationary expectations. The plan astonished the business community. It applauded the proposed end of indexation, but expressed anger and frustration over the new freeze. Nevertheless, business confirmed that it would comply with the new freeze as well, but Collor's credibility suffered badly. One business representative stated outright that inflation was no longer a question of anything but government credibility, and the government had none.

Through January 1991, the relations between Collor and the business community deteriorated. Business anger focused on three things: Collor's unwillingness to negotiate in good faith and the resulting loss of credibility; the costs and distortions created by the wage and price freeze; and the effects of recession. From January 31, the day Collor II took effect, until May 4, the day of Zelia Cardoso de Mello and her team's resignation, the business community openly expressed frustration. Throughout February, March, and April, Collor and his two top economic officials, Zelia Cardoso de Mello and Antonio Kandir, constantly fought with the business community. Business representatives angrily pointed out that the freeze was supposed to be temporary and instead had lasted long enough to produce serious price distortions. They claimed that they would kill their companies if they could not begin responding to price distortions. Unlike earlier freezes, the deep recession left firms with difficult cash flow problems, which made the distortions much more dangerous. Finally, they resisted government restrictions on wage adjustments. They argued that it was unrealistic not to adjust wages to inflation. For these reasons, the business community resorted more and more to illegal activities through March and April.

Emerson Kapaz, coordinator of PNBE, criticized Collor for squandering his credibility through imposed, rather than negotiated solutions.[68] He observed that the irony of Collor's government was that Collor was losing his credibility at the same rapid pace that he had shot up in the polls before the 1989 election. One representative, Aldo Lorenzetti (vice-president of FIESP and Indústrias Lorenzetti), charged the government's policy with pushing business to illegality to cope with wage and price pressure.[69] Other major figures of FIESP's Economic Council, such as Ricardo Semler, José Mindlin, and Antônio Ermírio de Moraes, concurred.[70] Citing concern over strikes and over the fact that workers were facing destitution, FIESP negotiated an illegal wage adjustment with the Metal Workers' Union of São Paulo.[71]

The recession continued to wear heavily on the business community. Charging that few businesses could last for long without some prospect for improvement, Amato tried to reopen a dialogue with Kandir and his team as they in turn sought support for Collor's legislative agenda. The principal focus of the meeting became a debate over whether Ermírio de Moraes meant his harsh criticisms of the Collor government and whether he was really going to suspend U.S.$4 billion worth of investments.[72]

Business representatives had legitimate concerns. The Instituto Brasileiro de Geografia e Estatística (IBGE) figures published in April 1991 revealed that industrial production had fallen 12 percent between February 1990 and February 1991, while open unemployment rose from 4.04 percent to 5.41 percent in the same period. According to one estimate, 40 percent of the country's largest firms were operating at a loss.[73] What particularly aggravated business representatives was the clear loss of

68. Emerson Kapaz, "Chega de Embrulho," *Exame,* March 6, 1991, p. 26.
69. Quoted in *Jornal da Tarde* (São Paulo), April 9, 1991, p. 4.
70. Quoted in *Journal da Tarde,* April 25, 1991, p. 10.
71. *Veja,* April 17, 1991, p. 18.
72. *Gazeta Mercantil,* April 26, 1991, p. 3.
73. Cited in *Jornal da Tarde,* April 21, 1991, p. 7.

monetary control as the state (at all levels of government) continued to spend out of control.[74]

With the failure of his social pact effort, the substantial business disgruntlement that Collor II and *Portaría 852* caused, and without a congressional majority, Collor faced a difficult situation. He needed to start reconstructing a base of support to help push his modernization program. On the other hand, he needed to contain inflation, maintain a fiscal balance, and avoid wage and price indexation to obtain favorable results in critical IMF negotiations. IMF standby loan negotiations affected all other pending private loans. Brazil badly needed the new outflow of capital, and Collor needed it politically, both for his credibility and for financing an ambitious welfare program aimed at the informal-sector poor, population.

In response, Collor made several adjustments. First, he once again clamped down hard on monetary expansion. Second, he unveiled a longer-term modernization plan to respond to criticisms that he was over-emphasizing inflation and failing to signal the government's policy commitments beyond stabilization. Thus, on the first anniversary of his government, Collor released the new project for national reconstruction, the *projetão* (essentially "the huge project"). The *projetão* restated Collor's commitment to modernizing the economy and laid out the new priorities for the government. Among other things, these included old offerings, such as a re-emphasis on privatization (which had not yet occurred) and fiscal reform, as well as new elements, such as the program for industrial competitiveness. The *projetão* also proposed a set of constitutional reforms. Collor claimed that without these reforms, he would be unable to address Brazil's long-standing structural problems. The reforms included a reworking of the distribution of revenues between the federal and lower levels and changes to rules governing the civil service.

The *projetão* laid out a legislative agenda for Collor's modernization program. The key elements to this agenda were port reform, a patent law, a fiscal reform, and a sweeping set of proposed constitutional amendments (dubbed the *emendão,* literally "giant amendment") that Collor claimed were necessary to truly modernize the country. Indeed, both the fiscal and port reforms depended on successfully negotiating the amendments. The amendments addressed crucial structural issues for the state:

74. Comments by Luiz Fernando Furlan (Sadia), in *Jornal da Tarde,* April 21, 1991, p. 7; Claudio Sonder (Hoechst do Brasil) and Olacyr de Moraes (Grupo Itamaraty) in *Jornal da Tarde,* April 23, 1991, p. 12.

the division of revenues between the state and lower levels of government; restrictions on state and municipal rights to issue debt paper; modification of civil service rules, especially job stability and retirement rules; an end to all restrictions on foreign investment; and opening reserved sectors, like mining, to foreign investment. With this project, Collor reminded Brazilians that he was concerned about more than just inflation. This project, he claimed, would bring his government back on the modernization track.

The *projetão* received initially positive responses from business groups whose own proposals differed little in substance from it. Collor's secretary of economic policy, Antonio Kandir, met with 144 business leaders to sell the package to the business community, which still felt bruised from Collor II. Although the *projetão* was well received in principle, the earlier *Portaría* 852 and the price freeze had badly eroded any business confidence in the words of the government.

MAY–DECEMBER 1991: THE *PROJETÃO* NEGOTIATIONS AND COLLOR'S LAST STAND

Collor's growing troubles in Congress and his credibility problems with business forced him to change his tactics. This third period, marked by a cabinet shuffle, witnessed Collor's last unsuccessful efforts to maintain congressional and business support for his program. He had already lost important segments of the business community. This last set of tactical failures pushed significant portions of the remaining industrial community into opposition.

His cabinet shuffle of May 4 introduced a new chapter into his politics: a kinder, gentler Collor who cooperated more and had more credibility (Collor himself referred to it as "his soft style"—*estilo soft*). The soft style included Collor's instructing ministers to open up coffers for public expenditures in exchange for votes. It included allowing the economy to heat up to buy back business support and possibly to create conditions for a social pact. Collor also formally brought the Liberal Front Party (PFL) into his government by appointing some of party boss Antônio Carlos Magalhães's people to cabinet positions.

Through April and May, Collor made several moves to increase his use of patronage to strengthen his hand in Congress. First, he tentatively offered to make it easier for the states to roll over their vast accumulated debt. Collor's tight money policy had stifled governors' easy relations with federal banks and banking authorities. In exchange for their support, Collor offered to open the coffers again, easing the states' difficult financial circumstances. He courted the governor of Rio de Janeiro, Leonel Brizola, and São Paulo's Luis Antônio Fleury. Brizola was among Collor's natural enemies. A politician of the old guard (Brizola was governor of Rio Grande do Sul during the 1964 coup), Brizola's profile was leftist, labor-oriented, virulently nationalist, and antimarket, but he was also an accomplished champion of his state's *descamisados* and a pragmatist. In exchange for Brizola's support, Collor handed him several gifts: the United Nations Environment Conference, significant public works programs, and the national launching of Brizola's pet project, the Cieps, schools for street children. To Fleury, Collor offered to open up the public works coffers and to invest in the state. Collor also restored Sarney's pet project, the Northwest Railroad, a substantial pork project popular in the poor north and by some estimates worth fifty votes alone.[75] Despite this flurry of efforts, Collor's political problems grew.

Collor's best bet rested on the most important new member of the new cabinet, former ambassador to the United States, Marcílio Marques Moreira. As new Minister of the Economy, Moreira committed himself to commercial liberalization, nonintervention, avoidance of shocks, and a credible, constant policy. He immediately proclaimed himself ready to end the freeze and promised an orthodox stabilization without surprises. True to his word, Moreira used the good news of 8 percent inflation in May as the impetus for ending the freeze. The business community entered into negotiations in sectoral chambers with Kandir's replacement, Dorothea Werneck. By the end of June, virtually all prices were free, and Werneck and Moreira had restored Collor's credibility in the business community, but the good news was short-lived.

Despite Collor's newfound willingness to play patronage politics, the legislature defeated, tabled, or watered down virtually his entire legislative program. By now, Congress was asserting itself more and more. The price for cooperation increasingly became both increased patronage and power sharing with Congress and other parties. From mid-1991, Collor continued to move toward appeasing Congress while protecting himself and his cabinet from congressional power-sharing demands.

Collor still maintained control of the public coffers. He still needed to

75. *Carta Política*, Ano 1, no. 1, p. 1.

contain inflation and to maintain a fiscal balance to satisfy IMF concerns. Thus, he maintained a tight money policy and recession as a balance against his increasing spending. Unlike Sarney who unabashedly poured resources into the North and Northeast, Collor played the northern governors against the southern governors, by limiting his payments to them. Finally, he continued to rely on the fragmentation of congressional opposition rather than all-out vote buying.

Congress repaid his patronage austerity by handing him defeat after defeat throughout the legislative session. His sole victories had little to do with him. The first successful privatization, Usiminas, had had the necessary legislation in place since April 1990. The other victory, the end of the computer market reserve, came in September with virtually every interest in the country lined up in favor of the legislation. In June, the independent bloc (PDS-PTB-PL) circulated a note criticizing Collor for the recession and for the lack of compensation for its support.[76] Instead, it sought the leader of the PMDB and heir apparent to the presidency, Orestes Quercia. In response, Collor turned again to the PDT and PSBD to try to include them formally in his government. Again, they turned him down.

By August, inflation had begun spiraling upward again, reaching 14 percent per month. The Congress began negotiating on the *emendão*, but Collor still lacked a congressional majority. Members of Congress quietly observed that Collor had the means to win the votes he needed, but that it would be expensive. Traditional patronage politics in the midst of Brazil's economic crisis undermined efforts to maintain a balanced budget and contain inflation. Winning the necessary votes required Collor's opening the coffers to public works and distributing funds widely enough to purchase 350 seats of the 584 total (Collor needed 60 percent rather than a simple majority to pass constitutional reforms).

Instead, Collor tried to buy the votes of the governors in the hope that their support would win him enough votes in Congress. On August 12, 1991, Collor met with all twenty-seven governors to hammer out an agreement. The key to this agreement was state debt. Collectively, the states owed some U.S.$70 billion dollars from loans as much as twenty years old. Servicing that debt strained the states' budgets. Traditionally, the cozy relations between the states and the Central Bank, Bank of Brazil, and other federal banks (such as the Caixa Econômica) meant an automatic rollover of their debt. The states emitted debt paper, which

76. *Carta Política*, Ano 1, no. 12, p. 4.

these banks bought with money graciously handed over by the federal treasury, which printed the money to cover the payments.[77] Collor's tight control of monetary policy squeezed that relation hard, giving him unusual leverage and the states' unusual financial difficulties.

The terms of the accord were as follows. First, Collor offered to leave off the *emendão* any proposal to transfer state receipts back to the federal government. Second, he proposed a fiscal reform that would increase taxes by lowering the rate and simplifying the system, thereby spreading the burden rather than raising taxes on those who already paid (workers and big business). Third, he offered to ease the restrictions on rolling state debt. Fourth, he offered to ease limits on state-level foreign borrowing. Finally, he offered to open the public works coffers and start investing in the states. In exchange, the governors promised to work out a long-term debt payment scheme; to maintain their spending within a fixed formula that limited payroll expenditures to 65 percent of receipts; and to support (or at least remain neutral on) Collor's legislative package. The successful negotiation became an instant public relations hit, but, the accord had some fatal problems. For one, the government needed 60 percent of the votes to pass Collor's amendments. The Left's opposition could muster 20 percent by itself, leaving very little margin for error. In addition, even the most influential governors, such as those of São Paulo, Paraná, and Rio de Janeiro, could not promise even a majority of their state's representatives. Moreover, almost immediately after making the deal, the governors started trying to separate rolling over their debt from the rest of the agreement. In any event, once Collor rolled over their debts, he would lose any leverage to enforce the deal. Finally, the contents of the proposal alienated too many political players. The governors began backing away from any commitment to help pass the package. In the end, no governor publicly supported it. The game fell back into Congress.

A look at the specific contents of the package reveals some of the political difficulties Collor faced. Measures like those lifting bans on foreign capital participation had become so consensual that even the PT accepted them. Other measures like those ending bank account protection from the government smacked of authoritarianism and provoked opposition. The most important measures, those dealing with bureaucratic reforms, tax reforms, and spending reforms, had virtually no support. For example, the measures ending civil service stability and changing the retirement

77. *The Economist,* December 7, 1991, p. 10.

benefits paid out met formidable opposition.[78] First, the civil service workers had one of the largest and best organized lobbies in Brazil. Brazil's peculiar rule permitting observers to vocally express themselves from the visitor's gallery during congressional debates had a chilling effect on debates. Second, the extraordinary importance of patronage at the state and city levels made support impossible for too many members of Congress.

At the time, an estimated 30 percent of sitting members of Congress planned to run in 1992's mayoral elections. Thus, the redistribution of federal revenues faced substantial opposition. For the same reasons as the added opposition of the governors, the measure proposing a redistribution of spending obligations to the cities and the states had no chance. Realizing that his strategy was not going to work, Collor opened up social pact negotiations again. In this case, Collor faced the upcoming *emendão* negotiations with poor support in Congress. He hoped to use a social pact to give him the base he needed to pass his reforms. This time, he included the governors, the political parties, and Congress in his negotiations. On the business side, IEDI had replaced the PNBE as his principal interlocutor. The process began this third time in meetings between Collor and a small group of prominent businesspeople, including Luis Carlos Mandelli of FIERGS, Amato, Albano Franco (president of the CNI), Paulo Cunha (president of IEDI), and Leon Max Feffer of IEDI. This group supported Collor's call for constitutional changes and presented a document with five points: first, a statement of support for Collor's policies and for a social pact as a means of overcoming the nation's problems; second, a call for urgent structural reforms to address the public sector's fiscal disequilibrium and to restore the credibility of the *cruzeiro* as well as an appeal to Congress to cooperate in this task; third, a commitment to stop using shocks as an anti-inflation mechanism; fourth, a commitment to stop resorting to high interest rates without fiscal reform; and fifth, an understanding that episodic attacks on inflation erode the government's credibility and make social actors defensive. That being the case, the document called for a commitment by the government to attack the base of inflation: public-sector finance.[79]

Both sides emerged satisfied from this meeting. The business representatives had supported Collor's constitutional amendments. Collor had

78. This reform problem has been discussed in great detail by Weyland, "How Much Political Power."

79. The entire document submitted to Collor can be found in the *Diário de Comércio e Indústria,* September 6, 1991, p. 7.

promised to put aside shock plans.[80] For business groups, which had branded the constitution a disaster before the ink was dry, Collor's proposals made sense, and for Collor, business's demands exactly coincided with his program. Although both sides emerged happy with their agreement, the negotiations were left where they really mattered: with the governors, Congress, and the parties.

It was at this level that the last effort at social pact making died. By mid-September, the magazine *Exame* ventured a prediction: the *entendimento* was dying in a zero-sum conflict, Collor would eventually act, and as usual the result would fall on business's head.[81] The article, published on September 18, appears prophetic in hindsight. Antônio Delfim Netto took a lonely position among his peers in Congress in publicly criticizing the social pact effort. In a column in the *Folha de São Paulo,* he observed that social pact negotiations included every item imaginable without limits and left the mess for Collor to veto.[82] Mockingly, he observed that "[w]e learned some time ago that when a project is the result of a 'leaders' accord' the result is probably suicidal." He concluded by arguing that without a reform of the electoral system, social pacts are pure illusions.

True to Delfim Netto's observations, the negotiations quickly came to naught. Despite the best efforts of individuals like Ceará Governor Ciro Gomes and even of Collor who openly wooed opposition parties, offered them seats in his cabinet, and expanded his patronage spending, the negotiations never produced anything even as remotely tangible as the 1990 documents. Eventually, several business and labor participants broke off their negotiations with the government, turning their work into an anti-Collor pact.

The last months of 1991 witnessed Collor's growing powerlessness in the face of a resurgent, but angry and opportunistic Congress. Collor continued to try to purchase limited support for his package. Among the key negotiators were the five leading contenders to succeed Collor: Lula (PT), Orestes Quercia (PMDB), Brizola (PDT), Antonio Carlos Magalhaes (PFL), and Tasso Jereissati (PSDB); none of whom were interested in ceding too much to the embattled president.[83] In turn, only Lula could actually claim to speak for his party's members in Congress. With Col-

80. *Diário de Comércio e Indústria,* September 6, 1991, p. 7.
81. *Exame,* September 18, 1991, p. 18.
82. Antônio Delfim Netto, "Entendimento Nacional," in *Folha de São Paulo,* September 11, 1991, p. 2.
83. *Carta Política,* Ano 1, no. 26, pp. 1–2.

lor's difficulties, a new strategy emerged in Congress and among the governors: power sharing.

The *emendão* came up for consideration in November 1992. By that time, both the Congress and Collor had ample complaints about each other. Congress charged the government with arrogance or worse for submitting a measure with forty-four constitutional amendments without establishing priorities. Rumors circulated that Collor wanted it to fail so that he could pull off a "soft" coup like Alberto Fujimori of Peru. Members of Congress charged that the government had not decided which minister was coordinating the government's effort—Moreira, Justice Minister Jarbas Passarinho, or Strategic Affairs Secretary Egberto Batista. In turn, Collor's team complained that the governors had backed off their deal and that there was nobody with whom to negotiate in Congress. Essentially, the political parties and party leadership had become irrelevant in the face of their own disorganization.

In late November, congressional leaders, angry and immobile, finally effectively killed the bill. They split the package into five different clusters of amendments. Then they tabled them without any timetable for resuming debate. This measure, effectively killing the package, passed easily. By the time of Collor's impeachment in December 1992, the Congress still had not considered the *emendão*.

Collor's strategy may not have been the best he could have chosen, but his weakness in Congress and the political price that Congress exacted for every negotiation made it a plausible one. Collor then threw all his political weight behind it. He repeatedly made the case in public that the amendments he proposed were necessary to effectively govern. He warned of looming ungovernability and reminded the Congress of his legitimacy via his 35 million votes. He warned that without the amendments, he could not make any program work.[84] Critics charged that there were alternatives to constitutional amendments to address fiscal imbalances, noting that some states had done it (notably Ceará). Some groups, particularly the PNBE, argued that in any event constitutional changes should take place in the context of widely participatory debates.[85] However valid the latter argument, the former holds little water. Ceará's governors, Tasso Jereissati followed by Ciro Gomes, had cleaned up the state's finances largely by not paying the salaries of public-sector workers

84. Collor's views on Brazil's governability problems are set out in Power, "The Pen Is Mightier Than the Congress."

85. PNBE, open letter opposing the *emendão*. Confidential author interviews PNBE members, October–November, 1991.

who did not show up for work (the maharajahs), but, under the provisions of the 1988 Constitution, that strategy became illegal.[86]

With the death of the *emendão*, Collor immediately faced a new crisis in Congress. The depth of the recession had produced much lower revenues than expected, and estimates for 1991 were for a budget deficit of 2 percent of GDP. The *emendão*'s proposed fiscal reforms fell with it, leaving Collor with no means to make up the shortfall. With the IMF standing over his head, Collor, and indeed Brazil, faced a potential disaster. Publicly admitting that the union was broke, Collor asked for an immediate emergency tax reform. Collor hoped to raise U.S.$12 billion dollars by year-end to impress the skeptical IMF negotiators. He proposed raising the tax rate on the highest income bracket to 35 percent from 25 percent, reindexing taxes (which Collor had ended and which alone had caused a U.S.$4 billion shortfall on federal revenues), and anticipating the collection date for the 1992 corporate income tax on big businesses.

Congress, still angry from the *emendão* negotiations and Collor's apparent about-face on the parliamentarism plebiscite, preferred not to give its support to the tax increase. Some members expressed concern about Collor's likely use of receipts to fund election war chests.[87] At the same time, declining tax receipts and shortfalls on expected privatization revenues had created serious financial difficulties. At stake were the IMF negotiations and several smaller states that depended exclusively on the federal government for revenues. Similarly, fiscal difficulties threatened municipal works programs vital to the mayoral elections at the end of 1992.

In the end, Congress came through with Collor's emergency tax bill. To secure its approval, Collor gave up his only powerful playing card, agreeing to unconditionally reschedule the states' and cities' U.S.$70 billion in accumulated debt. Furthermore, the Congress trimmed Collor's access to new resources by dropping the tax increase on the highest rate of personal income, a politically unpopular measure. Collor signed the new bill into law on December 31, 1991.

DECEMBER 1991–SEPTEMBER 1992: THE ROAD DOWN

Despite Collor's successful tax hike, he now faced much more determined business opposition than at any point in his administration. From Decem-

---

86. *Gazetinha* (GM International Edition, New York), September 16, 1991, p. 3.
87. *Carta Política*, Ano 1, no. 34, p. 4.

ber 1991 until his suspension, Collor steadily lost ground to an increasingly hostile Congress, public, and business community. Collor's tax increase promised U.S.$8 billion in revenues, which proved sufficient for him to manage an IMF agreement by January 1992. The country still needed serious tax reform, which depended on constitutional changes. Collor's resort to a tax increase on business coupled with Moreira's intense recessionary policy pushed business deeper into opposition.

By the end of 1991, the depth of recession had produced new dynamics in business attitudes. Amato publicly gave up on Collor, shifting his appeal to the Congress to do the right thing for the market. Business opposition coalesced around the governors, who led the political movement against the recession and, for the first time, against commercial liberalization. Among other public calls against the recession, Governor Luis Antônio Fleury Filho of São Paulo state led a vigil of hope with workers and business.[88]

For some industry representatives, the pressure to adjust without supportive conditions changed their political positions. Both public statements and private interviews revealed a growing opposition to lowering import tariffs from concern about the future. As one representative put it, opposition had become a question of survival.[89] These views emerged particularly in sectors such as machine tools and equipment and electroelectronics.

The change in attitudes is captured in surveys by the National Confederation of Industry conducted in 1992. The most striking results relate to the change in evaluation of the market opening. First, comparing the results to its previous survey in 1991, it concluded that the business evaluation of the pace of the opening had shifted from "moderate" to "fast."[90] This change occurred despite the relatively weak effects of imports. The depth of the recession clearly discouraged imports as much as it did consumption of domestic goods. Similarly, as opposed to Oliveira's earlier survey, only 31 percent of respondents in this survey reported that the market opening encouraged investments, and only half claimed to be ready to face foreign competition. Finally, also unlike Oliveira's earlier survey, the uncertainty of the economy registered as the most serious concern businesses faced (Table 5.2).

By 1992, 25 percent inflation per month, tremendous recession, tight

88. Reported in *Folha de São Paulo,* December 13, 1991, p. 1.

89. Interview, official of Brazilian Association of Electro-Electronics Producers (ABINEE).

90. CNI, "Abertura Comercial e Estratégia Tecnológica: A Visão de Lideres Industriais Brasileiras" (Rio de Janeiro, 1992).

Table 5.2.   Evaluation of commercial liberalization, 1992

Evaluation of Pace of Opening (very slow 1; very fast 6)			*Effect of Competition from Imports* (very little 1; very strong 6)		
		Distribution of Results			
Slow	(1–3)	37.7%	Little	(1–3)	72.5%
	(1–2)	9.2		(1–2)	51.2
Fast	(4–6)	60.7	Strong	(4–6)	26.0
	(5–6)	16.3		(5–6)	12.5

Effect on Investments		*Preparation for Foreign Competition* (Very unprepared 1; very prepared 6)		
Encouraged	31.7%	Unprepared	(1–3)	49.0%
Discouraged	11.9		(1–2)	20.2
No impact	48.3	Prepared	(4–6)	49.7
			(5–6)	24.7

Principal Obstacles to Adjustment

Very unimportant	1
Very important	6

	Distribution of Results		
	Unimportant (1–3)	(1–2)	Important (4–6)
Uncertainty about the economy	17.8%	7.3%	79.6%
Exchange rate	36.8	13.7	60.4
Domestic tax load	6.9	2.1	91.2
Absence of adequate financing	21.3	6.9	76.3

SOURCE: CNI: Abertura Comercial e Estratégia Tecnológica, 1992

money (real interest rates hit 7 percent per month), Collor's legislative failures, and the conversion of a promised tax reform into a simple tax hike badly eroded support for the president's program. Increasingly, business groups and governors turned on liberalization itself as fear of foreign imports grew. Nevertheless, Moreira held his line and even accelerated the pace of tariff reduction by moving the schedule ahead six months. Despite the unpopularity of his policies, Moreira continued to have high credibility. His successful negotiations with the IMF and his credibility in the international community lent him esteem and credibility at home. His strict avoidance of shocks and the consistency of his policy helped him as well. Although businesspeople had begun to resist liberalization, had grown concerned about the length of the recession, and were frustrated with Moreira's unwillingness to negotiate with them, they appreciated the stability and certainty he did offer. Werneck, the Secretary for Industry, added to the credibility of the team through her highly respected performance in the sectoral chambers.

Nevertheless, 1992 saw a new set of indicators that pointed to the changes in the political stance of the business community. Up until that time, few business organizations had publicly opposed the commercial opening and the neoliberal program in general. Now, however, more associations expressed concern and opposition to the pace and extent of the commercial opening as well as to the maintenance of the anti-inflationary recession.

Among the growing number of expressions of concern, two are particularly important. The first was the return to the public political arena of the automobile producers' association (ANFAVEA). The second turned around the election for a new president of FIESP, only the second contested election in its fifty-five-year history. ANFAVEA, probably justifiably, boasted of its ability to remove economic ministers at will throughout the 1980s, but despite being the single most powerful business organization in Brazil, it had remained very quiet about the Collor program until March 1992. This silence was surprising given that Brazilian producers (GM, Ford, Volkswagen, Fiat, Chrysler, and Mercedes-Benz) were notoriously inefficient and were already facing stiff competition on a global scale from Japanese and Korean producers. Even more surprising, in a government-business-labor seminar on modernizing the industry in January 1992, the auto producers indicated strong support for the program.

In March, ANFAVEA changed its position. Jacy Mendonça, the outgoing president of the association, fired the first volley in what eventually became a campaign against government policy, for the imposition of restrictive import quotas. He announced that the demand for cars in Brazil had a ceiling and that for every car imported, one would stop being produced domestically and five jobs would be lost. In a country where urban violence is rampant because of gross social and economic inequalities, his threat was not an idle one.[91]

Although ANFAVEA's return to open political activity was significant,

91. The auto industry ultimately succeeded in negotiating preferential treatment for itself under the Fernando Henrique Cardoso administration. The so-called auto industrial policy is discussed in greater length in Chapters 6 and 7, but it is notable that the auto assemblers are the only industrial sector in Brazil that was able to reverse, at least partially, the commercial liberalization process.

the dynamics around the presidential election in FIESP says more about the issues in the São Paulo business community at large. The dominant theme of this election was which candidate was capable of modernizing the corporatist federation. Both camps operated with the same analysis of the problems in the Brazilian economy and the role of FIESP. The widely held belief was that FIESP was simply incapable of leading the business community in defense of its interests. The most glaring fault was its inability to stand up before the government and propose solutions as well as oppose policies that the business community believed were hurtful. Among those policies were tax reform and the pace of modernization. The themes of this campaign were developed and discussed from January 1992, when the opposition candidate, PNBE coordinator Emerson Kapaz, declared, until July 29, 1992, the date of the election.

In addition to FIESP's growing opposition, two rival organizations began to express resistance. Two organizations had broken away from FIESP in the 1980s in protest against FIESP's ineffectiveness. One mentioned earlier, PNBE, was the revolt of small and young businesses; the second, the Instituto de Estudos parao Desenvolvimento Industrial (Institute for the Study of Industrial Development—IEDI), was the revolt of the biggest businesses in Brazil. IEDI in particular began to assert itself in 1992 as a leader of business opposition to the commercial opening. The movement of these two organizations into opposition is even more striking because Collor had actively sought them out earlier as interlocutors who represented "modern business" as opposed to FIESP or ANFAVEA.

In fact, interviews in late 1991 and 1992 with business leaders from both the so-called modern and backward (or corporatist) organizations revealed widespread opposition to Collor and the market opening. Increasingly, industrialists spoke of *selvagem capitalismo* ("capitalist wilderness," a term that spoke of a destructive form of capitalism) and *sucateamento* (literally "junking" or "scrapping"). A number of sectors pushed hard for changes to the pace of tariff reduction. Some highly mobilized and politically well connected sectors achieved some success. Most notably, toy makers, a sector highly involved in the PNBE, secured a delay in their sector's tariff reduction schedule.

In March 1992, Collor's troubles deepened. Pedro Collor, the president's brother, leveled charges of corruption against Collor and his campaign treasurer and good friend P. C. Farias. A congressional inquiry began to investigate the charges against Farias with the hope and expectation that the president would not be affected. In the carnival of charges, confessions, and investigations, Collor eventually emerged as a central figure in a parallel, corrupt government structure.

Faced with this array of attacks, Collor shifted course again. In April 1992, Collor passed a sweeping cabinet reform designed to address concerns about corruption and make new friends in Congress. Although he did not succeed in luring opposition PMDB and PSDB members into his cabinet, observers roundly applauded the quality of his appointments. The three most critical features of the reform were the appointment of the eminent coalition builder Jorge Bornhausen, the preservation of Moreira as economy minister, and the purge of the so-called Republic of Alagoas "kitchen cabinet." This latter move responded to congressional anger that the president's influence-peddling, war-chest–building backers held important posts in the cabinet. Congressman (and former finance minister) Delfim Netto dubbed this change as "Collor 3" (Collor 1 and 2 corresponding to the "hard" and "soft" styles before the shuffle). Despite receiving praise for the change, Collor was helped little by it.

With the deepening of the corruption scandal during May, June, and July, Collor ended up in a pure patronage deal with Antônio Carlos Magalhães of the PFL and governor of Bahia. In exchange for the second-largest party's support, Collor opened the coffers for northern and northeastern states (the PFL's primary base). Even so, with increasing evidence of his complicity in the corruption scheme, growing popular disapproval, and a free television hour for the November 1992 mayoral campaigns approaching, even the PFL abandoned Collor. In September 1992, the Congress suspended the president, and the vice-president, Itamar Franco, assumed office. Finally, in December, the Congress formally impeached Collor, ending his presidency and his modernization program.

In fact, the end of Collor's program had arrived by March 1992. Between March and September, Collor lost all credibility and spent most of his time dealing with the scandal. Moreira became the central figure, holding the government up by his credibility and integrity. Even the business community held a major political event in support of Moreira and against calls for his removal by political opponents. It explicitly rejected any suggestion of support for the embattled president.

The most telling sign was the final collapse of Collor's legislative efforts. A proposed tax reform in June became little more than another tax hike in the hands of a patronage-dependent Congress. Similarly, the Congress passed the proposed modernization of the port of Santos (the most expensive port in the world) after removing virtually all modernizing measures.[92] Aside from these two legislative failures, Collor did not introduce any new legislation.

Overall, except for privatization (which Franco substantially slowed on assuming office) Collor passed very little of his modernizing program through Congress. With public debt and deficit spending unresolved, stabilization failed utterly. With high, persistent inflation, a series of legislative failures, and the loss of credibility and business support, the modernization program was aborted. With the Congress hungrily eyeing presidential elections for 1994 and the lame duck nationalist Franco as president, modernization was effectively tabled until 1995.

The industrial community was left in a difficult position. Collor's political decline left it without any strategic orientation. Franco's accession to the presidency returned the Brazilian economy to its precommercial liberalization state. High inflation with indexation permitted easy financial speculation and passing high prices on to customers. Uncertainty about the future left firms reluctant to invest in new adjustment strategies and reluctant to shift to imported inputs. Many politically important segments had grown more reluctant to embrace neoliberal reform, yet no other alternative presented itself. As a consequence, industry entered a limbo, economically and politically, as it awaited some new indication of the country's policy direction.

---

92. Collor's failure to advance significant portions of his program is discussed in Suzigan and Villela, *Industrial Policy in Brazil.*

6

Recrafting the Coalition

Fernando Henrique Cardoso and the
Consolidation of Neoliberal Reform

Fernando Henrique Cardoso successfully recrafted the neoliberal coalition after Collor's impeachment and the Franco interregnum. Cardoso's
coalition linked voters grateful for the Real Plan's success with business
elites expecting greater legislative success than Collor had achieved. Yet
despite significant conjunctural advantages over Collor, Cardoso quickly
ran into many of the same political obstacles. As his legislative agenda
ground to a halt, industrial leaders in many organizations increased their
political pressure on the government while actively exploring coalitional
alternatives. Unlike Collor, Cardoso responded much better tactically. He
extended new benefits and incentives to industrialists and introduced a
re-election amendment that forced industrialists to actively choose between him and all other candidates. The moves reinvigorated political
support for Cardoso and maintained the industrial adjustment process.
This chapter examines Cardoso's tactical decisions and the resulting business responses.

SEPTEMBER 1992–FEBRUARY 1994: THE FRANCO PRESIDENCY AND ADJUSTMENT ON HOLD

The Brazilian Congress voted overwhelmingly to impeach President Fernando Collor on December 30, 1992. The vote transformed Vice-President Itamar Franco from interim to actual president of the republic.

Interviews in the business community in 1992 suggested a substantial degree of apprehension about Franco's competence. By early 1993, those apprehensions seemed warranted. Franco's term consisted of a disheartening mélange of failed and controversial policies and squandered opportunities. Franco could boast of only two real contributions: he appeared to be scrupulously honest, and he appointed Fernando Henrique Cardoso as finance minister in May 1993 and relinquished active governing to him.

Franco revealed his inadequacies as interim president through his appointment and frequent rapid replacements of, and tense relations with, his finance ministers. In October 1992, Franco surprised and disappointed business observers with his appointment of a little-known member of Congress, Gustavo Krause. Although not considered an ideal choice, business observers, foreign and domestic, took solace in Krause's expressed commitment to Moreira's policy agenda. It quickly became apparent, however, that Franco's strong populist tendencies conflicted with Krause's orthodox inclinations. Franco clashed with Krause over his proposed increase in fuel prices and his economic plan. Franco rejected the plan Krause developed in conjunction with Planning Minister Paulo Haddad as too Collor-like. By December 1992, Krause had had enough and quit. Despite their differences, Franco moved Haddad to the position.

Franco's next two ministers, Haddad and Rezende, together lasted five months. In that time, Franco announced a move away from a commitment to stabilization to renewing growth even at the expense of rising inflation. Privatization slowed as Franco made clear his lack of enthusiasm for the program. Not surprisingly, growth resumed again by mid-1993, but so did inflation. Through 1993, monthly inflation crept up from 25 percent in August 1992 under Collor to nearly 50 percent by March 1994.

Business groups retained their concern for long-term reform, but they also took advantage of short-term opportunities for profit. Collor's induced recession had proved difficult. The new context did not present a long-term solution, but Brazilian businesses knew how to profit under high inflation; adjustment efforts could remain on hold until the government credibly addressed the country's structural problems.

Interviews through 1992 also suggested that most businesspeople believed that several crucial opportunities remained for resolving Brazil's long-term problems: the 1993 plebiscite on the form of government; the 1993 constitutional review; and the 1994 presidential election. The 1988 Constitution had called for a plebiscite, to be held in 1993, on the form of government. Most Brazilian observers believed that a parliamentary system would serve Brazil better than presidentialism. As a result, many leading politicians, including Tasso Jereissati, PSDB, and Lula, PT, had been campaigning for parliamentarism. In fact, Jereissati, among other congressional leaders, had tried to use the plebiscite as a bargaining tool with Collor. In exchange for Collor's support on an early vote for parliamentarism, Jereissati and others offered to support his constitutional reforms. With Collor out of the picture and Franco showing no signs of effective presidential leadership, the leading candidates for parliamentarism also led in the polls for the country's next president. In a predictable turnabout, Jereissati and Lula joined Orestes Quercia, PMDB, another leading presidential contender, in the campaign for presidentialism. The plebiscite occurred in April 1993, and presidentialism won with 53 percent of the vote.

The second opportunity arose with the constitutional review and once again proved a disappointment. The writers of the 1988 Constitution, recognizing the flaws in their work, had mandated a review for 1993, during which members of Congress would have the opportunity to reconsider articles they found flawed. Slated to begin in October 1993, opponents succeeded in substantially delaying the process. Opponents, primarily the PT and the labor movement, successfully resisted what they labeled an assault on social rights and a betrayal of the country. Their resistance included an effective public relations campaign, court challenges, and violence in the Chamber of Deputies—from ripping the government's proposal in half, to tearing a microphone cord out of a desk—including at least one fist fight. In the end, the review process overwhelmingly failed. Members of Congress revealed that in the majority they supported constitutional reforms but would not vote for them.[1] To avoid having to make unpleasant choices, members of Congress stayed away from key votes again and again in numbers sufficient to deprive the Congress of the necessary quora. Furthermore, members of Congress swamped the congressional committee on the constitution and justice with seventeen thousand amendments and an additional twelve thousand subamendments. Of those, only thirty-two were ever read out of committee, and only six were approved. Of the six, only two had any real significance: the creation of the Social Emergency Fund (discussed below) and the reduction in the term of the president from five years to four.[2]

1. Survey evidence cited in Lamounier, "Brazil."
2. Discussed in Murillo de Aragão, "Ação dos grupos de pressão nos processos constitucionais recentes no Brasil" (paper presented at the Latin American Studies Association, Washing-

Business leaders made a concerted effort to influence the review process. Led by Jorge Gerdau Johannpeter (a founding member of the Liberal
Institute and IEDI), business leaders formed a coordination organization
called Ação Empresarial (Business Action). Ação Empresarial developed
a list of desired reforms and positions on proposed reforms and then actively pushed all business organizations to lobby on the common platform. The list had grown from discussions in the Liberal Institute and
thus reflected a business effort to push toward liberalizing the Brazilian
state and improving the state's fiscal balances. Interviews with industrialists revealed satisfaction with the organization, particularly the idea of a
coordinating group as opposed to renewing efforts to create a genuine
peak organization. Nevertheless, Ação Empresarial registered scarcely
any successes. Even a successfully coordinated lobbying campaign was
unable to overcome legislators' narrowly defined electoral priorities.

Perhaps the most important short-term success of the constitutional
review lay in the creation of the Social Emergency Fund. Responsibility
for its creation, a critical component of the success of the Real Plan of
1994, lay with Fernando Henrique Cardoso. Appointed Finance Minister
in May 1993, Cardoso soon took over the reins of government. This shift
represented a decisive retreat from Franco's populist tendencies to a renewed, determined commitment to stabilization. Cardoso took several
policy steps in 1993 and 1994, but probably none was as important and
skillfully effected as the passage of the Social Emergency Fund.

As noted earlier, the 1988 Constitution shifted roughly one-quarter of
the federal government's revenues to the states and municipalities without
accompanying spending obligations. This contribution was important to
Brazil's structural deficits. The Social Emergency Fund countered this
problem by recovering 20 percent of the federal government's revenues
for "social emergencies" for a period of two years. The fund was primarily a fiscal adjustment used to contain Brazil's fiscal deficit. It was not
a popular measure among members of Congress, and early indications
suggested that it would not pass. Cardoso, however, combined a set of

---

ton, D.C., September 28–30, 1995), 11. The other four increased the power of the Congress
to call bureaucrats to testify and permitted dual citizenship for Brazilians and ethics measures
for holder of elective offices. The last two in particular were meaningless given the extreme
weakness of ethics enforcement in Brazil's electoral system. For a discussion of the extraordinary difficulties in enforcing ethics requirements in Brazilian politics, see David Fleischer, "Attempts at Corruption Control in Brazil: Congressional Investigations and Strengthening
Internal Control" (paper presented at the Latin American Studies Association, Washington,
D.C., September 28–30, 1995).

bargains that dispensed patronage and substantially weakened the original proposal with effective hardball politics. Facing likely defeat, Cardoso took his campaign to television, where he pitted his high credibility against the dismal reputation of the Congress. Cardoso made his case to the public with the added threat that without passage of the Social Emergency Fund, he would quit. Cowed by this effective tactic, the Congress voted to grant him the fund.[3]

Cardoso made several other efforts to improve the state's fiscal situation. His first act as Finance Minister was to pass the immediate action program. The plan included sharp reductions in spending by the federal government, measures to crack down on tax evasion, which enjoyed some success, and measures to force the states to make payments on their massive, outstanding debt obligations. All told, the immediate action program played an important, albeit short-term, role in improving the government's 1994–95 tax revenues and expenditures. Tax revenues climbed from under 25 percent of GDP in 1992 and 1993 to over 31 percent in 1995, while the operational deficit dropped from a 2.2 percent deficit in 1992 to a 1.3 percent surplus in 1994.[4] Spending cuts amounted to U.S.$6 billion, while pressure to enforce the states' debt obligations promised an additional U.S.$2 billion.[5] Efforts to control state banks' practice of issuing credit were less successful.

Several other measures also performed less well. Cardoso tried yet another social pact, the "Agenda Brasil," which failed when both the CUT and the CGT walked out. He also reissued the controversial IPMF, a tax on all financial transactions. The new tax was expected to raise U.S.$600 million per month, but it provoked a minirevolt with cities and states refusing to pay it, banks threatening to circumvent it, and even the press publishing tricks to avoid it. As one prominent television announcer put it: "[T]he people of this country are tired of paying one more illegal tax so that afterward the money should be wasted and even stolen."[6] Eventually, the courts struck down the tax as illegal.[7]

Business adjustments came to a standstill in this context. Brazil re-

3. Even then the fund proposal was substantially watered down during negotiations with the Congress. Suzigan and Villela, *Industrial Policy in Brazil,* 104.

4. *Exame,* July 3, 1996, p. 30.

5. Baer, *Brazilian Economy,* 191–92.

6. Boris Casoy, news announcer for SBT News, August 25, 1993.

7. It is interesting to note that during 1991–92 a number of businesspeople joined a small but passionate movement endorsing the financial transaction tax, but they intended it as a substitute for the existing set of taxes. This instance illustrates the tendency of tax reform efforts to turn into simple tax hikes.

corded almost no new capital inflows. Productive investment slowed considerably as did privatizations, but businesses were able to survive. The Franco government allowed growth to resume, albeit with high and rising inflation. Businesses knew how to profit in this situation. Setting high profit margins on low volumes while engaging in financial speculation by lending to a desperate government was a familiar survival strategy for business. Nevertheless, business leaders understood in the 1980s that this strategy was not long term. Accordingly, they waited for a new reform program.

MARCH 1994–APRIL 1995: CONFIDENT CARDOSO AND ADJUSTMENTS RESUMED

In December 1993, Cardoso changed the course of the Brazilian political economy. Seeking to avoid the tendency of previous finance ministers to drop unannounced stabilization plans on Congress and society, Cardoso introduced to Congress a new stabilization proposal, the Real Plan.[8] The intention was to allow Congress and society time to discuss and digest the plan before any changes actually occurred. After fifteen years of failed and often extremely invasive stabilization plans, Brazilians were skeptical of government efforts to contain inflation. More important, they were conditioned to engage in speculative and opportunistic behavior when they thought a plan was impending. This was rational behavior on their part. Most Brazilian stabilization plans in the 1980s and 1990s had tended to violate contracts and to include wage and price freezes with arbitrary and unequal impact. As a consequence, it made sense for economic actors to try to anticipate stabilization plans by raising their prices or wages before the freeze.[9] Cardoso's effort to make the plan as transpar-

---

8. For full discussions of the technical details of the Real Plan, see Bresser Pereira, *Economic Crisis and State Reform*; Jeffrey Sachs and Álvaro Zini Jr., "Brazilian Inflation and the *Plano Real*," *World Economy* 19, no. 1 (1996): 13–38; Gesner Oliveira, "The Brazilian Economy Under the Real: Prospects for Stabilization and Growth" (paper presented at the Latin American Studies Association, Washington, D.C., September 28–30, 1995); a brief discussion in Baer, *Brazilian Economy,* 377–79; and Fishlow, "Is the Real Plan for Real?" in Susan Kaufman Purcell and Riordan Roett, eds., *Brazil Under Cardoso* (Boulder, Colo.: Lynne Rienner, 1997).

9. An excellent discussion of this dynamic can be found in Bresser Pereira, *Economic Reforms in New Democracies: A Social Democratic Approach* (New York: Cambridge University Press, 1993), 50–52.

ent and predictable as possible was an important step, which significantly eased the introduction of the plan.

In February 1994, Cardoso continued with the policy of easing the Real Plan into implementation by introducing the unit of real value (URV). Brazilians had survived and in fact prospered under high inflation by developing a sophisticated system of indexing prices and wages to the rate of inflation. A number of agencies, from universities to the government, produced units of reference to allow economic actors to adjust their contracts. The URV was a unit of reference pegged to the exchange rate and adjusted daily. The point was to create a unit of reference with greater stability and credibility than one pegged to Brazil's currency, without either the shock of a currency reform or the vulnerability to external shock entailed in a full-scale dollarization plan as in Argentina.

Under Cardoso, the government began to adjust its contracts and quote its prices with reference to the URV. Cardoso also encouraged private actors to do the same. Thus, over time, the URV became a mechanism to allow private actors to adjust their contracts in anticipation of the currency reform, but without the shock and without wage and price controls. The initial results were positive and expected from a technical point of view, but they were not politically popular. Initially, the implicit dollarization led to real price increases that were poorly received and poorly understood. Popular approval for the program remained below 40 percent into June 1994.

On July 1, the URV was converted into the new currency, the *real*. The rewards appeared almost immediately. By the end of July, inflation had fallen sharply from 46 percent in June, to 24.7 percent in July to 3.3 percent in August.[10] Not surprisingly, popular support for the plan rose from 37 percent approval in May to over 70 percent by the presidential election of October 1994.

The success of the *real* hinged on several factors. First, the developers of the Real Plan correctly saw the slow and transparent introduction of the plan as the key to solving the government's low credibility. The gradual introduction, coupled with its announcement three months before its implementation, provided a window of time for actors to adjust their contracts and prevented a situation in which parties felt that the currency reform had resulted in breaches of their contracts. It also minimized the efforts of private parties to gain advantage by raising prices in anticipation of the reform.

10. Data from Sachs and Zini, "Brazilian Inflation."

Second, the fiscal reform of 1993, through the immediate action program and especially through the Social Emergency Fund, gave the plan a solid fiscal base on which to stand. Previous efforts like the Cruzado Plan had failed partly because the government did not live up to its commitments to address its own fiscal imbalances. The result was that fiscal deficits helped to fuel a resurgence of inflation as well as to undermine the credibility of the reform. Given the strength of inertial inflation in Brazil, factors that decreased private actors' confidence only worked to reinforce rather than eliminate the memory of inflation.

A third crucial factor was the government's commitment to restrictive monetary policy. The Cardoso team through the Franco and Cardoso administrations remained committed to restraining monetary expansion. It maintained this policy even in the face of the sharp recession that hit by mid-1995 and in the face of the enormous inflow of foreign investment that resumed in 1993 and was still growing as of 1998. This policy area in particular presented a real challenge to the Cardoso government. Successive Brazilian governments had had difficulty controlling the creation of money by government banks such as the Bank of Brazil, Banespa (São Paulo), and Banerj (Rio de Janeiro), as well as private banks.

Finally, the success of the Real Plan depended on several legacies from Fernando Collor. First, Collor's trade liberalization program, initiated in 1990, reached its conclusion in 1994, exactly in time for the inception of the Real Plan. The result was that import competition undermined Brazilian producers' traditional ability to pass on costs to consumers. The most important piece of protection for economic actors trying to speculate or behave opportunistically during a stabilization plan had been the certainty that indexation allowed consumers to absorb rising prices while high tariff barriers guaranteed that consumers had no choice. Trade liberalization exacted a heavy toll from producers who ignored import competition. In fact, the initial success of the Real Plan sparked a boom of import consumption through the last quarter of 1994 and into the first quarter of 1995. The surge in demand effectively disciplined any producer inclined to raise prices speculatively.

A second legacy of the Collor period was that the state's fiscal situation was already in decent shape when Cardoso initiated his fiscal adjustment. Much of Collor's fiscal adjustment stemmed from the temporary freezing of payments and monetary correction on state debt, but Collor did leave behind him relatively small operational deficits and primary surpluses, in sharp contrast to the situation Collor inherited of small primary deficits and operational deficits in excess of 5 percent of the GDP.

Finally, Collor's last legacy was his corruption scandal and the budget scandal that immediately followed his downfall. The budget scandal had the potential to bring down almost half of Congress, but was contained to the seven most visible offenders (the "seven dwarfs") who were expelled in early 1993.[11] The result of these scandals was to deepen public mistrust of the Congress and to strengthen Cardoso's hand against it when he took his campaign for the Social Emergency Fund to the media. Cardoso exercised real political skill in passing the fund through Congress, but it is plausible that he would not have enjoyed such success without that advantage.

With the implementation of the Real Plan in February, Fernando Henrique Cardoso seemed an obvious choice for president. In 1986, the PMDB, the party of President José Sarney, had been able to capture the euphoria of the Cruzado Plan and translate it into electoral gains. Even if the *real* proved as ephemeral in its accomplishments as the *cruzado,* Cardoso would still be likely to benefit in the October election, but Cardoso remained noncommittal. His stated task was to make sure the Real Plan worked. The deadline to declare for Cardoso was April 1994, when he would have to resign from the cabinet. It came as little surprise when Cardoso resigned in April to assume the candidacy for the president for the PSDB. At the time of his decision, popular approval for the Real Plan remained relatively low, the public's evaluation of the Franco government remained relatively poor, and Cardoso's support was relatively meager.

With the dramatic drop in inflation that began in July 1994, Cardoso began to move in the polls. Three factors helped him: First, popular approval of the Real Plan soared from below 40 percent in May to over 70 percent by the election in October; second, both public approval of the Itamar government and general optimism about Brazil climbed dramatically with the drop in inflation;[12] finally, more and more voters became aware (through Cardoso's campaigning efforts) that Cardoso was responsible for the plan.

Cardoso's campaign did not rest exclusively on his stabilization plan. His campaign turned on five pledges.[13] He pledged to make a priority of agriculture, employment, security, education, and health. Each of these

11. Discussed in David Fleischer, "Attempts at Corruption Control in Brazil."
12. Rubens Figueiredo, "Opinião Pública, Intencionalidade, e Voto," *Opinião Pública* 2, no. 2 (1995): 75, 80.
13. Cardoso indicated his five promises by holding up his five fingers, one finger per promise, a move that many perceived as an underhanded attack on Lula, who had lost a finger as a metalworker.

corresponded to areas of deep concern among Brazilian voters, areas that Cardoso believed would improve through management of inflation and the state's fiscal dilemmas. Cardoso's campaign also benefited from an explicit coalition with two right-wing parties, the PFL and the Brazilian Labor Party (PTB), both of which withdrew candidates from the race. The Franco government helped as well, threatening to crack down on employers who raised prices or salaries. In addition, Ciro Gomes (PSDB) the new finance minister, was a close ally of Cardoso and a man openly contemptuous of Paulista industrialists. He protected the *real* by accelerating the tariff reduction process and by encouraging import consumption as a check on price increases. Finally, Cardoso also benefited from the well-publicized corruption allegations swirling around another of his potential challengers, Orestes Quercia of the PMDB.

The only real question left open on October 3, 1994, was whether Cardoso would win in the first round or beat Lula in the second round. With 54.3 percent of the vote in the first round, Cardoso won in every state but Rio Grande do Sul and the Federal District and won by a majority in all but four and the Federal District. Cardoso won among every age group, wage group, and educational level. By contrast, Lula obtained only 27 percent of the vote—one-half of Cardoso's tally in the first round. Unlike Collor, Cardoso benefited from the first concurrent legislative elections since 1950.[14] The assumption was that these "married" elections would weaken the strong corporatist element in the legislative elections. Instead, observers hoped that the national, issue-driven executive elections would influence the legislative ones.[15]

The effect of the concurrent elections is unclear, but the party system showed some signs of stabilizing in the 1994 elections. The number of parties represented in the Chamber of Deputies declined from nineteen to seventeen. Several smaller parties merged; first, the PDS and Christian Democratic Party (PDC) merged into the PPR, which then merged with the PP to form the PPB, the third-largest party in the Chamber with eighty-eight seats. As a result, the party composition of the Chamber

14. This may have been the most important constitutional reform of 1994. Shortening the presidential term to four years means that presidential and legislative elections always occur concurrently, which may in the long run alter the dynamic of legislative elections.

15. The logic underlying the hope that married elections might alter the character of legislative elections was that executive elections turn on national issues whereas legislative elections are driven by local, patronage, and clientelistic concerns. The hope was that marrying these elections would allow parties and candidates to insert national issues into the legislative election process, thereby enhancing the tendency to vote on programmatic issues at the expense of *corporativismo*.

changed from 1990 to 1994. What is more significant about the change is that the three largest parties alone accounted for 55 percent of the seats in the Chamber. Their votes, totaled with the results for the PSDB, the fourth-largest party in the Chamber, accounted for 67 percent of the seats. That total represented a majority sufficient to pass constitutional amendments (Table 6.1).

In addition to Cardoso's center-right alliance of the PFL, PMDB, the PPB, and the PSDB, he added the medium-size PTB. All told, his coalition could count on 73 percent of the Chamber votes. His coalition's dominance was mirrored in the Senate, where he and his allies held an overwhelming 83 percent of the seats. Finally, the Cardoso coalition held twenty-one of twenty-seven governorships. This dominance, combined with his dramatic first-round victory, made Cardoso appear unstoppable.

Cardoso's coalition also appeared much more solid than Collor's had because several of his coalition partners did not field a presidential candidate in the first round of the 1994 election. Thus, there appeared to be a united coalition behind defense of the Real Plan. In fact, polls of the new legislators' opinions on issues of constitutional reform seemed to support the optimistic view that Cardoso's legislative support was solid. Strong majorities supported constitutional reforms that privatized state companies, broke monopolies, ended reserves for domestic capital, and significantly altered the social security, tax, and administrative systems (Table 6.2).[16]

His formidable coalition appeared to give him a guarantee of greater success than his predecessors in passing constitutional reforms. When Cardoso took office in January 1995, he enjoyed approval ratings over 70 percent, and over 80 percent for the Real Plan, but he also enjoyed

Table 6.1.   Party composition of the Chamber of Deputies, 1987–1994

Party Size	1987	1990	1994
Large parties (81 and more)	2	2	3
Medium parties (31–80 seats)	4	6	4
Small parties (10–30 seats)	4	4	3
Microparties (less than 10)	11	8	7
Total number of parties	21	19	17

SOURCE: Adapted from *Estado de São Paulo*, various issues.

16. Lamounier and Edmar Bacha, "Democracy and Economic Reform in Brazil," in Joan Nelson, ed., *A Precarious Balance: Democracy and Economic Reforms in Latin America* (San Francisco: Institute for Contemporary Studies, 1994).

Table 6.2.   Distribution of seats, Chamber and Senate, 1994

Party	Chamber Seats	Senate Seats
PMDB*	107	22
PFL*	89	18
PPB*	88	11
PSDB*	62	11
PT	49	5
PDT	34	6
PTB*	31	5
PSB	15	1
PL	13	1
PC do B	10	—
PMN	4	—
PSD	3	—
PSC	3	—
PPS	2	1
PRN	1	—
PRP	1	—
PV	1	—
Total	513	81

SOURCE: Scott Mainwaring, "Parties, Electoral Volatility, and De-mocratization: Brazil Since 1982" (paper presented at the Latin American Studies Association, Washington, D.C., September 1995).
*Cardoso coalition member.

several other conjunctural advantages. First, continuing fear of Lula and the left in general meant that his coalition partners were likely to stay with him. Second, the peso crisis had hit just before he took office, and the resulting tequila effect appeared to reinforce the necessity of the reform agenda. Third, price stabilization had encouraged a significant inflow of capital so that Brazil sat on dollar reserves over U.S.$60 billion. The strength of Brazil's reserves gave it a substantial cushion against the brief outflow of capital that occurred in the wake of the peso crisis. It also permitted the overvaluation of the *real* through the exchange-rate anchor without threatening the balance of payments. Finally, 1995 was a year without elections at any level of government. Thus, the historic tendencies for political parties to focus on election tactics at the expense of the government would not resurface until the municipal elections of October 1996.

With all these strengths, Cardoso appointed a technically strong cabinet rather than one that doled out key posts to coalition members. Key ministries, such as Finance and Planning, went to the PSDB members,

Pedro Malan and José Serra. In addition, Cardoso's appointments to head the Central Bank, the BNDES, and the Bank of Brazil also reflected technical, not political, concerns.[17] The PFL, the PMDB, and the PTB did secure several ministerial posts. In addition, they secured many of the leading legislative positions, including presidents of both chambers, leader of the government in both chambers, and chair of the vital chamber committee on the constitution and justice.

Cardoso began his term with a full agenda. The peso crisis and the resulting tequila effect provoked a rapid outflow of foreign capital. Although that outflow reinforced the perception that reforms were necessary, it also presented an immediate serious policy problem for the Cardoso administration. In addition, by December 1994, it was clear that a significant banking crisis existed in the state-level banks. In particular, Cardoso had to intervene in the state banks of two of his key allies: Banespa, the state bank of São Paulo, governed by Mario Covas (PSDB), and Banerj, the state bank of Rio de Janeiro, governed by Marcello Alencar (PSDB). Together, the two banks had deficits nearing U.S.$3 billion dollars.[18] Interviews[19] revealed that the Cardoso administration knew the full extent of the banking crisis by August 1994, including the disastrous U.S.$5 billion dollar hole in the Bank of Brazil.

In addition to these substantial distractions, Cardoso made it clear that his priority was securing the long-term stability of the *real*. The solution to that was constitutional reforms that addressed the social security system, the civil service, and the tax system. In other words, Cardoso made clear that his stabilization plan depended on the exact set of reforms that Collor had attempted through the *emendão*. Although Cardoso had also campaigned on his commitment to social policy, he argued that stabilization was the linchpin of his social policy. Without resolution of the fiscal crisis of the state, there could be no progressive social policy.[20]

17. Discussed at greater length in Maria D'Alva Gil Kinzo, "The 1994 Elections in Brazil: Party Politics in the New Government" (paper presented at the Latin American Studies Association, Washington, D.C., September 1995), 10–13.

18. *Latin American Regional Reports, Brazil* (London), January 1995.

19. Confidential author interviews with multinational corporation executives, June 1996, São Paulo, who reported meeting with Cardoso in August 1994 and receiving briefings on the Real Plan, including expressions of concern that the banking crisis, especially in the Bank of Brazil, promised to be the most serious threat to the plan. These meetings increased executives' confidence that Cardoso was on top of his program and that, given time, he would successfully pass it through Congress.

20. Bresser Pereira, *Economic Crisis and State Reform,* makes the case that his and Cardoso's approach to economic policy is social democratic rather than neoliberal. Bresser Pereira argues that to resolve the fiscal crisis of the state, reforms that address budget deficits, responsi-

Unfortunately, Cardoso almost certainly overestimated the solidity of his alliance. The Congress's first act of the new legislative session was to approve a PT-sponsored bill that increased the minimum wage from seventy *reals* to one hundred *reals* per month. Aside from its potential inflationary impact, Cardoso opposed the bill because social security payments in Brazil were linked to the minimum wage rate. Cardoso protested that the bill threatened the state's finances by adding an extraordinary burden to the already-bankrupt social security system, but he approved legislation that increased legislative and executive salaries 100 percent. Cardoso and the Congress clashed over the bill through the month of February, but the Congress refused to back down on the measure. Finally, Cardoso vetoed the bill while leaving intact the 100 percent pay increase for the legislature and executive. This single decision was the most significant cause of Cardoso's tumble in public opinion polls to 36 percent in March 1995.[21]

Cardoso continued to struggle with Congress through February. In response, he moved to increase the representation of allied parties, notably the PMDB and PFL, in his government. Furthermore, he sought to improve his performance on social policy to counter growing public criticism. However, neither Cardoso's efforts in Congress nor his efforts at social policy helped his situation. On the congressional front, Cardoso froze federal hiring and cut U.S.$7 billion from the federal budget. Perceiving both as attacks on crucial sources of patronage resources for their electoral bases, members of Congress reacted angrily. On the social front, the Catholic Bishops' Conference released a report on poverty in Brazil with a scathing criticism of the government and its priorities. A poll in April 1995 revealed that 54 percent of Brazilians believed that Cardoso had not kept his promises on his social agenda.[22]

Cardoso drew additional criticism through his handling of the consequences of the tequila effect. By February 1995, most observers believed that the *real* had become significantly overvalued. The government was going to have to take some steps to halt the outflow of capital and to devalue the *real,* but Persío Arida, the Central Bank president, repeatedly insisted that the bank would make no such move. Finally, in early March, the bank introduced an exchange band to allow the *real* to float to a more

---

ble monetary policy, promotion of trade, and encouragement of competitiveness have to be passed. These reforms are also necessary for the development of a social pact that brings the poor into the process of development.

21. Cited in Kinzo, "The 1994 Elections," 14.

22. Brasmarket Poll, cited in *Lagniappe Letter* (Washington, D.C.), April 14, 1995.

realistic rate without sacrificing the exchange rate as an anchor on the currency. The move surprised and disappointed members of Congress. In particular, Antônio Delfim Netto, the architect of the Brazilian Miracle and its disastrous move to orthodoxy in the early 1980s, emerged as a leading critic of the government. Delfim, who increasingly became the voice of a disgruntled industrial class through late 1995 and 1996, hammered the government for its mismanagement of both the exchange band and its resolution of the tequila effect.

The Cardoso government used two mechanisms to ward off the worst of the tequila effect. First, the government sharply raised interest rates to curb consumer spending, thereby protecting against a depletion of foreign reserves and against a resumption of inflationary pressure. Second, the government raised tariff barriers on 109 products in the automotive and consumer electronics sectors to 70 percent to discourage imports and stem capital outflows. Stung by criticism that it had raised rates too far, the government responded in a few weeks by lowering rates on 23 of those products.

The decision on tariffs clearly illustrated criticisms expressed in the business community and voiced aggressively by Delfim. Critics charged that the government was operating without a strategic vision, which led to a lack of appreciation for the impact of its decisions at the micro-level. Auto imports had reached over 81,000 units in 1993 as tariffs fell to 20 percent. This figure represented almost three times the number of imported cars in 1992. The first quarter of 1994 saw close to three times the number of imports over the first quarter of 1993.[23] The result of this boom in import consumption was a dramatic increase in employment and in wages at import dealers.[24] The increase in tariffs had an immediate and disastrous impact on both. For critics like Delfim, it revealed that the government was not considering firms' need for predictability to successfully adapt to open trade.[25]

By early May, the Congress had handed Cardoso two more stinging defeats. In mid-March, the Chamber's crucial committee on the constitution and justice dismantled Cardoso's social security reform. Cardoso had presented a series of measures, including disconnecting the link between social security and the minimum wage, establishing retirement by years of contribution instead of years of service, setting a ceiling on pensions,

23. *Latin American Regional Reports, Brazil* (London), May 4, 1995, p. 4.
24. Confidential author interviews with representatives of the auto industry, June 1996.
25. Delfim, cited in *Veja,* May 3, 1995.

and restricting pensioners' ability to draw more than one pension or continue to work after drawing a pension. Cardoso insisted that the committee report the bill out as a whole to avoid members weakening its provisions.

Instead, the committee broke the bill into multiple sections. Eight members of the coalition from every party defected on the vote, with one coalition member suggesting that the government had to show more concern for people.[26] Various unions, notably the CUT, the CGT, and the Popular Movement's Central (CMP), orchestrated an effective campaign against the reform so that even though earlier polls suggested that members of Congress supported almost all the proposals in principle, they were not going to vote for a bill that clearly attacked vital, well-organized electoral constituencies. Meanwhile, the president of the Senate, José Sarney, warned the government that its reform agenda was producing legislative gridlock, which could only have undesirable results. Responding to the implied threat, the Cardoso government added tax and administrative reforms to the already-shelved social security reform. By May, it was clear that Cardoso's strategy for moving his reform agenda was not working.

MAY 1995–MAY 1996: THE ROAD DOWN REDUX?

Over the period from May 1995 to roughly June 1996, uncertainty grew as to Cardoso's ability to carry through his reform program. Cardoso's policy performance began well, but deteriorated throughout the period. As it did, the contradictions of this incomplete reform process began to hurt business interests badly. In response, industrialists' concerns and anger grew throughout the period, finally emerging in a range of venues by mid-1996.

Cardoso's initial success rode on the back of a tactical error by the left. On May 3, 1995, the oil workers' union, a key union in the CUT, went on strike. Labor unions played an important role in derailing social security reform. The oil strike appeared to be an opportunity to attack proposed privatization of the oil industry, notably Petrobrás. Forty-eight thousand workers went on strike, producing real shortages of heating and cooking oil relatively quickly. Striking workers threatened to quit if their wage demands, the explicit pretext of the strike, were not met.

26. Cited in *Latin American Regional Reports, Brazil* (London), May 4, 1995, p. 2.

The strike proved not only a serious miscalculation on the part of the left, but also an opportunity for political resuscitation for Cardoso. Backed by opinion polls that showed strong public hostility to the strikers and growing support for privatization, Cardoso struck back. After the court ruled the strike illegal, Cardoso called in the military to maintain order and to guarantee that workers who wished to return to work could do so. By the beginning of June, Cardoso had successfully broken up the strike.

His reaction to the strike marked a turning point in his strategy, which *Veja* noted with the headline "The government turns to the attack."[27] Cardoso publicly criticized his opponents and encouraged his cabinet to participate in the attack. Malan, a normally staid banker, denounced critics of the government as "gravediggers of the Real Plan." When faced with left-wing opposition to privatization, including some from his own party, Cardoso lashed out, calling the left "stupid."

In the period from May to October, he continued his verbal assault. He threatened that any party defections on key votes would cost that party government posts. He denounced the observers who described Brazil's slowing economy in the second half of 1996 as cowards, traitors, and pessimists and advised them to "shut up." He made several criticisms of the Congress, denouncing their patronage politics. Overall, the strategy seemed to work. Cardoso enjoyed his greatest period of legislative success from May 1995 to January 1996. Building on earlier success in liberalizing rules for the private sector and foreign capital in areas such as electricity, transports, ports, and postal services, he removed the constitutional obstacles to privatization in telecommunications, mining, energy, and shipping. By August, Cardoso had also ended the distinction between national and foreign capital. Privatizing Petrobrás proved a more difficult task, with the PT and PDT firmly opposed to privatization and nationalists of all parties joining them. Cardoso solved the impasse by offering to "flexibilize" the sector. Flexibilization promised to keep the company in state hands while permitting joint ventures and allowing competitors to enter the oil and natural gas sectors. Cardoso's compromise effectively isolated the hard-line nationalists and leftists and opened the door to private and foreign capital participation.

Cardoso also managed to get privatizations back on schedule by August 1996. Brazil's privatization program had generated far less revenues than aggressive privatizers such as Argentina, Chile, and Mexico. In fact,

27. *Veja*, May 3, 1995.

Collor and Franco together had generated less than U.S.$10 billion in revenues from all sales, well below the growth in public debt during the same period. Although the evidence suggested that the privatization program had succeeded in enhancing the competitive performance of privatized companies, it had not occurred very quickly and had done little to help ease fiscal deficits. The process slowed even more as a result of Franco's reticence about privatization. When Cardoso took office in January 1995, there were no firms ready for sale, but in May, the government announced an aggressive sell-off of petrochemical and power companies beginning in August 1995.

As the year drew to a close, Cardoso faced a renewed struggle over his reform agenda. By September 1995, the government began floating proposals for tax and administrative reform. The life of the Social Emergency Fund was ending, and Cardoso desperately needed a renewal of the fund to protect the state's finances. Through hardball politics and effective bargaining, Cardoso managed to secure a vote for a watered-down administrative reform in the Chamber committee on the constitution and justice. Nevertheless, further readings of administrative reform and any work on tax reform disappeared in negotiations over the Social Emergency Fund. The Cardoso government offered deals to roll over state-level debt in exchange for support on renewal of the fund. The government insisted that it needed two years to provide a safe window for continuing work on securing the *real*. The opposition to renewal, led by the senate president José Sarney, considered the period too long. Finally, in December, the Congress approved an eighteen-month renewal of the fund, now renamed the Financial Stability Fund. Although Cardoso won an important victory, he made no progress on the most crucial and most controversial of the constitutional reforms: tax, administrative, and social security reforms. As the Congress recessed until February, Cardoso faced a short window of time in which to work on the reform agenda before the October 1996 municipal elections took the political stage. Industrialists shared this concern.[28] In fact, the CNI's annual survey of business attitudes toward commercial liberalization suggested that business concern about policy uncertainty grew throughout 1995 over 1994.

By January 1996, growing uncertainty rested on doubts that Cardoso could pass his reform in the short time left to him. Congress would reconvene in February, a month made even shorter by *Carnaval*. In July, the

28. CNI, "Abertura Comercial e Estratégia Tecnológica" (Rio de Janeiro, 1995).

Congress would recess for the winter break. After that, all thoughts would turn to the October municipal elections. Early indications showed that as much as 40 percent of the sitting Congress might run for municipal office. Most of the Congress was likely to consider legislation exclusively in terms of its impact on the October elections. In economic terms, it was clear that Cardoso's window was growing narrower, too. The good news was that inflation remained low and even showed signs of decreasing, but the bad news posed a real threat to the continuity of the Real Plan. Most important, despite the Cardoso government's stringent fiscal policies, the fiscal deficit reached close to 5 percent of GDP in 1995. Early indications threatened an even higher deficit in 1996.

Industrialists were concerned because Cardoso faced two seemingly insurmountable problems. First, key budget items such as social security and payrolls continued to require real increases in spending. These increases more than offset the government's effort to clamp down on all other discretionary spending. Estimates of the deficit in social security alone exceeded U.S.$5 billion. Second, successful stabilization provoked a renewed enormous inflow of capital. At the beginning of 1996, Brazil's reserves stood again at roughly U.S.$50 billion after falling to U.S.$20 billion. To prevent this inflow of cash from driving up inflation, the Central Bank had to sterilize it by issuing domestic debt paper instead of cash. This tactic kept the money supply down but dramatically increased debt loads. Thus, the second source of Brazil's continuing deficit problem came from servicing this burgeoning debt.

In early March, with the Congress negotiating new, watered-down social security reform, Cardoso visited Mexico City and lashed out at Congress in a speech before the Mexican Congress. His criticism of the Brazilian Congress as overly concerned with patronage and private interests may have been entirely accurate, but Brazilian legislators received it poorly. Cardoso quickly discovered that the hardball phase was over. Through March and April, Cardoso fought to resuscitate social security reform after losing a key vote in March and then a court decision in April. He faced an even greater threat in calls for a Parliamentary Commission of Inquiry (CPI) into the banking crisis and growing revelations of the depth of corruption that existed in the financial system. By March 1996, it was clear that the government had known and concealed the depth of the scandal since 1994. Cardoso was forced to bargain desperately to stop the CPI and to get social security back on the agenda. Members of Congress made it clear that the price would be high. By the end of March,

Cardoso regained control by turning to new highs of patronage spending[29] and by drastically watering down his reforms.[30] Not surprisingly, this did not convince industrialists that Cardoso's reform agenda was on track.

This confusing performance was particularly disturbing because the combination of high interest rates and open markets made life difficult for most Brazilian firms. By late 1995 and early 1996, life at the micro-level had become increasingly challenging for much of the business community. Above all else, the combination of commercial liberalization with a failure to resolve Brazil's systemic costs, what industrialists called the Brazil cost, hurt a substantial number of businesses: those without the special protection obtained by the auto industry; those without access to foreign capital; and those left out of the boom of consumption in consumer goods sparked by successful stabilization. With the lowest-income segment enjoying the greatest gains from price stabilization, especially with basic staples prices rising slower than the rate of inflation, consumption of televisions, radios, washers, refrigerators, and cement hit all-time records, largely driven by the entrance of first-time consumers. For other producers, the benefits of the consumption boom were less noteworthy.

Brazil's uncompetitive costs were reflected in a number of crucial ways. First, the tax burden on production remained very high in Brazil. The staggering number of indirect taxes represented a significant source of uncompetitiveness. In turn, the number of indirect taxes reflected the state's continuing need to add new taxes to finance itself. A study by FIESP's department of the economy captures the impact of Brazil's tax burden, as well as the impact of its high real interest rate (Table 6.3).

Other indicators of industrial competitiveness supported FIESP's claims. In one study of the auto industry for the United Nations Economic Commission on Latin America, José Roberto Ferro noted that the total tax component of the price of a Brazilian car ranged from 23 percent for

29. Cardoso's return to patronage was widely commented on in the Brazilian press. There was nothing secret about it. The specific details of deals with members of the Congress appeared in the news. Tasso Jereissati, one of the president's closest allies, publicly confessed that there was no choice but to engage in *fisiologismo*. Meanwhile, the treasury announced it was swamped with demands by the PMDB; the PPB leader Espiridião Amin announced that the party would not vote on amendments to the social security reform until Cardoso came through on his promise to provide a minister.

30. Celso Martone, "Recent Economic Policy in Brazil Before and After the Peso Crisis," in Roett, ed., *The Peso Crisis: International Perspectives* (Boulder, Colo.: Lynne Rienner, 1996), is particularly critical of Cardoso's reform efforts. He argues that Cardoso erred in the order of the reforms he pursued as well as in their timidity.

Table 6.3. Brazil cost: Impact of taxes and financial cost on production (Percentage)

Taxes on financing	17.2
Financial cost	38.1
Taxes (IPI, ICMS, PIS, COFINS)	75.4
Total value added	100.0

SOURCE: SINDIPEÇAS, 1996.
NOTE: The study calculated costs assuming six stages of production, excluding the final marketing of the good, a 150-day production period, 30 days for payment at each stage, a 4% difference between real interest rates in Brazil and other countries (actually a modest assumption), loans of 45% of working capital, with IPI at 25% and ICMS at 18%.

"popular" cars to 34 percent for all others. This percentage represents an enormous difference between Brazil and other countries, for example, Argentina, France, and Italy, 16 percent; Germany, 12 percent; Japan, 8 percent; United States, 6 percent.[31] In a similar vein, Sergio Magalhães, president of ABIMAQ, reported that of the 1995 total of U.S.$18.7 billion of capital goods sales, taxes represented U.S.$2 billion.[32] Monthly interest rates on short-term loans averaged over 6 percent per month through 1995—on average over 5 percent above the rate of inflation per month.[33]

Despite low take-home pay, payrolls also embedded uncompetitive costs. One of the unfortunate realities of Brazilian economics is that Brazilian laborers take home very little pay while employers do not benefit from a low-wage situation. Brazilian firms must also pay a series of social obligations, notably the social security tax and the FGTS tax (among several others). Social obligations represented an additional 36 percent of workers' pay. Brazil's generous vacation pay, thirteenth salary (a legally mandated bonus month's pay), and other payments of paid leave added an additional 42 percent to payroll costs. Other social obligations and paid leave added an additional 15 percent. All told, legal obligations added 102 percent of wages to payrolls.[34] In addition to legal obligations, employers repeatedly noted nonlegal obligations, including meals, health

31. José Roberto Ferro, "A Indústria Automobilística no Brasil: Desempenho, Estratégias, e Opções de Política Industrial," ILDES/FES Policy Paper, no. 14; 1995, 30.

32. Cited in *Latin American Newsletters, Economy and Business* (London), October 1996, 3.

33. SINDIPEÇAS, "A Nova Ordem Mundial e a Conjuntura Brasileira," 1996.

34. SINDIPEÇAS, "A Nova Ordem."

plans, and transportation—all high costs that reflected the paucity of public service and all of which hurt labor productivity.[35]

Finally, despite six years of neoliberal promises of renewed infrastructure investment through privatization and improvement of government budgets, Brazil still suffered from an uncompetitive infrastructure. Brazil had among the least-efficient, most-expensive ports in the world. Concerns about energy supply led to repeated debates as to how much time the country had before it faced real shortages. Interviews with representatives in the energy sector revealed further concern that the law "flexibilizing" the oil sector left the task of defining the new rules for the sector in the hands of Petrobrás. Shell publicly warned that it would enter only if the rules were well designed.

Brazilian business leaders grew increasingly vocal about their concerns about how the Brazil cost affected adjustment efforts. They repeatedly made clear that the government's bet on foreign direct investment was coming at the expense of local production in the hands of Brazilian owners ("denationalization") and at the expense of small- to medium-size firms and employment. Some critics pointed out that Brazil could not become an export platform with an uncompetitive system.[36]

The 1995–96 data seemed to bear out these business concerns. Sectors like textiles, auto parts, machine tools and equipment, consumer electronics, and electrical appliances all showed substantial drops in employment. Bankruptcy requests increased over 300 percent from 1995 to 1996, with textile and machinery reporting particularly high rates.[37] Auto parts lost

35. Confidential author interviews throughout 1992 and 1996. In discussing micro-level adjustments, businesspeople frequently mentioned these issues as problems affecting labor productivity and therefore requiring employers' responses. What particularly galled many of the businesspeople who mentioned these issues was that in addition to providing these services, businesspeople paid high taxes, supposedly to provide the very services that employers had to provide privately. One textile firm owner observed to me in 1991 that he had calculated that if he did not have to pay the social obligations, he could have afforded to privately provide a substantially superior medical and dental plan, raise workers' salaries, and still reduce the price of his goods. I obviously make no claim as to the veracity of his calculations or as to any inclination to actually provide such care in the absence of social obligations. I merely cite it as illustrative of business attitudes with reference to these payroll costs. In general, there is agreement among many economists that payroll costs are high although how high is the subject of some dispute. A discussion of this dispute and alternative assessments of payroll costs is offered in Suzigan and Villela, *Industrial Policy in Brazil,* 129–30.

36. This point was made by Delfim, among others, at a seminar sponsored by FIESP and published in FIESP, *Notícias.* It was also a point made by the vice-president of CIESP and ABIMAQ, Mario Bernardini, who had a radio show on which he made these observations.

37. Bankruptcy data are reported routinely in FIESP *Notícias,* available on the Internet at http://www.fiesp.org.br (cited May 1997).

one-half the firms in the sector from 1990 to 1993 and halved again to 1996. The sector association, SINDIPEÇAS, estimated another gradual reduction in half by 2000. Remaining firms showed both significant efforts to improve quality and productivity and substantial results, but productivity gains lost ground in the face of real wage increases as well as real increases in payroll costs. Finally, a number of sectors reported very rapid increases in the volume of imports. The Association of Electro-Electronics Producers (ABINEE) estimated that imports would represent as much as 45 percent of the market by 1997:[38] a doubling of imports in two years.

Part of this process was inevitable and had been both understandable by and acceptable to Brazilian businesspeople in the early period of import liberalization. Brazilian businesspeople argued that the severity of the impact had been seriously exaggerated by several aspects of government policy, however. First, industrialists complained that high real interest rates had significant decapitalizing effects. Second, they charged that the uncompetitive costs associated with Brazil's tax burden and payroll expenses affected competition with imports and hindered exports. Finally, they complained about unfair trade practices (Brazil opened its markets without a dumping law on the books—something that a number of businesspeople remarked on with disbelief and dismay, particularly when the government finally ruled in mid-1996 that sectors like toys and textiles had suffered from significant dumping).

A review of changes in the three sectors analyzed in Chapter 3 shows some of the pressures facing the business community. By 1996, the auto parts sector faced profound changes. Sectoral representatives had expressed a certain degree of optimism in 1991–92, but by 1996, changes in the auto industry rendered much of that optimism invalid. As part of the globalization trend, auto producers in Brazil as elsewhere had shifted to "systems" suppliers.[39] Systems suppliers supplied completed systems, such as a complete chassis, as opposed to individual parts. Complete systems suppliers required very large scale, and the shift to systems suppliers provoked sharp contractions in the parts sector. As SINDIPEÇAS ob-

---

38. Imports represented 28 percent of the market in 1995, a jump from 13 percent in 1990. The estimate for 1996–97 came from an interview with a sectoral representative. The data was supplied by ABINEE as part of its routine data collection, but was not yet published.

39. A detailed discussion of the changes in the sector and the rise of the systems suppliers can be found in Anne Caroline Posthuma, "Industrial Restructuring and Skills in the Supply Chain of the Brazilian Automotive Industry" (paper prepared for the Latin American Studies Association, Guadalajara, 1997).

served, the globalization trend led to a situation in Germany in which 3 percent of producers supplied 84 percent of all parts. SINDIPEÇAS estimated that in the Brazilian industry, one-half of all firms in operation in 1996 had no hope of surviving. They further estimated that the sector would see a 50 percent reduction in employment by 2000.[40]

Auto parts representatives expressed particular concern with the Cardoso government's policy for the auto industry. The auto industry faced enormous increases in imports from 1993 to early 1995, some of which were imported by existing producers. The Brazil cost helped to prevent Brazilian auto producers from exporting to the United States and Europe. Instead, the industry continued to depend heavily on the domestic market with some exports to Latin America. The Cardoso government, seeking to promote the auto industry, raised tariffs on autos from 20 percent in 1994 to 32 percent in February 1995 and then again to 70 percent in May 1995. As part of the tariff increase in May, the government also reduced import tariffs on auto parts and machine tools to 2 percent.

Representatives of the auto parts industry complained that the tariff reduction was unnecessarily low and was an obvious blow to the industry's efforts to adjust. For their part, representatives of the auto industry complained that only 25 percent of domestic producers were competitive in both price and quality. In response, the auto parts industry maintained that it had made substantial improvements, but that increases in total labor costs offset those gains. According to SINDIPEÇAS, 40 percent of the sector was competitive in price terms. Furthermore, surveys in the sector showed that over 70 percent of firms were aware of the methods of improving quality and productivity, and over 50 percent were actively engaged in implementing them.[41]

For many industrialists, the sale of Metal Leve (one of the crown jewels in Brazilian industry's crown) demonstrated the problems with Cardoso's program. The sale quickly developed into one of the most dramatic events of the year in the Brazilian business community. Metal Leve, owned by one of Brazil's most influential entrepreneurs, José Mindlin, was one of Brazil's first multinationals with production and research operations in the United States. Metal Leve announced its sale in June to a consortium made up of a Brazilian competitor, Cofap, Bradesco, a Brazilian bank, and a German auto parts competitor, Mahle. Metal Leve had just won General Motors' annual global supplier award for both price and quality,

40. SINDIPEÇAS, "A Nova Ordem."
41. SINDIPEÇAS, "A Nova Ordem."

but it faced two problems. First, to remain competitive, the firm's need for capital forced it to consider taking partners. Mindlin publicly made it clear that he did not want to be a minority partner in his firm, particularly not with Cofap and Mahle as partners. Second, Metal Leve representatives claimed that Mahle had been dumping pistons in a predatory bid to drive the firm out of the market. Without antidumping measures in place, the firm had been forced into a destructive price war against Mahle, one that Metal Leve representatives did not believe they could win.

Besides becoming a symbol of the problems with Cardoso's policies for much of the business community, this situation reflected a growing trend in the sector. Mergers and acquisitions had become common throughout 1995–96, particularly in the auto parts sector and particularly with foreign partners. Many of the largest firms in the sector had announced mergers or acquisitions by mid-1996.[42] Despite the rapid influx of foreign auto parts firms, auto sales took a substantial downswing in the second half of 1996. At least one observer, J. D. Power, advised caution in entering the auto parts market because of probable overcapacity in the auto industry.

The mix of factors in 1996 was particularly difficult for machine tools and equipment. Labor costs represented roughly 40 percent of total costs. Thus, the continuous real increase in labor costs more than offset any productivity gains. ABIMAQ data revealed an accumulated increase of 64 percent in labor costs over the course of the *real* as compared to 39 percent inflation.[43] Finally, a series of financial factors battered the industry: the financial incentives available to importers through lags in payment periods; the scarcity of financing for capital goods sales—a critical factor in capital goods sales; and the cost of capital when available. In a comparison of the period January to April 1995 with January to April 1996, the sector recorded a 57 percent reduction in the grants made to the industry through Brazil's main capital goods–financing program, Finame.[44]

For representatives of the sector, a further problem was the fact that a

42. SINDIPEÇAS produced a table detailing changes among major firms in the sector, including fifteen acquisitions, most of which involved foreign capital and some of which included the participation of Bradesco, four major mergers, two joint ventures, and eight closings. The table was reproduced in the *Estado de São Paulo,* Sunday, June 16, 1996, p. B4.

43. ABIMAQ, unpublished data. SINDIPEÇAS, "A Nova Ordem," reveals the same relative increase in labor costs, although labor costs represent a smaller share of the total for the industry.

44. ABIMAQ, "Indicadores Conjunturais," April 1996.

substantial portion of foreign direct investment was in existing plants, not new ones. Import/export data revealed a sharp increase in imports from 1994 to 1996, yet a net decline in the total consumption of machine tools and equipment. In fact, the data revealed increases in both imports and exports for 1995 and 1996, but declines in local production for the domestic market revealed an 11 percent reduction in total consumption from 1995 to 1996.[45]

In response to the situation, ABIMAQ representatives pressed the Cardoso government to improve financing for the sector. In particular, sectoral representatives entered negotiations with the BNDES to increase the spread on loans available through the Finame program. Finame was a BNDES program to finance capital goods purchases, which worked by making the loans available through private banks. As of early 1996, sector officials were concerned that the low spreads on the loans were making them unattractive. The sector secured the agreement of the BNDES to increase the spreads to increase private banks' interest in lending Finame resources.

Finally, pulp and paper producers were in a much improved situation in 1996. The sector had suffered from a global and domestic recession during the period 1990–93, but prices began to improve after 1993 and as a consequence, so did profits. Even so, smaller firms in the industry began to feel the consequences of the mix of trade liberalization and high interest rates/overvalued exchange. Some had declared bankruptcy or Brazil's equivalent of U.S. Chapter 11 filing for protection from creditors. The industry faced two real problems. The first lay in the continuing infrastructure weaknesses, notably the concerns about the energy infrastructure. The second was that to remain competitive, the industry estimated the need to invest on the order of U.S.$13 billion.[46] Sectoral data revealed that the sector continued to be globally competitive, thanks in large measure to competitive raw material costs, but interest rates, depreciation costs, and transportation costs all hurt the sector's competitive position.[47] Sectoral representatives lobbied the Cardoso government, claiming that as important exporters it made sense to provide lower cost capital for new investments. In addition, they called for an end to taxes on exports, higher depreciation allowances, improved export credit and insurance, and improved financing for Finame. In June 1996, the Cardoso

---

45. ABIMAQ, unpublished data provided during confidential author interview.
46. ANFPC, "A Política de Desenvolvimento do Complexo Celulose-Papel: 1995–2005."
47. ANFPC, "A Política."

government came through with a new line of credit for the industry. Some outside business observers suggested that the new line was purely politics because pulp and paper, more than most industries, was well positioned to capitalize through the Brazilian stock market, where firms such as Klabín had already been listed, as well as through American depository receipts (ADRs). By 1996, Brazilian firms had obtained over U.S.$6 billion through issuing commercial paper directly in the United States. Whatever the case, the pulp and paper industry made the case that it needed the credit, and the Cardoso government came through.

The micro-level pressures discussed above led to growing business pressure for policy changes. Sectoral associations quietly pressed for reforms, individual businesses lobbied directly (prompting Malan's warning that those businesspeople crowding his corridors waiting for subsidies would not get any), and FIESP, together with the CNI, led the public campaign. The culmination of the public campaign came in May 1996 when the CNI and FIESP orchestrated the "March to Brasília." Between two thousand and three thousand businesspeople occupied the city, pressing the legislature and the government to pass the constitutional reforms. The intention was to push the Congress to recognize the urgency of the reform process and to press the government to recognize the urgency of passing measures to aid industry's adjustment efforts in the absence of reforms.

The March to Brasília was a historic event for the business community. Interviews with FIESP officials confirmed president Carlos Eduardo Moreira Ferreira's view that the march represented an important exercise of democracy for the business community. FIESP officials' views found wide support among members of the business community. In a survey conducted by FIESP, 98 percent of respondents thought that the march was important, while 77 percent approved of Moreira Ferreira's efforts to secure the labor centrals' support for the effort.[48] FIESP also published responses of various sectoral association leaders in São Paulo and elsewhere, which expressed strong satisfaction with the effort.[49] Private interviews suggested much more mixed views about the results. Sectoral leaders who had participated suggested that neither members of Congress nor the government had given a serious hearing to business representatives.

To satisfy the growing pressures he faced, Cardoso shuffled his cabinet at the end of April 1996. Francisco Dornelles, PPB, replaced Dorothea

48. FIESP, *Notícias,* May 13, 1996, pp. 10–11.
49. FIESP, *Notícias,* May 6, 1996, pp. 4–10.

Werneck as industry minister. Werneck, the architect of the 1992 auto accord, was well regarded by industry, but had no influence in the government and as a member of the PSDB was dispensable. Dornelles, appointed as a gesture to the PPB and industry, pledged his commitment to be the minister of industrialists. Former Communist Raúl Jungmann became the head of agrarian reform, which Cardoso raised to a cabinet post. Finally, the PMDB gained when Luiz Carlos Santos became the minister for political coordination. Even the government's most solid supporters decried the extent to which patronage had become the defining character of the government.

Despite Cardoso's efforts, his legislative performance barely improved. Although the Congress finally passed a new patent law, it soundly defeated Cardoso's efforts to advance agrarian reform and increase civilian control over the military. Perhaps most important, it delayed his renewed effort at social security reform to the end of June. When the Chamber finally passed the social security reform bill, it looked nothing like the government's original proposal. In fact, one prominent television newscaster dismissed it as a "reform of nothing." The Congress defeated both the government's relatively limited efforts (as well as Temer's even milder efforts) to set minimum ages for retirement, end correction for inflation, limit the size of pension payments, and end the special retirement for the military, teachers, university professors, members of Congress, and their state and municipal counterparts. Instead, the Congress left the military situation for regular law, preserved the benefits for the entire public sector including special privileges for teachers, professors, and politicians, and ended monetary correction for the private sector only. Shifting the burden onto private-sector workers alone held out little hope for the state's finances. As of June 1996, the National Institute for Social Security (INSS), the private-sector pension system, paid out U.S.$40 billion to sixteen million workers, while the government pension system faced annual payments of U.S.$20 billion to roughly one million workers.[50] One of the keys to Cardoso's defeats was the defection of coalition allies, including the PSDB, who were standing as candidates for mayor in the October elections.[51] The loss on social security ended Cardoso's efforts at constitutional reform for 1996.

50. Executive Secretary of the Ministry of Social Security José Cechim, cited in the *Estado de São Paulo,* June 9, 1996, p. 15.

51. Reported in the *Gazeta Mercantil,* June 25, 1996, p. 7. The government lost roughly fifty coalition votes on three key areas of the reform: age limits for retirement, an end to special retirement privileges for professors, and ceilings on pensions for the public sector.

Thus, by June 1996, Cardoso faced pressure on all fronts. Coalition partners, notably the PPB, continued to demand patronage payments and government posts. Hints of the 1998 presidential election arose as Paulo Maluf explicitly expressed his interest and Itamar Franco hinted at it. Business groups, led by the National Confederation of Industry and FIESP, grew increasingly agitated and angry at the lack of government responsiveness to their concerns. A strike of public-sector workers trapped Pedro Malan in his office. Finally, a massacre of landless squatters in the state of Pará forced agrarian reform specifically and social policy generally onto the top of the agenda.

JUNE 1996–1998: CARDOSO RESURGENT AND THE APPEASEMENT OF BUSINESS

By mid-1996, Cardoso faced a decidedly mixed situation. Several indicators suggested that Brazil had made tremendous gains under Cardoso and the *real*. Poverty had declined markedly, and it showed in record consumption of consumer goods. Inflation was dropping quickly and was projected to drop below 10 percent for 1996. Interest rates were slowly dropping as well, which promised real reductions in the government's fiscal deficit as debt servicing grew cheaper. Businesses projected investments up to U.S.$220 billion by 2003, with the auto industry planning U.S.$23 billion alone by 1999, and with promises of almost U.S.$9 billion slated for 1997. As a result of the enormous influx of foreign investment, both portfolio and direct, Brazilian reserves stood at roughly U.S.$60 billion. Finally, despite growing pessimism about the Real Plan, large numbers of voters still held Cardoso himself in high regard.[52]

On the negative side, Brazil faced some serious problems. Debt exceeded U.S.$200 billion dollars, doubling from 1994. Although the composition of the debt was changing so that the proportion of privately held debt was growing, the level of debt itself was still a serious preoccupation.[53] Furthermore, the government faced payments on over U.S.$30 billion in debt that matured in 1997. The debt to exports ratio was over 300

---

52. By August 1996 only 30 percent of the public thought the Real Plan was good, whereas 25 percent thought it was bad. *Folha de São Paulo* poll, cited in *Latin American Newsletters, Economy and Business* (London), August 1966, p. 3.

53. Martone, "Recent Economic Policy," 52–53.

percent, while interest to debt was roughly 20 percent.[54] The fiscal deficit promised to reach an excess of 4 percent for 1996 after months of Malan's predicting surpluses on the order of 2 percent of GDP. Real interest rates continued to be very high, although gradually declining. The trade deficit threatened to reach U.S.$5 billion by year-end, despite the government's earlier projections of a trade surplus.

From June to December 1996, more and more observers sounded warnings about the Real Plan. In June, the prominent and highly regarded economist Rudiger Dornbusch declared that the *real* was overvalued by 40 percent. His comments were widely reported and dismissed as unreasonable in both Brazil and New York, but they provoked an assault by the government, which suggested a defensiveness about the *real* incompatible with the confidence Malan and Cardoso projected publicly. Even the government's most consistent critics, especially Delfim Netto, thought 40 percent was too high. The more common perception was that the *real* was roughly 15 percent overvalued. Although government supporters quickly dismissed Dornbusch, other quieter critics made more credible arguments. In the same week as Dornbusch's announcement, the Bank for International Settlements (BIS) quietly sounded warnings as well. In August, *real* originators Andre Lara Resende and Edmar Bacha joined the chorus of economists alarmed by the lack of progress on permanent fiscal adjustments. Prominent economists (and former Central Bank presidents) Eduardo Gianetti Fonseca and Celso Martone published their concerns as well. Standard and Poor's rated Brazil's banking system as the riskiest in Latin America, a staggering statement given the hole in Mexico's banking sector after the peso crisis and the collapse in Venezuela's banking system. On another worrisome note, observers noted that banks and stores were finding ways to circumvent high interest rates to consumers by lowering interest rates on special checks (an overdraft protection system in Brazil that acts as an informal extension of credit) and by increasing the use of postdating checks as a means of extending store credit. This informal money creation was a strong indicator of the difficulties of establishing firm monetary control in Brazil.

Business interviews revealed strong dissatisfaction with the pace of reforms, and survey evidence showed that businesspeople blamed the executive and legislature equally.[55] In fact, in interviews in June 1996, businesspeople expressed strong anger at Cardoso for taking so long to

---

54. Reported in *Latin American Special Reports* (London), April 1996, p. 4.
55. FIESP survey in FIESP *Notícias,* April 1996, p. 17.

realize that the best strategy was to try to use regular law to reduce government expenditures and uncompetitive business costs. Several interviewees expressed frustration that their views had been repeatedly dismissed as the complaints of "cartorialists" and protectionists by arrogant and contemptuous government representatives. In particular, participants in FIESP's March to Brasília expressed frustration at their reception by both members of Congress and the administration.

Public opinion increasingly mirrored the business community's reaction. A Brasmarket/Ibope poll in June 1996 confirmed the general disappointment in the Cardoso government. Although large percentages still highly approved of Cardoso, his government received only a 3.3 score on a scale of 10. Sizable majorities found that Cardoso had not lived up to any of his promises, especially those on employment and security. Whereas 30 percent of respondents expressed the belief that democracy was proving to be the best course for Brazil, close to 35 percent disagreed. Over 18 percent supported a Fujimori-style coup that would close Congress, and an additional 15 percent supported an outright return of the military.[56]

In certain respects, this disappointment stood in opposition to the genuine accomplishments of the Real Plan. Research reported in June 1996 revealed that the rate of poverty in Brazil's large cities had improved dramatically. In the two years of the *real*, roughly five million urban dwellers had climbed above the poverty line.[57] The improvement in the standard of living for the poorer segments of society translated into new consumption of televisions, washing machines, beef and chicken, fast food, and building materials such as cement for home repairs and improvements. For many of these sectors, consumption hit all-time records in the two years of the Real Plan.[58]

Other indicators, however, showed the darker side of the government's economic policy. Despite the improvement in living standards, Brazil had grown more unequal through the 1990s. Although Cardoso's government bore no direct responsibility for the growth in inequality, other problems

56. Poll published in *Isto É,* June 1996, p. 26.

57. Changes in poverty levels reported in Sônia Rocha, "Renda e Pobreza: Os Impactos do Plano Real" (texto para discussão no. 439; Rio de Janeiro: IPEA [Instituto de Pesquisa Econômica Aplicada], December 1996).

58. Cardoso made a speech on the second anniversary of the plan in which he presented exaggerated data on the performance of the plan. The "error" caused somewhat of an uproar. Nevertheless, the *real* results of the Real Plan were impressive enough. The results are summarized in *Exame,* June 1996, pp. 12–22.

were direct consequences of his program. Official statistics put unemployment at 5.5 percent, but Brazil's official unemployment figures systematically underestimated the real rate. CUT's research arm, DIEESE, placed
the real rate above 15 percent. The DIEESE figure squared much better
with FIESP's own figures on monthly changes in employment, which revealed a loss of two million jobs since 1988. In addition, the originator
of the Real Plan, Edmar Bacha, suggested that another one million jobs
would disappear by 1999. On the business side, high real interest rates
in particular drove record bankruptcy filings. In 1995, the number of
bankruptcies increased roughly 40 percent over 1994. The first quarter of
1996 suggested a similar rate of increase. All told, the effect of real interest rates and competitive restructuring slowed the economy to an anemic
2.5 percent rate of GDP growth,[59] stark contrast to Malan's projections
of 6 percent growth in 1996 and 10 percent in 1997.

This mix of good and bad news left Cardoso with a complex relation
with the industrial community. Superficially, Cardoso had maintained a
good relation with big business throughout his first two years in office,
but under the surface, there were real tensions. A number of sectors faced
the significant micro-level problems noted above, for which only two solutions really existed: a rapid resolution of the reform agenda and thereby
a reduction in what the business community had come to call the Brazil
cost; or a return to an industrial policy that incorporated some measure of
protection. Industrialists in sectors such as machine tools and equipment,
consumer electronics and electrical appliances, pulp and paper, furniture,
textiles and apparel, toy makers, and auto parts complained that the government tended to dismiss their concerns as being the complaints of "cartorialists" and protectionists. Interviews with government officials and
representatives of multinational corporations (MNC) suggested that the
perception was an accurate reflection of at least some influential views in
the government.

By mid-1996, the trade data began to confirm the complaints of the
"cartorialists." A number of sectors once considered vital to Brazil were
suffering from import competition, not simply because of uncompetitiveness, but also through dumping, predatory pricing, and the extraordinary
financial incentives to import rather than buy locally, even when price
and quality were competitive. The principal problem for domestic pro-

---

59. Two and a half percent GDP growth is roughly equal to the rate of population growth.
Therefore, it represents almost no net gain. Although 2.5 percent is a respectable rate of growth
in the United States, it is not especially robust for Brazil, especially in a context of 15 percent
unemployment.

ducers was that the tariff reduction program, as designed, had intended a gradual reduction that granted time to adjust. In practice, though, tariff reduction behaved as if it had been a rapid liberalization because the depth of the recession from 1990 to 1992 had kept out imports. In 1993, the economy grew again, but uncertainties limited firms' adjustment efforts and sharply curtailed the activities of foreign investors. By the time prices and politics finally stabilized in 1994, the tariff schedule had already reached its conclusion. Brazilian firms had had limited time to adjust to import competition and suddenly faced a dramatic inflow of imports at a time when Brazil's average tariffs were lower than those of Japan or South Korea. To make matters worse, interest rates and the exchange rate combined to create strong financial incentives to import while making competitive adjustments difficult.

Brazilian producers' frustration smoldered through 1995 and erupted more visibly into protest in 1996. Quietly, several *sindicatos* mobilized at the same time, pressuring the government to alter its policies. By June 1996, signs of business frustration became much more apparent. On the one hand, the economic data told a worrying story, even though the commercial balance remained generally positive as of June. Sharp increases in imports, such as in textiles where imports climbed from U.S.$500 million dollars in 1992 to U.S.$3 billion by 1996 with an accompanying loss of one million jobs, were hard to dismiss. On the other hand, both the general press and business journals published repeated accounts of business frustration. *Custo Brasil* filled the news along with frequent reports of growing urban violence, rural landlessness, the more aggressive tactics of the MST, and the burden of high unemployment. All these reports added to the general sense of the high social price that the Real Plan was exacting.

In response to growing business agitation, the government slowly began to ameliorate conditions for business. In March 1996, the government increased the staff of its unfair trade office, Decom, from four to forty. Decom had come into existence only in May 1995 and with a staff of four had been unable to effectively investigate the complaints it had received. Shortly afterward, in May 1996, the government raised tariffs to 40 percent on textiles and toys and set minimum prices for textiles as a protective measure against dumping.

In June 1996, Cardoso shifted tactics again, even as social security went down to defeat. For months, government critics like Delfim and leaders in industry, such as Carlos Eduardo Moreira Ferreira, president of FIESP, had urged Cardoso to resort to measures that could improve the economic situation without constitutional reforms. In interviews during June 1996, industrialists repeatedly expressed dissatisfaction with Cardoso's tactical decisions for implementing economic reforms. Moreira Ferreira presented FIESP's proposals during the business march to Brasília in May, and important members of the business community continued to press them to Industry Minister Francisco Dornelles and Planning Minister Antonio Kandir.[60]

Cardoso announced the shift in strategy in June 1996 after consulting with government allies, notably the PFL. Beginning in June to July 1996, Cardoso proposed a series of measures to increase credit for small firms and firms in hard-hit sectors. He raised tariff protection for a series of sectors hit by dumping. He removed taxes that made exports uncompetitive and discouraged capital investments. He moved more aggressively to force states to meet debt obligations and acted to sell off bankrupt state banks. He cut government payrolls through layoffs of workers without civil service protection and through a voluntary retirement program. He also resisted public-sector pay increases. Finally, he aggressively increased the pace of privatization. In June, the government announced two BNDES lines of credit: U.S.$500 million for small and microenterprises and U.S.$1 billion for export financing for nine sectors badly hit by import competition, including shoes, textiles, auto parts, and furniture. Although few businesspeople seemed to think that the measures had much impact, in particular the U.S.$1 billion credit line that limited loans to U.S.$10,000 per firm, they appreciated the gesture. Finally, in September, the government eradicated the tax on goods and services (ICMS) and lowered import taxes on capital goods. For businesspeople, these actions represented a real effort that was long overdue. In particular, the removal of the ICMS and the elimination of the tax on exports of machine tools and equipment pleased exporters. Similarly, interviews with members of the business community suggested that the lines of credit the government extended to smaller and more vulnerable firms was a positive gesture, if not a real source of assistance. Nevertheless, the measures clearly worked

60. The details of the proposals FIESP presented can be found in FIESP, *Notícias,* May 6, pp. 8–10, May 27, pp. 11–15, and June 3, 1996, pp. 10–13. They closely corresponded to what the government actually attempted in the ensuing months. Among the most important recommendations were to postpone the constitutional reform process and focus on improving systemic competitiveness. This could be done through normal law changes to the tax system to remove tax components from the price of exports and to reduce the tax component on crucial, basic industrial inputs. A full description of Cardoso's industrial policy measures up to 1996 is in Suzigan and Villela, *Industrial Policy in Brazil.*

to forestall quietly but rapidly growing opposition to Cardoso from May to July 1996.

Cardoso's efforts through late 1996 to placate the business community seemed to effectively reduce the level of visible frustration. Nevertheless, room for alternative coalitions existed. The venue for laying out the alternatives was the municipal elections, particularly the São Paulo election, in October 1996. Cardoso worked hard to argue that the elections were about local issues, but his own efforts to promote his allies belied his claims. The PT, in its municipal elections, made its appeal based on the need for a more effective policy to protect domestic industry. Although it accepted the need for a market opening, it argued in exactly the terms the business community used: the opening had to be managed properly to allow for competitive restructuring. Cardoso's greatest asset in confronting the PT's pitch was that the PT also rejected much of the constitutional reform agenda that made an alliance between labor and business virtually impossible. On the right, Delfim Netto had become one of the most consistent defenders of industry from 1994 to 1996. Delfim was also one of the architects of Maluf's presidential bids, and by late 1996, Delfim was designing an economic program for the PPB calling for more aggressive promotion of exports with more effective protection of industry. At the conclusion of the voting, neither the PT nor Cardoso's allies appeared strong, but, Paulo Maluf's effort to promote his handpicked successor left him looking like a serious rival. His successful support of the unknown Celso Pitta was doubly surprising given Pitta's lack of name recognition and charisma as well as his race: black in a predominantly white city.

Cardoso immediately shifted his attention to the growing threat from Maluf (and other presidential possibilities, including Jaime Lerner [PMDB], the popular former mayor of Curitiba, and Lula). Throughout Cardoso's presidency, he had flirted with re-election but had endeavored to appear disinterested in the discussion when it repeatedly surfaced through 1994 and 1995. With his reform agenda badly stalled, the municipal elections appearing unsupportive, and Maluf's and Delfim's blatant coalition-building efforts, Cardoso turned his attention fully to the issue.

The re-election issue was an effective tactical choice for Cardoso. In essence, raising the re-election issue forced the business community to choose between him and his contenders. Cardoso suffered some political setbacks in the wake of the municipal elections. Nevertheless, he remained the most credible presidential candidate. Maluf appeared as Cardoso's most serious challenger, but in interviews, industrialists expressed doubts about his ability to build beyond his São Paulo base. Cardoso at the very least was credibly committed to the reform process. In interviews, industrialists frequently voiced the opinion that given time, Cardoso had a chance to push the reform agenda incrementally. Faced with the need to choose, industrialists chose Cardoso. Carlos Eduardo Moreira Ferreira promptly declared that the president had his support and probably 90 percent of his members as well. Cardoso also benefited from the continued reliable support of Luis Eduardo Magalhães, who vowed to bring the issue to a vote before his term as president of the Chamber expired in January 1997. Cardoso also stood to benefit from the interest of the newly elected mayors, many of whom would be interested in re-election if it applied to municipal offices as well. Furthermore, rifts in the PMDB and the PPB showed that if Cardoso was willing and able to pay the patronage price, there were sufficient votes for sale to buy the re-election amendment. Ultimately, the amendment passed, although tainted by a vote-buying scandal in which Cardoso's minister of communication, Sergio Motta, was implicated (although not indicted). Cardoso successfully resecured business support despite his apparent shift away from domestic industrialists. That shift reflected what appeared to be a general trend in the economy.

Cardoso's mixed relation with the business community worked for a number of reasons. First, despite some of the criticisms of his government, the Cardoso administration maintained good communications with the business community. Unlike Collor, who repeatedly reviled the business community and overtly excluded them, Cardoso and his ministers repeatedly appeared in FIESP to address business elites. As the Collor period demonstrated, access counts for a great deal to business leaders, and the Cardoso government made certain that business had it.[61] Second, business leaders believed that the reform agenda was central to enhancing the competitiveness of the economy, and if Cardoso did not do it, it was not clear who would. In research conducted by FIESP, business respondents confirmed that growth could not resume without reforms and awarded the Real Plan an average score of 7.2 on a scale of 10.[62] The PT was the most aggressive political voice condemning the neoliberal path. Although business leaders may have agreed with the PT's condemnation of trade liberalization, they were equally put off by the PT's defense of measures that maintained the fiscal crisis, such as the social security system. As for

61. This is one of the central claims made by Payne in *Brazilian Industrialists.* The evidence from this study overwhelmingly supports her claims.

62. FIESP, *Notícias,* April 15, 1996, p. 17.

Maluf, he not only had a limited political base, but he became mired in corruption troubles of his own.

Third, the business community was more fragmented in 1996 than it had been for years.[63] The business community had sharp internal cleavages in the 1980s while ISI-corporatism was collapsing and in the period leading to the rise of neoliberal policies, but criticism of the role of the state and the need for a resolution of the fiscal crisis tended to unite business. By 1996, neoliberalism had generated a much more distinct set of winners and losers. Leading banks, pension funds, and securities firms joined many multinationals and importers as beneficiaries of Cardoso's policies. Firms like Bradesco and Goldman Sachs participated heavily in the wave of mergers and acquisitions and prospered from the enormous profit potential that leveraging differences in interest and exchange rates offered to firms that could obtain dollars abroad. Similarly, MNCs enjoyed tremendous competitive advantages over local producers through much cheaper costs of capital and the luxury of being able to import or produce locally, depending on the cost advantage. Finally, lags in payment periods for importers (between payments from final customers and payments to foreign suppliers) allowed them to profit financially from satisfying Brazilians' fondness for imported merchandise. In short, any firm or businessperson who could obtain dollars abroad stood to gain from the situation between 1994 and 1996. On the opposite side, domestic producers too small to secure very low cost financing or too dependent on the domestic market suffered tremendously. Thus, small- to mid-size producers in sectors such as textiles, machine tools and equipment, and auto parts bore the brunt of Cardoso's policies. His palliatives, including limited protection and credit lines, eased the situation somewhat. Many of these domestic firms managed by entering into a strategic association with foreign capital. Thus, even these firms remained dependent on the reform process.

Finally, Cardoso tended to benefit from the tendency of Brazilian businesspeople to express optimism about the future. In the research noted above, 81 percent of respondents observed that they thought the Real Plan would consolidate. Only 3 percent thought otherwise, while 9 percent thought it already had. This represents a much stronger degree of optimism than popularly felt. In a similar question at roughly the same

---

63. This fragmentation was observed and commented on as well by Payne, "Brazilian Business."

time, research by Ibope found that nearly one-half the respondents thought that it was too early to tell if the plan would work.

Despite this expression of confidence, it is important to remember that business respondents expressed similar confidence in both the Cruzado Plan of 1986 and the Collor Plan in 1990. In both cases, business optimism only eroded as inflation returned. In the research noted above, while expressing such high levels of confidence, 66 percent of respondents also expressed the belief that the continuation of high budget deficits compromised the plan. Only 20 percent expressed the belief that the government would succeed in reducing the deficit. In 1992, when pressed for sources of optimism, business interviewees stated that even if Collor did not resolve the country's problems, leaders would resolve them in the 1993 plebiscite, or the constitutional review, or in the 1994 elections. In 1996, when pressed, business interviewees typically mentioned two reasons for optimism, often citing them together. First, many respondents reasonably noted that the reform process was difficult and it was unrealistic to expect rapid progress. These respondents observed that Cardoso had made some progress, had demonstrated genuine commitment to the process, and that with time (especially if he succeeded in standing for re-election), he would complete the reforms. Second, a number of respondents also observed that the principal beneficiaries of stabilization had been the poorest segment of Brazilian society. Business representatives repeatedly expressed the view that their voting weight coupled with the realization that they had been paying the greatest share of the inflation tax would pressure politicians to pass the reform agenda.

Other research on popular attitudes, conducted by Ibope and by the National Confederation of Industry (CNI), does not support the latter source of optimism. In May 1996, research by Ibope on attitudes toward the *real* found that lower education respondents did not place much importance on issues related to the reform.[64] For example, while higher educated respondents overwhelmingly identified loss of control of public spending as the primary danger to the *real,* less educated respondents placed virtually no importance on public spending. In fact, less educated respondents identified issues closer to the PT and domestic business groups' agendas: high interest rates, unemployment, and recession. Whereas more educated respondents saw the behavior of politicians as

64. Unpublished Ibope poll, "Pesquisa de Opinião Pública sobre Assuntos Gerais," May 1996. The poll surveyed 2,000 voters across Brazil from May 22–28, 1996, with results broken down by gender, age, and education.

central to the consolidation of the plan, less educated respondents again placed little importance on it. Perhaps most important, 21 percent of less educated respondents were unable to identify any obstacle to the Real Plan. Research by the CNI confirmed the lack of understanding of the importance of Cardoso's reform agenda: 70 percent of less educated respondents did not know what the constitutional reforms were.[65]

Thus, Cardoso finished 1996 in a vulnerable position. He had secured business support. Brazil had succeeded in drawing enormous amounts of foreign investment, which had played an important role in giving Cardoso the room to operate politically. Without the tremendous reserves and foreign investment in government debt paper, Cardoso, early in his term, would have faced a fiscal and perhaps balance-of-payments crisis. Nevertheless, politically, Cardoso had not accomplished even a significant fraction of what he and most observers agreed he should accomplish. His failure to reform the constitution revealed itself in alarming numbers: U.S.\$210 billion in debt; a fiscal deficit in the area of 4 percent; real interest rates that remained, despite their gradual decline, over 10 percent per year; a trade deficit of U.S.\$5 billion; and no certainty that the government would contain either debt or the deficit in 1997.

These elements put Cardoso in a bind. In the absence of a real fiscal adjustment, Cardoso had to continue to rely on interest rates and the exchange rate as artificial stabilizers of the *real*. The good news for Cardoso was that the Congress remained as fractured, venal, and patronage dependent as ever at the end of 1996. The significance for Cardoso and Brazil was that a legislative coalition for re-election and reform was available. If Cardoso could win re-election, then the incremental "muddling through" strategy could well succeed.

---

65. Unpublished survey data, made available during confidential author interview, June 1992, São Paulo.

7

Lessons from Brazil

Sustainable Reforms and the Development Consequences of
Private Business Power

As the Cardoso government moved through 1997, its coalition seemed to
gain strength. The industrial adjustment process forced firms to make
choices that deepened their dependence on continuation of the reform
process. By contrast, firms that could not competitively adjust were being
displaced rapidly. Thus, the neoliberal reform process appeared to have
consolidated, but the onset of the Asian financial crisis revitalized the
debate on the sustainability of reform. This chapter considers how the
industrial adjustment process entrenched business's commitment to the
neoliberal reform process and what that commitment means for assessments of business power. Finally, it explores how private-sector decisions
have influenced Brazil's development course.

DESCENT INTO THE ASIAN FLU

The year 1997 began with a number of threats to Cardoso's government.
The previous year, 1996, had closed with a much higher commercial
deficit than expected—over U.S.$5 billion. GDP growth remained moder-
ate while public-debt growth was staggering. In 1996, GDP growth was
roughly 4 percent, whereas public debt had risen from U.S.$120 to
U.S.$200 billion. Public deficits had come down somewhat from
1995—to roughly 4 percent of GDP—but remained too high by all ac-

counts. Finally, real unemployment, as measured by the IBGE or DIEESE, remained around 16 percent with little promise of coming down quickly.

On the political front, Cardoso faced a number of problems. The constitutional reform agenda had barely advanced through 1996. As a consequence, the government continued to rely on a combination of high real interest rates and an overvalued exchange rate to maintain the stability of the *real*. Despite popular and business confidence about the future, the government's measures continued to exact a high price, particularly high rates of bankruptcy and unemployment, constrained economic growth, and the continuing favoring of imports over domestic products as well as exports.

Cardoso also faced the beginnings of presidential electoral competition. One early example came from nationalist opposition over the proposed privatization of the Companhia Vale do Rio Doce, one of the jewels in Brazil's parastatal crown: Itamar Franco appeared to be using the issue as a platform for his own presidential ambitions. Cardoso also faced a more dangerous opposition in Paulo Maluf. Maluf's success in the 1996 municipal elections in São Paulo emboldened him in his attacks on the government. Delfim Netto, a fellow party member, acted as his economic adviser. Delfim had spent 1996 repeatedly visiting business associations to make the apparently well-received case that the Cardoso government was mismanaging the economic reform process. Delfim's criticisms focused on the exchange rate, interest rates, and failure to orient constitutional reforms toward increasing domestic competitiveness. With Delfim's support, Maluf offered an economic reform program that proposed a more careful integration with the global economy.

Cardoso's tactical response in the latter half of 1996 had however effectively eliminated the most critical threats. Between June 1996 and early 1997, the government put its incremental approach in place as it passed a series of laws that eased the fiscal burden on exporters and small and microenterprises. The government introduced a system of fiscal credits that compensated exporters for payments of the tax on the circulation of goods and services (ICMS) and payroll taxes (PIS/PASEP and COFINS). In addition, the administration introduced several new lines of BNDES credit and imposed various restrictions on imports in hard-hit sectors. These measures directly responded to business criticisms about exporting taxes, inadequate financing, and unfair trade practices.

Cardoso's decision to push for a re-election amendment proved equally effective. By early 1997, it was clear that, faced with a choice, politicians and industrialists preferred Cardoso. Politicians lined up to make sure they remained in favor with the government. Paulo Maluf's fortunes changed as a corruption scandal implicated both him and his handpicked successor, Celso Pitta. Cardoso eventually bought off Maluf as well as Jaime Lerner, a popular former mayor of Curitiba and another potential rival. Despite a vote-buying scandal in the Congress, the re-election amendment passed by mid-1997.

With these victories in hand, Cardoso renewed his efforts at constitutional reform. Through late 1997, he managed to maneuver a moderate administrative reform through the preliminary rounds of congressional voting. He also introduced a tax reform bill that received high marks from the industrial community. Although it did not go as far as most observers believed it should, industrial leaders, such as Fernando Bezerra of the CNI, praised it for its primary focus on economic competitiveness.

Cardoso's tactical maneuvers effectively rebuilt industrialists' support for his government. Through 1997, business confidence and production rose, and investments continued, even though many business respondents still expressed concern about constitutional reform and the viability of the *real*. Groups such as FIESP, FIERGS, and the CNI continued to mobilize businesspeople to push for more rapid constitutional reforms.

Nevertheless, Cardoso's incremental approach appeared justified in the economic indicators. Inflation was estimated at less than 5 percent for the year. Industrial production rose dramatically over 1996. Although capital goods production declined 15.9 percent in 1996, it rose by 3.7 percent in 1997.[1] In fact, with privatizations continuing, the anticipated opening of the telecommunications industry, and renewed investment provoked by industry confidence, ABDIB and the BNDES identified over U.S.$180 billion in investments planned for the period between 1997 and 2005.[2] Transport materials, including auto parts, increased production by 10.9 percent.[3] In 1996, production had declined by only 0.3 percent, but net receipts had fallen in the auto parts sector by on average over 20 percent.[4] Pulp and paper production continued a relatively constant moderate pace of growth—3.3 percent in 1997 and over 2.2 percent in 1996.[5] Overall, manufacturing production grew 4.4 percent in 1997, climbing from only 1 percent growth in 1996.

1. Industrial Production Indicators, *Brazilian Central Bank Bulletin,* December 1997.
2. *Gazeta Mercantil, International Weekly Edition* (New York), October 13, 1997, p. 16.
3. *Gazeta Mercantil,* October 13, 1997, p. 16.
4. Data from *Gazeta Mercantil,* Balança Anual, 1996–97, p. 258. The decline translated into accumulated net losses of over 140 million *reals.*
5. *Brazilian Central Bank Bulletin,* December 1997.

Cardoso also put into place an infrastructure investment plan with both political and economic benefits. The plan, Brazil in Action, called for over U.S.$50 billion dollars in investments in areas such as telecommunications, energy, transportation, sanitation, and health.[6] The plan addressed widespread concerns about the country's declining infrastructure, including the industrial community's identification of infrastructure problems as a major source of investment risk.[7] The program also had crucial electoral benefits. The decision-making process was centered in the president's office with daily updates provided through the Internet. This process gave the president extraordinary control over spending. Although there was no evidence as of this writing that the president manipulated spending in any way, the government authorized over U.S.$2 billion dollars (U.S.$6 million per day from January to December) for twenty major projects to be concluded around the time of the 1998 presidential elections.[8]

Industrialists' satisfaction appeared in their high levels of confidence. According to one poll conducted by the National Confederation of Industry, over 70 percent of respondents believed that their firms had good chances of succeeding.[9] Of those, 30 percent reported that their confidence had increased a lot, while 32 percent reported that their confidence increased only a little. Only 12 percent reported having lost confidence.

In October 1997, the Asian flu arrived in Brazil. Just as the Mexican peso crisis of December 1994 had rocked other emerging markets, the onset of a financial crisis in Asia led skittish foreign investors to retreat from the Brazilian market. Between October 27 and October 30, close to U.S.$8 billion left the country. Brazilian Brady bonds, the principal instrument for trading Latin American debt, lost 30 percent of their value, while the São Paulo stock exchange lost 26 percent of its value. In an effort to contain the outflow of dollars, the Central Bank doubled interest rates and frantically intervened in the dollar market to protect the value of the *real*.

Thus, Brazil finally faced the kind of situation that analysts had feared throughout the course of the Real Plan. Nevertheless, the initial noncha-

6. Ministry of Planning and Budget, "Brasil em Ação." Internet document available at http://www.seplan.gov.br (cited December 1996).

7. CNI survey on investment. Internet document, November 1996, available at http://www.cni.org.br (cited November 1996).

8. *Gazeta Mercantil, International Weekly Edition* (New York), December 1, 1997, p. 4.

9. CNI/Ibope poll. Pesquisa de Opinião; Aspectos Econômicos. Internet document, May 1997, available at http://www.cni.org.br (cited June 1997).

lant government response surprised the business community. In his first press conference after the shock, Cardoso stated his confidence in the Brazilian economy, minimized the severity of the shock, and expressed his belief that the interest rate hike would be unrecessionary. Others were less sanguine. Paulo Maluf called the interest rates "pornographic"; the PT forecast the end of the *real*.[10] Foreign investors expressed disbelief at the government's apparent denial, while domestic industries cut production, scrapped sales and production plans, and unloaded stockpiles. Although the government initially dismissed the events of late October as a botched amateur speculative attack on the *real,* other interpretations suggested that Brazil was more vulnerable than most observers thought.

By November 10, the government appeared to have reached a similar conclusion. Cardoso introduced an emergency fiscal plan designed to reduce the budget deficit by U.S.$20 billion through a host of tax increases and spending cuts. He also called for a more rapid resolution of the constitutional reforms lagging in Congress. The effects of the package were brutal, landing heavily on the middle class. Nevertheless, Cardoso publicly stated that his re-election did not matter in the face of the need to protect the country and the currency. Indeed, the mix of tax hikes, interest-rate increases, spending cuts, withdrawal of fiscal incentives, and maintenance of the exchange-rate policy raised a crucial question: How sustainable was the reform process?

This book has argued that economic factors alone do not account for business behavior. Political signals play an important role in helping industrialists evaluate their preferences. In particular, I have highlighted how industrialists' perceptions of government performance in the present shape their expectations about and preferences for the future. This argument would expect business support for Cardoso to reflect the perceptions of his ability to maintain his policy commitments—not just economic factors such as interest rates or growth.

The early indication seemed to bear out this prediction. Public opinion polls in December 1997 showed declining rates of public approval of Cardoso, although still around 57 percent. José Dirceu, national president of the PT, gleefully predicted a second round in the 1998 presidential election, but early indications also suggested that much of the political establishment, including many governors, still supported Cardoso.[11] In fact,

---

10. Reported in *Gazeta Mercantil International* weekly edition, November 10, 1997, p. 3.
11. Reported in *Gazeta Mercantil International* weekly edition, November 17, 1997, p. 4.

even Paulo Maluf expressed his support as he shifted his ambitions to the São Paulo governorship.

In addition, many representatives of the business community expressed support. These public pronouncements also warned that the government could not maintain interest rates at such high levels for long. Nevertheless, they praised the president for the speed and boldness of his actions. A *Gazeta Mercantil* report found that many top executives from leading firms expected a poor first semester in 1998, but would not reschedule investments.[12] For example, representatives from capital goods, chemicals, and petrochemicals specifically noted that their investments were long term and thus unaffected by what they believed was only a short-term emergency.

In the ensuing weeks, the Congress passed most of Cardoso's emergency package, with some resistance to certain items such as the elimination of fiscal incentives in the Manaus Free Trade Zone and the increase in the income tax. Moreover, the Congress finally passed the administrative reform bill. Negotiations over two years had weakened the bill substantially, but the administration did expect to begin reaping fiscal benefits— over U.S.$7 billion in savings per year—in the medium term.[13]

By December, business confidence in the plan and the future appeared even higher. A poll conducted by the *Jornal do Brasil* found 81.7 percent reporting high expectations for 1998.[14] At the same time, José Roberto Mendonça de Barros, the secretary of economic policy, offered encouraging words by noting that interest rates could not and would not stay high for long. He concluded by predicting that January 1998 would be a critical month for determining Brazil's success.[15] Would the pro-reform coalition collapse if the emergency measures did not prevent a deepening crisis?

THE SUSTAINABILITY OF NEOLIBERAL REFORM

By the late 1990s, the analytical trend had moved from studying the emergence and successful implementation of reforms to the sustainability of

12. Reported in *Gazeta Mercantil International* weekly edition, November 17, 1997, p. 10.
13. Reported in *Gazeta Mercantil International* weekly edition, November 24, 1997, p. 3.
14. Reported in the *Jornal do Brasil*, December 21, 1997, p. 1.
15. Reported in *Gazeta Mercantil International* weekly edition, November 24, 1997, p. 7.

reforms. For the purposes of this book, there are two underlying questions. First, how durable is business support for economic reforms? Second, how capable is the government of maintaining a broad, electoral coalition in favor of reform? The answer to the first question has generated two contrasting opinions. On the one hand, Rodrik has argued that once reforms have begun and firms have had time to adjust, business support stabilizes.[16] On the other hand, Pastor and Wise, examining Mexico, have argued that economic fragility makes support for neoliberal reform much more uncertain.[17] The evidence for this book leads to the same conclusion as Rodrik's.

The stability of business support lies in three changes as the reform process proceeded. First, once price stability set in and Cardoso looked as if he would carry through the reform process, industrial firms began adjusting rapidly. The choice of strategy was not always the preferred outcome. Nevertheless, once firms chose, to some extent it locked them into a particular adjustment course that depended on continuation of the existing policy. Second, as the adjustment process continued, influence shifted in the business community generally and the industrial community specifically. Thus, many players who lost out in the adjustment process simply lost influence as well. To illustrate the first point, it is helpful to reconsider the emergent pattern in the three sectors analyzed earlier. In each of the three sectors (machine tools and equipment, auto parts, and to a much lesser extent pulp and paper), market conditions and government policy led firms to pursue particular strategies. Those strategies subsequently shaped the market in ways that make it difficult to conceive of a retreat from neoliberal reform, no matter how painful those reforms may be.

Pulp and paper in 1990 was among the most competitive sectors in the global economy. Thus, neoliberal reform per se was never a significant threat. Nevertheless, concerns about Fernando Collor and problems in the commercial liberalization (namely, concerns about dumping, inadequate investment conditions, and decaying infrastructure) led key members of the sector to mobilize against Collor. Leading members of the sector joined Carlos Eduardo Moreira Ferreira's FIESP campaign in which concern about liberalization figured prominently. Leading members of the sector participated in IEDI's secretive coalition-building efforts. Finally, the sectoral association ANFPC (renamed BRACELPA in

---

16. Rodrik, "The Rush to Free Trade," 83.
17. Pastor and Wise, "Origins and Sustainability," 487–89.

1997), devoted much effort to lobbying for improved financing from the BNDES, which it secured in 1992 and then again in 1996.

At the level of the market, the sector remained largely unchanged from 1990 to 1997. In 1997, there were 220 companies operating 255 plants, a slight increase in the number of companies and a slight decrease in the number of plants from 1990. Both exports and imports rose sharply over the period, particularly after the Real Plan, when domestic consumption increased by 33 percent over the period 1993–97. The ANFPC and the BNDES jointly estimated that the sector needed to invest roughly U.S.$13 billion between 1996 and 2005 to meet domestic demand and maintain exports.[18] As of 1997, the BNDES and the ANFPC estimated that roughly U.S.$3 billion of investments had begun,[19] of which 800 million was in capital goods.[20] Thus, overall, the sector had not committed itself to irreversible changes, but the pulp and paper sector was always much less likely to oppose neoliberal reform.

That situation was much less true for auto parts and machine tools and equipment. By 1997, the auto parts sector had significantly suffered as a result of the commercial liberalization process. The number of firms in the sector had halved and sharp contractions in numbers were anticipated for the future as well. Although parts production had on average climbed over the period 1993–97, many firms had operated at losses. Furthermore, the sector had experienced a rapid process of "denationalization" of control—shifting of ownership from domestic to foreign firms. These effects stemmed largely from changes in the global auto industry and from explicit government policy. In turn, these changes made a reversal of policy unlikely, regardless of the 1998 presidential election.

As noted in Chapter 6, the auto industry's shift to complete systems suppliers radically altered the character of supply relations. Thus, the confidence that the auto parts sector expressed in 1993 reflected invalid assumptions about the structure of supply. The shift to systems producers demanded intense capital investments to achieve competitive economies of scale. The need for increases in size for "first tier" producers pressured domestic firms to seek foreign partnerships.[21]

18. Angela Regina Pires Macedo and Maria Goretti A. de Carvalho, "Forest Products: Pulp and Paper—The Impact of the 'Real' Plan," BNDES. Internet document available at http://www.bndes.gov.br (cited December 1997).

19. Macedo and de Carvalho, "Forest Products."

20. Genilson Fernandes Santana, "A Indústria de Bens de Capital" (Secretariat of Political Economy Paper, December 1997, Appendix F).

21. Discussed in Angela Maria Medeiros M. Santos and Claudia Soares Costa, "A Reestru-

The shift to systems suppliers also represented a change in the power relations between the two sectors. As Posthuma has noted, the new production system allowed assemblers multiple supply options: systems suppliers, single part suppliers, imported parts or systems, in-house production, and subcontracting relations.[22] The options gave the auto industry tremendous leverage against parts suppliers. This leverage allowed the assemblers to push costs on to suppliers, leading to substantial operating losses in the sector.

Government policy sharply exacerbated the inequality of the relations. In 1994, the auto industry played its most important trump card. Threatening to invest in Argentina to export to Brazil, the industry succeeded in obtaining an "industrial policy" to encourage it to stay in Brazil. The 1995 industrial policy consisted of protection (70 percent for domestically produced cars), some fiscal incentives, and extraordinary tariff reductions on auto parts and capital goods (anywhere from 0 to 2 percent). Parts producers also noted that the high interest rates, overvalued exchange rates, and procedural lags in import payments created strong incentives to import, regardless of the prices of domestic goods. Similarly, the absence until 1996 of antidumping rules or an office to enforce them made unfair trade practices hard to combat. Government decisions thus sharply exacerbated the effects of the change in supply relations.

To be fair, the government decision translated into a commitment from assemblers to remain in Brazil and to export to the other Mercosur countries. It also led to promises of roughly U.S.$20 billion in investments in the auto industry by 2002. In the period following the introduction of the Real Plan, auto consumption rose dramatically, spurred by the introduction of lower priced vehicles and favorable credit conditions for auto purchases.

Nevertheless, it is also fair to ask whether the government had any other choice. Clearly the issues of high interest rates and overvalued exchange rates were dependent on congressional approval of constitutional reforms. Without that approval, the Cardoso administration had little alternative to secure the *real*. The administration also demonstrated a willingness to use tariff and nontariff barriers at various times. The auto industry policy sharply discriminated on tariffs between firms that produced locally and those that did not, even in the face of protests from

---

turação do Setor de Auto-Peças," BNDES study, Internet document, available at http://www.b-ndes.gov.br (cited July 1996).

22. Posthuma, "Industrial Restructuring."

Argentina and threats from the United States, Korea, and Japan. The government resorted to tariffs as an emergency response to long-ignored charges of dumping in sectors like textiles and toys. In late 1997, the government used administrative blocks to delay imports as a way to contain the commercial deficit.

The government could have used tariff and nontariff barriers to discourage firms from relocating to Argentina and could easily have restructured the policy so that it would hit domestic suppliers less sharply. In any event, not only were these requests from the suppliers' sectoral associations ignored, but they were dismissed as the complaints of cartorialists and oligopolists. The requests were heeded only when the commercial balance began its steep decline through 1996, by which time it was almost certainly too late to change the auto industry policy.

The results have clearly emerged. Besides the dramatic decline in the number of firms producing, other changes have also been rapid. Between 1991 and 1996, employment in the sector declined from 255 thousand workers to 192 thousand. Imports have increased at a much faster rate than exports—on average 27 percent per year from 1991 to 1996 versus 9 percent per year for exports. Imports increased from U.S.$844 million in 1991 to nearly U.S.$3.5 billion by 1996, while exports rose from U.S.$2 billion to U.S.$3.5 billion by 1996. Firms were also actively engaged in improving quality and productivity. Research by SINDIPEÇAS revealed that by 1996 nearly 75 percent of 250 sampled firms were implementing ISO-9000 certification programs, the same percentage was conducting supplier-training programs, nearly 70 percent were developing statistical process control programs, nearly 65 percent were implementing just-in-time, and nearly 50 percent were developing total quality control programs.[23]

The most striking change was the rapid shift in ownership. Domestic firms sought foreign partners as a solution to the significant challenges facing them after 1995. Firms pursued three options: outright acquisition by a foreign firm, mergers, and joint ventures. Between 1995 and 1997, some leading firms in the sector pursued this strategy. As a consequence, market factors and government policy led to a new clustering of interests that make any retreat from supporting neoliberal reform unlikely. In fact, given the size of the investments that both the assemblers and the parts

23. Data reported in Angela Maria Medeiros M. Santos and Claudia Soares Costa, "A Reestruturação do Setor de Auto-Peças," BNDES study. Internet document, available at http://www.bndes.gov.br (cited November 1996).

producers have undertaken (nearly U.S.$6 billion by parts producers alone between 1991 and 1996), the sector depends on continuing success in implementing reforms in Brazil (Table 7.1).

Although the data for machine tools and equipment are less precise than those for auto parts, similar trends have been observed. Economists agree that the capital goods sector is critical for absorbing and diffusing new technology, but the Cardoso administration made no effort to protect or promote it until mid-1997. The BNDES did work with the sectoral association to improve financing conditions under the bank's FINAME program, but interest rates remained a disincentive for private banks to participate in the program. As the BNDES did not directly lend itself, the unwillingness of private banks to participate led to a substantial decline in loan disbursements from 1994 to 1996.[24] Aside from that program, no other government incentives, promotion, or protection existed. Moreover, the government's efforts to reduce import taxes on capital goods and to lower tariff protection through the auto industry policy heightened the impact of neoliberal reform.

As a consequence, both the number of firms and the level of employment fell sharply from 1990 to 1997. At the same time, the sector made significant efforts to improve productivity and quality of production. Between 1992 and 1996, receipts per employee in the sector rose from U.S.$90,000 to over U.S.$115,000. Capital goods exports rose from 7.7 percent of production in 1989 to an estimated 17.9 percent in 1997.[25]

Imports told another story. In 1989, imports measured only 11.9 percent of total domestic production. By 1996, they had reached 52.9 percent, and the estimate for 1997 was as high as 77.6 percent. The rise in imports posed a stark choice for producers in the sector. If they were to compete, they needed to achieve globally competitive production standards, but the period 1990–96 presented wildly erratic demand for capital goods, and high inflation affected the period 1990–94. As a consequence of these two factors, firms in the sector found it difficult to plan or implement more than defensive or reactive adjustments. Even after the Real Plan, the sector still faced exorbitant financial costs, both for itself and for customers—a significant factor in capital goods competition. The sector suffered from a lack of well-qualified labor. Finally, as mentioned above, government policy favored consumption of capital goods over promotion of domestic production.

---

24. Santana, "A Indústria."
25. Data reported in Santana, "A Indústria."

Table 7.1. Mergers and acquisitions in the auto parts sector

Acquisitions:

Buyer	Purchase
Brosol	Forin, Metalúrgica Micro, Ferragens Haga
Bradesco	Brosol
Iochpe Maxion	Brosol
Mastra	De Maio Gallo
Cofap	Kadron
Mahle	Ind. Iwega
Mahle and Cofap	Metal Leve
Sachs	Borg Warner
Mannesman	Sachs
Plascar	Plavigor, Carto, Mangotex
BTR	Plascar
Acesita	Sifco
Enermex	Durex
Dana Corp.	Braseixos
Dana Corp.	Simesc, Wiest
Bradesco	Tupy
Usiminas	Brasinca
SPS	Metalac
Rassini	Fabrini
Bosch	Bendix
Randon Part.	Fras-le
Eaton	Clark
Delphi Packard	Sielin

Joint Ventures:
  Acil *and* Pianfei, Irausa, Sommer
  Arteb *and* Sico
  Trambusti Naue *and* Woodbridge
  Du Pont *and* Renner
  Alcoa Al. Brazil *and* Alcoa Fujikura Ltd.
  Sonave *and* Circle International
  Varga Freios *and* Albarus

Mergers:
  Getoflex *and* Dunlop
  Donaldson *and* Filtobras
  DHB *and* Maxidrive
  Bosch *and* Allied Signal
  Allied Signal *and* Bendix, Jurid, Garret
  Lucas Ind. *and* Varity Corp.

SOURCE: Angela Maria Medeiros M. Santos and Claudia Soares Costa, "A Reestruturação do Setor de Auto-Peças," BNDES study. Internet document, available at http://www. bndes.gov.br (cited July 1996).

The resulting strategies turned largely on differing associations with foreign capital. First, a large number of multinational firms bought into the sector, through either acquisitions or joint ventures. Second, many domestic producers turned to assembling premanufactured kits rather than producing their own product. Finally, a large number of firms stopped producing locally and became licensed importers and distributors (or changed the mix of their distribution to include some of their own production and some imports). In fact, in a CNI survey, machine tools and equipment producers noted that roughly 50 percent of imports in their markets were distributed by local producers.[26] Naturally, many firms simply closed operations. One trend emerging from these responses was that higher technology—higher value-added production—moved out of Brazil, leaving behind the more labor-intensive portion of the industry.

The consequence of these rapid changes, particularly in the latter two sectors, was a greater fragmentation in the industrial community. One segment of industry suffered tremendous harm from the way that neoliberal reform occurred in Brazil. The pace of change, once the reform process and inflation stabilized, forced all firms to respond rapidly. As a result, many leading domestic firms sought partnerships with foreign capital, linking them more solidly with the global economy. Many multinational corporations (MNC) entered the economy, also strengthening the connection to the global economy. Finally, many weaker domestic firms sought associations with foreign capital as well, thus tying them to a commercial liberalization strategy. By 1997, the industrial community appeared to have foreclosed many alternative strategies. Their choices left them dependent on successful resolution of the constitutional reform process, as reflected in the intensity with which a wide array of business associations continued to call for reforms through the 1995–97 period.[27]

In addition, the industrial community was likely to continue supporting neoliberal reform because of changes in political and economic influence. As the reform process unfolded, many leading industrialists under the ISI-corporatist model appeared to have lost their ability to protect and promote the industrial community, either because their firms declined in importance or because they themselves were associated with foreign capital.

The most striking example of this was the sale of Metal Leve to the

---

26. CNI, *Abertura Comercial e Estratégia Tecnológica: A Visão dos Líderes Industriais Brasileiras em 95*, 16.

27. An excellent review of business positions and concerns, with significant support from prominent Brazilian economists, is the FIESP publication "O Custo do Atraso," FIESP/CIESP, June 1997.

German giant auto parts maker, Mahle, discussed in Chapter 6. Other crucial examples abound, some of the most telling of which come from an inspection of IEDI in 1997. Abraham Kasinsky of Cofap, one of Brazil's most important firms and one of the leading auto-parts firms, teamed with the German MNC Mahle to acquire Metal Leve, at one time represented by fellow IEDI member Celso Lafer. One year later, Mahle simply consumed Cofap. Also in the auto-parts sector, Ivonchy Iochpe took over Maxion as part of an effort to acquire sufficient scale to compete. The move left the new company, Iochpe-Maxion, in dire financial condition. Paulo Villares's giant operation scaled down significantly and essentially became a subcontractor. Bardella, facing serious financial problems, was involved in a massive reorganization. Ricardo Semler's operations were in financial difficulties. Other members of IEDI were succeeding, however. Gilberto Dupas became one of the most highly regarded consultants, for example, playing a lead role in brokering the Metal Leve buyout. Eugenio Staub attached his fortunes to the Amazon Export Promotion Zone–based Eletros—an organization that largely served the lobbying interests of Amazon-based MNCs. José Ermirio de Moraes Filho joined foreign investors to position himself for the privatization of telecommunications.

When interviewed in 1996, many industrialists observed that the new leaders in the business community differed from the old guard of family-owned industries. Industrialists identified two sources of new leaders. First, several industrialists observed that the emerging professional executive class, many of whom worked in multinationals, had assumed a new importance. By their testimony, this group identified more with the model and mode of behavior of an advanced economy. The second group frequently mentioned was new leaders in the financial market. For example, Bradesco Bank, a leading institution in the merger and acquisition wave of the mid-1990s, was noted as an example.

Although this sampling of opinion was limited in size, the answers seemed supported by the empirical events discussed above. These speculative observations suggested that many industrialists most likely to push for a retreat from neoliberal reform were increasingly losing their prominence and their voice. The *Estado de São Paulo* described the sale of Metal Leve as the turning over of a page in history—the end of an era.[28]

Even if the industrial community was unlikely to retreat from the neoliberal reform process, the larger population could still defeat it electorally. Large majorities expressed satisfaction with their lives and confi-

---

28. *Estado de São Paulo,* June 13, 1996, p. 1.

dence in the future through 1997, but, unemployment, health service, education, land reform, crime, and corruption remained areas where voters did not rate Cardoso's government highly. If the *real* were to collapse, it would be easy to conceive of the emergence of an anti-Cardoso, anti-neoliberal reform coalition. As of 1997, it was not clear to what extent any real alternative program was available for an opposition government. Brazil's fiscal problems demand solutions, and in the short run probably any government would be heavily reliant on foreign capital inflows. In any event, speculating on the larger electoral issues surrounding economic reform is beyond the scope of this book. On the surface, it does not appear that the Brazilian business community has had significant influence on broader electoral outcomes. One question that this raises is how powerful is business?

HOW POWERFUL IS BUSINESS IN LATIN AMERICA?

Business in Latin America has been alternatively depicted as passive and weak and as deeply privileged and extremely powerful. These contrasting views have depended on what was being examined. Analysts examining issues related to the market, competition, risk taking, and hegemonic leadership in pushing for a liberal, capitalist society have tended to see Latin American business as passive and dependent. Analysts examining democratic stability, regime change, and the persistence of uneven capitalist development have identified business as extraordinarily powerful and privileged. Naturally, there is some truth in both sets of claims.

The question of business power in Latin America has not been the subject of the kind of sustained debate that has occurred with reference to politics in advanced industrial democracies, particularly the United States. The U.S. debate turned on whether business was an unusually privileged group or merely one among many with no special claim to extraordinary privilege.

On the one hand, scholars such as Charles Lindblom focused on the structural power of business in a market economy.[29] Responsibility for investment and job creation lies with private actors. Democratically

---

29. Charles Lindblom, *Politics and Markets* (New York: Basic Books, 1976), 152–56. This section reviews the implications of what Lindblom refers to as "corporate discretion on delegated decisions."

elected politicians depend on good economic performance for their success. Consequently, businesspeople can extract concessions from politicians on a routine basis and in an inequitable way. Furthermore, these private actors escape democratic control because democratic capitalism delegates decision making over crucial welfare functions to the private sector. Finally, Lindblom observed that business added to this power by having an overwhelming advantage in the quantity of lobbying organizations and available lobbying funds.

By contrast, Robert Dahl's classic *Who Governs* (1961) presented the most elegant and enduring depiction of relative equality of interests.[30] Dahl's analysis does not deny the economic advantages of the business class, but his discussion of democratic politics identifies a series of alternative power sources. Thus, individuals or groups with intense preferences and knowledge may bring special resources to bear in well-defined issue areas relevant to them. Time, energy, passion, education, media attention, as well as money and skill all interact in unpredictable ways to produce winners in political conflicts. One of the most powerful resources in democracies is voters. Although largely uninvolved and not even necessarily informed, voters respond to political messages and through their numbers are able to thwart even the most passionate and skillful interests. As a consequence, politicians always have to respond to what they believe voters prefer, even without any overt political mobilization or clear evidence of public preferences.

In *Fluctuating Fortunes,* Vogel (1989) attempted to reconcile these competing views of business power by framing power as a variable that shifts over time and issue area.[31] Vogel argued that business power increased in hard economic times when the public was more likely to grant concessions to the private sector in the hope of spurring new growth. Conversely, the public and politicians were more likely to favor adding regulatory burdens in times of prosperity. Vogel further argued that business power increased when political issues affected the business community as a whole, thus prompting a united front among various business organizations.

The analysis in this book suggests that these three views are not totally incompatible. At the core of Lindblom's analysis lie two central claims: First, businesses have significant discretion in decisions with critical public welfare consequences. Firms make crucial decisions about whether,

---

30. Robert Dahl, *Who Governs* (New Haven: Yale University Press, 1961).
31. David Vogel, *Fluctuating Fortunes* (New York: Basic Books, 1989).

how, and where to invest, as well as how many and what kind of workers to employ. Democratic capitalism allows firms a great deal of discretion over these decisions, yet they have enormous consequences for growth and distribution of wealth. Second, even developmental or interventionist states depend heavily on the private sector to drive the economy. Thus, even if businesses do not attempt to extract concessions, democratic politicians have to worry about private-sector performance for electoral reasons.

Nevertheless, these constraints set relatively broad parameters for politicians' and business behavior. As this book shows, the Cardoso administration made fundamental choices about which parts of the private sector to favor and how to do so. The wide variety of ways in which successive Brazilian governments have tried to influence investment decisions and protect or not protect different sectors reveals how much latitude Lindblom's constraints allow.

In fact, much of Collor's and Cardoso's behavior is best understood with reference to Dahl's observations on the power of voters as an influence on politicians' behavior. Cardoso in particular has maintained the vitality of the *real* and its attack on inflation as the centerpiece of his administration. All other policy choices have been subordinated to securing the currency. This has made perfect sense politically given Brazil's history of inflation and its disproportionate impact on the large mass of poor Brazilian voters. Thus, Cardoso has ignored industrialists' concerns whenever they conflicted with interest-rate and exchange-rate policy.

Even Cardoso's policy concessions can be understood in terms of electoral concerns. His use of tariff and nontariff barriers, tax incentives and exemptions, and extensions of new lines of credit all link to concerns about employment, growth, and the commercial balance (with its implications for the currency). Most of the concessions that industrial sectors received from Cardoso after mid-1996 were items they had been demanding for some time. Cardoso relented in a context of mounting legislative difficulties, decreasing popular support, and rising business restlessness.

The relative lack of business power becomes even clearer when we consider electoral results. Business groups did not successfully elect their preferred candidates in the 1989 election. Ultimately, their shift to support Collor against Lula was inconsequential in the former's victory. In fact, Collor distanced himself from the business community as part of his campaign strategy. Similarly, business support for Cardoso was not significant in electing him in 1994. Cardoso would not have won without the success of the *real* and his ability to claim credit. In the same way, business support for Cardoso in 1998 is unlikely to affect the electoral outcome in any notable way.

In addition, the business community has been unable to influence congressional voting on constitutional reform since it first appeared on the legislative agenda in 1991 (not to mention its failure to effectively influence the writing of the document in the first instance). Despite repeated efforts, improved lobbying efforts, and substantial, ongoing mobilizations in favor of reform, legislators have followed their narrower electoral concerns. Business groups' only successes have come through narrow, particularistic organizations and even then primarily through privileged contacts in the bureaucracy.

For some analysts, this fragmentation represents only a partial limit on business influence. Businesses cannot influence the broader political process, but they remain powerful and effective at protecting their private interests. For example, Weyland noted that organizational fragmentation in the business community allowed businesses to protect tax privileges against efforts to address equity concerns.[32] Echoing this argument, Diniz and Boschi observed that the business community had failed to produce a modern leadership.[33] They reported that business leaders themselves have complained that organizational fragmentation has enhanced *jogos dos interesses* (jockeying for personal gain) over collective lobbying efforts. Thus, businesses were able to promote their private interests at the expense of a "modernizing" agenda.

Other analysts, following Vogel, have seen fragmentation as a weakness. For example, Payne argued that natural divisions in the business community make it hard for business elites to mobilize in the absence of a clear threat to private investment.[34] Business elites can overcome their organizational fragmentation, ideological differences, and internal competition only when the threat affects the community at large and individual action is unable to resolve the problem.

Organization clearly matters. The way that business interests are organized affects whose interests are represented and how effectively they are represented. Organizational factors, however, are less determinative of business influence than are regime structure and electoral politics. The way that the regime structures access determines how much influence business has over what issues, and how business exercises it. In turn, this

32. Weyland, *Democracy Without Equity: Failures of Reform in Brazil* (Pittsburgh: University of Pittsburgh Press, 1996).
33. Diniz and Boschi, "Lideranças Empresariais."
34. Payne, *Brazilian Industrialists*, 153–59.

influence varies with politicians' electoral strategies. This point is the missing piece in Vogel's effort to reconcile Dahl and Lindblom. Vogel noted that public perceptions play a crucial role in determining to what extent business can extract concessions. Yet, it is politicians' perceptions of voter preferences that really matter. Business mobilization and lobbying only work to the extent that politicians believe voters support efforts to promote business or that business mobilization influences the outcome of electoral competition. When the opposite is true, business unity and organizational coherence matter little. Even had IEDI and FIESP succeeded in effectively leading the entire industrial community, they would have faced a fragmented state and politicians whose political priorities conflicted with industrialists' preferences.

The preceding discussion suggests that politicians do not need to worry about crafting support for neoliberal reform. As long as they can muster political support from key electoral constituencies, business groups have no choice but to go along. As Lindblom noted, however, business is not like all other social groups in one important aspect: Private decisions about business strategies have crucial public welfare implications. Even if politicians have the political room to ignore business concerns, business as a class remains powerful in that its decentralized choices can lead to undesirable outcomes.

DEVELOPMENTAL CONSEQUENCES OF BUSINESS STRATEGIES IN BRAZIL

In 1978, eight leading industrialists issued the Democratic Manifesto of the Bourgeoisie. The Manifesto was a letter printed in the *Gazeta Mercantil*. Among various points made, the writers stressed the need for a national dialogue on development. The writers urged the military government to withdraw so that all important actors could openly and democratically discuss what development policy should emphasize. Five years later, the group (with some additions) issued a renewed call for a national discussion of development and industrial policy. Six years after that, this same group joined with IEDI and renewed its appeal.

These industrial leaders believed that the country's economic crisis could be resolved only through a coordinated effort between business and the state. As a developing country, it was important for Brazil to explicitly identify strategic sectors and to identify mechanisms for promoting them. These industrial elites were particularly concerned about absorption of new technology, correcting the gap between "backward" and "modern" sectors and integrating with the global economy on competitive terms.

In fact, the BNDES shared their concern. Through the late 1980s, the bank issued a series of documents entitled "Competitive Integration" making the same case. This position expressed itself in the bank's approach to privatization, which emphasized competitiveness rather than financial considerations. Finally, these views expressed themselves in the industrial policy proposal of Antonio Kandir, Fernando Collor's first planning secretary and later Fernando Henrique Cardoso's minister of planning.

Unfortunately, the discussion never took place. Cardoso communicated much more effectively with the industrial community, particularly through Kandir and Minister of Industry Francisco Dornelles. As Payne noted, communicating with the industrial community is of vital concern.[35] However, it helped to maintain political support, it did not translate into any effective discussion of development priorities. As a consequence, Brazilian industrialists were left to make private decisions without reference to any strategic framework. Commercial liberalization led firms to embrace a host of competitiveness-enhancing measures. Brazilian firms increased productivity, embraced new quality production techniques, and undertook new investments in technology and new productive capacity.

A host of other factors led to less encouraging private decisions. First, the continuation of commercial liberalization without successful resolution of the country's fiscal problems exacerbated the advantages already accruing to foreign capital and imports. Inefficient taxation, high capital costs, an overvalued exchange rate, decaying infrastructure, and uncompetitive payroll costs have all shaped industrialists' private strategic choices. In addition, relative government indifference to repeated expressions of concern about national industry has also provided clear signals to domestic industrialists. Finally, despite Cardoso's achievements in stabilizing the economy and maintaining his political course, there remain underlying concerns about the resolution of the country's fiscal problems. This fact has also shaped business strategies.

This cluster of concerns has led to four trends with potentially suboptimal consequences. First, the industrial community has primarily oriented

35. This observation is one of the crucial and central conclusions of Payne, *Brazilian Industrialists*.

itself toward the domestic market despite the government's efforts to promote exports. Several interviewed industrialists commented that the Brazil cost was significant enough that the country was not likely to serve as an effective export platform in the medium term. Even multinational executives, for whom the Brazil cost was less onerous, believed that the combination of infrastructure weaknesses and domestic taxes (including payroll taxes) made exports a subordinate strategy. Instead, interviewed industrialists repeatedly pinned their growth expectations on hopes that the internal market would continue to expand. This interview evidence was supported by a CNI survey that found that most firms were investing for the domestic market.[36] This tendency raises some concerns, however. First, the government has had to increase fiscal deficits to minimize tax costs on exports. The administration's announced expectation was that rising exports would reduce the commercial deficit and thereby justify the fiscal losses.

Yet, this trend points to continuing commercial deficit problems. In fact, by the end of 1997, projections for the commercial deficit had come down for the year and for 1998 but only because Cardoso's austerity package had brought projected GDP growth down to 1 percent. If not for that, the commercial deficit was on a track of continuing increases. The result is that Brazil remains caught, either having to restrain GDP growth or risking balance-of-payments problems. Furthermore, the country faces real risks to the *real* as long as it continues to run large commercial deficits that require offsetting capital inflows.

A related problem points to limited growth without continuously improving income distribution. The initial success of the Real Plan had a one-time effect of rapidly improving income distribution for the large mass of the working population.[37] Without inflation's regressive redistributive effect, many consumers entered the market for the first time. As a consequence, a wide variety of consumer goods hit record consumption levels in the first two years of the plan, but this does not represent sustainable growth without continued efforts to improve income distribution. As one interviewed MNC consumer durables executive noted, future growth depends on the lowest income categories (Class D) to consume like Class

36. CNI survey on investments. Manuel R. Agosin reports the same conclusion in Manuel R. Agosin, ed., *Foreign Direct Investment in Latin America* (Washington, D.C.: Inter-American Development Bank, 1995).

37. The limitations of the Real Plan are discussed in Timothy J. Power and Timmons Roberts, "A New Brazil? The Changing Sociodemographic Context of Brazilian Democracy," in Kingstone and Power, eds., *Democratic Brazil*.

C, and Class C to consume like Class B, and so on. Otherwise, this pattern of consumption stops once low-income consumers complete their first (and only) purchases of a wide range of consumer goods (notably televisions, radios, washing machines and other white line goods, concrete for home improvements).

The second concern is that this orientation to the domestic market also points to the potential for surplus capacity in a number of key sectors. Sectors such as automobiles and televisions have attracted large investments from nearly all important producers in the world. Representatives of these sectors expressed doubt that the market could support all these players without constantly improving income distribution. In particular, several MNC executives observed that a critical dynamic driving foreign direct investment was competition among MNCs to gain (or maintain) a position in Brazil's potentially vast internal market. According to this view, the risk of not entering Brazil, and thereby losing profit potential to rival MNCs, was greater than the risk of suffering losses should the *real* collapse. Although this dynamic has probably played a positive role in attracting large numbers of producers in the short term, it sets up the probability of some sort of rationalization (and consequently loss of producers and jobs) of these sectors in the medium to long term.

Third, trends in various sectors point to some degree of denationalization of ownership and loss of control in key areas of technology. Mergers and acquisitions became increasingly common through the 1995–98 period. Although the majority of these transactions occurred among domestic firms, many represented foreign buyouts. Some sectors, notably auto parts, witnessed extensive shifts in the composition of ownership. In many other sectors, foreign companies bought into or acquired important industry leaders, for example, Monsanto's acquisition of agroindustry leader Agroceres. In other sectors, notably capital goods, many local producers shifted from domestic production to distributing imports or assembling kits. Both author interviews and BNDES reports suggest that this move has tended toward ending production of high-technology, higher value-added goods. Instead, local producers have continued labor-intensive, lower technology production. The 1997 BNDES study of capital goods particularly expressed concern as the sector is commonly viewed as a critical conduit of technological innovation.[38]

As of this writing in 1997, the evidence remains too fragmentary to reach firm conclusions, but the evidence suggests that a recomposition of

38. For example, see Santana, "A Indústria."

the triple alliance is taking place. Peter Evans, in his depiction of the triple alliance, suggested a relation wherein MNCs provided technical know-how and capital.[39] These firms entered into high-technology, capital-intensive industries, whereas local producers were relegated to labor-intensive production and to roles as junior partners supplying political and internal market connections. Finally, the state provided large-scale production of basic inputs such as naphtha or steel. These three roles provided a stable alliance in which all three partners flourished.

The triple alliance always described a general framework that varied substantially by sector, and this remains true as of 1997. It also appears as if the country's emerging development model is becoming much more reliant on foreign capital, however. With increasing state withdrawal, foreign capital has entered into steel production, aircraft production, and petrochemicals and is poised to enter telecommunications and the energy sector (natural gas and oil). The presence of foreign capital has become stronger in auto parts, consumer electronics, agroindustry, and capital goods and has increased among transport assemblers. Pulp and paper remains one of the few sectors without notable entrance of new foreign investment.

Although economic theory does not suggest anything wrong with this state of affairs, the literature on development suggests that this trend may be undesirable. Certainly, Latin America's earlier experience in the liberal export period suggests both economic and political risks to excessive dependence on foreign capital. Foreign capital limited the political space to forge accommodations between elite and nonelite classes. Economically, the dominance of foreign capital limited the ability of governments to shape development as well as to promote absorption of technology and the local capacity to develop it. In this period of globalization and neoliberal dominance, foreign investment has been welcomed as a crucial engine of growth, but developing countries in the future may come to regret their extensive reliance on firms that define their production strategies outside the country, have no loyalty or commitment to the host country, and in fact may shift production relatively easily out of the country.[40]

The fourth related concern is that interviews with industrialists in a variety of sectors suggest that many firms have left exit options should the *real* collapse. Many interviewed industrialists noted that they were in

39. Evans, *Dependent Development,* 113–21.
40. The complex and variable effects of financial globalization are discussed in comparative perspective in Leslie Elliott Armijo, *Financial Globalization and Democracy in Emerging Markets* (New York: St. Martin's Press, 1999).

a position to quickly move from local production to imports, particularly because many firms entered the market by purchasing existing operations rather than investing in new capacity. As a consequence, this lower-cost, risk-averse strategy gained an entry for MNCs, provided them with an existing distribution network, and facilitated an exit option should the *real* fail. The evidence for this trend also remains suggestive as of this writing. The pattern of foreign direct investment and the character of merger and acquisition activity tend to support this conclusion. Similarly, such lower-cost investment seems to be reflected in relatively low levels of investment as a percent of GDP. The CNI and ECLA estimated that private-sector investment in the period 1995–97 represented 3 to 3.5 percent of GDP—slightly above the period 1990–93, roughly even with the percentage over the last decade (3.4 percent), and well below the rate of 4.5 percent of GDP for the 1972–80 period.[41]

LESSONS FOR STUDYING ECONOMIC REFORM FROM THE BRAZILIAN CASE

This book has traced the ways that the Brazilian business community faced the economic reform process and the way that the political process shaped the dynamics of business support. Two critical questions for future research and reflection emerged from the research. Research on business politics and free trade would benefit from a combination of formal, deductive modeling and qualitative, comparative research. Second, the evidence also raises some questions about the claims of the large, and growing, institutionalist literature. Studies of political institutions, particularly party systems, have raised profound concerns about the durability, quality, and governability of countries with poor constitutional designs. Yet, the evidence suggests that the effects of party systems on the economy are not so clear-cut.

Deductive Versus Inductive Methods

The occasionally acrimonious debate between formal modeling and qualitative research sometimes obscures the natural middle ground: that the

41. CNI survey on investments.

two methods can be complementary as opposed to purely rival methods. Deductive models offer certain clear advantages. First, formalism contributes to analytic work through its insistence that scholars make their assumptions explicit and that they precisely specify causal hypotheses. In this regard, formal models help to crystallize and clarify our thinking about causal relations. Second, formal methods allow scholars to encompass more cases in their analyses than qualitative methods can. The danger is that formal models may be too mechanical—though qualitative methods may fall into the same trap. Analysts must be careful about deriving preferences from static scores on some variable or set of variables. Treating preferences as given, as this method often does, can oversimplify reality too much and consequently misunderstand the much more complex dynamics that occur around trade reform.[42]

Qualitative research is not inherently better, but modeling can benefit from the advantages of the comparative method. For example, as discussions of "process tracing" have noted, comparative, qualitative research is well suited to tracing the way that a complex set of variables may interact and influence one another. This approach can be helpful in understanding the politics of free trade. Social coalitions may be fluid, and mechanical derivations of preferences based on static, material characteristics may not capture the range of factors that influence actors' definitions of their preferences. As a consequence, politicians may have ample opportunity to shape preferences through a variety of appeals. Moreover, the operationalization of seemingly simple variables may not be so simple in reality. For example, Alt, Frieden, Gilligan, Rodrik, and Rogowski expressed a belief that explaining the politics of free trade lies in specific-factors–based models. On the face of it, specific factors seems like an easy variable to operationalize and generate scores for relevant actors. Yet, by Alt and colleagues' own account, specific factors represents a remarkably difficult variable to define and measure. The review authors noted that few efforts have been made to examine how to measure specificity and those that have been made tend to be circular and/or labor intensive and qualitative in character.[43] One significant problem of factor specificity is that a vast number of factors can create specificity, including political privileges—something widely dispersed in a highly politicized market

---

42. A similar critique of classical political economy approaches is in Schamis, "Distributional Coalitions."

43. Alt, Frieden, Gilligan, Rodrik, and Rogowski, "The Political Economy of International Trade," 704–9.

such as Brazil.[44] Furthermore, as the evidence in Chapter 3 suggests, such benefits can help promote competitiveness (as they did with pulp and paper) or may detract from it (as with machine tools and equipment and to a lesser extent autos and auto parts).

In general, efforts to understand the politics of free trade can benefit from a larger body of qualitative research that can illuminate some of the complex interactions that take place during the reform process. Several factors contribute to making the reform process sufficiently nuanced and contingent so that it is difficult to predict how business groups will respond to economic change. For one, markets are remarkably supple institutions that allow for significant adjustments. Markets are not perfectly malleable: They are constrained by technological and sectoral qualities and the way that regime structure and growth strategies influence those qualities. Because the interactions of technology, sectoral characteristics, regime structure, and development strategy do not yield unique solutions, analysts have to examine the way that businesspeople respond at the micro-level and the way that specific policies and the political process affect their strategic considerations. Finally, business organizations play a critical role in influencing which business interests have a voice and which do not, and in what ways they express their voice. Yet, business organizations are not static, and without an analysis of how business interests are aggregated and represented, it is difficult to make claims about how business groups respond to the economic reform process.

Future research should consider the influence of at least three different problems for explaining the politics of free trade. First, the context matters. The behavior of industrial elites in the politics of Latin American free trade has been poorly explained, as noted in Chapter 1. Part of the reason is that industrialists have made their choices in times of crisis. Crises have a large impact on how actors see their preferences. Tornell has argued that crises weaken opponents of reform. Fernandez and Rodrik have argued that crises may lead actors to prefer the status quo. Less has been said, however, about how crisis may induce industrialists to prefer reform policies, even in the face of significant adjustment challenges. This context is different from early efforts to promote industrialization in Latin America or even in the United States. In that earlier context, nascent industries required protective tariffs whereas competitive commodity exporters rabidly opposed them. Similarly. struggles over tar-

44. The way political privilege can create specificity emerges strikingly in Armijo, "Inflation and Insouciance."

iff policy in the United States during the 1980s occurred in a context of strong import competition for mature, but highly differentiated industries. Thus, understanding the politics of free trade requires more consideration of how context influences industrialists' perceptions of their preferences.

Second, understanding the politics of free trade requires careful specification of the relative actors. More economistic approaches tend to treat actors as owners of factors, but that is not sufficient. Treating the unit of analysis as a factor owner ignores that the factor owner may be embedded in social networks, in a specific firm, and in interest associations. Thus, the character of business organizations and the character of the firms both matter. For example, economic groups play an important role in many developing countries and certainly in Latin America. Economic groups may have holdings in a variety of sectors and may be users of many different kinds of factors. As a consequence, they may be available for a wide array of alternative policy programs and tariff structures.[45] Origin and size of firms matter as well. One issue that rose repeatedly, primarily in the later research in 1996, was unequal access to capital and especially cheap capital. One MNC executive noted that his firm could obtain financing at a rate of 0.25 percent plus LIBOR (London Interbank offer rate)—vastly cheaper than any financing available in Brazilian financial markets. Large domestic firms also enjoyed comparative advantages in raising international capital at lower costs than smaller domestic firms. Given the enormous importance of capital costs for competitive restructuring, origin and size of firms matter a great deal. Interest associations matter as well. As noted in Chapter 1, some analyses of Latin American reform have identified ways in which organizations privileged some interests while excluding others. As the evidence from the Brazilian case has demonstrated, business organizations can and do change. When they change, they may affect which interests have a voice and which interests do not. How and why this happens and how it influences the reform process merit further attention as well.

The third area for further reflection is the way that political access is structured and how that access influences the reform process. Does the nature of political competition influence the character of business organizations and business lobbying? Work by Alt and Gilligan (1994) focused

---

45. Two important considerations of economic groups in Latin America are Eduardo Silva, *State and Capital in Chile*; and Francisco Durand, *Incertidumbres y Soledad: Reflexiones sobre los Grandes Empresarios de América Latina* (Peru: Fundación Friedrich Ebert, 1996).

on the interaction among domestic political institutions (majoritarian versus nonmajoritarian), collective action costs, and factor specificity. Daniel Verdier (1994) observed that lobbying and interest-group formation reflect how open the political system is to particularistic interests and how the electoral process influences trade policy debates. These crucial considerations are important for further reflection. The structure of access influences the ease of exerting influence and the size of the rewards from lobbying. The structure of access determines how well executives can insulate themselves from business lobbying or conversely how well they can insulate business from other political pressures. Ultimately, the ability of the business community to shape the reform process and the way it may shape it depend on the structure of political access. These features rest heavily on domestic political institutions.

For example, Brazil's domestic political institutions have discouraged coherent policy development while encouraging particularistic lobbying at the expense of encompassing organizations. Brazil's fragmented party system has made it difficult for business to shape the larger reform process. The collective action obstacles are formidable, and the rewards are diffuse. By contrast, any large firm or group of large firms (such as Eletros) can lobby well-placed bureaucrats in Brazil's fragmented state at very little cost. In return, it can hope to obtain substantial rewards. Industrialists may want a clear, strategic vision, and they may support a definitive reform program, but they can only hope to realistically obtain highly specific, narrow benefits. In turn, executives compete in a volatile political arena. Voters' concerns are paramount and offer only limited insulation to executives seeking to negotiate clear policy alternatives.

A distinct contrast is what Eduardo Silva has called Chile's "pragmatic neoliberalism."[46] Chile's much more centralized bureaucracy and disciplined parties provide mechanisms for more coherent bargaining over policy design. As a consequence, Chile has been able to pursue a vigorously market-liberalizing program while incorporating a series of protections, including capital controls, a well-crafted social safety net, and safety nets for domestic producers. State structure and party system characteristics profoundly affect what the trade reform process looks like as well as how durable and encompassing pro-free-trade reform will be. Further research on how variations in the state and accompanying political institutions influence trade dynamics is warranted.

46. Two cases that conform more to Brazil's erratic pattern of complex and unstable bargains between executives and business are discussed in Conaghan, "The Private Sector," and Corrales, "Corporate Choices."

How Political Institutions Influence Reform

The New Republic's political system has benefited scholars by being so poorly designed that it has provided ample opportunity for analytical work, but the concern with institutional design goes well beyond Brazil. Scholars have debated and analyzed the effects of presidentialism, multipartism, decree authority, and the impact of regime type on growth. Much of this literature has expressed concern about the quality of political institutions and their effect on democratic deepening and durability as well as the capacity to govern effectively. Analysts like Haggard and Kaufman and Mainwaring and Scully have identified particularly worrisome governability problems in the political party system. Countries like Brazil, Bolivia, Ecuador, and Peru are hypothesized to be especially vulnerable to a host of governability problems.

Whatever the political consequences of these party system perversities, the economic consequences are less easy to pin down. For example, Brazil has managed to reduce inflation from rates in the thousands through much of the early 1990s to less than 10 percent per year from 1996 to 1998. Bolivia's rate of inflation averaged below 15 percent for the decade between 1987 and 1996. Both Peru and Ecuador were able to contain inflation and fiscal deficits. All four countries have enjoyed mostly moderate growth rates since the mid-1990s. The average annual inflow of foreign capital roughly doubled between the period 1987–91 and the period 1992–96.[47] Executives have been able to finesse solutions to ungovernability problems. Those solutions have been adequate to renew private investments.

Industrialists have also proved very adaptable. During interviews in 1991–92, industrialists repeatedly claimed that the chaos of Brazilian political economy taught them how to adapt to rapidly changing circumstances. Events to this writing seem to have confirmed this claim. Brazilian industrialists found a wide range of solutions to market challenges, new market niches, innovative ways to address labor-management concerns. They devised joint ventures, participated in mergers and acquisitions, changed their product lines, and pursued a wide range of competitiveness- and productivity-enhancing strategies. As a consequence, a large number of leading (and not leading) Brazilian firms survived through the 1990–98 period despite adverse policy conditions.

47. Data calculated from the Inter-American Development Bank Annual Report, 1997, part four, Statistical Appendix.

This adaptability suggests that Brazilian industrialists were open to many alternative policy coalitions. Governments seem to have had room to craft alternative programs even though neoliberalism has appeared politically inevitable. Scholars have questioned the possibility of pursuing social democratic or neostructuralist programs. Some have suggested that the interests of capitalists and the possibility of capital flight have sharply limited that possibility. Yet neither domestic nor multinational executives expressed hostility to a continuing role for state promotion of growth. Industrialists sought a stable investment climate with a predictable policy trajectory. Even among multinationals, executives expressed the desire for the administrations to create a strategic framework to orient future investments and adjustment decisions.

In such a framework, industrialists have demonstrated an ability to find solutions to their micro-level problems. The pattern of support and opposition to free trade in Brazil points to the need for governments to maintain good communications between policymakers and industry leaders. Through good communication and careful policy design, politicians have had the opportunity to pursue programs that mix some elements of protection, state promotion, and even redistribution. In fact, Cardoso's government arrived at such a program in an ad hoc way. Business concerns about the growth of the domestic market suggest that there has been ample room to go farther.

Thus, party systems do matter for economic performance because they shape governments' capacity to provide a strategic framework for private industry. Brazilian governments lack the ability to craft policy programs that deviate from neoliberal orthodoxy in a coherent way. By 1997, the evidence of economic and social indicators suggests that getting prices right was simply not sufficient. Growth rates remained modest in most of Latin America, whereas poverty, inequality, and regional disparities remained serious problems for all Latin America. In addition, most Latin American nations remained vulnerable to sharp capital outflows, such as occurred in Mexico with the peso crisis of 1994–95. Technological innovation and spending on research and development remained underdeveloped as did education spending. All these problems required leadership and coherent policy direction of a kind that Brazil's fragmented, chaotic polity seemed hard pressed to produce. The contrast between Chile's well-crafted "pragmatic neoliberalism" and Brazil's stumbling, unpredictable pragmatism is striking.

The result of Brazil's stumbling ad hoc pragmatism is a mix of sometimes contradictory policies. For example, Brazil has sought to encourage exports—a central plank of neoliberal reform and a vital element in Brazil's effort to contain its current account deficit. Export incentives, however, add to the fiscal deficit (moving toward an estimated 7 percent of GDP in the election year 1998) and violate another central precept of neoliberal reform—elimination of government incentives that distort the market. Cardoso, like Collor before him, initially hoped to encourage exports through a thorough tax reform aimed at removing systemic sources of uncompetitiveness. His inability to do so left critical sources of uncompetitiveness embedded in the tax system, and these could be offset only through extensive government rents.

In another contradiction, the Collor and Cardoso governments insisted that local industrialists had to adjust to compete in the new economic environment. Both governments (especially Cardoso's) suggested that the responsibility to compete was entirely in private hands. Yet, government policy left interest rates at exorbitant levels, and the exchange rate favored importers. Granted, the need to protect the country's dollar reserves, and by extension the currency, drove the interest-rate and exchange-rate policies. Nevertheless, these policies made micro-level adjustment difficult, especially in view of the absence of reforms oriented to ameliorating what Brazilian industrialists called the Brazil cost. In turn, these policies contributed to unemployment and bankruptcies, without generating surpluses for improvements in social policy. In short, the erratic quality of policy produced significant policy contradictions, distinctly suboptimal outcomes, and no clear strategic vision of the future.

In the absence of a strategic framework, private actors are left to their own devices. Private actors pursue their own individual strategies, regardless of the consequences for public welfare. With poorly functioning political institutions, private actors must solve their market problems in ways that protect them from uncertainty about the future policy directions and government performance. Unfortunately, those private solutions may lead to less than optimal solutions. Ultimately, the price of such weakly crafted solutions is support from industrialists who may limit public welfare by maintaining one eye on the exit.

Bibliography

Abrucio, Luiz Fernando. 1994. "Os Barões da Federação: O Poder dos Governadores no Brasil Pos-Autoritário." Master's thesis, Universidade de São Paulo.

Acuña, Carlos. 1995. "Business Interests, Dictatorship, and Democracy in Argentina." In Ernest Bartell and Leigh Payne, eds., *Business and Democracy in Latin America*. Pittsburgh, Pa.: University of Pittsburgh Press.

Addis, Caren. 1999. *Taking the Wheel: Auto Parts Firms and the Political Economy of Industrialization in Brazil*. University Park: The Pennsylvania State University Press.

———. 1995. "Emerging Forms of Industrial Governance: Promoting Cooperation Between Small and Large Firms in Brazil." Paper presented at the Latin American Studies Association, Washington, D.C., September 28–30.

———. 1990. "Auto Parts, Made in Brazil." In Luciano Coutinho and Wilson Suzigan, eds., *Desenvolvimento Tecnológico da Indústria e a Constituição de um Sistema Nacional de Inovação no Brasil*. Campinas, IPT/FECAMP contract; Instituto de Economia / UNICAMP.

Agosin, Manuel R., ed. 1995. *Foreign Direct Investment in Latin America*. Washington, D.C.: Inter-American Development Bank.

Alesina, Alberto, and Allan Drazen. 1991. "Why Are Stabilizations Delayed?" *American Economic Review* 81, no. 5: 1170–88.

Alt, James; Jeffry Frieden; Michael Gilligan; Dani Rodrik; and Ronald Rogowski. 1996. "The Political Economy of International Trade: Enduring Puzzles and an Agenda for Inquiry." *Comparative Political Studies* 29 (December): 689–717.

Alt, James, and Michael Gilligan. 1994. "The Political Economy of Trading States." *Journal of Political Philosophy* 2:165–92.

Ames, Barry. 1995a. "Electoral Rules, Constituency Pressures, and Pork Barrel: Bases of Voting in the Brazilian Congress." *Journal of Politics* 57 (May): 324–43.

———. 1995b. "Electoral Strategy Under Open-List Proportional Representation." *American Journal of Political Science* 39 (May): 406–33.

———. 1994. "The Reverse Coattails Effect: Local Party Organization in the 1989 Presidential Election." *American Political Science Review* 88, no. 1: 95–111.

———. 1987. *Political Survival: Politicians and Public Policy in Latin America*. Berkeley and Los Angeles: University of California Press.

Aragão, Murillo de. 1995. "Ação dos Grupos de Pressão nos Processos Constitucionais Recentes no Brasil." Paper presented at the Latin American Studies Association, Washington, D.C., September 28–30.

Armijo, Leslie Elliott. 1999. *Financial Globalization and Democracy in Emerging Markets.* New York: St. Martin's Press.

———. 1996. "Inflation and Insouciance: The Peculiar Brazilian Game." *Latin American Research Review* 31, no. 3: 7–46.

Associação Brasileira da Indústria de Alimentação. 1991. "Fome: A Grande Vergonha Nacional." São Paulo.

Associação Brasileira da Indústria de Máquinas e Equipamentos. 1990. "Brasil 1987–1990: Máquinas-Ferramentas para Trabalhar Metais e Carbonetos Metalicos–Pesquisa Industrial." ABIMAQ, Divisão de Economia e Estatistica 14, no. 14.

———. 1989a. "Política Industrial para a Indústria de Máquinas e Equipamentos no Brasil." São Paulo: ABIMAQ. December.

———. 1989b. "Bens de Capital Mecanicos: Comercio Exterior." ABIMAQ, Divisão de Economia e Estatistica 15, no. 15.

———. 1989c. "Acordos e Revisões de Acordos de Participação Nacional Homologados pela CACEX, 1975–1989." ABIMAQ, Divisão de Economia e Estatistica 7, no. 8.

Bacha, Edmar L., and Pedro Malan. 1989. "Brazil's Debt: From the Miracle to the Fund." In Alfred Stepan, ed., *Democratizing Brazil: Problems of Transition and Consolidation.* New York: Oxford University Press.

Baer, Werner. 1995. *The Brazilian Economy: Growth and Development.* New York: Praeger.

Banco Nacional de Desenvolvimento Econômico e Social. 1991a. "Programa Nacional de Desestatização." May.

———. 1991b. "Política Industrial." Numero Especial, Acompanhamento dos Atos. Centro de Pesquisas e Dados.

———. 1989a. "Integração Competitiva: Uma Estratégia para o Desenvolvimento Brasileiro." Área de Planejamento. November.

———. 1989b. "Integração Competitiva: Uma Nova Estratégia para a Industrialização Brasileira." Paper presented by Luiz Paulo Vellozo Lucas, Chief of the Planning Department, at the United Nations Industrial Development Organization Technical Meeting, Vienna, April 4–7.

Banuri, Tariq, ed. 1991. *Economic Liberalization: No Panacea.* Oxford: Clarendon Press.

Bartell, Ernest. 1995. "Perceptions by Business Leaders and the Transition to Democracy in Chile." In Ernest Bartell and Leigh Payne, eds., *Business and Democracy in Latin America.* Pittsburgh, Pa.: University of Pittsburgh Press.

Bartell, Ernest, and Leigh Payne, eds. 1995. *Business and Democracy in Latin America.* Pittsburgh, Pa.: University of Pittsburgh Press.

Barzelay, Michael. 1986. *The Politicized Market Economy: Alcohol in Brazil's Energy Strategy.* Berkeley and Los Angeles: University of California Press.

Becker, David G. 1990. "Business Associations in Latin America: The Venezuelan Case." *Comparative Political Studies* 23 (April): 114–38.

Berger, Suzanne. 1981. "Regime and Interest Representation: The French Traditional Middle Classes." In Suzanne Berger, ed., *Organizing Interests in Western*

Europe: Pluralism, Corporatism, and the Transformation of Politics. New York: Cambridge University Press.

Bier, Amaury G.; Leda M. Paulani; and Roberto P. Messenberg. 1988. "O Desenvolvimento em Xeque: Estado e Padrão de Financiamento no Brasil." In Lourdes Sola, ed., *O Estado da Transição: Política e Economia na Nova Republica.* São Paulo: Vértice, Editora Revista dos Tribunais.

Binder, Leonard. 1971. *Crises and Sequences in Political Development.* Princeton: Princeton University Press.

Bonelli, Regis, and Pedro Malan. 1987. "Industrialization, Economic Growth, and Balance of Payments: Brazil, 1970–1984." In John Wirth, Edson de Oliveira Nunes, and Thomas E. Bogenschild, eds., *State and Society in Brazil: Continuity and Change.* Boulder, Colo.: Westview Press.

Booz, Allen, and Hamilton. 1990. "Estratégia Setorial para a Indústria Automobilistica no Brasil." São Paulo: Booz, Allen, & Hamilton / União pela Modernização da Indústria de Autopeças / SINDIPEÇAS. November.

Boschi, Renato Raul. 1990. "O Arco-Íris da Modernização: Do Brasil Novo á República Velha." In IUPERJ, Cadernos de Conjuntura, no. 34/35. November–December.

———. 1979. *Elites Industriais e Democracia: Hegemonia Burguesa e Mudança Política no Brasil.* Rio de Janeiro: Graal.

Brazil, Government of. 1991. "Desregulamentação, Ano I." Presidência da República.

———. 1990. Ministério da Economia, Fazenda, e Planejamento. "Diretrizes Gerais para a Política Industrial e de Comércio Exterior." June 26.

———.1986. Grupo Interministerial de Política Industrial. "Política Industrial." July.

Bresser Pereira, Luis Carlos. 1996. *Economic Crisis and State Reform in Brazil: Toward a New Interpretation of Latin America.* Boulder, Colo.: Lynne Rienner Publishers.

———. 1991. "Populism and Economic Policy in Brazil." *Journal of Interamerican Studies and World Affairs* 33 (Summer): 1–21.

———. 1978. *O Colapso de um Aliança de Classes.* São Paulo: Brasiliense.

Bresser Pereira, Luis Carlos; José Maria Maravall; and Adam Przeworski, eds. 1993. *Economic Reforms in New Democracies: A Social Democratic Approach.* Cambridge: Cambridge University Press.

Brooke, James. 1992. "Looting Brazil." *New York Times Magazine,* November 8, p. 30.

Business International Corporation. 1990. "Coping with Crisis in Brazil: Business Under Collor." New York: Business International Corporation.

Cameron, Stevie. 1994. *On the Take: Crime, Corruption, and Greed in the Mulroney Years.* Toronto: McFarlance, Walter & Ross.

Canak, William, ed. 1989. *Lost Promises: Debt, Austerity, and Development in Latin America.* Boulder, Colo.: Westview Press.

Cardoso, Eliana, and Ann Helwege. 1991. "Populism, Profligacy, and Redistribution." In Rudiger Dornbusch and Sebastian Edwards, eds., *The Macroeconomics of Populism in Latin America.* Chicago: University of Chicago Press.

Cardoso, Fernando Henrique. 1986. "Entrepreneurs and the Transition Process: The

Brazilian Case." In Guillermo O'Donnell, Philippe C. Schmitter, and Laurence Whitehead, eds., *Transitions from Authoritarian Rule: Comparative Perspectives*. Baltimore: Johns Hopkins University Press.

————. 1964. *Empresário Industrial e Desenvolvimento Econômica*. São Paulo: Difusão Européia do Livro.

Cardoso, Fernando Henrique, and José Rubens de Lima Figueiredo Jr. 1992. "Reconciling the Capitalists with Democracy." Paper presented at the Conference on Economic Reform and Democratic Consolidation, Forli, Italy, April 2–4.

Castro, Paulo Rabello, and Marcio Ronci. 1991. "Sixty Years of Populism in Brazil." In Rudiger Dornbusch and Sebastian Edwards, eds., *The Macroeconomics of Populism in Latin America*. Chicago: University of Chicago Press.

Centeno, Miguel A. 1995. *Democracy Within Reason: Technocratic Revolution in Mexico*. University Park: The Pennsylvania State University Press.

Chalmers, Douglas A.; Maria Carmo Campello de Souza; and Atilio A. Boron, eds. 1992. *The Right and Democracy in Latin America*. New York: Praeger.

Cohen, Stephen S., and John Zysman. 1987. *Manufacturing Matters: The Myth of the Post-Industrial Economy*. New York: Basic Books.

Coleman, William, and Wyn Grant. 1988. "The Organizational Cohesion and Political Access of Business: A Study of Comprehensive Associations." *European Journal of Political Research* 16:467–87.

Collier, David. 1979. "Inducements Versus Constraints: Disaggregating Corporatism." *American Political Science Review* 73 (December): 967–86.

Collier, David, ed. 1979. *The New Authoritarianism in Latin America*. Princeton: Princeton University Press.

Collier, David, and Ruth Berins Collier. 1991. *Shaping the Political Arena: Critical Junctures, the Labor Movement, and Regime Dynamics in Latin America*. Princeton: Princeton University Press.

Conaghan, Catherine. 1995. "The Private Sector and the Public Transcript: The Political Mobilization of Business in Bolivia." In Ernest Bartell and Leigh Payne, eds., *Business and Democracy in Latin America*. Pittsburgh, Pa.: University of Pittsburgh Press.

————. 1990. "Retreat to Democracy: Business and Political Transition in Bolivia and Ecuador." In Diane Ethier, ed., *Democratic Transition and Consolidation in Southern Europe, Latin America, and Southeast Asia*. Bassingstoke, Eng.: Macmillan.

————. 1988. *Restructuring Domination: Industrialists and the State in Ecuador*. Pittsburgh, Pa.: University of Pittsburgh Press.

Conaghan, Catherine, and James M. Malloy. 1994. *Unsettling Statecraft: Democracy and Neoliberalism in the Central Andes*. Pittsburgh, Pa.: University of Pittsburgh Press.

Confederação Nacional da Indústria. 1992. "Abertura Comercial e Estratégia Tecnológica: A Visão de Lideres Industriais Brasileiras." Rio de Janeiro, May.

————. 1991a. "Abertura Comercial e Estratégia Tecnológica: A Visão de Lideres Industriais Brasileiras." Rio de Janeiro, May.

————. 1991b. "Sistema de Acompanhamento de Indicadores de Competitividade." Departamento Econômico, no. 1, June.

————. 1990. "Políticas de Indústria e de Comércio Exterior." Seminar given in Brasília, July.

———. 1989. "Abertura Comercial e Estratégia Tecnológica: A Visão de Lideres Industriais Brasileiras." Rio de Janeiro, May.

———. 1988. "Competitividade Industrial: Um Estratégia para o Brasil." Rio de Janeiro, May.

Corrales, Javier. 1998. "Coalitions and Corporate Choices in Argentina, 1976–1994: The Recent Support for Privatization." *Studies in Comparative International Development* 32, no. 4: 24–51.

Cotler, Julio. 1995. "Political Parties and the Problem of Democratic Consolidation in Peru." In Scott Mainwaring and Timothy Scully, eds., *Building Democratic Institutions*. Stanford, Calif.: Stanford University Press.

Coutinho, Luciano, and João Carlos Ferraz. 1995. *Estudo da Competitividade da Indústria Brasileira*. Campinas: Papirus/Editora da Universidade Estadual de Campinas.

Cruz, Hélio Nogueira da, and Marcos Eugênio da Silva. 1990. "A Situação de Bens de Capital e Suas Perspectivas." In Luciano Coutinho and Wilson Suzigan, eds., *Desenvolvimento Tecnológico da Indústria e a Constituição de um Sistema Nacional de Inovação no Brasil*. Campinas, IPT/FECAMP contract; Instituto de Economia / UNICAMP.

Cruz, Sebastião C. Velasco e. 1984. "Os Empresários e o Regime: A Campanha contra a Estatização." Ph.D. dissertation, University of São Paulo.

Dias, José Luciano de Mattos. 1991. "Legislação Eleitoral: Situação e Perspectiva de Reforma." In *Regimes Eleitorais e Sistemas Partidários*. IUPERJ, Cadernos de Conjunto, no. 43, August.

Dimenstein, Gilberto. 1988. *A República dos Padrinhos: Chantagem e Corrupção em Brasília*. São Paulo: Editora Brasiliense.

Diniz, Eli. 1990. "Economia, Política e Democracia sob a Gestão Collor: Uma Difícil Articulação." In IUPERJ, Cadernos de Conjuntura, no. 34/35, November–December.

Diniz, Eli, and Renato Raul Boschi. 1992. "Lideranças Empresariais e Problemas Do Estratégia Liberal no Brasil." In Eli Diniz, ed., *Empresários e Modernização Econômica: Brasil Anos 90*. Florianópolis: Editora da UFSC/IDACON.

———. 1990. "Brasil: Um Novo Empresariado? Balanço de Tendências Recentes." Paper presented at the Conference on the New Business in Latin America, Santiago, Chile, November 14–17.

———. 1987. "Burocracia, Clientelismo e Oligopólio: O Conselho Interministerial de Preços." In Olavo Brasil de Lima Jr. and Sergio Henrique Abranches, eds., *As Origens da Crise: Estado Autoritário e Planejamento no Brasil*. São Paulo: Vértice, Editora Revista dos Tribunais.

———. 1979. *Agregação e Representação de Interesses do Empresariado Industrial: Sindicatos e Associações de Classes*. Rio de Janeiro: Edições IUPERJ.

———. 1978. "Burocracia, Clientela e Relações de Poder: Aplicação de Modelo Teórico ao Estudo das Relações entre o Empresário e o Setor Público (o Caso do Conselho Interministerial de Preços). Instituto Universitario de Pesquisas do Rio de Janeiro Working Paper no. 1/78.

Diniz, Eli, and Olavo Brasil de Lima Jr. 1986. *Modernização Autoritaria: O Empresariado e a Intervenção do Estado na Economia*. Brasília: IPEA-CEPAL.

Dinsmoor, James. 1990. *Brazil: Responses to the Debt Crisis*. Washington, D.C.: Inter-American Development Bank.

Dix, Robert. 1992. "Democratization and the Institutionalization of Latin American Political Parties." *Comparative Political Studies* 24 (January): 488–511.

Dominguez, Jorge. 1982. "Business Nationalism: Latin American National Business Attitudes and Behavior Towards Multinational Enterprises." In Jorge Dominguez, ed., *Economic Issues and Political Conflict: U.S.–Latin American Relations*. London: Butterworth.

Doner, Richard F. 1992. "Limits of State Strength: Towards an Institutionalist View of Economic Development." *World Politics* 44 (April): 398–431.

Dornbusch, Rudiger, and Sebastian Edwards, eds. 1991. *The Macroeconomics of Populism in Latin America*. Chicago: University of Chicago Press.

Dreifuss, René. 1987. *1964: A Conquista do Estado: Ação Política, Poder e Golpe de Classe*. Petrópolis: Vozes.

Dresser, Denise. 1991. "Neopopulist Solutions to Neoliberal Problems: Mexico's National Solidarity Program." San Diego: Center for U.S.-Mexican Studies, Current Issue Brief No. 3.

Durand, Francisco. 1996. *Incertidumbres y Soledad: Reflexiones sobre los Grandes Empresarios de América Latina*. Peru: Fundación Friedrich Ebert.

———. 1995. "From Fragile Crystal to Solid Rock: The Formation and Consolidation of a Business Peak Association in Peru." In Ernest Bartell and Leigh Payne, eds., *Business and Democracy in Latin America*. Pittsburgh, Pa.: University of Pittsburgh Press.

———. 1994. *Business and Politics in Peru: The State and the National Bourgeoisie*. Boulder, Colo.: Westview Press.

Echeverri-Gent, John. 1993. "The Dynamic Constraints of India's Economic Reform: A Critique of Game-Theoretical Approaches to Interest Representation." Paper presented at the American Political Science Association, Washington, D.C., September 3–6.

Erber, Fábio Stéfano, and Roberto Vermulm. 1992. "Ajuste Estrutural e Estratégias Empresariais—Um Estudo dos Setores Petroquímico e de Máquinas-Ferramenta no Brasil." Unpublished study. Banco Nacional de Desenvolvimento Econômico e Social / Universidade de São Paulo.

Erickson, Kenneth Paul. 1977. *The Brazilian Corporative State and Working Class Politics*. Berkeley and Los Angeles: University of California Press.

Ethier, Diane, ed. 1990. *Democratic Transition and Consolidation in Southern Europe, Latin America, and Southeast Asia*. Bassingstoke, Eng.: Macmillan.

Evans, Peter. 1995. *Embedded Autonomy: States and Industrial Transformation*. Princeton: Princeton University Press.

———. 1992. "Predation, Embedded Autonomy, and Adjustment." In Stephan Haggard and Robert Kaufman, eds. *The Politics of Economic Adjustment*. Princeton: Princeton University Press.

———. 1979. *Dependent Development: The Alliance of Multinational, State, and Local Capital in Brazil*. Princeton: Princeton University Press.

Evans, Peter; Dietrich Rueschemeyer; and Evelyne Huber Stephens, eds. 1985. *States Versus Markets in the World System*. Beverly Hills, Calif.: Sage Publications.

Federação Brasileira das Associações de Bancos. 1991. "O Impacto da Carga Tributaria na Taxa de Juros." September.

Federação da Indústria do Estado de São Paulo. 1997. "Fórum das Reformas: A Nação Tem Pressa." June 23.

———. 1991. "A Faculdade para Determinar os Preços: Mercado ou Governo?" *Cadernos Instituto Roberto Simonsen* 19 (May).

———. 1990a. "FIESP/CIESP, A Serviço da Indústria." March.

———. 1990b. *Livre para Crescer*. São Paulo: Cultura Editora Associados.

———. 1990c. "Orgãos e Dirigentes, 1989–1992." April.

———. 1989. Aide Memoire, no. 177, December 22.

———. 1988a. "Evolução do Texto sobre Alguns dos Direitos dos Trabalhadores durante os Trabalhos Constituintes." October.

———. 1988b. "A Intervenção do Estado no Domínio Econômico na Nova Constituição." *Cadernos Instituto Roberto Simonsen* 4 (December).

———. 1987a. "Considerações sobre o Documento 'Política Industrial e Diretrizes Setoriais' a que se Refere a Portaria no. 12, de 13.02.87 do Ministério de Indústria e Comércio." Departamento de Economia. June.

———. 1987b. "Política Industrial." Departamento de Economia. November.

———. 1986. "O Voto Distrital na Perspectiva de uma Nova Constituição." *Cadernos Instituto Roberto Simonsen* 1 (December).

———. 1985. "A Defesa da Livre Iniciativa e Controle da Intervenção do Estado na Constituinte." Seminar given at the Instituto Roberto Simonsen, November.

Fernandez, Raquel, and Dani Rodrik. 1991. "Resistance to Reform: Status Quo Bias in the Presence of Individual-Specific Uncertainty." *American Economic Review* 81, no. 5: 1146–55.

Ferro, José Roberto. 1990. "Para Sair da Estagnação e Diminuir o Atraso Tecnológico da Indústria Automobilística Brasileira." In Luciano Coutinho and Wilson Suzigan, eds., *Desenvolvimento Tecnológico da Indústria e a Constituição de um Sistema Nacional de Inovação no Brasil*. Campinas, IPT/FECAMP contract; Instituto de Economia / UNICAMP.

Figueiredo, José Rubens de Lima, Jr. 1995. "Opinião Pública, Intencionalidade e Voto." In *Opinião Pública* 2, no. 2: 73–82.

———. 1992. "Verdades e Mitos sobre a Cultura Brasileira." In Bolivar Lamounier, ed., *Ouvindo O Brasil: Uma Análise da Opinião Pública Brasileira Hoje*. São Paulo: Editora Sumaré.

———.Unfinished master's thesis, Universidade de São Paulo.

Figueiredo, Ney Lima. 1992. "A Imagem do Empresariado." In Bolivar Lamounier, ed., *Ouvindo O Brasil: Uma Análise da Opinião Pública Brasileira Hoje*. São Paulo: Editora Sumaré.

Fiori, José Luis. 1990. "Dezembro 1990: O Impasse Político da Razão Tecnocrática." IUPERJ, Cadernos de Conjuntura, no. 34/35, November–December.

Fishlow, Albert. 1997. "Is the Real Plan for Real?" In Susan Kaufman Purcell and Riordan Roett, eds., *Brazil Under Cardoso*. Boulder, Colo.: Lynne Rienner Publishers.

———. 1989. "A Tale of Two Presidents: The Political Economy of Crisis Management." In Alfred Stepan, ed., *Democratizing Brazil: Problems of Transition and Consolidation*. Oxford: Oxford University Press.

———. 1973. "Some Reflections on Post-1964 Brazilian Economic Policy." In Alfred Stepan, ed., *Authoritarian Brazil*. New Haven: Yale University Press.

Fleischer, David. 1995. "Attempts at Corruption Control in Brazil: Congressional Investigations and Strengthening Internal Control." Paper presented at the Latin American Studies Association, Washington, D.C., September 28–30.

Flynn, Peter. 1993. "Collor, Corruption, and Crisis: Time for Reflection." *Journal of Latin American Studies* 25:351–71.

Foxley, Alejandro. 1983. *Latin American Experiments in Neoconservative Economics*. Berkeley and Los Angeles: University of California Press.

Frieden, Jeffry. 1991. *Debt, Development, and Democracy: Modern Political Economy and Latin America, 1965–1985*. Princeton: Princeton University Press.

Fritsch, Winston, and Gustavo H. B. Franco. 1994. "Import Compression, Productivity Slowdown, and Manufactured Export Dynamism." In G. K. Helleiner, ed., *Trade Policy and Industrialization in Turbulent Times*. New York: Routledge.

Gall, Norman. 1991. "The Floating World of Brazilian Inflation. " Instituto Fernand Braudel, São Paulo, September.

Gamarra, Eduardo A., and James M. Malloy. 1995. "The Patrimonial Dynamics of Party Politics in Bolivia." In Scott Mainwaring and Timothy Scully, eds., *Building Democratic Institutions*. Stanford, Calif.: Stanford University Press.

Garcia, Odair Lopes. 1990. "Análise da Indústria Brasileira de Máquinas e Acessórios Têxteis." In Luciano Coutinho and Wilson Suzigan, eds., *Desenvolvimento Tecnológico da Indústria e a Constituição de um Sistema Nacional de Inovação no Brasil*. Campinas, IPT/FECAMP contract; Instituto de Economia / UNICAMP.

Geddes, Barbara. 1995. "The Politics of Economic Liberalization." *Latin American Research Review* 30, no. 2: 195–214.

———. 1994. *Politician's Dilemma: Building State Capacity in Latin America*. Berkeley, Calif.: University of California Press.

Gibson, Edward. 1992. "Conservative Electoral Movements and Democratic Politics: Core Constituencies, Coalition Building, and the Latin American Right." In Douglas A. Chalmers, Maria Carmo Campello de Souza, and Atilio A. Boron, eds., *The Right and Democracy in Latin America*. New York: Praeger.

Goldthorpe. John, ed. 1984. *Order and Conflict in Contemporary Capitalism: Studies in the Political Economy of Western European Nations*. Oxford: Clarendon Press.

Gourevitch, Peter. 1986. *Politics in Hard Times: Comparative Responses to International Economic Crises*. Ithaca, N.Y.: Cornell University Press.

Gouvêa, Leila Villas Boas. 1991. *Política Industrial—Modernização ou Sucateamento?* São Paulo: Círculo do Livro.

Grindle, Merilee S., and John W. Thomas. 1991. *Public Choices and Policy Change: The Political Economy of Reform in Developing Countries*. Baltimore: Johns Hopkins University Press.

Gros, Denise Barbosa. 1992. "Empresariado e Ação Política na Nova República: Os Institutos Liberais de São Paulo e Rio Grande do Sul." In Eli Diniz, ed., *Empresários e Modernização Econômica: Brasil Anos 90*. Florianópolis: Editora da UFSC/IDACON.

Guilhon Albaquerque, José Augusto. 1991a. "Le Presidentialisme Plébiscitaire et L'Instabilité de Democraties." Série Comparada 1, Política Internacional Comparada. Universidade de São Paulo, June.

———. 1991b. "Presidencialismo no Brasil É Receita para o Caos." In *Carta Política* 1 (July): 6.

Haggard, Stephan. 1990. *Pathways from the Periphery: The Politics of Growth in the Newly Industrializing Countries*. Ithaca, N.Y.: Cornell University Press.

Haggard, Stephan, and Robert Kaufman. 1995. *The Political Economy of Democratic Transitions*. Princeton: Princeton University Press.

———. 1992. "The Political Economy of Inflation and Stabilization in Middle-Income Countries." In Stephan Haggard and Robert Kaufman, eds., *The Politics of Economic Adjustment: International Constraints, Distributive Conflicts, and the State*. Princeton: Princeton University Press.

———. 1989. "Economic Adjustment in New Democracies." In *Fragile Coalitions: The Politics of Economic Adjustment*. New Brunswick, N.J.: Transaction Books.

Haggard, Stephan, and Robert Kaufman, eds. 1992. *The Politics of Economic Adjustment: International Constraints, Distributive Conflicts, and the State*. Princeton: Princeton University Press.

Haggard, Stephan, and Steven Webb, eds. 1994. *Voting for Reform: Democracy, Liberalization, and Economic Adjustment*. Oxford: Oxford University Press.

Haggard, Stephan; Sylvia Maxfield; and Ben Ross Schneider. 1997. "Theories of Business and Business-State Relations." In Sylvia Maxfield and Ben Ross Schneider, eds., *Business and the State in Developing Countries*. Ithaca, N.Y.: Cornell University Press.

Hagopian, Frances. 1990. "Democracy by Undemocratic Means?" *Comparative Political Studies* 23 (July): 147–70.

———. 1986. "State Capitalism and Politics in Brazil." Helen Kellogg Institute Working Paper no. 63. University of Notre Dame. February.

Hall, Peter. 1986. *Governing the Economy: The Politics of State Intervention in Britain and France*. Cambridge: Polity Press.

Hardin, Russell. 1982. *Collective Action*. Baltimore: Johns Hopkins University Press.

Heredia, Blanca. 1995. "Mexican Business and the State: The Political Economy of a Muddled Transition." In Ernest Bartell and Leigh Payne, eds., *Business and Democracy in Latin America*. Pittsburgh, Pa.: University of Pittsburgh Press.

Hinchberger, William R. 1992. "Coalition Quandary: Collor, Liberalization, and Brazilian Political Elites." Master's thesis, University of California at Berkeley.

Hollingsworth, J. Rogers, and Robert Boyer, eds. 1997. *Contemporary Capitalism*. Cambridge: Cambridge University Press.

Humphrey, John. 1982. *Capitalist Control and Workers' Struggles in the Brazilian Automotive Industry*. Princeton: Princeton University Press.

Ianni, Octavio. 1981. *A Ditadura do Grande Capital*. Rio de Janeiro: Editora Civilização Brasileira.

Instituto des Estudos para o Desenvolvimento Industrial. 1992a. "Modernização Competitiva, Democracia e Justiça Social." *Mudar para Competir*. June.

———. 1992b. "A Nova Relação entre Competitividade e Educação: Estratégias Empresariais." *Mudar para Competir*. January.

———. 1991. "Carga Fiscal, Competitividade Industrial e Potencial de Crescimento Econômico." *Mudar para Competir*. August.

———. 1990. *Mudar para Competir*. June.

International Advisory Services Group. 1991. "The Tax Burden and Effective Rates of Protection for Various International Producers." Washington, D.C.: International Advisory Services Group. May.

Jenkins, Rhys. 1987. *Transnational Corporations and the Latin American Automobile Industry.* London: Macmillan.

Johnson, Chalmers. 1982. *MTIT and the Japanese Miracle.* Stanford, Calif.: Stanford University Press.

Kanitz, Stephen Charles. 1991. "O Peso da Carga Tributária nas Empresas." Study conducted for the periodical *Exame.* São Paulo.

Karl, Terry Lynn. 1986. "Petroleum and Political Pacts: The Transition to Democracy in Venezuela." In Guillermo O'Donnell, Philippe C. Schmitter, and Laurence Whitehead, eds., *Transitions from Authoritarian Rule: Latin America.* Baltimore: Johns Hopkins University Press.

Katzenstein, Peter J. 1985. *Small States in World Markets: Industrial Policy in Europe.* Ithaca, N.Y.: Cornell University Press.

Katzenstein, Peter J., ed. 1978. *Between Power and Plenty: Foreign Economic Policies of Advanced Industrial States.* Madison: University of Wisconsin Press.

Kaufman, Robert. 1988. *The Politics of Debt in Argentina, Brazil, and Mexico: Economic Stabilization in the 1980s.* Berkeley, Calif.: Institute of International Studies.

———. 1977. "Corporatism, Clientelism, and Partisan Conflict: A Study of Seven Latin American Countries." In James Malloy, ed., *Authoritarianism and Corporatism in Latin America.* Pittsburgh, Pa.: University of Pittsburgh Press.

Keck, Margaret. 1989. "The New Unionism in the Brazilian Transition." In Alfred Stepan, ed., *Democratizing Brazil: Problems of Transition and Consolidation.* Oxford: Oxford University Press.

Keeler, John. 1993. "Opening the Window for Reform: Mandates, Crises, and Extraordinary Policy-Making." *Comparative Political Studies* 25, no. 4: 433–86.

Kingstone, Peter R., and Timothy J. Power, eds. 2000. *Democratic Brazil: Institutions, Actors, and Processes.* Pittsburgh, Pa.: University of Pittsburgh Press.

Kinzo, Maria D'Alva Gil. 1995. "The 1994 Elections in Brazil: Party Politics in the New Government." Paper presented at the Latin American Studies Association, Washington, D.C., September 28–30, pp. 10–13.

Kornblith, Miriam, and Daniel H. Levine. 1995. "Venezuela: The Life and Times of the Party System." In Scott Mainwaring and Timothy Scully, eds., *Building Democratic Institutions.* Stanford, Calif.: Stanford University Press.

Krasner, Stephen. 1985. *Structural Conflict: The Third World Against Global Liberalism.* Berkeley and Los Angeles: University of California Press.

Kuczynski, Pedro Pablo. 1988. *Latin American Debt.* Baltimore: Johns Hopkins University Press.

Kugelmas, Eduardo, and Brasílio Sallum Jr. 1993. "O Leviathan Accorrentado." In Lourdes Sola, ed., *Estado, Mercado, e Democracia: Política e Economia Comparadas.* São Paulo: Paz e Terra.

Lal, Deepak, and Sylvia Maxfield. 1993. "The Political Economy of Stabilization in Brazil." In Robert Bates and Anne O. Krueger, eds., *Political and Economic Interactions in Economic Policy Reforms: Evidence from Eight Countries.* Cambridge: Blackwell Publishers.

Lamounier, Bolivar. 1996. "Brazil: The Hyperactive Paralysis Syndrome." In Jorge J. Dominguez and Abraham F. Lowenthal, eds., *Constructing Democratic Governance: Latin America and the Caribbean in the 1990s.* Baltimore: Johns Hopkins University Press.

———. 1991. "Opção Parlamentarista e a Governabilidade." *Carta Política* 1 (May 6–12): 6.

———. 1990. "Antecedentes, Riscos e Possibilidades do Governo Collor." In Bolivar Lamounier, ed., *De Geisel a Collor: O Balanço da Transição*. São Paulo: Editora Sumaré.

———. 1989. "*Abertura* Revisited: The Impact of Elections on the *Abertura*." In Alfred Stepan, ed., *Democratizing Brazil: Problems of Transition and Consolidation*. Oxford: Oxford University Press.

Lamounier, Bolivar, ed. 1990. *De Geisel a Collor: O Balanço da Transição*. São Paulo: Editora Sumaré.

Lamounier, Bolivar, and Edmar Lisboa Bacha. 1994. "Democracy and Economic Reform in Brazil." In Joan Nelson, ed., *A Precarious Balance: Democracy and Economic Reforms in Latin America*. San Francisco: Institute for Contemporary Studies.

Lamounier, Bolivar, and Alexandre Hubner Marques. 1992. "A Democracia Brasileira no Final da 'Decada Perdida.' " In Bolivar Lamounier, ed., *Ouvindo O Brasil: Uma Análise da Opinião Pública Brasileira Hoje*. São Paulo: Editora Sumaré.

Laplane, Mariano Francisco. 1990. "Diagnóstico da Indústria Brasileira de Máquinas-Ferramenta." In Luciano Coutinho and Wilson Suzigan, eds., *Desenvolvimento Tecnológico da Indústria e a Constituição de um Sistema Nacional de Inovação no Brasil*. Campinas, IPT/FECAMP contract; Instituto de Economia / UNICAMP.

———. 1988. "Competitive Assessment of Brazilian Industrial Robots and Computer Numerical Control Industries." Unpublished paper, Universidade Estadual de Campinas / Instituto de Economia.

Leopoldi, Maria Antoinetta. 1984. "Industrial Associations and Politics in Contemporary Brazil." Ph.D. dissertation, Oxford University.

Lima, Olavo Brasil de, Jr., and Sergio Henrique Abranches, eds. 1987. *As Origens da Crise: Estado Autoritário e Planejamento no Brasil*. São Paulo: Vértice, Editora Revista dos Tribunais.

Little, Ian; Tibor Scitovsky; and Maurice Scott. 1970. *Industry and Trade in Some Developing Countries: A Comparative Study*. Oxford: Oxford University Press.

Locke, Richard. 1995. *Remaking the Italian Economy*. Ithaca, N.Y.: Cornell University Press.

Maciel, Claudio Schuller. 1990. "Padrão de Investimento Indústrial nos Anos 90 e Suas Implicações para a Política Tecnológica." In Luciano Coutinho and Wilson Suzigan, eds., *Desenvolvimento Tecnológico da Indústria e a Constituição de um Sistema Nacional de Inovação no Brasil*. Campinas, IPT/FECAMP contract; Instituto de Economia / UNICAMP.

Mainwaring, Scott. 1995. "Parties, Electoral Volatility, and Democratization: Brazil Since 1982." Paper presented at the Latin American Studies Association, Washington, D.C., September 28–30.

———. 1992. "Dilemmas of Multiparty Presidential Democracy: The Case of Brazil." Working paper no. 174. Notre Dame, Ind.: Kellogg Institute for International Studies, March.

———. 1991. "Politicians, Parties, and Electoral Systems: Brazil in Comparative Perspective." *Comparative Politics*, October.

Mainwaring, Scott, and Timothy Scully. 1995. *Building Democratic Institutions.* Stanford, Calif.: Stanford University Press.

Mainwaring, Scott, and Matthew S. Shugart. 1997. *Presidentialism and Democracy in Latin America.* New York: Cambridge University Press.

Malloy, James. 1979. *The Politics of Social Security in Brazil.* Pittsburgh, Pa.: University of Pittsburgh Press.

Malloy, James, ed. 1977. *Authoritarianism and Corporatism in Latin America.* Pittsburgh, Pa.: University of Pittsburgh Press.

Manzetti, Luigi. 1994. *Institutions, Parties, and Coalitions in Argentine Politics.* Pittsburgh, Pa.: University of Pittsburgh Press.

Martin, Scott. 1991. "(Re)Constructing the Missing Links: Production Regimes, Flexible Restructuring, and the Labor Movement in Brazil and Mexico." Paper presented at the Congress of the Latin American Studies Association, Washington, D.C., April 4–6.

Martins, Luciano. 1968. *Industrialização, Burguesia Nacional e Desenvolvimento.* Rio de Janeiro: Saga.

Martone, Celso L. 1996. "Recent Economic Policy in Brazil Before and After the Peso Crisis." In Riordan Roett, ed., *The Peso Crisis: International Perspectives.* Boulder, Colo.: Lynne Rienner Publishers.

———. 1995. "The Collapse of Banespa: or, How to Dissipate Public Money." Fernand Braudel Institute of World Economics Paper, São Paulo.

Maxfield, Sylvia. 1997. *Gatekeepers of Growth: The International Political Economy of Central Banking in Developing of Growth.* Princeton: Princeton University Press, 1997.

Maxfield, Sylvia, and Ben Ross Schneider. 1997. *Business and the State in Developing Countries.* Ithaca, N.Y.: Cornell University Press.

McDonough, Peter. 1981. *Power and Ideology in Brazil.* Princeton: Princeton University Press.

McQuerry, Elizabeth. 1995. "Economic Liberalization in Brazil: Business Responses and Changing Patterns of Behavior." Ph.D. dissertation, University of Texas at Austin.

Milner, Helen V. 1988. *Resisting Protectionism: Global Industries and the Politics of International Trade.* Princeton: Princeton University Press.

Milner, Helen V., and David B. Yoffie. 1989. "Between Free Trade and Protectionism: Strategic Trade Policy and a Theory of Corporate Trade Demands." *International Organization* 43 (Spring): 239–72.

Miori, Celso. 1991. "Outlook for the Brazilian Economy: The Challenges for the Brazilian Automotive Industry and the Outlook for the Electronics Industry and the Retail Sector." São Paulo: Celso Miori Assessoria Empresarial. June.

Montero, Alfred. 1999. "Devolving Democracy? Political Decentralization and the New Brazilian Federalism." In Peter R. Kingstone and Timothy J. Power, eds., *Democratic Brazil: Institutions, Actors, and Processes.* Pittsburgh: University of Pittsburgh Press.

———. 1997. "Shifting States in Uneven Markets: Political Decentralization and Subnational Industrial Policy in Contemporary Brazil and Spain." Ph.D. dissertation, Columbia University.

Motta, Francisco. 1979. *Empresários e Hegemonia Política.* São Paulo: Editora Brasiliense.

Moura, Alkimar R. 1990. "Rumo a Entropia: a Política Econômica, de Geisel a Collor." In Bolivar Lamounier, ed., *De Geisel a Collor: O Balanço da Transição*. São Paulo: Editora Sumaré.

Muszynski, Judith, and Antonio Manuel Teixeira Mendes. 1990. "Democratização e Opinião Pública no Brasil." In Bolivar Lamounier, ed., *De Geisel a Collor: O Balanço da Transição*. São Paulo: Editora Sumaré.

Nelson, Joan, ed. 1990. *Economic Crisis and Policy Choice: The Politics of Adjustment in the Third World*. Princeton: Princeton University Press.

———. 1989. *Fragile Coalitions: The Politics of Economic Adjustment*. New Brunswick, N.J.: Transaction Books.

Nicolau, Jairo César Marconi. 1991. "Representatação Proporcional: É Preciso Mudar?" In *Regimes Eleitorais e Sistemas Partidários*. IUPERJ, Cadernos de Conjunto, no. 43, August.

Nóbrega, Maílson da. 1992. "Presença do Estado na Economia e na Sociedade." In Bolivar Lamounier, ed., *Ouvindo O Brasil: Uma Análise da Opinião Pública Brasileira Hoje*. São Paulo: Editora Sumaré.

Nunes, Edson de Oliveira, and Barbara Geddes. 1987. "Dilemmas of State-Led Modernization in Brazil." In John Wirth; Edson de Oliveira Nunes; and Thomas E. Bogenschild, eds., *State and Society in Brazil: Continuity and Change*. Boulder, Colo.: Westview Press.

Nylen, William. 1992. "Small Business Owners Fight Back: Non-Elite Capital Activism in Democratizing Brazil, 1978–1990." Ph.D. dissertation, Columbia University.

———. 1992. "Liberalismo para Todo Mundo Menos Eu: Brazil and the Neoliberal Solution." In Douglas A. Chalmers, Maria Carmo Campello de Souza, and Atilio A. Boron, eds., *The Right and Democracy in Latin America*. New York: Praeger.

Oliveira, Gesner. 1995. "The Brazilian Economy Under the Real: Prospects for Stabilization and Growth." Paper presented at the Latin American Studies Association, Washington, D.C., September 28–30.

———. 1993. "Condicionantes e Diretrizes de Política para a Albertura Comercial Brasileira." IPEA Texto para Discussão, no. 3 (September).

Olson, Mancur. 1971. *The Logic of Collective Action: Public Goods and the Theory of Groups*. Cambridge, Mass.: Harvard University Press.

Packenham, Robert A. 1992. "The Politics of Economic Liberalization: Argentina and Brazil in Comparative Perspective." Paper presented at the American Political Science Association, Chicago, September 3–6.

Pastor, Manuel, Jr., and Carol Wise. 1994. "The Origins and Sustainability of Mexico's Free Trade Policy." *International Organization* 3:459–89.

Payne, Leigh. 1995. "Brazilian Business and the Democratic Transition: New Attitudes and Influence." In Ernest Bartell and Leigh Payne, eds., *Business and Democracy in Latin America*. Pittsburgh, Pa.: University of Pittsburgh Press.

———. 1994. *Brazilian Industrialists and Democratic Change*. Baltimore: Johns Hopkins University Press.

Petras, James; Fernando Ignacio Leiva; and Henry Veltmeyer. 1994. *Democracy and Poverty in Chile: The Limits to Electoral Politics*. Boulder, Colo.: Westview Press.

Posthuma, Anne Caroline. 1997. "Industrial Restructuring and Skills in the Supply Chain of the Brazilian Automotive Industry." Paper prepared for the Latin American Studies Association, Guadalajara.

Power, Timothy J. 1999. "Political Institutions in Democratic Brazil: Politics as a Permanent Constitutional Convention." In Peter R. Kingstone and Timothy J. Power, eds., *Democratic Brazil: Institutions, Actors, and Processes*. Pittsburgh, Pa.: University of Pittsburgh Press.

———. 1998. "The Pen Is Mightier Than the Congress: Presidential Decree Power in Brazil." In John Carey and Matthew Soberg Shugart, eds., *Executive Decree Authority: Calling Out the Tanks or Filling Out the Forms*. New York: Cambridge University Press.

———. 1991. "Politicized Democracy: Competition, Institutions, and 'Civic-Fatigue' in Brazil. " *Journal of Interamerican Studies and World Affairs* 33 (Fall): 75–112.

Power, Timothy J., and Timmons Roberts. 1999. "A New Brazil? The Changing Sociodemographic Context of Brazilian Democracy." In Peter R. Kingstone and Timothy J. Power, eds., *Democratic Brazil: Institutions, Actors, and Processes*. Pittsburgh: University of Pittsburgh Press.

Pöyry, Jaakko. 1991. "Perspectivas e Oportunidades para a Indústria de Papel e Celulose Latino-Americana." São Paulo. Jaakko Pöyry / Associação Nacional dos Fabricantes de Papel e Celulose. June.

Price Waterhouse. 1992. "Série Tendencias Economicas XI." January–April.

Przeworski, Adam. 1991. *Democracy and the Market: Political and Economic Reforms in Eastern Europe and Latin America*. Cambridge: Cambridge University Press.

Ramos, Alberto Wunderler. 1990. "Reavaliação do Sistema Nacional e da Infra-Estrutura Pública de Normalização Técnica, Metrologia, e Qualidade." In Luciano Coutinho and Wilson Suzigan, eds., *Desenvolvimento Tecnológico da Indústria e a Constituição de um Sistema Nacional de Inovação no Brasil*. Campinas, IPT/FECAMP contract; Instituto de Economia / UNICAMP.

Remmer, Karen. 1993. "The Political Economy of Elections in Latin America, 1980–1991." *American Political Science Review* 87 (June): 393–407.

———. 1986. "The Politics of Economic Stabilization: IMF Standby Programs in Latin America, 1954–1984." *Comparative Politics* 19 (October): 1–24.

Rezende, Francisco. 1987. "O Crescimento (Descontrolado) da Intervenção Governamental na Economia Brasileira." In Olavo Brasil de Lima Jr. and Sergio Henrique Abranches, eds., *As Origens da Crise: Estado Autoritário e Planejamento no Brasil*. São Paulo: Vértice, Editora Revista dos Tribunais.

Rocha, Sônia. 1996. "Renda e Pobreza: Os impactos do Plano Real." Texto para discussão, no. 439. Rio de Janeiro: IPEA (Instituto de Pesquisa Econômica Aplicada). December.

Rockman, Bert A. 1984. *The Leadership Question: The Presidency and the American System*. New York: Praeger.

Rodrik, Dani. 1989. "Promises, Promises: Credible Policy Reform via Signalling." *Economic Journal* 99 (September): 756–72.

Rogowski, Ronald. 1989. *Commerce and Coalitions: How Trade Affects Domestic Political Alignments*. Princeton: Princeton University Press.

Rosenn, Keith. 1990. "Brazil's New Constitution: An Exercise in Transient Constitutionalism for a Transitional Society." *American Journal of Comparative Law* 38, no. 4: 773–802.

Roxborough, Ian. 1992. "Inflation and Social Pacts in Brazil and Mexico." *Journal of Latin American Studies* 24, no. 3: 1–26.

———. 1992. "Neo-Liberalism in Latin America: Limits and Alternatives." *Third World Quarterly* 13, no. 3: 421–40.

Sabel, Charles. 1982. *Work and Politics*. New York: Cambridge University Press.

Sachs, Jeffrey, and Álvaro Zini Jr. 1996. "Brazilian Inflation and the *Plano Real*." *World Economy* 19, no. 1: 13–38.

Salgado, René. 1987. "Economic Pressure Groups and Policy-Making in Venezuela: The Case of FEDECAMARAS Reconsidered." *Latin American Research Review* 2, no. 30: 91–121.

Sallum, Brasílio. 1988. "Por Que Não Tem Dado Certo: Notas Sobre a Transição Política Brasileira." In Lourdes Sola, ed., *O Estado da Transição: Política e Economia na Nova Republica*. São Paulo: Vértice, Editora Revista dos Tribunais.

Santos, Fabiano Guilherme Mendes. 1991. "A Questão da Proporcionalidade no Brasil: Lições da Vida." In *Regimes Eleitorais e Sistemas Partidários*, IUPERJ, Cadernos de Conjunto, no. 43, August.

Schamis, Hector E. 1999. "Distributional Coalitions and the Politics of Economic Reform in Latin America." *World Politics* 51, no. 2: 236–68.

———. 1992. "Conservative Political Economy in Latin America and Western Europe: The Political Sources of Privatization." In Douglas A. Chalmers, Maria Carmo Campello de Souza, and Atilio A. Boron, eds., *The Right and Democracy in Latin America*. New York: Praeger.

Schmitter, Philippe C. 1977. "Modes of Interest Intermediation and Models of Societal Change in Western Europe." *Comparative Political Studies* 10, no. 1: 7–38.

———. 1971. *Interest Conflict and Political Change in Brazil*. Stanford, Calif.: Stanford University Press.

Schneider, Ben Ross. 1998. "Elusive Synergy: Business-State Relations and Development." *Comparative Politics* 31, no. 1: 101–22.

———. 1997. "Organized Business Politics in Democratic Brazil." *Journal of Interamerican Studies and World Affairs* 39, no. 4: 95–127.

———. 1993. "The Elusive Embrace: Synergy Between Business and the State in Developing Countries." Paper presented at the American Political Science Association, Washington, D.C., September 2–5.

———. 1992. "Privatization in the Collor Government: Triumph of Liberalism or Collapse of the Developmental State?" In Douglas A. Chalmers, Maria Carmo Campello de Souza, and Atilio A. Boron, eds., *The Right and Democracy in Latin America*. New York: Praeger.

———. 1991a. "Brazil Under Collor: Anatomy of a Crisis." *World Policy Journal* 8 (Spring): 321–47.

———. 1991b. *Politics Within the State: Elite Bureaucrats and Industrial Policy in Authoritarian Brazil*. Pittsburgh, Pa.: University of Pittsburgh Press.

———. 1990a. "Collor's First Year: The Stalled Revival of Capitalist Development in Brazil." IUPERJ, Cadernos de Conjuntura, no. 34/35, November–December.

————. 1990b. "The Politics of Privatization in Brazil and Mexico: Variations on a Statist Theme." New York: Columbia University–New York University Consortium Center for Latin American and Caribbean Studies, Conference Paper no. 23.

————. 1987. "Framing the State: Economic Policy and Political Representation in Post-Authoritarian Brazil." In John Wirth; Edson de Oliveira Nunes; and Thomas E. Bogenschild, eds., *State and Society in Brazil: Continuity and Change*. Boulder, Colo.: Westview Press.

Scully, Timothy R. 1992. *Rethinking the Center*. Stanford, Calif.: Stanford University Press.

Shadlen, Kenneth. 1997. "Small Industry and the Mexican Left: Neoliberalism, Corporatism, and Dissident Populism." Paper presented at the American Political Science Association, Washington, D.C., August.

Shapiro, Helen. 1994. *Engines of Growth: The State and Transnational Auto Companies in Brazil*. Cambridge: Cambridge University Press.

Sheahan, John. 1987. *Patterns of Development in Latin America: Poverty, Repression, and Economic Strategy*. Princeton: Princeton University Press.

Shugart, Matthew Soberg, and John M. Carey. 1992. *Presidents and Assemblies: Constitutional Designs and Electoral Dynamics*. New York: Cambridge University Press.

Silva, Eduardo. 1996. *The State and Capital in Chile: Business Elites, Technocrats, and Market Economics*. Boulder, Colo.: Westview Press.

————. 1992. "Capitalist Regime Loyalties and Redemocratization in Chile." *Journal of Interamerican and World Affairs* 34 (Winter): 77–117.

Sindicato Nacional da Indústria de Componentes para Veículos Automotores. 1992. "Guia Brasileño de los Exportadores de Autopiezas." São Paulo.

Singer, André. 1990. "Collor na Periferia: a Volta por Cima do Populismo?" In Bolivar Lamounier, ed., *De Geisel a Collor: O Balanço da Transição*. São Paulo: Editora Sumaré.

Singer, Paul. 1989. "Democracy and Inflation in the Light of the Brazilian Experience." In William Canak, ed., *Lost Promises: Debt, Austerity, and Development in Latin America*. Boulder, Colo.: Westview Press.

Skidmore, Thomas. 1977. "The Politics of Economic Stabilization in Postwar Latin America." In James Malloy, ed., *Authoritarianism and Corporatism in Latin America*. Pittsburgh, Pa.: University of Pittsburgh Press.

————. 1967. *Politics in Brazil, 1930–1964: An Experiment in Democracy*. Oxford: Oxford University Press.

Smith, William C. 1991. "State, Market, and Neoliberalism in Post-Transition Argentina: The Menem Experiment." *Journal of Interamerican Studies and World Affairs* 33 (Winter): 45–82.

————. 1989. "Heterodox Shocks and the Political Economy of Democratic Transition in Argentina and Brazil." In William Canak, ed., *Lost Promises: Debt, Austerity, and Development in Latin America*. Boulder, Colo.: Westview Press.

Smith, William C.; Carlos H. Acuña; and Eduardo A. Gamarra, eds. 1993. *Democracy, Markets, and Structural Reform in Latin America: Argentina, Bolivia, Brazil, Chile, and Mexico*. New Brunswick, N.J.: Transaction Publishers.

Soares, Luiz Eduardo. 1990. "Governo Collor: Autonomia da Conjuntura Política." In IUPERJ, Cadernos de Conjuntura, no. 34/35. November–December.

Soares, Sebastião José Martins; Walter Aluisio Morais Rodrigues; and José Clemente de Oliveira. 1990. "O Setor Celulose-Papel." In Luciano Coutinho and Wilson Suzigan, eds., *Desenvolvimento Tecnológico da Indústria e a Constituição de um Sistema Nacional de Inovação no Brasil*. Campinas, IPT/FECAMP contract; Instituto de Economia / UNICAMP.

Sola, Lourdes. 1988a. "Heterodox Shock in Brazil: Técnicos, Politicians, and Democracy." *Journal of Latin American Studies* 23:163–95.

———. 1988b. "Choque Heterodoxo e Transição Democrática sem Ruptura: Uma Abordagem Transdisciplinar." In Lourdes Sola, ed., *O Estado da Transição: Política e Economia na Nova Republica*. São Paulo: Vértice, Editora Revista dos Tribunais.

———. 1982. "The Political and Ideological Constraints to Economic Management in Brazil, 1945–1964." Ph.D. dissertation, Oxford University.

Soto, Hernando de. 1989. *The Other Path: The Invisible Revolution in the Third World*. London: I. B. Taurus.

Souza, Maria do Carmo Campello de. 1992. "The Contemporary Faces of the Brazilian Right: An Interpretation of Style and Substance." In Douglas A. Chalmers, Maria Carmo Campello de Souza, and Atilio A. Boron, eds., *The Right and Democracy in Latin America*. New York: Praeger.

———. 1989. "The Brazilian 'New Republic': Under the 'Sword of Damocles.' " In Alfred Stepan, ed., *Democratizing Brazil: Problems of Transition and Consolidation*. Oxford: Oxford University Press.

Stepan, Alfred, ed. 1989. *Democratizing Brazil: Problems of Transition and Consolidation*. Oxford: Oxford University Press.

———. 1978. "Political Leadership and Regime Breakdown: Brazil." In Juan J. Linz and Alfred Stepan, eds., *The Breakdown of Democratic Regimes: Latin America*. Baltimore: Johns Hopkins University Press.

———. 1973. *Authoritarian Brazil: Origins, Policies, and Future*. New Haven, Conn.: Yale University Press.

Suzigan, Wilson. 1992. "As Fraquezas da Política de Exportação do Governo." *Carta Política*, ano ii (March 30–April 5): 6.

———. 1991. "Situação Atual da Indústria Brasileira e Implicações para a Política Industrial." Unpublished paper, December 4, distributed at the Universidade de São Paulo.

———. 1986. *Indústria Brasileira: Origem e Desenvolvimento*. São Paulo: Editora Brasiliense.

Suzigan, Wilson; José Rubens Dória Porto; Ana Lucia Gonçalves da Silva, eds. 1989. *Seminário de Avaliação da Política Nacional da Informática*. Universidade Estadual de Campinas; Instituto de Economia / Núcleo de Economia Industrial e da Tecnológia.

Suzigan, Wilson, and Anibal Villela. 1997. *Industrial Policy in Brazil*. Campinas: UNICAMP / Instituto de Economia.

Teixeira, Mendes; Antonio Manuel; and Gustavo Venturi. 1995. "Eleição Presidencial: O Plano Real na Sucessão de Itamar Franco." *Opinião Pública* 2, no. 2: 39–48.

Thacker, Strom. 1997. "Big Business, the State, and Free Trade in Mexico: Interests, Structure, and Political Access." Paper presented at the American Political Science Association, Washington, D.C., August.

Tornell, Aaron. 1995. "Are Economic Crises Necessary for Trade Liberalization and Fiscal Reform: The Mexican Experience." In Rudiger Dornbusch and Sebastian Edwards, eds., *Reform, Recovery, and Growth: Latin America and the Middle East*. Chicago: University of Chicago Press.

Verba, Sidney. 1971. "Sequences and Development." In Leonard Binder, *Crises and Sequences in Political Development*. Princeton: Princeton University Press.

Verdier, Daniel. 1994. *Democracy and International Trade: Britain, France, and the United States, 1860–1990*. Princeton: Princeton University Press.

Vianna, Luiz Werneck. 1991. *De Um Plano Collor a Outro*. Rio de Janeiro: Editora Revan.

———. 1990. "Governo vs. Pacto Social e Político: A Hipotese da Dualidade de Poderes." In IUPERJ, Cadernos de Conjuntura, no. 34/35, November–December.

Vogel, David. 1989. *Fluctuating Fortunes: The Political Power of Business in America*. New York: Basic Books.

———. 1977. "Why Businessmen Distrust Their State: The Political Consciousness of American Corporate Executives." *British Journal of Political Science* 8:45-78.

Wallerstein, Michael. 1980. "The Collapse of Democracy in Brazil: Its Economic Determinants." *Latin American Research Review* 15, no. 3: 340.

Waterbury, John. 1989. "The Political Management of Economic Adjustment and Reform." In Joan Nelson, ed., *Fragile Coalitions: The Politics of Economic Adjustment*. New Brunswick, N.J.: Transaction Books.

Weyland, Kurt. 1996a. *Growth Without Equity: Failures of Reform in Brazil*. Pittsburgh, Pa.: University of Pittsburgh Press.

———. 1996b. "How Much Political Power Do Economic Forces Have? Conflicts over Social Insurance Reform in Brazil." *Journal of Public Policy* 16, no. 1: 59–84.

———. 1992. "The Dispersion of Business Influence in Brazil's New Democracy." Paper presented at the American Political Science Association, September 3–6.

Whiting, Van. 1993. "Economic Liberalization and Democratic Politics: A Comparison of India and Mexico." Paper presented at the American Political Science Association, September 2–5.

Wilensky, Harold. 1987. *Democratic Corporatism and Policy Linkages: The Interdependence of Industrial, Labor-Market, Incomes, and Social Policies in Eight Countries*. Berkeley: Institute of International Studies, University of California.

Wilson, Graham K. 1990. *Business and Politics: A Comparative Introduction*. Chatham, N.J.: Chatham House Publishers.

Wirth, John; Edson de Oliveira Nunes; and Thomas E. Bogenschild, eds. 1987. *State and Society in Brazil: Continuity and Change*. Boulder, Colo.: Westview Press.

Wise, Carol. 1997. "The Trade Scenario for Other Latin American Reformers in the NAFTA Era." In Carol Wise, ed., *The Post-NAFTA Political Economy: Mexico and the Western Hemisphere*. University Park: The Pennsylvania State University Press.

Zysman, John. 1985. *Government, Markets, and Growth: Financial Systems and the Politics of Industrial Change*. Ithaca, N.Y.: Cornell University Press.

NEWSPAPERS, PERIODICALS, AND JOURNALS

ABIMAQ, *Infomaq*
ABINEE, *Informativo*
ANFAVEA, *Anuário Estatístico*
ANFPC, *Papel e Celulose*
ANFPC, *Relatório Estatístico*
Brazil Service
Business Latin America
Carta Política
Diário de Comércio e Indústria
Diário do Grande ABC
Diário Popular
The Economist
Exame
Estado de São Paulo
FIESP/CIESP, *Notícias*
Folha da Tarde
Folha de São Paulo
Gazeta Mercantil
Gazetinha (Gazeta Mercantil International Edition)
Isto É
Isto É Senhor
Jornal da Tarde
Jornal do Comércio
Latin Finance
Pensamento (Pensamento Nacional das Bases Empresariais)
Senhor
SINDIPEÇAS, *Desempenho do Setor*
SINDIPEÇAS, *Notícias*
Veja
Visão

Index